Children on the Streets of the Americas

Association François-Xavier Bagnoud

Children on the Streets of the Americas

Homelessness, Education and Globalization in the United States, Brazil and Cuba

edited by
Roslyn Arlin Mickelson

Routledge
London and New York

Published in 2000 by
Routledge
29 West 35th Street
New York, New York 10001

Published in Great Britain by
Routledge
11 New Fetter Lane
London EC4P 4EE

10 9 8 7 6 5 4 3 2 1

Permissions Acknowledgments
4.   Stronge, James H., "A Long Road Ahead: A Progress Report on Educating Homeless Children and Youth," *Journal of Children & Poverty,* 3, (2). © 1997 by The Institute for Children and Poverty. Reprinted with permission.
15.   Reprinted/adapted by permission of the publisher from J. Anyon, *Ghetto Schooling: A Political Economy of Urban Reform* (New York: Teachers College Press, © 1997 by Teachers College, Columbia University. All rights reserved), pp. 1-15.

Library of Congress Cataloging-in-Publication Data

Children on the streets of the Americas : homelessness, education, and globalization in
   the United States, Brazil, and Cuba/New subtitle (by Routledge)/
   Mickelson, ed.
      p.   cm.
   Includes bibliographical references (p.) and index.
   ISBN 0-415-92321-2 (hb). — ISBN 0-415-92322-0 (pb)
   1. Street children—Brazil—Social conditions. 2. Street children—Cuba—Social conditions. 3. Street children—United States—Social conditions. 4. Street children—Education—Brazil. 5. Street children—Education—Cuba. 6. Street children—Education—United States. 7. Street children—Services for—Brazil Case studies. 8. Street children—Services for—Cuba Case studies. 9. Street children— Services for—United States—Case studies.
   I. Mickelson, Roslyn Arlin, 1948- .
   HV887.B8C475   1999
   362.74—dc21
                                                                                    99-22989
                                                                                        CIP

Contents

Illustrations

Abbreviations

ACP	A Child's Place
AFDC	Aid to Families with Dependent Children
BLS	Bureau of Labor Statistics
CBIA	Fundação Centro Brasileiro para a Infância e a Adolescência (Brazilian Center for Childhood and Adolescence)
CDC	Child Development Center of the American Family Inn's Preschool Program
CDF	Children's Defense Fund
CEPAL	Comisión Económica para América Latina y el Caribe (Economic Commission for Latin America and the Caribbean)
CIMs	Círculos Infantiles Mixtos (mixed daycare centers)
CMS	Charlotte-Mecklenburg Schools
ECA	Estatuto da Criança e do Adolescente (The Children and Adolescents Act, 1990)
ED	U.S. Department of Education
EITC	Earned Income Tax Credit
FEBEMs	Fundaçoes Estuduais de Bem-Estar do Menor (State Foundations for the Welfare of Minors)
FMC	Federacíon de Mujeres Cubanas (Federation of Cuban Women)
FORUM–DCA	Forum de Defesa dos Direitos da Criança e do Adolescente (The Child and Adolescent Rights Forum)
FUNABEM	Fundação Estadual do Bem-Estar do Menor (National Foundation for the Welfare of Minors)
FGV	Getúlio Vargas Foundation
GDP	Gross Domestic Product
GED	General Education Degree
GNP	Gross National Product
HFH	Homes for the Homeless
HUD	Housing and Urban Development
IBASE	Brazilian Institute of Social and Economic Analysis
IBGE	Instituto Brasileiro de Geografia e Estatística (Brazilian Institute of Geography and Statistics)
IDB	International Development Bank
IDEA	Individuals with Disabilities Act
IEP	Individualized Education Plan
ILO	International Labor Organization
IMF	International Monetary Fund
INS	Immigration and Naturalization Service
JTPA	Job Training Partnership Act Program
KOOL-IS	Kids Organized on Learning in School
LBA	Legião Brasileira de Assistência (Brazilian Welfare Legion)
LEA	Local Educational Authorities

MINED	Ministerio de Educación (Cuban Ministry of Education)
MNMMR	Movimento Nacional de Meninos e Meninas de Rua (National Movement of Street Boys and Girls of Brazil)
NAFTA	North America Free Trade Agreement
NGO	Nongovernmental Organization
NIC	Newly Industrializing Country
NLC	National Law Center on Homelessness and Poverty
PNAD	Pesquisa Nacional por Amostra de Domicílios (National Survey of Sample Households)
PNBEM	Política Nacional por Bem-Estar dos Menores (National Policy for the Welfare of Minors)
SAM	Serviço Assistência a Menores (Assistance Service to Minors)
SEA	State Educational Authorities
SSI	Supplemental Social Security Income
TANF	Temporary Assistance to Needy Families
UJC	Unión de Jóvenes Comunistas (Youth Branch of the Communist Party)
UN	United Nations
UNESCO	United Nations Educational, Scientific, and Cultural Organization
UNICEF	United Nations Children's Fund
WTO	World Trade Organization

Foreword

Marian Wright Edelman

O ne of the most disturbing problems facing the global village as it lurches toward the twenty-first century is the tragedy of homeless children. Unlike some aspects of poverty such as inadequate education, nutrition, and medical care, homelessness is all too visible, its adult and sometimes child victims frequently found on the streets of the poshest of urban shopping districts. And while there may be many among the well-housed who are quick to attribute the homelessness of adults to these individuals' short-comings and failures, even the most heartless cannot blame a homeless child for his or her situation. However, the blamelessness of these children and the visibility of their plight has yet to evoke a comprehensive public policy response in the United States, Brazil, and many other countries.

As someone who had taught and traveled throughout the United States and worked with homeless children in North Carolina, Roslyn Arlin Mickelson, the editor of this fine volume, was no stranger to this devastating problem. But it is doubtful this compilation would have ever been conceived—let alone produced—were it not for the incident she recounts in the introductory chapter about her first night in Rio de Janeiro. Just as that incident 8,000 miles from home made her think more sharply about her experiences in the United States, I believe this book will help all of us focus more clearly on the plight of homeless and street children.

Children on the Streets of the Americas shows us the face of homelessness in Brazil, Cuba, and the United States. The United States is the quintessentially developed country, while Brazil is the rapidly developing one; both are characterized by concentrations of extreme affluence and extreme poverty. Cuba is much poorer than either Brazil or the United States, but some indicators of child and adult well-being surprisingly surpass those of the other two. Whatever the differences among the three, they all are affected by the increasingly globalized economy. These similarities and differences shape the contours of homelessness in the three countries. In the best traditions of comparative sociology and public policy research, this book describes these contours and draws inferences about appropriate responses by both the public and private sectors.

Homeless and street children are, in the final analysis, extremely poor children. It thus makes little sense to talk about such children, and policies to address their educational and social needs, without talking about poverty in each of the three countries and how poverty is affected by worldwide economic developments and the policies of agencies such as the International Monetary Fund and the World Bank. As a result, macrosolutions—government policies aimed at alleviating poverty and its consequences—emerge as the sine qua non of any comprehensive attempt to address the problems of homeless children.

As a supplement to such comprehensive macrosolutions, and in the absence of such attempts (an all-too-frequent state of affairs), microsolutions are also important. The case studies in Parts III and IV do an especially effective job of exploring why some short-term or micropolicies are more effective than others. And this is where education has an important role to play in the lives of homeless and street children.

The book's discussion of education emphasizes that schools have the opportunity as well as the necessity of fulfilling more than traditional academic roles. To succeed as academic institutions as well as to address the needs of homeless and street children, schools must develop collaborative relationships with nongovernmental organizations (NGOs), and others to provide a wide range of services for homeless and street children. The notion of education must be expanded to include informal programs as well. Yet no matter how successful schools might be in providing even the broadest array of services, these efforts will amount only to running full speed to stay in the same place in the absence of more comprehensive macropolicies aimed at providing decent jobs and affordable housing and eliminating racial and gender discrimination.

The effectiveness of the book's comparative analysis and the relevance of its policy recommendations reflect the group of international, multiethnic, eminent scholars who have contributed chapters to this volume. This book exemplifies the importance of thinking globally and acting locally. I hope it will find a wide audience, especially among policymakers, and that it will inspire them to do the same.

Acknowledgments

This book has been five years in the making, and like other such enterprises, it was truly a collaborative effort. I am most grateful to all the Brazilian and U.S. contributors who provided superb original research and patiently endured the sometimes grueling process of bringing this volume to life. The Brazilian chapters were written in Portuguese and were translated into English by Donna Sandin. The translation would not have been possible without the generous support of the Association François-Xavier Bagnoud. The Rockefeller Foundation provided me a month-long residency at the Bellagio Center on Lake Como, Italy, where I was able to complete a large portion of this manuscript. I finished the book while I was a visiting scholar at the Stanford University School of Education. I am grateful to these institutions for their support.

I am indebted to many, many colleagues, friends, and family members for their support and assistance over the years as this project moved from a concept to a book. I wish to thank Ann Altman, Mona Arlin, Jean Anyon, Mario J. Azevedo, Diane E. Davis, Susan Duncan, Annelle Houk, Howard Haworth, Bo King, Miriam Lyons, Sheryl L. Lutjens, Colleen McInerney, John Meyer, Carolyn Seligson Mickelson, William M. Park, José Neistein, Paula Razquin, Frances Schwartz, Larry Suter, Kathy Tindell, Michael M. Weinstein, Jerry Wolfe, and Lucilia Silveira Writer. I could not have completed this book without the assistance of my dedicated graduate students Anne E. Velasco and Tiffany L. Waits. The indispensable critical commentary and support of Stephen Samuel Smith, my husband and colleague, kept me focused on the really important issues in work and life. Seeing our children, Ginny and David, develop into delightful young adults has been profoundly satisfying to me. Watching their journey through childhood has increased my fury that so many of the Americas' children suffer conditions that needlessly and cruelly stunt their lives. Finally, I wish to dedicate this book with love and respect to those who first inspired me, my parents Louis Mickelson (1917-1995) and Hannah Arlin, and to my brothers Larry (1957-1989) and David.

Roslyn Arlin Mickelson
Palo Alto, California
February 1999

Part I: Introduction

Figure 1.1　Map of the Americas (UNC Charlotte Cartography Lab)

1

Globalization, Childhood Poverty, and Education in the Americas

Roslyn Arlin Mickelson

The wide sidewalks of central Rio de Janeiro are beautiful mosaics of white, gray, and black stone. Each major boulevard has its own unique pattern. During my first night in Rio, sometime in June 1994, my *carioca* friends took me to dinner in a chic section of town.[1] After our sumptuous meal, we strolled along the sidewalks holding bags filled with the remains of our generous dinner. The evening air was pleasantly balmy; the titter of al fresco diners' conversations blended with distant music and motor vehicle noise as we walked. At a particular corner, I stopped to admire the window displays of a designer bathroom fixture store. A half dozen bathrooms—with their perfectly color-coordinated commodes, bidets, sinks, towels, wallpapers, and tile floors—dazzled me. The window embodied the glamorous, fashionable Rio of popular songs and cinema.

But reflected in the window's glass I caught a glimpse of another side of Rio. Two thin, small boys about 10 years old were preparing for bed on the sidewalk a dozen meters away from the front of the window where I stood admiring commodes and bidets. I turned around, transfixed by the scene. In the dim evening light, their skin and hair and dusty, faded clothing blended into a honey-brown blur. They were shoeless and wore only cotton T-shirts and shorts. Their bed was a flattened cardboard box that they unfolded on the mosaic sidewalk. Occasionally, well-heeled *cariocas* exiting the nearby grocery store placed some money or packaged food on their bed of cardboard. The boys tucked the wads of money, actually worth only pennies, into their pockets.[2] They ate some of the donated food and saved the rest. Then they lay down and pulled their knees up under their shirts for warmth. Facing each other, they snuggled close and went to sleep.

Mesmerized by this scene, I was also struck by its contradictions: their squalor amidst our comfort; the designer bathrooms in the window and the cardboard beds on the sidewalk. Was I a witness or an accomplice to their tribulation? Agitated and frustrated, I naively asked my friends what I could do. What did they do?

Certainly, this was not the first time I'd seen street children. I have lived in several major U.S. cities; I have traveled throughout Latin America. During my 2 months in Brazil, I saw many more street children. I spent an afternoon in a *favela* (shantytown), walking though narrow streets and paths, bombarded by intense sights and sounds of the neighborhood, and odors from garbage and debris that never would be hauled away by the city. I toured one section under the vigilant eyes of small boys with large guns. "They work for the drug dealers," explained my guide who lived there. I visited numerous programs for street children in several cities, and when it was possible, I chatted with children I encountered. But no Brazilian children I saw left their impression on me more forcefully than the sleeping boys on their cardboard bed. They seemed to embody the central contradictions of poverty amidst wealth, of uneven development, and of the global economy's underside.

Six months earlier, I had spent 2 weeks in Cuba, where street children simply were not part of the urban landscape, even in the tourist haven of Old Havana. I saw Cuban children in schools or parks, or with their teachers on field trips. I observed them in parades and musical reviews. I had the opportunity for formal and informal visits to schools in the provinces of Havana and rural Pinar del Río. One school in Havana left a profound impression on me. Estado de Cambodia was both a conventional neighborhood primary school and a *hogar,* a group home for orphaned, abandoned, or parentless Cuban children.[3]

Estado de Cambodia is located in the once-exclusive Havana residential neighborhood of Miramar. Miramar today is a mix of well-kept and beautiful art-deco buildings adjacent to sad, deteriorating structures. Some homes are bordered by manicured lawns and flower gardens. The school itself is located in a former single-family home built of stucco and covered with a red tile roof. It looks more like a house than a school. Estado de Cambodia's facilities consist of two houses; one is the school that I visited, and the other is the group home where the resident students live.

From the spacious front porch decorated with a wall-sized black-and-white photo of a much younger, smiling Fidel holding a child in his arms, my colleague and I entered the school's reception and office areas. Once these rooms were the living room and dining rooms of the house. Now they are furnished with worn antique tables, mirrors, and cabinets as well as with more traditional office furniture. We continued through to a large rectangular courtyard that served as a meeting area where children assembled and performed. Classrooms faced the courtyard on four sides. Their walls were lined with assorted bookshelves, posters, and educational visuals. Children eagerly welcomed the distraction of foreign guests and, upon their teacher's cue, loudly greeted us in unison.

I accompanied one class to their noon meal. As children waited to enter the cafeteria, they peppered me with questions while I showed them photos of my own family. Meals and snacks were served in the former garage, now converted into a kitchen and dining area packed tightly with tables covered by colorful oil cloths. Children ate a meal of rice, beans, fish stew, and milk. After lunch, the children returned to the main building, unfolded their canvas cots, and rested under the shade of the patio.

The children of Estado de Cambodia who had no families were indistinguishable from those who had parents. Even though this took place during the austere Special Period in Peacetime following the end of Soviet aid, I saw nothing during my visit to the school that made me question what I had read about Cuba's successes in education and public health. My impressions of the children at Estado de Cambodia and the dozen or so schools I visited put flesh and bones on those favorable statistics.

My ruminations about street children in Brazil and children without families in Cuba forced me to think more critically about the homeless children in my own city, Charlotte, North Carolina. Homeless children in Charlotte are almost always members of homeless families who have not shared in the greater metropolitan area's prosperity. Charlotte has enjoyed tremendous economic and population growth during the last 2 decades. The city is a major financial center and the headquarters of the largest bank in the United States, Bank of America. Yet, at the same time that the city's economy has boomed, many poor families, lured by the gleam of Charlotte's prosperity, have encountered low-wage entry-level jobs and unaffordable rents. As is true elsewhere across the United States, the number of homeless families with children in Charlotte has grown in the last 2 decades.

Despite the community's wealth and educational resources, homeless children faced multiple obstacles before they could receive the education to which they were entitled. When Charlotte school officials first learned that homeless children in adult shelters were not enrolled in school, they initially resisted the need for programmatic attention to their problems. Educators, social workers, and community groups pressed ahead and eventually established a collaborative program for homeless children in a church basement. Several years later, it became a formal program of the local school system.[4]

My recollections gave rise to several questions. What are the commonalities and differences in the life circumstances and educational opportunities of homeless and street children in Brazil, Cuba, and the United States? I wondered to what extent the different patterns of education and child well-being I observed have to do with globalization. Are there connections among poverty and homelessness in the United States, the global economy, and the plight of the two boys I saw sleeping on their cardboard bed on the sidewalk in Rio de Janeiro? Where does education fit into this constellation of issues? What policies and practices effectively address the immediate needs of homeless and street children, and what structural transformations are necessary for long-term social change?

The answers I found divide into several themes. Globalization and the intertwined political economies of Latin American countries and the United States simultaneously create wealth and poverty in all three nations. While the causes and conditions of poverty differ, Brazilian, Cuban, and U.S. street and homeless children invariably stand as extreme manifestations of that poverty. All three states respond to the presence of these children with domestic policies and practices that reflect their society's core values and priorities. The final point concerns the place of education in the lives of homeless and street youth. While high-quality education programs are essential for street and homeless children's present lives and future opportunities, education alone will not resolve the dilemma of the social inequality that fundamentally underlies their plight.

In the following sections, I synthesize several bodies of research that make the necessary connections among these themes. I begin with a discussion of the globalization of the world's economy within a capitalist framework, and the roles played in that process by the International Monetary Fund (IMF) and the World Bank. Using Brazil, Cuba, and the United States as examples, I connect the effects of globalization and the neoliberal policies of the IMF and World Bank to increases in poverty and wealth in both the developed and developing world. Greater levels of income polarization associated with globalization then bring us to the question of homeless and street children, who are, in the final analysis, very poor children. The last section of this essay considers the role of education in the lives of homeless and street children within the context of the emerging global informational economy.

GLOBALIZATION, CAPITALISM, AND THE EMERGING WORLD ECONOMIC ORDER

During January 1999, while the Brazilian economy buckled in crisis, I lived in Palo Alto, California. Palo Alto is in the heart of California's Silicon Valley and is the home of Stanford University. Whenever I walked along University Avenue in the city's primary entertainment and business district or through the Stanford Shopping Center—both designed for the whims of the consumers whom Saskia Sassen (1991) labels the "compulsive spending classes"—I was struck by the palpable opulence of the community. The polarization between the poor and affluent in Palo Alto was also visible to me. No poor actually live in the city itself, although occasionally, homeless men will panhandle for money there. Poor people live in East Palo Alto, 4 miles east down University Avenue separated by U.S.

Highway 101 from the prosperous, palm-lined avenues of the wealthy. The largely Latino and African-American population of East Palo Alto attends separate schools, too.

I followed the unfolding Brazilian financial crisis in major U.S. newspapers: "Brazil Devalues Further, and Stocks Soar 33 Percent" (Schemo 1999a); "Brazil's Slide Stuns Markets" (Blustein 1999); "IMF, US Officials Warn Brazil to Keep Its Economic Promises" (Stevenson 1999). Even the *Charlotte Observer* featured the story, "Brazil Crisis Worries NC Firms" (Hopkins 1999). In mid-January, Brazil's finance minister and central bank president flew to Washington to assure the United States and the IMF that appropriate austerity measures would be taken to prevent default on international loans and the continued free fall of the currency (Safatle 1999; Sekles 1999). The *real* and the Brazilian stock market temporarily stopped their descent and the Dow Jones average rebounded. It seemed that the linkages among globalization, the emerging capitalist world economic order, and the connections between the political economies of the United States and Brazil could not be clearer. I was wrong. They became even more explicit in February when Brazil announced, shortly after a visit to Brazil by the deputy managing director of the IMF, that Arminio Fraga Neto would become the new president of the central bank. Fraga Neto, who directs Brazil's monetary policy, had served as a fund manager for U.S.-based international financier George Soros's Quantum Emerging Growth Fund since 1993 (Schemo 1999b).

The observation that the United States has a profound effect on the Brazilian economy (and the economies of other Latin American nations) is neither novel nor trenchant. Eduardo Galeano (1997[1973]) and others (Baer 1995, Stillwaggon 1998, Thorp 1998) have chronicled this centuries-old relationship. But this set of events neatly captures contemporary manifestations of this historic relationship as well as multiple aspects of the globalization of the world's economy.

Globalization's essential quality is the increased mobility of capital. Among the consequences of this mobility are the tendency for multinational firms to locate production and assembly plants across many countries, to obtain financing in the international capital markets, and to market goods and services worldwide. Telecommunications and computers create the material infrastructure that permits firms to conduct business independently of the physical location of the corporation (Adams 1997).

Globalization is multidimensional in its effects. It creates great wealth, and as it spreads, its process challenges the state in new ways. Advances in technology and communications beam information and U.S. popular culture into the lives of people throughout the developing world. So while globalization raises the standard of living for many, it also raises the expectations of what people consider the minimum standards for housing, education, and medical care. Dreams of a better life, in conjunction with economic forces associated with industrialization, push people from rural areas and draw them to cities.

Globalization itself is merely one aspect of the emerging world economic order. Paul Krugman describes the world economy as a system, a complex web of feedback relationships, not a chain of one-way effects (1996: 53). In the new world economy, the most dynamic source of wealth generation is the creation of new knowledge that is then applied broadly to human activity by means of enhanced technology and organizational procedures for information processing. Not only is this informational economy global in scope, its structure and logic define a new international division of labor within this emerging world economic order (Castells 1993).

Globalization of the production system means that various countries may be classified according to the relative size of the workforce that is competitive on the global level. The emerging global economy is hourglass in shape: at the top are those who work in the high-tech, high-wage informational economy; those in the lower portion work in the low-wage, low-tech formal service (McDonald's), retail, and production sectors (e.g., maquiladores), and the growing informal sectors (street vendors). The majority of the globally competitive labor power is found in the developed nations. In the peripheralized industrial countries of Latin America, small elite segments of the productive system are competitive in the above sense. Increasingly, this division of labor polarizes a nation's workforce between rural and urban areas and within cities. Those with capital or who can manipulate technology and symbols are one side of the divide; those who have neither remain on the other side.

We gain a glimpse of the information and technology infrastructure in Brazil, Cuba, and the United States from Tables 1.1 and 1.2. Using the United States as a point of comparison, we see that in science and engineering research and development, Cuba is in a better position to enter the global economy than is Brazil, but still lags behind the United States. In other respects, those that involve technology and trade, Brazil is somewhat better positioned. However, compared to the United States, both Brazil and Cuba have tremendous distances to travel in order to enter the global economy as a partner.

Differences like these widen the gap between developed and developing world (Adams 1997). Before he became the president of Brazil, Fernando Henrique Cardoso cautioned against thinking of the South as on the periphery of the capitalist core, tied to the center in the classical relationship of dependence. He also rejected the view of the South as locked into a "dependent-associated" relationship whereby multinational firms transfer parts of the productive system to developing countries in which local firms linked to foreign capital then take over production. Instead, he warned of a crueler phenomenon: either the South invests heavily in research and development and endures the "information economy" metamorphosis, or it becomes unimportant, unexploited, and unexploitable (Cardoso and Faletto 1979). If developing nations fail to articulate with the new world economic order, then Cardoso saw the danger of their "quaternization" (Cardoso 1993).

International financial institutions play an important part in the restructuring of the world economy. During the last 3 decades, the policies of the International Monetary Fund and the World Bank have been shaped by the political economy of the United States and, in turn, have shaped the political economies of Brazil and Cuba. In doing so, the IMF and World Bank have affected economic and domestic policies, the distribution of wealth and poverty, and each nation's capacity to address the consequences of inequality. Homeless and street children are, in the final analysis, manifestations of a

Table 1.1   Science and Technology Indicators: Brazil, Cuba, and the United States

Indicator	Mean of Years 1981–1995[a]		
	Brazil	Cuba	U.S.
1. Scientists and engineers in R&D per million persons	165	1369	3732
2. Technicians in R&D per million persons	58	878	—
3. % GNP for R&D	.4	.9	2.5[a]

Sources: World Bank, *World Development Indicators* (1998).
[a] 1994 only for U.S. (UNESCO 1997).

Table 1.2   Information and Technology Indicators: Brazil, Cuba,
and the United States

Indicator (circa 1995)	Brazil	Cuba	U.S.
Daily newspapers	45	120[a]	228
Mobile phones per 1,000 persons	16	0	165
Faxes per 1,000 persons	1.7	—	64.6
Radios per 1,000 persons	222	241	—
TVs per 1,000 persons	289	200	806
Personal computers per 1,000 persons	18.4	—	362.4
Internet hosts per 1,000 persons	4.2	.06	442.1

Source: World Bank, *World Development Indicators* (1998).
[a] Cuban newspapers are state controlled.

nation's poverty. Thus, to understand the phenomenon of homeless and street children in the Americas, we must examine in greater complexity the history and operations of these two world financial institutions.[5]

BRETTON WOODS INSTITUTIONS AND THE GLOBAL ECONOMY

The global informational economy requires coordination. The institutional foundations for the necessary oversight began at the end of World War II. Bretton Woods institutions—the International Monetary Fund and the World Bank—provided the framework for the conduct of international economic policy in the postwar period and were a major factor in setting the tone of world economic development for the next half century. They set the rules for global trade (prior to the creation of the World Trade Organization) and created an international regime based on U.S. dominance of the world economy (Adams 1997; Amin 1997; Chossudovsky 1997; Polak 1994; Sassen 1991; Thorp 1998).

The IMF was conceived as a stabilization fund whose main purpose was to promote, through the use of its resources, exchange rate stability and adjustments to short-term disequilibria. The World Bank's niche was conceived to be reconstruction finance, especially the physical infrastructure, but development finance eventually became its raison d'etre. Initially, social investments in education, housing, or water and sanitation were not considered productive and therefore not eligible for loans (Adams 1997; Polak 1994). By the 1970s, new guidelines widened the scope of leading and permitted loans for agriculture and education. Since then, the World Bank has lent billions of dollars for education projects in more than 100 countries.

During the 1970s, developing countries' debt burdens rose steeply. The inflation caused by the oil crisis, the recession that followed, and additional borrowing to service interest on existing loans and to pay dividends on foreign investments created a cycle of debt. The processes underlying the growth of Third World debt were accompanied by an ideological shift in developed countries from the postwar Keynesian consensus toward the neoliberalism pushed by Reagan and Thatcher, and fueled by the fall of communism in Eastern Europe. Such views gave full play to free-market economic policies that included deregulation, privatization, cutting back the role of the government in the economy, import liberalization, removal of price controls, and huge cuts in government spending on social services and education (Carnoy 1999; Stillwaggon 1998).

Since the early 1980s, the macroeconomic stabilization policies of the IMF and the World Bank have included structural adjustment "shock therapy" programs. The impact of structural adjustment, including the derogation of social rights of women and environmental destruction, have been amply documented (Baer 1995; Bello 1993; Cardoso and Helwege 1997; Chossudovsky 1997; Cornia et al. 1987; Kakwani et al. 1990; Thorp 1998). Structural adjustment also has contributed to the destabilizing of national currencies and the crippling of economies in many developing countries.[6]

Adjustments occur principally through wages and labor markets, and extreme cuts in social spending. The burden of structural adjustments falls on already malnourished, ill-housed and unhealthy people (Stillwaggon 1998). Writing about Pinochet's Chile, where neoliberal reforms were crafted by University of Chicago–trained economists, the writer Isabel Allende observes that entrepreneurs and investors were in paradise as they enjoyed the benefits of the free market without troublesome unions; workers were plentiful, cheap, and submissive. Almost everything in Chile was privatized, including hospitals and schools.[7] And the government still intervened in the economy, but always in favor of the capitalists. "This savage capitalist revolution came out of the hides of the poor," charges Allende (1999: 27).

Martin Carnoy notes that a number of empirical studies, including several conducted by the World Bank, have shown that IMF and World Bank policies are associated with increased poverty, inequality of income and wealth, and slow or negative economic growth (1999: 23). While they have had dubious results with respect to the economic growth of developing countries, neoliberal macroeconomic stabilization policies have contributed to the impoverishment of millions of people (Adams 1997; Cardoso and Helwege 1997; Stillwaggon 1998; Thorp 1998).

Since the 1990s, monetarism has been applied across the board to global economic restructuring, including policies in the developed countries. Whereas the domestic macroeconomic policies of Bush, Clinton, Major, Blair, and Chirac are less harsh than those imposed on the South, the theoretical and ideological underpinnings are broadly similar. The consequences are skyrocketing corporate profits and economic growth—especially in the United States—in conjunction with the economic marginalization of large sectors of the population in the developed world. This is in part due to the hourglass economies of developed nations that are increasingly bifurcated into high-tech, high-wage jobs in financial and information sectors and low-wage jobs in service, retail, and some manufacturing. In addition, the relocation of production away from the central cities to suburban or offshore locations contributes to greater urban joblessness. As social expenditures are curtailed, many achievements of the welfare state have been reversed, leaving millions without adequate support for minimal levels of well-being (Bureau of Labor Statistics 1998; Children's Defense Fund [CDF] 1998).

GLOBAL ECONOMIC RESTRUCTURING AND INCOME POLARIZATION

The multiple processes and effects of global economic restructuring are perhaps most evident in major cities, especially those that Saskia Sassen calls global cities (1991, 1998). In cities, the effects of domestic and international migration intersect with the transforming capital-labor relationships. Racial and gender hierarchies are expressed in the reconstituting division of labor. The ways that the governments of Brazil, Cuba, and the United States mediate these processes and their effects can be seen in comparisons of social, educational, and economic well-being.

The Transforming Division of Labor

Major cities serve as the command posts for the world economy (Sassen 1991). Global cities have specific social structures where the capital-labor relationship has been reorganized: at the top are a small number of symbolic and financial workers who use technology and earn high wages and typically work for global firms; next is a middle class of professionals followed by a large working class that provides services to middle class and elite workers; at the bottom is a growing class of poor people, often the working poor. Immigrants from abroad and rural areas add to this mix. In urban areas of developing countries, Third World women's participation in the labor force has increased as urbanization and industrialization unfold. As low-skill jobs that pay living wages disappear in global cities, increasing numbers of uneducated poor urban residents are impoverished (Sassen 1998; Wilson 1996).

Sassen argues that employees of the multinational firms who arrive in the global cities contribute to the polarization of classes. The gentrified, compulsive spending classes, as Sassen characterizes them, require low-paid part-time workers to service their lifestyle. This lifestyle drives wedges between the rich and the poor, between urban and rural areas, and intensifies polarization within cities. In Latin America, the middle class as well as the rich live behind bars and gates; the streets have become the space of the poor (Hecht 1998). The growth in the United States of home security services in private homes and gated communities reflects the emergence of the same class polarization.

The informal sector of the economy grows in conjunction with rural migration to the cities. The underground (illicit) economy only partly overlaps with the informal sector. The informal economy involves the production of goods and services that are licit but produced outside the regulatory apparatus covering zoning, health and safety, or minimum wages (Sassen 1991). This pattern also appears in the United States, where an informal economy has flourished in inner cities and rural areas for decades.

Poverty and Quality of Life

There are growing disparities in income, wealth, and living standards within countries as well as between countries. Disparities are the outcomes of the economic histories of individual nations in interaction with regional dynamics such as the long-standing relationship between the United States and the Southern Hemisphere, and worldwide economic shocks like the oil embargo of the 1970s or the Asian economic crisis of the 1990s. Economic restructing and globalization of the world's economy, the neoliberal economic policies widely adopted during the last 2 decades, and their effects on domestic policies and programs contribute as well. Economies are affected by the policies of the global financial institutions that control and manage these processes. The globalization of poverty since the early 1980s, then, is not necessarily a consequence of scarce human or material resources. In fact, Brazil and the United States are wealthy nations. Rather, income polarization is intimately related to domestic policy choices of the government and actions of the civil society in response to the larger domestic and international economic context.

A series of comparisons among indicators of social, economic, and human well-being in Brazil, Cuba, and the United States illustrates these trends. Table 1.3 compares aspects of the economies of Brazil and Cuba. We can see that both nations have severe, albeit very different, economic problems. Table 1.4 shows that in most comparisons of living standards Brazil and Cuba fall far below the United States. Not surprisingly, Cuba has a much more egalitarian distribution of income. However, as we see in Tables 1.5 and 1.6, in the

Table 1.3 Economic Indicators: Brazil and Cuba

Indicator (circa 1995)	Brazil	Cuba
1. Annual rate of inflation in CPI[a] (mean, 1990–1995)	1,270	—
2. Commodity concentration index 1995	10.1	54.6
3. Import volume 1995 (US$millions 1970 prices)	11,601	510
4. Net barter of trade	60	118
5. Export volume growth (1900–1995)	2.7	1.9
6. Income terms of trade (purchasing power of exports)	429	45
7. Vehicles per 1,000 persons	88	47
8. Electrical energy kilowatt per person (1993)	1614	1017
9. Telephone density (lines per 1,000 persons 1990)	95	57
10. Railroad (kilometer of track per square kilometer of land 1995)	3.6	41

Source: Rosemary Thorp, *Progress, Poverty, and Exclusion: An Economic History of Latin America in the Twentieth Century* (1998).
[a] Consumer price index

areas of public health, adult, child, and infant well-being, Cuba equals and sometimes exceeds the attainment of the United States. Brazil comes in last on virtually every indicator except child malnutrition. In almost every comparison, Brazil has the least favorable indicators. Given the relative comparative resources of Brazil, Cuba, and the United States, these comparisons underscore the importance of state policy choices, rather than the absolute wealth of a country, for the health, education, and well-being of citizens. The dynamics of the poverty in the three nations are quite different, as are the effects of the globalized world economy on their political economies.

Table 1.4 Indicators of Income Inequality: Brazil, Cuba, and the United States

Indicator (circa 1995)	Brazil	Cuba	U.S.
1. Per capita GNP (US$)	$4,400	—	$28,020
2. Per capita GDP (US$ 1970 ppp prices)[*a]	$809	$480	$7,742
3. Population density per sq. km.	20	100	30
4. Per capita kg. oil consumption	772	949	7,905
5. Gini coefficient[b]	60.1	—	40.1
6. Percentage share of income received by poorest 10% of population	.8	—	1.5
7. Percentage share of income received by richest 10% of population	47.9	—	28.5
8. Percent of children aged 10–14 in labor force	16	0	0

Sources: An asterisk (*) indicates data are taken from the appendices in Thorp 1998. All other data come from the World Bank's *World Development Indicators* (1998).
[a] ppp = purchasing power parities
[b] Gini coefficients measure the extent to which the distribution of income among individuals or households within an economy deviates from a perfectly equal distribution. A Gini coefficient of 0 indicates a perfectly equal distribution, while one that is 100 represents a perfectly unequal one.

Table 1.5   Public Health Indicators: Brazil, Cuba, and the United States

Indicator (circa 1995)	Brazil	Cuba	U.S.
1. Life expectancy at birth—males—yrs	63	74	74
2. Life expectancy at birth—females—yrs	71	78	80
3. Prevalence of child malnutrition (%)	7	8	0
4. % Population w/ access to sanitation	41	66	85
5. % Population w/ access to safe water	72	93	90
6. % Population w/ access to health care	—	100	—
7. % Population smoking—male	40	39	28
8. % Population smoking—female	25	25	23
9. Births per woman	2.4	1.6	2.1
10. % Births attended by health staff	52	100	100

Source: World Bank, *World Development Indicators* (1998).

Poverty in Cuba

Sugar monoculture, shaped first by Spain and then by the United States, defined Cuban economy and society prior to the revolution of 1959. The period between independence from Spain and 1959 was marked by the intensification of both sugar monoculture and economic dependence on the United States. In 1880, 80 percent of Cuban sugar went to the United States; this rose to an annual average of 98 percent between 1899 and 1912. In the early part of the twentieth century, 53 percent of U.S. sugar came from Cuba. U.S. mills produced 60 percent of Cuban sugar and owned 22 percent of Cuban national territory. National City Bank of New York owned more than 50 Cuban sugar mills in 1921 (Thorp 1998: 77–79). Sugar was so woven into the fabric of Cuba's political economy, even after the revolution, attempts at economic diversification failed. With U.S. markets gone following the post-1959 rupture in U.S.-Cuban relations, Cuba turned to the USSR for markets and support.

Table 1.6   Adult, Child, and Infant Health Indicators: Brazil, Cuba, and the United States

Indicator (circa 1995)	Brazil	Cuba	U.S.
1. Low birth weight babies per 100,000 births	113	8	7
2. Infant mortality per 100,000 births	36	8	7
3. Maternal mortality rate per 100,000 births	160	36	12
4. Child mortality <5 yrs per 100,000	42	10	8
5. Child mortality >5 yrs.—males per 100,000	8	—	2
6. Child mortality >5 yrs.—females per 100,000	9	—	2
7. Adult mortality per 100,000—males	181	94	102
8. Adult mortality per 100,000—females	123	78	85
9. % Child immunization—measles	78	100	89
10. % Child immunization—DPT	83	100	94

Source: World Bank, *World Development Indicators* (1998).

Cuba has a population of more than 11 million citizens, 79 percent of whom live in urban areas (World Bank 1998). Since 1959, Cubans have successfully forged a new national identity, provided health care and education for the new nation, and become a force in geopolitics that influenced history in southern Africa and Latin America during the last quarter of the twentieth century. But Cuba is suffering from the effects of its own economic errors, the U.S. embargo, and the demise of its patron, the USSR. The 1992 Cuban Democracy Act and the 1996 Helms-Burton amendment to it tightened the U.S. embargo of Cuba coincident with the end of Soviet aid and trade with the Eastern bloc.[8]

Since 1991, the Cuban economy has been in deep crisis, and the government is effectively bankrupt (Eckstein 1994). State wages have not risen in line with increases in prices that followed the demise of Soviet subsidies. The informal economy has grown since the economic crisis worsened. For example, many professionals also work in the informal sector. Cuba is moving toward a dual economy defined by dollars: those who have them and those who do not.

But Cuban poverty is different in kind and extent from poverty in either Brazil or the United States. In addition to relatively narrow income inequality, polarization is less marked between rural and urban areas and within cities than in most other Latin American countries (Eckstein 1994; Lutjens 1996). Food is both subsidized and rationed, and those with dollars are able to buy more food in dollar stores. Moreover, health care, education, housing, and transportation are provided to citizens free or at subsidized prices. Nevertheless, some Cubans without dollars experience hunger.

Annually, Cuba garners about $US1.4 billion in hard currency from tourism and another $800,000 through gifts sent by relatives (McKinley 1999). About 50 percent of Cubans obtain dollars either through gifts from relatives abroad or tips from jobs in the formal economy (like tourism), or from licit and illicit activities in the growing informal economy (black-market sales of cigars, rum, and sex). And the informal sector, especially in tourist areas, has begun to flourish. Workers in the informal sector can earn far more than those earning state salaries. These changes have stimulated types of polarization not found since 1959.

It is difficult to evaluate dispassionately Cuba's economic development since the 1959 revolution for two reasons. First, there is tremendous ideological dogmatism on many sides, and second, comparative data are difficult to obtain. Nevertheless, until 1985, Cuba succeeded in achieving modest economic growth along with substantial distributional equity (Eckstein 1994; Rodríguez and Carriazo Moreno 1990). Recently, the Cuban state has pursued an economic course that engages the global economy via market relations and a commercial logic that, in some cases, supplants socialist mechanisms. Cuba seeks to implement market-oriented reforms without sacrificing the post-1959 gains in the areas of education, health, the reduction of rural/urban inequalities, and the reduction of race and gender inequalities. While children, pregnant women, the sick, and the elderly continue to enjoy special protection, in Cuba, as in the rest of the Americas, the threat of poverty is most acute for women, people of color, and the poorest in cities and rural areas. It is worth noting that market reforms were disastrous for the Russian economy and society, and neoliberal restructuring throughout Latin America has had devastating effects on the poor; Cuba soon may experience similar consequences.

Poverty in Brazil

Brazil has been described as Bel-India because it combines in one country the wealth of Belgium and the oppressive poverty of the subaltern continent (Hecht 1998; Scheper-Hughes 1992). The nation of 161 million people has the fifth largest land mass, the ninth largest economy, and the second worst income distribution in the world (Brazil's Gini coefficient of 60.1 is exceeded only by tiny Sierra Leone's 62.0). Even before the onset of the 1999 financial crisis, 66 percent of Brazilians lived in poverty (World Bank 1998: 5), and while 76 percent of Brazilians live in cities, rural areas are disproportionately poor (Baer 1995; World Bank 1998). Income concentration is stark: 10 percent of the population receives 48 percent of the income; the poorest 10 percent of the people receive less than 1 percent of the income (IBGE 1999a, 1999b, 1999c). Official unemployment figures show a 15-year low of 8 percent, but nongovernmental labor analysts put the number at 19 percent, and in certain poorer regions of the country, the rate is higher.[9] Class and race intersect in Brazil as they do in the United States: darker-skinned Brazilians are disproportionately poor.[10]

In Brazil, the established landholding system (the latifundio/monoculture system) not only has aggravated the chronic problem of low rural productivity through the waste of land and capital but has also stimulated the stream of unemployed workers toward the cities. New factories in emerging market nations like Brazil lure rural migrants seeking industrial wages and better lives. Too often, rural underemployment turns into urban unemployment.

Brazil's economic growth during the past decades has not transformed it into an advanced industrial society. Nor have the government, civil society, or the market stemmed the growth of poverty despite numerous initiatives intended to do so (Baer 1995; Hecht 1998). In real terms, the minimum wage of Brazilians fell by one-third between 1980 and 1988 (Rizzini et al. 1994). The 1980s debt crisis was devasting to the poor and working classes (Arruda 1994). The Brazilian state employs legions of civil servants, including teachers, who earn extremely low salaries (Hecht 1998; Plank 1996). Many in the middle and working classes hold several jobs. Families with multiple wage

Figure 1.2 An indigenous Guarani family travels great distances from their *favela* in the outskirts of São Paulo to work on the streets in downtown business and middle-class neighborhoods on market days. Pedro Vicente, his wife, and their three sons sell *palmettos* (hearts of palm) and carved wood handicrafts. (Photo by Fúlvia Rosemberg.)

earners in the formal sector still struggle to maintain a modest lifestyle. Those outside the formal economy are forced to work odd jobs in the informal economy. Children become essential wage earners in this economic context. This is why so many Brazilian children work in the streets—the site of most informal economic activity such as selling food or trinkets, working as a guide, guarding parked cars, helping parents who work on the streets, making *jeitinhos* (crafty solutions to ordinary problems), begging, and petty thievery. In these ways, children contribute to their families' subsistence and, in some cases of those truly homeless children, their own survival.

These long-standing difficulties of the poor are likely to be exacerbated by the economic crisis of 1999. It is noteworthy that the 1999 financial crisis was precipitated by the refusal of Itamar Franco, the governor of the state of Minas Gerais, to make debt payments to the central government for 90 days. His actions emboldened other governors to follow. In some states, more than 80 percent of revenues go to public payrolls. Another 13 percent go to debt service, leaving only 7 percent of the government's budget for schooling, roads, and social services. Because Brazil's foreign debt has ballooned to US$228 billion, the IMF's contingencies attached to recent loans require the central government to pass legislation limiting state spending on personnel to 60 percent of the budget (Fritsch 1999; Schemo 1999a). Such cuts hurt both those who lose their jobs through structural adjustment "rightsizing" of the government and those receiving fewer services. Public school teachers and students are directly affected by such cuts (Carnoy 1999).

Urban and rural poverty cause environmental as well as human degradation (Baer 1995; Pino 1996; Stillwaggon 1998). A large percentage of the urban and rural populations live in dangerous physical environments and do not have access to health and sanitation services. Uneven development forces the urban poor to concentrate in inadequate urban space. For example, because *favelas* are often in illegal areas, they have little infrastructure such as roads, sewage, or garbage collection. The water used by residents is untreated and often full of pathogens. This situation of cramped living in unsanitary conditions is associated with high levels of endemic diseases. Moreover, the type of building on hillsides typically associated with *favelas* results in environmental degradation. *Favelas* in Rio de Janeiro and São Paulo frequently experience landslides during the rainy season.

U.S. Poverty

While the performance of the U.S. economy in the last 5 years of the century has created economic growth, the poor have not shared the benefits. Corporate profits rose while inflation and interest rates fell. Official unemployment rates are the lowest in decades. But the booming U.S. economy masks the continuing struggles for survival that the poor face.

Since 1989, the United States has five times more billionaires, but 4 million more poor children (CDF 1998). How can this be? First, compensations for top corporate executives have swelled. In 1997, the chief executives of the 365 largest U.S. firms earned an average of 326 times the pay of the average factory worker, almost eight times the ratio in 1965 (Gold 1999). Second, employment statistics reflect all employed people, including those working less than 20 hours per week and those earning less than a living wage. More than 12 million full-time workers are paid wages lower than levels necessary to support a family. There is no consistent evidence that real wages have kept up with inflation, and a great deal of data suggests they have not. Third, the official unemployment rate typically underestimates the actual number of people without jobs. Unemployment statistics are notoriously inaccurate because they report only those actually still seeking work. A better measure is joblessness, a concept that includes those who have dropped out of the labor force. So while in December 1998, 6 million people (about 4.3 percent) were counted as unemployed, it is likely the true number of jobless is several times that (BLS 1998).

William J. Wilson has described how the U.S. labor market has twisted against those who live in poor neighborhoods (1996, 1987). There has been a nationwide transformation of the job market in inner cities, especially for poorly educated workers. Skilled jobs that pay living wages and benefits have been relocated either to the suburbs, the sunbelt, or overseas. The growth of jobs in cities has been largely in the tertiary sector (finance and information sectors). People with high levels of skills and credentials are competitive for these. Poor, inner-city residents typically do not have the credentials and skills to compete for such jobs. At the same time, there has been some growth in minimum-wage, dead-end service and retail jobs, and in many locations there are not even enough of these for the available low-skill labor pool. The lack of skills and education among the poor, especially in inner cities, and the changing labor market there reflect the intersection of race and class in the process of economic marginalization of millions of Americans because almost all major U.S. cities are racially segregated (Massey and Denton 1993; Sugrue 1996).

Despite rising corporate profits, there are proportionately more poor children in the United States in 1999 than there were in the 1970s. The United States has a population of 265 million people, 76 percent of whom live in urban areas. In 1973, 14.4 percent of children in the United States were poor. In 1998, almost one in four children grew up in poverty and one in eleven children grew up in extreme poverty.[11] Two-thirds of poor children have parents who work (Sherman et al. 1998). And while they are disproportionately members of minority groups, three-fifths of poor American children are white.

Poverty is the result of the interaction between structural forces, tragic circumstances, and, sometimes, bad choices. But many people who are not poor suffer from personal and familial crises. More important than individual factors in creating poverty are structural processes: the restructured globalizing economy, an inadequate minimum wage, a lack of affordable housing, transportation, or child care, and, of course, the gaping holes in the social safety net.

One of the most serious of these factors is the new federal "welfare-to-work" program, Temporary Aid to Families with Children (TAFC), that replaced Aid to Families with Dependent Children (AFDC). In 1996, the federal government abolished its largest social transfer cash assistance program, AFDC, and replaced it with TAFC. The central provisions of TAFC included lifetime limits on benefits and a requirement that recipients transition to school or work within 2 years. At the same time, food stamps were cut for poor immigrants (later to be restored), and supplemental social security income (SSI) for the elderly and disabled was cut. Earned income tax credits (EITC) helped those who work, but did not compensate for lost income and benefits.

The Children's Defense Fund and the National Coalition for the Homeless (NCH) report that while some former welfare recipients found work and some families were lifted from poverty, there is another side to the picture. Since 1996, there has been an increase in the number of children in extreme poverty among those families who left welfare. Between 1995 and 1997, 552,000 fewer children lived below the official poverty line; but in the same period, the families of 394,000 children had incomes below the bottom half of the poverty-level income distribution (CDF 1998; Homes for the Homeless 1998; National Coalition for the Homeless 1998).

Given the minimum-wage jobs they typically find, families who leave welfare are even less likely to afford rent than those remaining on welfare. For example, in New Jersey, one of the most expensive states in which to live, people must spend 78.6 percent of their minimum-wage job for the cheapest rent; in Missouri, one of the least expensive states, people have to pay 44.5 percent of net income for rent (CDF 1998: 113). Former welfare families who are homeless cite the loss of welfare benefits as a contributing factor (Sherman et al. 1998: 14–18).

CHILDHOOD POVERTY AND LIFE ON THE STREETS

While poverty in Brazil, Cuba, and the United States is related to each nation's unique political economy, its history, and its position in the hemisphere, there are certain common social and economic consequences of poverty that the poor tend to share. Children who work on the streets do so because there are no places for them in the formal economy and they or their families depend upon their earnings for survival. Poor children who live on the streets or in shelters do so because they and their families have no homes. It is not a tautology to say that homelessness is fundamentally due to a lack of housing (Kozol 1988). People lack housing because they cannot afford what is available, and what they can afford is not available. In all three countries, there is simply an inadequate supply of housing for poor and low-income people.[12]

Housing markets are very different in the three countries. In the United States, almost all housing is market driven; in Cuba it is not (yet); in Brazil there is a combination. In Brazil, the free-market housing is comingled with squatting. This means not only market dynamics but also political and social forces explain housing patterns. Because the housing markets in the three countries are so different, so too are the spatial relationships between home and work. Squatters who build in a *favela* on the hills behind the high rises can walk to work; those who squat in outlying *favelas* must ride public transportation for hours to reach their place of work in the business district. In such cases, sleeping on the street becomes a practical solution to an everyday problem. In the United States, almost all major cities are segregated by race and class, concentrating and isolating the poor (Wilson 1996). The paucity of jobs that pay living wages in inner cities (many firms have relocated abroad, to the sunbelt, or to suburbs) and the extraordinarily tight affordable housing market for low-wage workers contributes to increasingly greater distances between where the poor live and work.

Globalization contributes to the diminished supply of affordable housing for the poor in a number of ways. Gentrification of urban areas began well before the globalization of the world's economy. But globalization forces contribute to the dynamics of gentrification. In the United States, there is a growing tendency among landlords to convert poor people's domiciles into more lucrative residences for the middle-class professionals who arrive in major cities as part of the expanding high-tech, information-age workforce that is increasingly concentrated in global cities (Janofsky 1999; Sassen 1998). High-income gentrification creates jobs in the labor-intensive low-wage, service sector. Both in the United States and developing countries, this labor force is composed primarily of domestic and international Third World women migrants. So at the same time that affordable low-income housing stock is shrinking, globalization processes create conditions that promote the formation of a low-wage service and manufacturing labor force in global cities. Many of these workers become homeless because of a combination of their low wages and the paucity of affordable housing.

Problems of poverty, homelessness, and life on the streets are not individual phenomena. Rather they are, as Elliot Liebow observed, a social class phenomena (1993). In each country, there are unique forces that shape the contours of poverty, homelessness,

and the societal responses to these. Two decades of corrupt military dictatorship stimulated Brazilian industrialization, while it destroyed much of the rural environment. Both
processes provoked rural to urban migration. Along with huge debt burdens that Brazil
accumulated during the 1980s, these factors generated the incredible income polarization that manifests, in its basest form, as children working and living on the street (Baer
1995; Pino 1996; Plank 1996, Scheper-Hughes 1992).[13] In the United States, the globalizing economy, the reduced role of the federal government in housing and urban development, and the drastic reductions in social welfare spending contributed to a context
where greater numbers of the poor, including the working poor, become homeless.
Cuba's bankrupt economy, its battle with the 37-year-old U.S. embargo, the dissolution
of the Soviet bloc, its gradual entry into the global market, and its nascent market
reforms all contributed to conditions wherein some children and youth now turn to the
street for a livelihood.

Who Are the Children on the Streets of the Americas?

Homeless and street children are both visible and invisible. It is extremely difficult to
accurately count them because the size of the population is always changing. By virtue
of their living conditions, they are a moving target. Definitions used by educators, social
workers, or government officials vary by country and time period. Children who work
and congregate in the streets may be domiciled. In developing countries, ill-clothed and
barefoot street children do not appear much different from other poor children who
have homes in *favelas* or barrios; in developed countries, adolescents living on the
streets adhere to youth culture norms for clothing, jewelry, hairstyle, and body adorn-
ment just as do their counterparts with homes.

Brazil

The vast majority of Brazilian street children are not truly homeless. They are forced to
work or live intermittently in the streets by extreme economic and familial crises (see Klees
et al. this volume; Rosemberg this volume; Hecht 1998). A fraction of street children live
with their parents on the streets; typically, they are in transit from rural to urban centers.

A small fraction of all Brazilian street children truly live without parents on the
streets. Often such children create a fictive family unit among their associates on the
streets. Brazilian journalist Gilberto Dimenstein's work graphically portrays the most
horrific aspects of their exploited lives (1991). Tobias Hecht's ethnography of the street
children in northeastern Brazilian cities of Recife and Olinda captures a more nuanced
version of their street existence. His portrait reveals the Hobbesian nasty, brutish aspects
as well as certain of street life's appealing qualities—for example, networks of support,
availability of food and clothing to steal, and freedom from parental guidance (1998).
Hecht disabuses his readers of the more sanguine view of life on the streets, citing the
tragic histories of many of the children he studied during his ethnographic work.

Cuba

Although a developing nation, until recently Cuba had "clean streets." While Cubans are,
indeed, strained by the economic crisis, virtually no children live or formally work on
Cuban streets. This is because of the elaborate Cuban social welfare system that serves as
a tightly woven safety net even during the continuing economic crisis. Consequently,
few Cuban children suffer from the underlying grinding poverty endured by more than
60 percent of Brazilian children and 23 percent of U.S. children.

The introduction of the new commercialism that commenced during the Special Period in Peacetime has created fresh problems for Cuban families already stressed by long-term economic crisis. The explosive growth of the tourist industry (more than 1 million tourists visited Cuba in 1996) created markets for illicit street life, including prostitution among young women and men (Cabezas 1998) There has also been an increase in the number of children besieging tourists by either begging or hawking merchandise or services in the informal sector. However, these children are not homeless; they have homes, schools, medical care, and food. These developments are likely due as much to the "dollarization" of the Cuban economy as to its globalization.

There are some minors who do not or cannot take advantage of the elaborate social welfare and educational system in Cuba. Others are orphaned or abandoned. And while they are evidence of the new polarization of Cuban society, children working on the streets are still rare. There is little formal research on the subject. Lutjens (this volume) cites one study that counted about 40 street children per week in the tourist sections of Old Havana, and about 20 identified in other areas of the city.

The United States

According to the U.S. Department of Education's report to Congress, in the course of the year 1997, an estimated 630,000 children were homeless (1999). This number is consistent with several previous counts of homeless children between the ages of 6 and 17. This count reflects only families that passed through public or private agencies serving the homeless and whose children were enrolled in school. The figure does not represent the number who were homeless on any given day. That total is extremely difficult to calculate because it requires knowing the length of time a family remained homeless.

Another group of homeless youth, estimated to be about 300,000, are adolescents living on the streets. These are homeless and familyless youths. They are not part of the estimated 2.8 million youths who run away from home for periods of time and then return (National Coalition for the Homeless 1998: 2). Some youths become homeless with their families after a financial crisis. Later they are separated from others by shelter or child welfare policies. Other youths leave because of family violence—including sexual abuse, or because they have been rejected by parents due to their sexual orientation.

Crucial Distinctions

We must recognize, therefore, that not all street youths are homeless and that not all homeless children live on the streets. It is also useful to distinguish between homelessness in developing and developed countries. In developed countries like the United States, the vast majority of children living on the streets are teenagers who have run away from or have been pushed out of unbearable domestic situations (see Posner this volume; Ruddick 1996). Younger homeless children in developed countries typically are members of homeless families that live in their cars or in shelters, or double up with relatives and friends. In developing countries like Brazil, most street children are not truly homeless; the majority live and work on the streets and intermittently return to their family's domicile. However, in developing countries there are genuinely homeless children who have neither families nor homes. Children as young as 5 live in the streets (Blunt 1994; Hecht 1998).

There is, then, no single definition of street children, and it important to make the analytic distinctions among their various life circumstances. The definition used by UNICEF states, "Street children are those for whom the street (broadly speaking) more than their families has become their real home, a situation in which there is no protection,

supervision, or direction from responsible adults" (Blunt 1994: 237). From this definition, policy analysts have made several refinements: *Children of the street* have no
contact with their family members and live independently. These homeless children are
the exception. *Children on the street,* who make up the vast majority of street children
in the developing world, maintain some relationship with their family. They return home
daily, weekly, monthly, or when they are sick or need help.

These distinctions emphasize the fact that a majority of street children in the developing world are not necessarily either homeless or familyless. In fact, in the developing
world, they are likely to have a relationship with their family—typically their mothers and
siblings. Street children often provide an important portion of the family's income (Blunt
1994; Easton et al. 1994; Hecht 1998). Street children and runaway youth are active
agents who have made choices. This is not a romanticized notion of free will; rather, it is
a recognition of the social context of these children's lives. In some instances, contributing to the family's income is an important part of the child's identity. Similarly, living on
the street may be a better alternative to life in an abusive home or a crowded *favela* hours
from the city center where the child works.

In the developed world, the majority of homeless children are members of homeless
family units. Typically, homeless children and their families will be domiciled either in a
shelter or their car, or temporarily housed with relatives. Rarely do U.S. children and their
parents literally sleep on streets or in public places. Homeless adolescents are an important exception. They fit the definition of *children of the streets.* Homeless adolescents
who live on the streets, working, begging, socializing, and occasionally trading sex for
money, constitute a sizable portion of the population of homeless youths in America.

Government Responses to Homeless and Street Children

The recent increase in homeless children worldwide is a consequence of a number of
forces including domestic and international economic restructuring, the transition to
the global capitalist informational economy, the polarization of income and wealth, and
the disappearance of social safety nets associated with neoliberal economic policies. It
is useful to consider these processes as extensions to the global level of the Western
transition from traditional to industrial—now postindustrial—societies. The massive
social transformations that we see in Brazil today and the resulting growth of street children are similar in many ways to the Western European experience. Historically, the
flow of people from rural to urban areas and the increasing numbers of poor people,
especially children in public places, generated actual and perceived disorder, including
fear of crime by rogue children.

In one way or another, through their domestic policies, governments have always
mediated the impact of such major transformations. There is a certain historical continuity between the past and present measures employed by the Brazilian, Cuban, and U.S.
states to control and serve poor children. One solution has always been repression, ranging from curfews, to incarcerations, to exterminations. Today, the range of state responses
to the homeless and street populations includes extermination (unofficial, of course),
malign neglect, and a host of formal and informal programs that often involve collaborations with NGOs or religious institutions like those discussed in the chapters
in this book. Until the passage of the Child and Adolescent Statute in 1990, Brazil held
street children in "child welfare institutions" along with youths convicted of crimes. U.S.
prisons and youth detention centers continue to hold significant numbers of adolescents. While Cuba is somewhat different in that the population of street youth is very

small, it institutionalizes some delinquent youth deemed incorrigible. These differences notwithstanding, public education is virtually a universal policy and programmatic response to poor, homeless, and street children,—(at least in principle).

POVERTY AND EDUCATION

Although virtually all countries profess to honor children's rights to education, socially unequal outcomes are, nonetheless, one of the most widely enduring realities of our time (Connell 1994). In the United States and Brazil, schooling provided for poor children is markedly different from that provided for more affluent children. Not only do the poor receive less education but also their education, more often than not, is qualitatively inferior to the schooling provided for their more privileged counterparts.

Not surprisingly, homeless and street youth everywhere are the least likely to receive formal or informal educations (Anderson et al. 1995; Blunt 1994; Plank 1996).[14] The difficulty street and homeless children face in obtaining education is linked to the spatial dislocations that shape their lives. Just as poor people's spatial dislocations from employment interfere with their participation in the labor force, the shelters or *favelas* in which homeless and street children live make it even more difficult for them to attend school. Thus, changes in the dynamics of urban housing markets that are linked to globalization indirectly complicate homeless and street children's access to any education.

Education and the Individual

What kind of educations do poor, homeless, and street children need? There are two perspectives from which to approach the relationship between poverty and education: from that of the individual child and from that of the nation in which the child lives. The first concerns the role of education in lifting individuals from the mire of their poverty. The second involves the relationship between education and development. Increasingly answers to both aspects of the question must take into account the global informational economy context.[15]

From the perspective of individuals, the value and purpose of education must be broader than merely labor market preparation. At the World Conference on Education for All held in Jomtien, Thailand, in 1990, nations affirmed the place of education among the human rights recognized by the United Nation's Universal Declaration of Human Rights (World Conference on Education for All 1990). The state and civil society in each nation have a moral responsibility to educate all children irrespective of their gender, race/ethnicity, socioeconomic status, handicap, or region of residence. Citizens require education for democratic participation in civil society. Education is integral to human enlightenment and development. And as the great Brazilian educator Paulo Freire, has argued, education can contribute to personal and social transformation (1973).

At the same time, almost all children will work during their lives (many already do), and those with greater skills have a better chance of entering the formal labor market where their wages will be relatively higher. Given that the emerging global division of labor reflects the informational economy's bimodal distribution of high-tech informational age and low-tech service, manufacturing, and retail jobs, future workers who lack credentials and skills for higher-end jobs will be unable to enter the informational economy. While those with educations may still be relegated to irrelevance by macroeconomic forces, those without skills and training have even less opportunities. Most of them will become irrelevant to the formal economy and will be condemned to work in the informal sector.

Table 1.7   Indicators of Education and Literacy: Brazil, Cuba, and the United States

Indicator (circa 1995)	Brazil	Cuba	U.S.
1. % Adult illiteracy—males >15 yrs.	17	4	0
2. % Adult illiteracy—females >15 yrs.	17	5	0
3. % Enrolled primary education	90	99	96
4. % Enrolled secondary education	19	59	96
5. Mean years education attainment—males	8	12	16
6. Mean years education attainment—females	8	13	16
7. Pupil teacher ratio	23/1	14/1	16/1
8. % GNP for education	4.6[a]	6.6[b]	5.3[c]

Source: World Bank, *World Development Indicators* (1998).
[a]In 1989, UNESCO, *Statistical Yearbook* (1997).
[b]In 1990, UNESCO, *Statistical Yearbook* (1997).
[c]In 1993, UNESCO, *Statistical Yearbook* (1997).

Comparative Indicators

How successful are Brazil, Cuba, and the United States in providing education to their children? Comparative educational indicators appear in Table 1.7. Although, as Iris Rotberg cautions, international comparisons may be problematic if samples, tests, and indicators are not comparable (Viadero 1998), Table 1.7 nevertheless suggests several patterns. Overall, educational indicators for the United States exceed those for the other two countries. However, in almost every comparison, Cuban educational outcomes are more like those of the United States than Brazil, although Cuba is a much poorer country than either of the others. Cuban educational achievements reflect the priority given to education in public policy.[16]

   Whether the government is socialist or capitalist, domestic policies, like education, reflect choices and societal values. Despite the nation's enormous wealth and resources, public education in Brazil fails most children (Plank 1996; Stromquist 1997; Verhine 1998).[17] David Plank maintains that *clientelismo* in the public schools has corrupted Brazilian education (1996). Public sector jobs, including those in education, are routinely treated as private booty by civil servants (Hecht 1998). Structural adjustment austerity conditions for international loans have also hampered Brazilian efforts to provide adequate public schooling. As a consequence of these and other factors, the government provides poor Brazilians with very few educational opportunities. The U.S. public school system (actually 15,000 separate school systems) does a very mixed job of educating children. Middle-class and wealthy children typically receive extremely good public educations compared to what poor students receive (Anyon 1997; Kozol 1991; Mickelson and Smith 1994; Natriello et al. 1990). U.S. public education is marked by state and regional disparities, but the most important one is the urban/suburban cleavage because it is so highly correlated with race. Most large urban districts serve racial and ethnic minority students. Clearly Cuba is a poor nation and educational achievements have not altered that fact. But Cuba's relative poverty as a nation has not stopped its schools from educating the majority of that country's students to relatively high levels. Moreover, unlike Brazil and the United States, where urbanicity is highly related to educational outcomes, in Cuba there are far weaker urban and rural differences (Casassus et al. 1998).

If the relationships between education and individual poverty are not fixed, then we must ask whether educating poor, homeless, and street children is the solution to their plight. The answer is conditional. What kind of education does the child receive? Will the student's skills and credentials be suitable for entry into the formal economy? Are there racial and gender barriers in the job market? Are there available jobs that pay a living wage for those with educations? If the answers are no, then education is not even a partial solution to homeless and street children's situations. Will education in the long term enhance the child's life chances? Education alone is indeterminate. Therefore, the imperative for educating poor, street, and homeless youth must not rest on utility functions of schooling. Education is a matter of children's rights as human beings.

Education and Development

Just as education's curative power is prescribed as the necessary balm to heal a person's wound of poverty, education is widely considered the gateway to national development. Orthodox development theory gives a central role to investment in public education for national economic growth. National education policies and the international financing of development programs have been influenced by the faith in the ameliorative power of more and better schooling (Meyer 1986). Although the evidence is equivocal, nations with relatively better educated workforces are considered better able to compete in the global economy. The relationship between education and national development, as Brown and Lauder observe, both contradicts and corresponds to the human capital model (1996). Whether education stimulates development depends a great deal upon the policy orientation of the state and the nature of its political economy.

Given the reality of the global economy, what kinds of educational systems will support national development while advancing individual growth, a person's ability to make a living and to participate in democratic society? Joel Spring asks if it is possible to balance national goals and individual interests to create schooling for individuals that does not reduce them to mere resources (1998). Will education designed for global economies narrow or increase the polarization within societies and between nations? The future wealth of nations—measured in terms of quality of life, and social justice, as well as treasure—depends upon whether the answers to these questions challenge inequalities of power that underlie the maldistribution of education, income, and opportunities to live a life of dignity and meaning (Brown and Lauder 1996).

It is here that the question of the state enters the globalization-street-and-homeless-children-education nexus. The processes and consequences of economic transformations, including globalization, are mediated by the government. Whether the government is capitalist or socialist, it is the government's actions or inactions that directly affect education and homelessness, often by the degree to which it is involved in the provision of subsidized housing, public education, employment, and other social welfare services. It is here that we see the differences between the Brazilian, Cuban, and U.S. states: their structures, the extent to which they are involved in service provision (housing, employment, education, health care), and the public policy choices that they have made. It is critical that we recognize the importance of domestic policy *choices* for the fate of street and homeless children in the Americas. In the end, the Brazilian, Cuban, and U.S. states' adaptations to the new educational demands of global capitalism are not fixed—they will involve choices.[18] Martin Carnoy maintains that states can provide access to schooling more equally, improve the quality of education for the poor, and produce knowledge more equally within a globalized economy. That states generally choose not to offer more equitable education is at least partly the result of ideological preferences, not merely the result of the objective economic consequences of globalization (1999: 62–63).

As the political economies of the nations of the Americas integrated into the global economy during the last 2 decades, public and private actors have begun to reconstitute national education systems—for better or worse—in ways that articulate schooling with the global informational economy's structure and logic (Carnoy 1999; Ray and Mickelson 1993; Spring 1998). It is not at all clear that the children I saw on their cardboard bed in Rio, or in the *hogar* in Havana, or in the mainstream educational program in Charlotte, ever can be lifted from their poverty by education reformed to align with the global economy. Nor is it clear where or how they will fit into the new international division of labor that is emerging within the global economic order. It is clear, though, that without an education, they surely will be left behind.

THE STRUCTURE OF THE BOOK

The book is organized into six parts. This introductory chapter is Part I. The chapter sketches the living conditions and educational obstacles confronting poor, homeless, and street children within each nation. It flags the sociological dimensions of poverty in the three countries, and identifies the different challenges that each faces as it encounters the globalizing world economy. In Part II, chapters by Nelly Moulin and Vilma Pereira, Sheryl Lutjens, and James Stronge offer detailed analyses of the status of poor and homeless children and the education they receive in Brazil, Cuba, and the United States, respectively.

The chapters in Part III address the role of the state in matters of child well-being, the schooling they receive, and education policy. Steven Klees, Irene Rizzini, and Anthony Dewees describe the transformation of Brazilian national policy toward street and working children during the 1980s and 1990s. Irving Epstein engages the underlying dependency assumptions governing the education of homeless children and youth in the United States. Yvonne Rafferty reviews the legal entitlements to appropriate education of U.S. homeless children. Fúlvia Rosemberg critiques worldwide discourse that trivializes and distorts the realities of children's lives on the streets. The final chapter in Part III, by Rebecca Newman and Lynn Beck, looks at the intersection of a popular school reform—higher standards—and the education of homeless students in California.

Across the Americas, a variety of programs serve homeless and street children: some are offered by the government; others are public-private partnerships; a number have religious affiliations. Seven case studies of programs for homeless and street children appear in Part IV. These chapters illustrate various approaches to serving the educational and social needs of these youths. Some programs are exemplary; others leave much to be desired. All the programs are limited in that they leave intact the structural basis of homeless and street children's plight; that is, their poverty. Sheryl Lutjens offers a case study of a Cuban program, Maria Yon and I describe A Child's Place in Charlotte, North Carolina; and Fernanda Almeida and Inaiá Carvalho discuss Projeto Axé from Salvador, Brazil. Ralph Nuñez's case study of the Brownstone School is set in New York; while Amelia Queiroz and Ligia Elliot's program, Projeto Semear, is in Rio de Janeiro. Marcy School, discussed by Jean Anyon, is located in Newark; and Murilo Moreira Silva's case study of Programa Curumim is from Belo Horizonte, Brazil.

Although all homeless and street children are, by definition, needy in multiple ways, the chapters in Part V examine those who are even more marginalized than most. Lori Korenik and her colleagues address the issue of educating homeless children with disabilities. Ana Huerta-Macías and her coauthors analyze the plight of homeless undocumented immigrant children in El Paso with their case study of one such family and the Gateway School's response to them. Marc Posner discusses adolescents who live on the streets of America. The international community expressed shock and revulsion upon learning of the death squad murders of sleeping street youth on the steps of Rio de Janeiro's Candelária Cathedral in 1994. Martha Huggins's and Myriam Mesquita's analysis of the murder of street children is an appropriate end to the section on the Americas' most excluded youth.

In the final part of the book, I draw comparisons among the countries, programs, and policies discussed in the previous sections and attempt to synthesize the major themes and policy lessons offered by the contributors. I conclude with recommendations for micro- and macropolicies to address the immediate needs of homeless and street youth and offer some reflections on long-term solutions. One finding pervades all the lessons found in the other chapters: while education is essential, alone it is insufficient for resolving the vexing problems facing children on the streets of the Americas.

NOTES

1. Natives of Rio de Janeiro call themselves *cariocas,* a moniker they use with great pride.
2. In June 1994, the Brazilian *real nova* was valued at about 6,800 to the dollar. Inflation ran about 30 percent per month. Each day, newspapers reported the new exchange rate and the minimum wage. On July 1, 1994, Brazil converted its currency to the *real,* the value of which was pegged to the dollar.
3. In the last 2 years, street children have begun to work (begging and hawking merchandise) in tourist sections of Havana. See Sheryl Lutjens for a discussion of this and of *hogares,* the group homes for parentless Cuban children.
4. See my and Maria Yon's chapter for a more detailed treatment of this case study.
5. The problems of homeless children in Canada are relevant to this volume about street children in the Americas. In fact, the number of Canadian homeless families with children is growing. For example, a 1999 report by a task force convened by the mayor of Toronto describes the unprecedented numbers of homeless families with children in Canada's largest and most diverse city (Golden 1999).
6. Economist Jeffrey Sachs, of Harvard's Institute for International Development, criticized the IMF's policies: "We put Brazil through two years of unnecessary hell on the basis of terrible recommendations" (Phillips 1999).
7. Martin Carnoy analyzed the effects of privatization on Chile's schools since Pinochet's coup d'état in the 1970s (Carnoy 1998). He found that vouchers failed to do what proponents claimed, there was no persuasive evidence of the superiority of private schools, and children from higher-income groups were most likely to utilize private schools. Importantly, higher-income groups benefited as income from teachers, whose salaries were cut, was shifted to profits for entrepreneurs running the private schools. John Witte's evaluation of the Milwaukee, Wisconsin, voucher plan shows that after 5 years, there are no clear positive effects for private schools (1998). These findings, and the overwhelming achievements of the Cuban public school system (Casassus 1998), raise serious questions about the wisdom of market solutions to educational problems. As Sally Power and Geoff Whitty observe with respect to market solutions to the education of homeless children in the UK, "It is hard to see how the same distributive mechanism can be both cause and solution" (1996: 9).
8. In January 1999, President Clinton announced the relaxation of restrictions on trade, travel, and communication between the United States and Cuba (Weiner 1999).
9. The portrait of Brazilian wealth and poverty is based on IBGE's Synthesis of Indicators from the Brazilian National Household Sample Survey–PNAD of 1997. The survey was taken a few months before the Asian financial crisis that triggered the Brazilian crisis. Data were posted on the internet on December 9, 1998 (http://www.ibge.gov.br).
10. Race, racism, and social inequality are topics of epic dimensions and intense debate in Brazil as they are in the United States (Andrews 1991; Degler [1971] 1986; Fontaine 1985; Fernandes

1965, 1979; Harris 1964; Hecht 1998; Needell 1996). W. E. B. DuBois's prescient observation that the problem of the twentieth century is the problem of the color line is as true for Brazil as it is for the United States. Many years ago, Brazilian sociologist Florestan Fernandes (1979, 1965) argued that skin color correlates with wealth in Brazil; the country's rigid class structure relegates blacks and people of mixed race to the lower classes.

Most scholarly investigations of the relationship among race and class in Brazil report the myth that class, not race, is the important dynamic in Brazilian social stratification no empirical basis for. For example, Edward Telles (1994) found that as industrial development and education increased, Brazilian racial inequality decreased, but only for those in blue-collar jobs. Levels of racial inequality for white-collar occupations were unaffected, or even heightened, as levels of education and industrialization increased. Not surprisingly, most Brazilian street children today are what North Americans define as black. In the Brazilian racial parlance, street children range from *morenos* (dark or brown) to *pretos* (black) (Hecht 1998). Brazilian racism is not a minor social problem.

Cuban society is also multiracial and continues to struggle with the legacy of racism. Observers of Cuban society note both the overall reduction of institutional and individual racism since the revolution and the persistence of racial inequality across most social, economic, and political indicators.

11. U.S. poor are those whose household incomes fall below the official poverty line. Household income refers to the sum of the total weekly earnings of all persons living in a household. The poverty line reflects the amount of money the federal government calculates as the minimum necessary for acquiring the basic necessities. In 1997, the poverty line for a U.S. family of three was $12,802. In 1955, the federal government estimated the amount a household needed to maintain adequate nutrition. Since then, the poverty line is regularly adjusted for inflation and modified for family size. Extreme poverty is defined as family income below the lower half of the poverty line.

12. There are strong connections between the issues of public housing and the homeless. Martha Burt's *Over the Edge: The Growth of Homelessness in the 1980s* (1992) is an excellent treatment of the interrelationship between the two problems. Also see Christopher Jencks's *The Homeless* (1994). Julia César Pino provides a descriptive discussion of the growth of *favelas* in Rio de Janeiro (1996).

13. *Death without Weeping* (1994), Nancy Scheper-Hughes's ethnography of sugarcane workers in northeastern Brazil, vividly captures the lived reality of contemporary sugar monoculture's contribution to the corruption of rural Brazilian society and people's lives. In her account of migration of Bom Jesus residents seeking a better life, she records how people are pushed by latifundio exploitation and pulled by urban myths of prosperity.

14. We cannot understand education for poor and homeless children apart from the nature of the education system in each country. Robert Cowen and Maria Figueiredo's chapter on Brazil; Rolland G. Paulston and Cathy C. Kaufman's chapter on Cuba; and Susan F. Semel, Peter W. Cookson Jr., and Alan R. Sadovnik's chapter on the United States in the *International Handbook of Educational Reform* (1992) are excellent overviews of the three systems of education. Several recent books provide detailed, nuanced treatments of this subject. For Brazil, I relied heavily upon David Plank's *The Means of Our Salvation* (1996), and for Cuba, Sheryl Lutjens's *State, Bureaucracy and the Cuban Schools* (1996). Jean Anyon's *Ghetto Schooling: A Political Economy of Urban School Reform* (1997), Jonathan Kozol's *Savage Inequalities* (1992), and Gary Natriello, Edward McDill, and Aaron M. Pallas's *Schooling Disadvantaged Children* (1990) offer insight into the nature of the obstacles faced by families and educators in U.S. central cities.

15. The complex relationship between education and development has generated a vast body of scholarship. See Martin Carnoy and Joel Samoff et al., *Education and Social Transformation in the Third World* (1990); Bruce Fuller's *Growing Up Modern: The Western State Builds Third World Schools* (1995); John Meyer's chapter "Types of Explanation in the Sociology of Education," in Richardson's *Handbook of Theory and Research in Sociology of Education* (1986); O'Doyle et al., *Education and Development: Lessons from the Third World* (1993); and Nelly Stromquist's *Literacy for Citizenship* (1997).

16. The depth and breadth of Cuban educational achievements are also evident in results from a UNESCO study of language and math achievement among 15 Latin American countries. The First Comparative International Study of 3rd-grade math and 3rd- and 4th-grade language achievement was released in November 1998. Researchers report some small, nonsignificant variation among countries on all three tests. Cuba is the exception. In both language and math in all comparisons, the Cuban mean score was two standard deviations above the regional mean. The report also indicates that in all countries, there were large and significant differences between rural and urban areas, with rural students scoring significantly worse than urban ones (about one standard deviation). Again, Cuba is an exception in that urban and rural differences are small. The report indicated private school students performed better than public school students in math, but not in language. However, the authors hasten to point out that in Cuba, all schools are public. The Latin American Laboratory of Evaluation of the Quality of Education was created in 1994 by UNESCO in order to carry out comparative studies of education in the region. It is jointly funded by the Interamerican Development Bank, the Ford Foundation, and the regional office of UNESCO in Santiago, Chile, where it is also headquartered (Casassus et al. 1998).

17. The failure of the Brazilian education system forms the pivot of the plot of the 1998 Brazilia film *Central Station.* The main character, Dora, is a retired schoolteacher who makes her living writing letters for illiterate Brazilians. The film's denouement takes place as she reads to three illiterate brothers—one child and two young men—a letter written by their father.

18. I am indebted to Diane Davis, Sheryl Lutjens, John Meyer, Stephen S. Smith, and Michael Weinstein for their trenchant criticisms of earlier versions of this chapter. I am responsible for any errors of fact and interpretation.

REFERENCES

Adams, Nassau A. 1997. *Worlds Apart: The North-South Divide and the International System.* London: Zed Books.

Allende, Isabel. 1999. "Pinochet without Hatred." *New York Times Magazine,* Jan. 24–26.

Amin, Samir. 1997. *Capitalism in the Age of Globalization: The Management of Contemporary Society.* London: Zed Books.

Andrews, George Reid. 1991. *Blacks and Whites in São Paulo, Brazil, 1888–1988.* Madison: University of Wisconsin Press.

Anderson, Leslie M., Matthew I. Janger, and Karen L. M. Panton. 1995. *An Evaluation of State and Local Efforts to Serve the Educational Needs of Homeless Children and Youth.* Washington, D.C.: U.S. Department of Education, Office of the Undersecretary.

Anyon, Jean. 1997. *Ghetto Schooling: A Political Economy of Urban Educational Reform.* New York: Teachers College Press.

Arruda, Marcos. 1994. "Brazil: Drowning in Debt." Pp. 44–51 in *Fifty Years is Enough: The Case against the World Bank and the International Monetary Fund,* edited by Kevin Danaher. Boston: South End Press.

Baer, Werner. 1995. *The Brazilian Economy: Growth and Development.* 4th ed. Westport, Conn.: Praeger.

Bello, Walden. 1993. *Dark Victory.* Oakland, Calif.: Institute for Food and Development Policy.

Blunt, Adrian. 1994. "Street Children and Their Education: A Challenge for Urban Educators." Pp. 237–61 in *Education and Development: Lessons from the Third World,* edited by Vincent D'Oyley, Adrian Blunt, and Ray Barnhardt, Calgary, Canada: Detselig Enterprises, Ltd.

Blustein, Paul. 1999. "Brazil's Slide Stuns Markets." *San Francisco Chronicle,* 14 Jan., A10.

Brown, Phillip, and Hugh Lauder. 1996. "Education, Globalization, and Economic Development." *Journal of Educational Policy* 11: 1–24.

Bureau of Labor Statistics (BLS). 1998. *Economy at a Glance.* Washington, D.C.: U.S. Department of Commerce. http://www.bls.gov/eng.text.html.

Burt, Martha. 1992. *Over the Edge: The Growth of Homelessness in the 1980s.* Washington, D.C.: The Urban Institute.

Cabezas, Amalia Lucía. 1998. "Discourses of Prostitution: The Case of Cuba." Pp. 79–86 in *Global Sex Workers,* edited by Kamal Kempadoo and Jo Doezema. New York: Routledge.

Cardoso, Fernando Henrique. 1993. "North-South Relations in the Present Context: A New Dependency?" Pp. 149–60 in *The New Global Economy in the Information Age: Reflections on Our Changing World,* edited by Martin Carnoy, Manuel Castells, Stephen S. Cohen, and Fernando Henrique Cardoso. University Park: Pennsylvania State University Press.

Cardoso, Fernando Henrique, and Enzo Faletto. 1979. *Dependency and Development in Latin America.* Berkeley and Los Angeles: University of California Press

Cardoso, Eliana, and Ann Helwege. 1997. *Latin America's Economy: Diversity, Trends, and Conflicts.* Cambridge: MIT Press.

Carnoy, Martin. 1998. "National Voucher Plans in Chile and Sweden: Did Privatization Reforms Make for Better Education?" *Comparative Education Review* 42: 309–37.

—— 1999. *Globalization and Educational Restructuring.* Paris: International Institute of Educational Planning.

Carnoy, Martin, Joel Samoff, Mary Ann Burris, Anton Johnston, and Carlos Alberto Torres. 1990. *Education and Social Transition in the Third World.* Princeton, N.J.: Princeton University Press.

Casassus, Juan, Juan Enrique Froemel, Juan Carlos Palafox, and Sandra Cusato. 1998. *First Comparative International Study.* Report of the Latin American Laboratory of the Quality of Education. UNESCO-Santiago: Regional Office for Latin America and the Caribbean, Nov. http://ns.unesco.cl/lab/estudio.htm

Castells, Manuel. 1993. "The Informational Economy and the New International Division of Labor." Pp. 15–44 in *The New Global Economy in the Information Age: Reflections on Our Changing World,* edited by Martin Carnoy, Manuel Castells, Stephen S. Cohen, and Fernando Henrique Cardoso. University Park: Pennsylvania State University Press.

Children's Defense Fund (CDF). 1998. *The State of America's Children: Yearbook 1998.* Washington, D.C.: Author.

Chossudovsky, Michel. 1997. *The Globalization of Poverty: Impacts of IMF and World Bank Reforms.* Panang, Malaysia: Third World Network.

Connell, R. W. 1994. "Poverty and Education." *Harvard Educational Review* 64: 125–49.

Cornia, Giovanni Andrea, Richard Jolly, and Frances Stewart. 1987. *Adjustments with a Human Face.* Oxford, Eng.: Clarendon Press.

Cowen, Robert, and Maria Figueiredo. 1992. "Brazil." Pp. 51–68 in *International Handbook of Educational Reform,* edited by Peter W. Cookson Jr., Alan R. Sadovnik, and Susan F. Semel. New York: Greenwood.

Degler, Carl. [1971] 1986. *Neither Black Nor White: Slavery and Race Relations in Brazil and the United States.* Madison: University of Wisconsin Press.

Dimenstein, Gilberto. 1991. *Brazil: War on Children.* Translated by Chris Whitehouse. London: Latin America Bureau.

D'Oyley, Vincent, Adrian Blunt, and Ray Barnhardt. 1994. *Education and Development: Lessons from the Third World.* Calgary, Canada: Detselig Enterprises, Ltd.

Easton, Peter, Steven J. Klees, Sande Milton, George Papagiannis, Art Clawson, Anthony Dewees, Hartley Hobson, Bayard Lyons, and Judy Munter. 1994. *Asserting the Educational Rights of Street and Work Children: Lessons from the Field.* Report submitted to the Urban Section UNICEF, New York. Tallahassee, FL: Center for Policy Studies in Education.

Eckstein, Susan Eva. 1994. *Back from the Future: Cuba under Castro.* Princeton, N.J.: Princeton University Press.

Fernandes, Florestan. 1965. *A Integração do negro na sociedade de clases.* São Paulo, Brazil: Dominus Editora.

—— 1979. "The Negro in Brazilian Society: Twenty-Five Years Later." Pp. 103–121 in *Brazil: Anthropological Perspectives,* edited by M. Margois and W. Carter. New York: Columbia University Press.

Fontaine, Pierre-Michel, 1985. *Race, Class and Power in Brazil.* Los Angeles: Center for Afro-American Studies.

Freire, Paulo. 1973. *Pedagogy of the Oppressed.* New York: Seabury Press.

Fritsch, Peter. 1999. "Brazil Jolted as Governor Balks on Federal Debt. International Markets React." *Wall Street Journal,* 8 Jan., C15.

Fuller, Bruce. 1991. *Growing Up Modern: The Western State Builds Third World Schools.* New York: Routledge.

Galeano, Eduardo. [1973] 1997. *Open Veins of Latin America: Five Centuries of the Pillage of a Continent.* 25th Anniversary Edition. New York: Monthly Review Press.

Gold, Daniel. 1999. "Pressing the Issue of Pay Inequality." *New York Times,* 7 Feb., BU11.

Golden, Anne. 1999. "Taking Responsibility for Homelessness: An Action Plan for Toronto." Report of the Mayor's Homelessness Action Task Force, Jan.

Harris, Marvin. 1964. *Patterns of Race in the Americas.* New York: Walker and Company.

Hecht, Tobias. 1998. *At Home in the Street: Street Children of Northeast Brazil.* New York: Cambridge University Press.

Homes for the Homeless (HFH). 1998. *Ten Cities: 1997-1998: A Snapshot of Family Homelessness across America.* New York: Author.

Hopkins, Stella M. 1999. "Brazil Crisis Worries N.C. Firms." *Charlotte Observer,* 15 Jan. http://www.charlotte.com.

Instituto Brasileiro de Geografía e Estatísticos (IBGE). 1999a. *Minimum National Social Indicators Set: Education and Life Conditions.* http://www.ibge.gov.br.

—— 1999b. *Minimum National Social Indicators Set: Demographic Aspects.* http://www.ibge.gov.br.

—— 1999c. *Minimum National Social Indicators Set: Labor and Income.* http://www.ibge.gov.br.

Janofsky, Michael. 1999. "The Dark Side of the Economic Expansion: The Poor Wait Longer for Affordable Housing, Government Finds." *New York Times,* 7 Mar., Y24.

Jencks, Christopher. 1994. *The Homeless.* Cambridge: Harvard University Press.

Kakwani, N., E. Mankonnin, and J. Van der Gaag. 1990. *Structural Adjustments and Living Conditions in Developing Countries.* PRE Working Paper WPS 407. Washington, D.C.: Brookings Institution.

Kozol, Jonathan. 1991. *Savage Inequalities.* New York: Crown.

—— 1988. *Rachel and Her Children: Homeless Families in America.* New York: Fawcett Columbine.

Krugman, Paul. 1996. *Pop Internationalism.* Cambridge, Mass.: The MIT Press.

Liebow, Elliot. 1993. *Tell Them Who I Am: The Lives of Homeless Women.* New York: Penguin.

Lutjens, Sheryl L. 1996. *The State, Bureaucracy, and the Cuban Schools: Power and Participation.* Boulder: Westview.

Massey, Douglas S., and Nancy A. Denton. 1993. *American Apartheid: Segregation and the Making of the Underclass.* Cambridge: Harvard University Press.

McKinley, James C. 1999. "In Cuba's New Dual Economy, Have-Nots Far Exceed Haves." *New York Times,* 11 Jan., A1.

Mickelson, Roslyn A., and Stephen Samuel Smith. 1994. "Education and the Struggle against Race, Class, and Gender Inequality." Pp. 289-303 in *Race, Class, and Gender,* 2d ed., edited by Margaret Andersen and Patricia Hill-Collins. Belmont, Calif.: Wadsworth.

Meyer, John. 1986. "Types of Explanation in the Sociology of Education." Pp. 341-359 in *Handbook of Theory and Research in Sociology of Education,* edited by John G. Richardson. Westport, Conn.: Greenwood.

National Coalition for the Homeless. 1998. *Safety Network* 17: 1-4

Natriello, Gary, Edward L. McDill, and Aaron M. Pallas. 1990. *Schooling Disadvantaged Children: Racing against Catastrophe.* New York: Teachers College Press.

Needell, Jeffrey D. 1996. "Continuities and Change: A Century of Adaptation in Brazil." *Journal of Urban History* 22: 509-15.

Paulston, Rolland G., and Cathy C. Kaufman. 1992. "Cuba." Pp. 131-49 in *International Handbook of Educational Reform,* edited by Peter W. Cookson Jr., Alan R. Sadovnik, and Susan F. Semel. New York: Greenwood.

Phillips, M. M. 1999. "Brazil Takes Risky Move to Allow Currency to Continue Floating." *Wall Street Journal,* 18 Jan.

Pino, Julia César. 1996. "Dark Mirror of Modernization: The Favelas of Rio de Janeiro in the Boom Years, 1948-1960." *Journal of Urban History* 22: 419-53.

Plank, David N. 1996. *The Means of Our Salvation: Public Education in Brazil, 1930-1995.* Boulder: Westview.

Polak, Jacques J. 1994. *The World Bank and the IMF: A Changing Relationship.* Washington, D.C.: Brookings Institution.

Power, Sally, and Geoff Whitty. 1996. "Divided Responsibilities: The Education of Homeless Children in the UK." Paper presented at the meeting of the Comparative and International Education Society, Williamsburg, Va., 6-10 Mar.

Ray, Carol A., and Roslyn A. Mickelson. 1993. "Restructuring Students for Restructured Work: The Economy, School Reform, and Noncollege-bound Youth." *Sociology of Education* 66 (1): 1-23.

Rizzini, Irene, Irma Rizzini, Monica Muñoz Vargas, and Lidia Galeano. 1994. "Brazil: A New Concept of Childhood." Pp. 55-99 in *Urban Children in Distress: Global Predicaments and Innovative Strategies,* edited by Cristina Szanton-Blanc. Florence: UNICEF.

Rodríguez, José Luis, and George Carriazo Moreno. 1990. *Erradicación de la pobreza en Cuba.* Havana: Editorial de Ciencias Sociales.

Ruddick, Susan M. 1996. *Young and Homeless in Hollywood: Mapping Social Identities.* New York: Routledge.

Safatle, Claudia. 1999. "Juros altos vevitar inflação." *Jornal do Brasil,* 20 Jan., 13.

Sassen, Saskia. 1991. *The Global City: New York, London, Tokyo.* Princeton, N.J.:Princeton University Press.

———. 1998. *Globalization and Its Discontents.* New York: Basic Books.

Schemo, Diana Jean. 1999a. "Brazil Devalues Further, and Stocks Soar by 33 Percent." *New York Times,* 16 Jan.

———. 1999b. "In Surprise Move, Brazil Names Soros Ally to Head Bank." *New York Times,* 3 Feb.

Scheper-Hughes, Nancy. 1992. *Death without Weeping: Daily Life in Northeast Brazil.* Berkeley and Los Angeles: University of California Press.

Sekles, Favia. 1999. "Brasil ainda perde reservas. Malan pede mais calma." *Jornal do Brasil,* 20 Jan. 13.

Semel, Susan F., Peter W. Cookson Jr., and Alan R. Sadovnik. 1992. "United States." Pp. 443-73 in *International Handbook of Educational Reform,* edited by Peter W. Cookson Jr., Alan R. Sadovnik, and Susan F. Semel. New York: Greenwood.

Sherman, Arloc, Cheryl Amey, Barbara Duffield, Nancy Ebb, and Deborah Weinstein. 1998. *Welfare to What? Early Findings on Family Hardship and Well-Being.* Washington, D.C.: Children's Defense Fund and National Coalition for the Homeless.

Spring, Joel. 1998. *Education and the Rise of the Global Economy.* Mahway, N.J.: Lawrence Erlbaum.

Stevenson, Richard W. 1999. "I.M.F., United States Officials Warn Brazil to Keep Its Economic Promises." *New York Times,* 16 Jan.

Stillwaggon, Eileen. 1998. *Stunted Lives, Stagnant Economies: Poverty, Disease, and Underdevelopment.* New Brunswick, N.J.: Rutgers University Press.

Stromquist, Nelly. 1997. *Literacy for Citizenship.* Boulder: Westview.

Sugrue, Thomas J. 1996. *The Origins of the Urban Crisis: Race and Inequality in Postwar Detroit.* Princeton, N.J.: Princeton University Press.

Telles, Edward E. 1994. "Industrialization and Racial Inequality in Employment: The Brazilian Example." *American Sociological Review* 59: 46-63.

Thorp, Rosemary. 1998. *An Economic History of Latin America in the Twentieth Century.* Washington, D.C.: Interamerican Development Bank.

UNESCO. 1997. *Statistical Yearbook.* Paris: UNESCO.

U.S. Department of Education. 1999. *Report to the Congress for the Stewart B. McKinney Homeless Assistance Act.* Washington, D.C.: Author.

Verhine, Robert E. 1998. "The Financing of Primary Schooling in Brazil: An Analysis of Local Realities and National Trends." Paper presented at the World Congress of Comparative Education Societies, 12-16 July, Cape Town, South Africa.

Viadero, Deborah. 1998. "New Questions Raised About Validity of TIMMS Comparisons." *Education Week* (May 27): 7.

Weiner, John. 1999. "Anti-Castro Exiles Won Limit on Changes." *New York Times,* 6 Jan., A8.

Witte, John F. 1998. "The Milwaukee Voucher Experiment." *Educational Evaluation and Policy Analysis* 20: 229–52.

Wilson, William Julius. 1987. *The Truly Disadvantaged: The Inner City, the Underclass, and Public Policy.* Chicago: University of Chicago Press.

———. 1996. *When Work Disappears: The World of the New Urban Poor.* New York: Alfred A. Knopf.

World Bank. 1998. *World Development Indicators.* New York: Author.

World Conference on Education for All. 1990. *Final Report: World Conference on Education for All.* Jomtien, Thailand: Interagency Commission.

Part II: Children on the Streets of Brazil, Cuba, and the United States: A Status Report

2

Families, Schools, and the Socialization of Brazilian Children:
Contemporary Dilemmas that Create Street Children

Nelly Moulin and Vilma Pereira

In every culture, families have initial responsibility for socializing their children. It is the duty of the family to furnish at least minimal conditions for their offsprings' physical survival and psychological, intellectual, and social development. The structure and basic value system of Brazilian families have been weakened by repeated economic crises and the social transformations associated with development. Since the "economic miracle" of the 1970s, Brazil's economy has undergone successive recessions that have impoverished the wage-earning classes.

Such drastic economic and social changes have had a profound effect on the socialization of all Brazilian children. Schools, responsible for shaping citizens and preparing children for entry into the economy, have assumed some of the socialization functions previously performed by the family. But Brazilian schools are unable to perform satisfactorily their traditional duties to mold citizens and workers.

How does Brazilian society fill these gaps? This chapter focuses on the role of the government and civil society, especially the roles of families, the schools, nongovernmental organizations, and street educators in fostering the development and socialization of children. We examine the ways in which recent Brazilian laws have attempted to support the actions taken by government and nongovernment organizations to socialize and protect children and adolescents. We point out the structural and transitory factors that influence these processes and, in the final analysis, also reinforce Brazilian social inequalities because they fail to address their underlying causes.

CHANGING BRAZILIAN FAMILIES

The patriarchal family, organized around large landowners, constituted the foundation of economic and political power in Brazil, not only during the colonial and imperial periods but also in the early days of the republic. Patriarchal families brought together under one roof a husband, wife, sons, daughters, lineal and collateral blood relatives, as well as godchildren and others who had been accepted into the family. In this model, paternal power over all family members was absolute and was exercised in an authoritarian fashion.

Until the end of the nineteenth century, the population at the other extreme of the social scale was made up of slave laborers who inhabited a common area, called the *senzala* (slave quarters), on the *fazenda* (estate). Slaves were not allowed to form traditional family units. However, the fact that many slaves came from matriarchal African societies likely influenced family life among slaves and later among their descendants.

Between the powerful landowning elite and the miserable class of slaves moved a certain number of free workers, bureaucrats, and merchants. Their families were also marked by a strict hierarchy in which family members maintained unrestricted obedience to the male head. In all social classes, women were excluded from citizenship and denied civil, legal, and political rights. Their world was restricted to the home, and their duties were domestic.[1] Although carried out under the authority of the *pater familia*, the task of socializing the children was women's work. In the absence of schools, as was commonly the case in rural society, female family members also provided formal instruction in basic literacy. Very often, both in rural and urban areas, the home was the site for learning some kind of trade.

Beginning in the 1930s, a series of transformations changed the profile of Brazilian society. Brazil's struggle to develop transformed the economy from an essentially agricultural one, based on an export monoculture, to the predominantly industrial one of today. At the same time, Brazil experienced far-reaching demographic and social changes.

Between 1940 and 1970, Brazil's population doubled and its concentration shifted from rural to predominantly urban areas. In 1940, 31.24 percent of the population was urban. In 1970, for the first time, more than half of the population (55.98 percent) was urban. Twenty years later, 75.60 percent of the population lived in urban areas (Brazilian Institute of Geography and Statistics [IBGE] 1991). More recently, the 1995 National Survey of Sample Households (Pesquisa Nacional por Amostra de Domicílos [PNAD]), found 78.99 percent of the population living in urban areas (IBGE–PNAD 1996).

This demographic shift was just one of the factors that affected Brazil's population during the past 50 years. Industrialization and the consequent formation of an urban proletariat, the influence of the media in the shaping of customs, the campaigns to liberate women, and women's expanded role in the labor force are among the factors that influenced the structure of the modern Brazilian family. The urban Brazilian family changed from an extended to a nuclear form. The traditional model of the family still can be found in the less-industrialized areas, or in urban areas where there is a concentration of migrants from rural areas (Souza Campos 1985).

CONTEMPORARY BRAZILIAN FAMILIES

Although the nuclear family remains the most common form, research indicates that several models of family organization coexist in the Brazilian social context (Castelo Branco 1989; Gomes 1994; Novaes 1991; Szymanski 1992). Escaping from the concepts of a "nuclear" or "complete" family, Helena Castelo Branco constructed, instead, a descriptive typology "that . . . reproduce(s) the most important empirical manifestations of the family arrangements most frequently found in Brazilian society" (1989: 10). She found that the nuclear family still was the dominant form, but there has been an increase in the number of families headed by women.

Heloisa Szymanski argues that contemporary Brazilian families are "matrifocal," a model defined as "one organized around the woman when there is no male companion, but that assumes a patriarchal model when one is present" (1992: 6). Szymanski found that it is common for poor urban women to change partners while maintaining the family unit consisting of the mother and her children. Szymanski interprets this as a form of "marginalization of the man" that correlates with two historical factors we have already mentioned: the matriarchal heritage of some slave groups; and the prohibition of the formation of families during the slavocracy.

Census data from 1980 indicated that about 11 percent of households were headed by women (IBGE 1989). The most recent census (IBGE 1991) found that the average for the country had risen to 21.65 percent and that the highest percentages were found in the states of Rio de Janeiro (26.73 percent) and Sergipe (26.26 percent). Data gathered in 1995 confirmed this trend. A PNAD survey found, on average, 22.9 percent of families have female heads of households (IBGE 1996).

Moreover, as the modern family shifted from extended to nuclear, it also lost something in terms of marital stability. The increase in divorce in recent decades is one of the factors that has contributed to greater numbers of families headed by women. The causes of this trend vary from one Brazilian state to another. In Rio de Janeiro, as in other metropolitan areas, the growth can be attributed to cultural changes that have made women more independent from men in terms of survival and ability to care for children. In the states of the Northeast, especially the semiarid regions where droughts are endemic, the main reason for women becoming the head of the family has been the intense flow of men in search of better jobs and a higher standard of living toward Brazil's industrial hubs in the South and Southeast.

SOCIOECONOMIC PROFILE OF THE CONTEMPORARY BRAZILIAN URBAN FAMILY

Reality almost never corresponds to migrants' expectations. Accelerated urban growth in Brazil occurred in a disorganized fashion and with chaotic results. The lack of urban planning led to housing and running-water shortages, as well as inadequate transportation, schools, health care, and sewer systems. Overpopulation created surpluses of labor, especially unskilled labor. Having no way to survive, poor and miserable people set up households in *favelas* and *mocambos* situated on the hillsides, in swampy areas, or on the outskirts of large cities.[2] No social or economic policy has been able to reverse this situation. On the contrary, *favelas* have been expanding with the passage of time.

By the end of the 1960s, the authoritarian economic model imposed by the military dictatorship induced the "Brazilian miracle," a decline in the inflation rate coupled with significant economic growth. This model was based on a heavy concentration of income and capital in the hands of the elites and reliance on foreign capital. However, the fragility of the "miracle" was revealed by several factors, including the petroleum crisis of 1973. For the next 20 years, this economic model not only generated an astonishing increase in external debt but also aggravated the unemployment problem. That social crisis seriously affected the working class, whose wages were frozen, while the inflation rate rose geometrically. Inflation eroded worker purchasing power, lowered living standards, and made workers, as a class, poorer and poorer, and more and more miserable. During the 1980s and in the early 1990s, civilian administrations developed and implemented several new economic plans. None were able to rehabilitate Brazilian finances and avoid recurrent recessions.

In June 1994, under the presidency of Itamar Franco, with Fernando Henrique Cardoso as minister of planning (in 1995 Cardoso would be elected president), a monetary reform was instituted as the starting point for a new economic plan. A new currency—the *real*—was introduced, along with a number of other measures in the areas of taxes, government administration, and social security intended to ensure the economic plan's success. However, because these reforms depended upon congressional approval that had not yet been put to a vote as of early 1999, the policies have not been implemented.

Some positive effects of the monetary reform were immediately visible—a decline in the inflation rate to 9.2 percent in 1996 from a 1993 high that had topped 2,700 percent (Getúlio Vargas Foundation [FGV] 1996, 1997). As a consequence, there was a significant increase in the purchasing power of the new currency. On the other hand, the *real* plan has not been able to create new jobs, to spur economic growth without recession, or to promote a more equitable distribution of income.

Three major factors have helped the Brazilian state to cope with the worldwide economic crisis of 1998 and the flight of foreign capital that supported Brazilian monetary policy during the first 4 years of Cardoso's presidency (1994-1998). First, even though he was campaigning for reelection, Cardoso drastically cut the 1998-1999 domestic budget, stating, "I prefer to save the *real* than to be reelected." Second, at the time that the 1998 economic crisis was sweeping through Asia and Russia, Brazil had already commenced the privatization of state properties such as electric power and telephone companies, iron mines, and railroads. These enterprises were sold to foreign investors whose hard currency entered the Brazilian economy. Third, there has been a clear effort on the part of old and new European and North American investors to help Brazil escape the world financial crisis, largely because in doing so, the investors would save their own capital.

On October 4, 1998, Cardoso was reelected, even though the electorate anticipated greater budget cuts. The results of the Brazilian election were well received by the Brazilian and international financial worlds. While the inflation rate continued at about 2 percent in 1998, the internal recession and Brazilian unemployment rate remained stagnant (*Jornal do Brasil* 1998).

Wage scales still do not allow workers to live decently. Studies on the living conditions and welfare of Brazilian families indicate that a family consisting of the head and four dependents needs at least R$750 per month to get by. For example, 1991 census data showed that the monthly wages of about 80 percent of family heads were below that level. Most heads of families in Brazil (67.76 percent) earned no more than three minimum monthly wages.[3] Before the 1998 world economic crisis, recent figures indicated a positive trend. Although the number of wage earners receiving between three and ten monthly minimum wages had risen, income is still highly concentrated in Brazil (Monteiro 1996).

In recent years, more family members have entered the labor force in order to increase family incomes. As a result, the numbers of women entering the the labor market jumped 30 percent between 1981 and 1987 (Castelo Branco 1989). Whereas upper-income Brazilian women who work outside the home are relieved of domestic chores and child care by their paid domestic servants, in lower-class families low educational and skill levels do not permit women to earn wages high enough to hire servants. Poor and working-class women must appeal to charitable institutions for free day care or preschools so that their children are cared for while they enter the labor force. Then they bear the burden of domestic chores as a second job. As is true elsewhere in the world, the early introduction of children into nurseries, day care centers, and preschools transfers the responsibility for early socialization from the family to institutions.

The problems in supporting a family faced by the head of the typical Brazilian family has led to solutions that jeopardize family organization, stability, and members' health, as well as the socialization and schooling of the children. In order to boost his or her earnings, a family head must either work longer days, or join the informal economy during hours when he or she should be resting or pursuing leisure activities. This routine limits family fellowship and results in the fraying of interpersonal relationships. Furthermore, one must consider how the excess workload negatively affects a worker's physical health and emotional equilibrium. Across Brazilian society, economic conditions have made it more difficult for families to socialize their children.

CHILDREN IN THE LABOR FORCE

The role of children and adolescents in the Brazilian labor force is also significant. In 1987, the PNAD family survey found that, on average, 30 percent of youth in the 10-to-17-year-old age group worked. The figure ranged from 24.3 percent in urban areas to 43.1 percent in rural areas. A 1995 survey of households reported that almost 5 million children between the ages of 10 and 14 (30 percent of that age group) were working and that there were 5 million young workers between ages 15 and 17—half the population in that age cohort (Melo 1996). The percentage of youth in the labor force varies with the families' socioeconomic status; for example, the rate of children's economic activity declines as family income rises (Castelo Branco 1989). Poorer children are the most likely to be young workers.

In 1995, the PNAD first included individuals in the 5-to-9-year-old age bracket in its survey of the economically active population. The data gathered reveal the most perverse of situations. Out of a total of 16.3 million Brazilian children aged 5 to 9, 522,185 are already in the labor force. What is more serious is that 481,335 (or 92.2 percent) were not earning any pay, which means they were treated as slave labor (Melo 1996). The majority of those boys and girls (255,679, or 49 percent) worked from 15 to 39 hours a week; 226,790 (43.4 percent) worked up to 14 hours; and 21,215 were working more than 40 hours a week.

According to the survey results, in the absence of paid employment, the child follows parental examples and looks for work in the informal economy—working on the street as a vendor, shoe-shine boy, seller of candies or knickknacks, loading and pulling shoppers' carts at open-air markets, or guarding cars. The street exerts a strong attraction, inasmuch as it offers a series of alternative activities from which a child can earn a living and supplement family income. We should point out that although socioeconomic factors carry a lot of weight, they are not the only reasons that encourage children to gather in the streets. The weak attraction of school, a lack of family affection, or even the violence that a child may be enduring within the family tend to pull him or her away from the home and onto the street.

THE ROLE OF THE SCHOOL IN THE SOCIALIZATION OF THE CHILD

Although illiteracy has declined in Brazil, if school-age children continue to enter the labor force, then it will be difficult for Brazil to achieve a fully literate population in the near future. According to the 1991 census 20 percent of Brazilians older than the age of 15 were illiterate, while in 1995 an estimated 16.20 percent of people over the age of 10 were illiterate (IGBE 1996). However, out of a total of 522,185 child laborers age 5 to 9, 406,742 (77.9 percent) are enrolled in and attending school.

Brazilian schools serve more than 30 million children and adolescents. The profile of the Brazilian school is not particularly auspicious. By law, the federal government must invest at least 18 percent of annual tax revenues on education, while the states and cities must spend not less than 25 percent. Those funds are to be allocated to public and community schools, including church- or charity-supported schools. However, schools function ineffectively because of poor financial management and frequent strikes by severely underpaid public school teachers. Furthermore, due to lack of planning, the number of schools in urban areas has not kept pace with urban growth. Poorly paid elementary teachers are unable to take refresher courses and are forced to look for additional income to enhance their living conditions. These circumstances—out-of-date schools, too few schools, too few seats for new enrollments, teacher strikes—are indicative of the educational system's inability to meet its responsibilities.

Of those who enter first grade, and fewer than half make it into second grade. Later, only one quarter reach the fourth grade, fewer than 10 percent finish secondary school (Freitag 1980). According to the 1991 census, only 5.7 percent of Brazilian families were headed by someone who had completed 15 or more years of study, that is, college level. Most heads of household had not gone past the basic grades, and 24.4 percent either had less than one year of schooling or were illiterate.

Public schools are largely unsuccessful in socializing their students for another reason. Terezinha Carraher and others (1991) found that schools fail to take advantage of the body of knowledge accumulated by the students outside of the school; they fail to build on the knowledge and rationale of the students so as to expand it; schools are not aware of the skills that children of the lower classes must have if they are to survive in big cities; they do not recognize the difficulties in shifting from oral to written expression; and educators do not reflect on the differences in opportunities for learning among children from various social strata in order to redesign appropriate curricula.

STREET CHILDREN: EVOLUTION OF THE CONCEPT

As we have seen, a chaotic trajectory of urbanization shaped the growth of major Brazilian cities. A disorganized migratory flow of people from the poorer regions of the country to the industrial centers, deficiencies in the urban infrastructures, and urban overpopulation gave rise to large surpluses of workers. These forces are directly related to unemployment, low wages, the need for breadwinners to earn an extra income, women working outside the home, and children entering the job market at an early age. These factors set the stage for the disintegration of the traditional family, which, coupled with the bankruptcy of the school system, greatly contributes to the presence of boys and girls in the streets.

At the end of the 1970s, the term *street children* (*meninos de rua*) came into use in reference to poor and working-class children and adolescents who used the streets as their living, working, and recreational space. Until then, poor young people 18 or under found outside their homes, wandering the streets, or even those housed in assistance institutions were all called *minors*.[4] This was a pejorative label, inasmuch as the term was often associated with adjectives such as abandoned, needy, delinquent, at risk, or marginalized. Previous literature from the 1950s through the 1970s had referred to them with the terminology found in the Juvenile Code of 1927 and, later, in the 1979 Juvenile Code. Here they were referred to as marginalized minor, institutionalized minor, vagrant minor, or minor worker (Brazilian Center for Childhood and Adolescence [CBIA] 1993).

The pillars of the new concept of street children rest on the 1979 research by Fisher Ferreira and others, which reported that part of that population still maintained some kind of links to their families of origin.[5] The term *street boys and girls* (*meninos e meninas de rua*) first alerted us to the presence of both genders on the streets, highlighting the problem of street girls. Later, two different definitions emerged: children and adolescents *of* the street (*crianças e adolescentes de rua*), those who set up housekeeping on the main arteries or main commercial streets of urban zones; and the children and adolescents who were in transit *on* the street as part of their survival strategy (*crianças e adolescentes na rua*). The latter still had some kind of connection with their families, and many returned home frequently.

The conceptual distinction between children *of* the street and children *on* the street drawn in a 1989 Bogotá meeting on street children highlights the links to the family that Paulo Freire previously had emphasized. At that meeting, *children of the street* were defined as children and adolescents to the age of 18 and living in urban zones and who claim the streets as their principal residence in substitution of the family—even if tenuous ties remain. Life on the street, even if hazardous, is their primary source of growth and socialization (CBIA 1993). For these reasons, *children in the street* were called "children in a survival strategy." These are children and adolescents up to age 18 who, although maintaining family ties, are developing outside the family, in the street where they spend most of their time. Furthermore, they engage in activities designed to ensure their survival, both in the formal and informal economies—or even in the illegal economy. They may or may not receive remuneration, and what they do receive may be earmarked for themselves, their family, or even third parties (CBIA 1993).

Some research shows that children and young people of/on the street retain some links to their families of origin or their reference groups (Fisher Ferreira 1979, cited in CBIA 1993; Pinto et al. 1983). During the 1980s, studies on the status of poor children in Brazil identified a host of contributing factors leading to their marginalization: their need to generate income; the disintegration of traditional family forms; truancy from school; and the ostracism of children and adolescents by their families (Alvim and Valladares 1988; Rizzini and Rizzini 1991).

In 1987, a study by Maria Tereza Almeida reported the presence in the streets of both *working* and *nonworking* boys and girls. More recently, Alda Judith Alves-Mazzotti (1994) identified two subgroups among the *workers:* those who maintained a connection to some company (delivery boys/girls, messengers, newspaper vendors, helpers, and so on); and those in the informal sector who simply circulate in an open space as street vendors or as car guards.

Fúlvia Rosemberg (1994) conducted research in the city of São Paulo on the relationships between boys and girls of/on the street and their families, their residences, and their work. She reported a variety of conditions: some children and adolescents live with their families on the streets—these are the street dwellers; others simply accompany parents who are working in the streets (and may or may not help earn an income) and, like their parents, return home. Some street children maintain a connection with their families and work sporadically in the streets (at open-air markets, or near their homes); and others maintain the connection but work frequently in the streets. Some children work in the streets only occasionally, while residing with their families and attending school regularly. Still others, in spite of maintaining the connections with their families, work in the streets and eventually sleep in the streets. Then there are others who live without families in the streets for only a short period during their childhood or adolescence; finally, there are those who live in the streets for a major part of their childhood and adolescence.

Published counts of the numbers of street children are full of contradictions. Some experts claim there are thousands of children on the streets of big cities such as Rio de Janeiro or São Paulo. Others state that fewer than 1,000 children are actually living on the streets of those same cities. Both counts may be correct. One need only observe the diversity of relationships between those children and the street, family, and work in order to realize how difficult it must be to classify and register them. The fact that this is a nomadic population makes it even harder to count them. For these reasons, there is no accurate or comprehensive picture of the total size and location of this portion of Brazil's population (Rosemberg 1994).[6]

BRAZILIAN LAWS PERTAINING TO CHILDREN AND ADOLESCENTS

The 1990 Child and Adolescent Statute (Federal Law 9.069) is based mainly on the new constitution's vision of children's rights. Article 227 of the 1988 Brazilian Constitution states:

> It is the duty of the family, of society, and of the state to assure the child and the adolescent, as a matter of absolute priority, the right to life, health, nutrition, education, leisure time, vocational training, culture, dignity, respect, liberty, and the fellowship of the family and community, in addition to making them safe from any form of neglect, discrimination, exploitation, violence, cruelty and oppression.

The law is also the result of of a broad-based social movement on behalf of young people.[7] This pathbreaking legislation significantly changed the Brazilian legal panorama. The statute provides for full protection of children and adolescents. A *child* is considered to be a person under the age of 12; an *adolescent* is a person between the ages of 12 and 18. Full protection encompasses the observance of basic human rights and the assurance of opportunities that permit children to develop physically, mentally, morally, spiritually, and under social conditions of freedom and dignity (Article 3 of the statute).

The statute defines the duties of the family, society, and the government to ensure the fundamental rights of children listed in Article 227 of the Constitution. It also provides guidelines for effective observance of the rights of children and adolescents; the functioning of assistance agencies and their programs; protective measures; penalties for misdemeanors and crimes; and access to the courts. Among the statute's guidelines for the implementation of the rights of children and adolescents is the establishment of national, state, and municipal councils. These are decision-making and oversight bodies featuring balanced public participation by representatives of government agencies and civil society. Their work is financed by specific national, state, and municipal funds that are eligible to receive a portion of income tax revenues, as well as federal and state appropriations of funds (Article 88 of the statute). In short, the key features of the Child and Adolescent Statute of 1990 include equality of treatment, universal service, special priority attention to individuals who are still developing as people, and insistence on holding the family, society, and the government responsible for observing the rights of children and adolescents.

Implementation of the statute is proceeding very slowly throughout Brazil. Stewardship councils *(conselho tutelar)* empowered to implement the law at the local level are being set up, and other organizations are adapting to the provisions of the new law. Increasingly, people are starting to fight for their rights. However, there are obstacles to full implementation of the statute. Existing data indicate that although structures exist to provide full service to Brazilian children, in practice, the needs of children and adolescents are still not being met.

NONGOVERNMENTAL ORGANIZATIONS (NGOs)

Brazilians' concerns about the misery of poor children are long-standing. Although religious and charitable organizations were already in place during the nineteenth century, community groups also formed in order to assist those who lacked resources. Social assistance and specific legislation aimed at minors, however, dates from the twentieth century. As the problem became more extensive, the number of social assistance institutions grew. Ultimately, they were joined by the nongovernmental organizations.

NGO is a generic term referring to commercial, partisan, citizen-oriented, but not governmental, entities (Franco 1994). NGOs currently engage in the emerging practice of alternative development, as well as more traditional activities that ameliorate poverty, misery, and hunger. Franco refers to creative or alternative practices in contrast to more traditional ways to cope with the problems. Some of the institutions work with needy children, others with street children. Most of the projects are directed at children who live with their families in *favelas* in the midst of big cities and their shabby outskirts. The goal of those that work with youth is to protect children and adolescents who are at risk from being drawn into illegal activity. At the same time, NGOs emphasize schooling, acquisition of occupational skills, job placement, and actions that boost self-esteem and foster socialization among targeted children (Valladares and Impelizieri 1992).

The total number of institutions that serve children and adolescents in Brazil, the scope of their activities, and their history—as well as their effectiveness—are still unknown. For example, Valladares and Impelizieri (1992) identified 620 NGOs in Rio de Janeiro. They then classified them by type of institution and services offered: (a) alternative education projects; (b) social assistance agencies; (c) boarding homes; (d) residents' associations; (e) job-training projects; (f) shelters; (g) centers for the defense of human rights; (h) schools and day-care centers; and (i) coordinating bodies that finance and supervise a subgroup of projects that share the same principles. Of these 620 institutions, only 43 dealt specifically with street children, and of these, only 3 were founded prior to 1984.

In the final analysis, while NGOs intend to help ameliorate the problems of street children and adolescents, by and large, they have instead perpetuated their problems because NGOs fail to help children get off the streets, to redirect them to their families, or to support their families (UNICEF 1992).

THE ROLE OF STREET EDUCATORS

The need to have someone in the street who is able to initiate a dialogue with the contingent of street boys and girls was recognized early in the 1980s in numerous sectors of Brazilian society. The need was realized not only at the government agencies—such as the National Foundation for the Welfare of Minors (FUNABEM)—but also in the private sector, particularly NGOs associated with the Catholic Church. Early in 1982, FUNABEM began a project in partnership with the Social Action Department of the Ministry of Social Welfare and with UNICEF, entitled the Alternative Project for Assistance to Street Children. The project featured interns trained specifically to deal with street boys and girls. Depending on their abilities and skills, the interns would establish a personal connection with street children, supply some of their food needs, and get closer to the boys and girls. In addition to the humanitarian goals, interns sought "to reduce hunger as a driving force behind theft and other similar acts" (FUNABEM 1987: 3). This pioneering project influenced the establishment of assistance projects, both government-sponsored and others, throughout Brazil. However, after 1988, when UNICEF withdrew its financial support, FUNABEM discontinued the effort.

During this period, street educators, trained by the Catholic agencies located throughout Brazil, were guided in their social work and educational practices by the teachings of Christ and by pastoral principles of solidarity and sharing. In their work, the street educators sought to establish themselves as agents who

> respect the individuality of the child, his values, and his expectations. With genuineness, and truth, consistency. . . . Not crossing the boundaries of the child's vital space, which is real, unless the child wants this, unless he permits it. To do otherwise would be to violate that space. [They] wait for the "magic moment" when the child lets down his defenses. [They] have historic patience in initiating the process. (CBIA 1993: 18)

In the early 1980s, agencies and organizations involved in assisting Brazilian street children met to exchange and debate their experiences. The First Latin American Seminar on Community Alternatives for Street Children was held in Brasília from June 13 to June 16, 1984. It resulted in the formation of the National Movement of Street Boys and Girls of Brazil (MNMMR). As part of the conditions of the seminar, the profile of the street educator was drawn based on a significant contribution by Paulo Freire, who emphasized that the work of the street instructor will always have political, ideological, and pedagogical content. Moreover it must be oriented toward "thinking about practice, for an educational philosophy of growth rather than conversion," one that "is not accomplished without the transformation of the concrete reality that is generating the injustices" (Ramos 1995: 7). Freire described street educators as people who are perceptive and sensitive to the underlying causes of the problems of street children; respect the individual nature of others; possess a sense of mutual aid; are flexible and encouraging; do not try to "domesticate" the child or adolescent; work with the group in a group; do not try to suppress the accusations made by the young people; try to provide concrete conditions to help children overcome their situations; and develop education as a process of exchanging experiences (FUNABEM 1985).

Even at that time, street educators were selected more for their empathy and ability to identify with the children than for their academic background. However, all this work was always done *in the street* as a palliative effort. Despite all its progress in developing a profile of the ideal street instructor and determining the nature of his actions, the seminar put no emphasis on the task of *removing* the children and adolescents *from the streets* and setting them on the path to gaining their rights and citizenship. There was no frontal attack on the causes.

CONCLUSION

The prospects for poor Brazilians' economic futures are not very bright in the short run. In 1997, most Brazilian heads of households had less than 4 years of schooling and earned less than R$360 per month. In 1998, poor children had a very good chance of being expelled by the educational system and forced to work at an early age and often in the streets. These untrained, illiterate children will, at best, become unskilled workers competing in a globalized labor market that is becoming more and more oriented toward technology. They will most likely be underemployed or work in the informal sector.

Progress, stumbling blocks, and arbitrariness mark the course of socialization and assistance to Brazilian children and adolescents. Brazilian society has awakened to one of the by-products of the social problems we have described—the street children. And although people have battled to enact fairer laws, the actions proposed by existing laws still remain to be put into practice. The picture we have described shows that the social, political, economic, and pedagogical conditions under which comprehensive assistance is provided to children and adolescents cry out for immediate reformulation. Yet comprehensive assistance cannot be accomplished without the transformation of the concrete reality that generates the injustices.

NOTES

1. The legal model of the Brazilian family, according to the 1916 Civil Code, was that of the patriarchal family in its most conservative sense. All power was concentrated in the hands of the man/husband, who legally represented the family in dealings with the state and with society. A married woman was considered incompetent to make decisions about her children or to administer her property (even her own inherited property). This situation was not changed until 1962, when Law No. 4.721, known as the Married Woman Statute, was enacted.

2. *Favelas* (shantytowns), found in the Southeast, and *mocambos* (huts in the woods—the term originally referred to refuges used by slaves), found in the Northeast, are precarious dwelling units built of alternative materials (junk, straw, packing crates) in areas that have no sanitary infrastructure.

3. Brazil measures most incomes in terms of the equivalent number of (monthly) minimum wages, rather than as a weekly wage or annual salary. In May 1998, one minimum wage was approximately R$130, roughly equivalent to US$130. The government reviews the minimum wage each year on May 1, Labor Day. Most workers are paid only once a month. In rural areas, and even in urban areas at times, the lower-class workers are paid weekly.

4. Assistance institutions are philanthropic organizations (NGOs), often associated with the Catholic Church, which provide temporary housing and care for children. Unlike the government institutions where street children were previously compelled to live, children enter these voluntarily.

5. See Alvim 1991; Fisher and Gonçalves 1989 (cited in CBIA 1993); and Rizzini 1986 (cited in CBIA 1993).

6. See Rosemberg's chapter in this volume for a comprehensive and nuanced discussion of these issues.

7. See the chapter by Klees, Rizzini, and Dewees for an analysis of this movement and its effects on Brazilian domestic policy.

REFERENCES

Almeida, Maria Tereza F. de. 1987. "Os meninos estão na rua." *Projeto alternativas de atendimento aos meninos de rua: é possível educar na rua?* Rio de Janeiro: FUNABEM.

Alves-Mazzotti, Alda Judith. 1994. "Do trabalho à rua: uma análise das representações sociais produzidas por meninos trabalhadores e meninos de rua." In *Tecendo Saberes,* edited by Centro de Filosofia e Ciências Humanas. Rio de Janeiro: Diadorim Editora Ltda.

Alvim, Maria Rosilene B., ed. 1991. *Da violência contra o "menor" ao extermínio de crianças e adolescentes.* Rio de Janeiro: NEPI/CBIA.

Alvim, Maria Rosilene B., and L. P. Valladares. 1988. *Infância e sociedade no Brasil: uma análise da literatura.* Rio de Janeiro: ANPOCS. Mimeographed.

Brazilian Center for Childhood and Adolescence (CBIA); Ministry of Social Welfare. 1993. *"Meninos de rua": uma redução analítica da pobreza.* June. Rio de Janeiro: CBIA/DIEST. Mimeographed.

Carraher, Terezinha et al. 1991. *Na vida dez, na escola zero.* São Paulo: Cortez.

Castelo Branco, Helena Alvim. 1989. *Família indicadores sociais (1981–87).* Rio de Janeiro: Brazilian Institute of Geography and Statistics (IBGE).

Constitution of the Federative Republic of Brazil. 1988. Brasília Senate Printing Office.

"Estatuto da Criança e do Adolescente." 1990. Brasília Senate Printing Office.

Franco, Augusto de. 1994. *Redefinindo as ONG.* Belo Horizonte. Mimeographed.

Freitag, Barbara, 1980. *Escola, estado e sociedade.* São Paulo: Moraes.

Fundaçao National do Bem-Estar do Menor (FUNABEM) [National Foundation for the Welfare of Minors]. 1985. *Paulo Freire e educadores de rua: uma abordagem crítica.* Rio de Janeiro: FUNABEM/UNICEF/SAS.

———. 1987. "Projeto alternativas de atendimento aos meninos de rua: 1987." *É possível educar na rua?* FUNABEM/UNICEF/SAS.

Getúlio Vargas Foundation (FGV). 1996. "Compasso de espera." *Conjuntura Econômica* 50(1): 10-11. Rio de Janeiro: FGV.

———. (FGV). 1997. "Crise, estabilização e pobreza." *Conjuntura Econômica* 51(1): 22-26. Rio de Janeiro: FGV.

Gomes, Jerusa Vieira. 1994. "Socialização primária: tarefa familiar?" *Cadernos de Pesquisa* 91: 54-61.

Instituto Brasileiro de Geografia e Estatística (IBGE) and UNICEF. 1989. *Crianças e adolescentes: indicadores sociais 1.* Rio de Janeiro: Author.

Instituto Brasileiro de Geografia e Estatística (IBGE) 1991. *Censo demográfico 1991: características gerais e instrução.* Rio de Janeiro: Author.

———. 1996. *Pesquisa nacional por amostra de domicílios* (PNAD) [National Survey of Sample Households]: *Síntese de indicadores.* Rio de Janeiro: Author.

Jornal do Brasil. 1998. "Indicadores." 10 Oct., 18.

Melo, Murilo Fiuza de. 1996. "Brasil escraviza meio milhão de crianças." *Jornal do Brasil,* 25 Dec., 4.

Monteiro, Marion. 1996. "Os ganhos da estabilidade." *Jornal do Brasil,* 6 Sept., 12.

Novaes, Maria Salete N. 1991. *Direito à convivência familiar e comunitária.* Brasília: Ministry of Social Action.

Pinto, Lucia Luiz, et al. 1983. *Batalhadoras de rua: nós e elas, elas e nós.* São Paulo: Fundação Carlos Chagas.

Ramos, Lilian M. P. de Carvalho. 1995. *Educador social de rua: Um novo segmento para a velha categoria de educador popular?* Presented at the Encontro Anual da Associação Nacional de Pesquisa em Educação—ANPED. GT 6. Caxambu: Educação Popular. Mimeographed.

Rizzini, Irene, and I. Rizzini. 1991. "Menores institucionalizados e meninos de rua: os grandes temas de pesquisa da década de 80." Pp. 69-90 in *O trabalho e a rua: crianças e adolescentes no Brasil urbano dos anos 80,* edited by Ayrton Fausto and R. Cervini. São Paulo: Cortez.

Rosemberg, Fúlvia. 1994. "Estimativa de crianças e adolescentes em situação de rua na cidade de São Paulo." *Cadernos de Pesquisa* 91: 30-45. São Paulo: Fundação Carlos Chagas.

Souza Campos, M. C. S. 1985. *Educação: agentes formais e informais.* São Paulo: EPV.

Szymanski, Heloisa. 1992. "Trabalhando com famílias." *Cadernos de Ação* 1. São Paulo: Pontifical Catholic University of São Paulo/CBIA.

UNICEF. 1992. "Educação para todos: contribuições e desafios de Jomtien." Latin American Meeting of NGOs. *Contexto & Educação* 7(26): 21-74.

Valladares, Lícia, and F. Impelizieri. 1992. *Invisible Action: A Guide to Non-Governmental Assistance for Underprivileged and Street Children of Rio de Janeiro.* Rio de Janeiro: IUPERJ.

3

Schooling and "Clean Streets" in Socialist Cuba: Children and the Special Period

Sheryl L. Lutjens

In a world where structural dynamics and state neglect have contributed to a growth in poverty, homelessness, and violence by—and against—youth, the absence of street children in Havana has distinguished postrevolutionary Cuba.[1] The streets of Cuba's two-million-plus capital reflect the priorities and policies of the 1959 revolution, as well as the socialist commitments formalized in the early 1960s. More specifically, transformation in the economy and the pursuit of social justice created a context in which the care and education of all children became a constitutional responsibility of the state, mass organizations, and individuals. Yet the economic crisis of the 1990s, labeled the Special Period in Peacetime, has threatened the educational system and the egalitarian commitments of Cuban socialism. How have children been affected by crisis and the reforms that are adjusting Cuba to the new global order of the 1990s?

This chapter uses education to explore the distinctive role of the Cuban state with regard to children. It begins with an overview of change after 1959, presenting indicators of child welfare and well-being that reflect structural reforms and the crucial place of educational policies in Cuba's state-directed project of social transformation. The economic crisis associated with the collapse of socialist trade and the strengthening of the U.S. embargo, as well as Cuban responses, are then explained by exploring the consequences of the Special Period for children and their education. Cuban reforms have prioritized international tourism, and with success (more than 1 million visitors in 1997) has come an increasing number of children who implore visitors for pens, money, candy, or gum. Yet "there are no *niños de la calle* [street children]," said one official of the Federation of Cuban Women (Federación de Mujeres Cubanas—FMC) in 1995; the children who ask for gum, she noted, have schools, a place to live, medical care, and food (Berges 1995).[2] Conclusions about these—and other—children in Cuba must be placed in the context of state policies, schooling, and the "clean streets" that have characterized postrevolutionary society.

REVOLUTIONARY CHANGE AND CHILDREN

The 1959 revolution dramatically altered the conditions of childhood in Cuba. Nationalist and then socialist policies targeted the problems created by dependent capitalist development, creating formal opportunities and new protections for children of all colors and classes. In the process, state policies confronted the legacy of the past, as well as ongoing U.S. efforts to isolate and undo the revolution. Education has had a prominent role in reclaiming childhood in Cuba, and the revolution's successes offer a striking contrast with the sad realities of the life—and death—of children in the streets of Latin America's major cities.

Before 1959, the lives of children were defined by the complex dynamics of class, race, gender, and geography. Sugar was the core of a dependent economy, one shaped by slave production and four centuries of Spanish colonial control, followed by more than 50 years of U.S. neocolonialism under the Cuban republic. By the 1950s, ownership of land and infrastructure was concentrated (13 North American estates controlled 47.2 percent of sugar lands); foreign trade was oriented by U.S. markets and marketeers (the U.S. received 60 percent of Cuban exports and counted for 71 percent of imports); and Havana, in turn, was a thriving commercial and cultural center that contrasted sharply with rural life and its own metropolitan peripheries (Rodríguez and Carriazo Moreno 1990). While 20 percent of Cubans lived in Havana, the city accounted for more than half the value of national production—including sugar. At the same time, the easternmost province of Oriente had 31.9 percent of the population and only 15 percent of national production (Hardoy 1975). One-third of the workplace was un- or underemployed in 1953, and though Cuba ranked high among Latin American countries with regard to GNP and industrialization, rural life benefited little from twentieth-century advances (Rodríguez and Carriazo Moreno 1990). Rural housing lacked most amenities—including potable water—diets were poor, and there was but one rural hospital on the island. Conditions for the urban poor were similarly bad.

Education was maldistributed as well. Of those aged aged 10 to 49, 22.3 percent were illiterate, while only 45.9 percent of primary-age and 8.7 percent of secondary-age children were enrolled in 1952–53 (Rodríguez and Carriazo Moreno 1990). The 1940 Cuban Constitution, a product of the failed 1933 revolution, had nationalist and humanitarian goals, as well as an article devoted to the rights of children. Yet family law was rooted in the Spanish civil code in place from 1868 to 1950 (including the distinction between illegitimate and legitimate children), and poverty, unequal access to basic health and education, street labor such as shoe shining and thievery, institutionalized racism, and patriarchal family practices informed the divergent realities of Cuban children.

The revolutionary movement of the 1950s promised to eliminate these and other injustices and to fulfill the nationalist aspirations of the 1940 Constitution. Agrarian reform, housing reform, the abolition of gambling, prostitution, and speculative accumulation, and the nationalization of property were among the early measures aimed at creating a new Cuba. Change provoked U.S. responses and a Cuban alliance with the Soviet Union; by 1962 a hemispheric economic embargo was in place. Planning quickly became the institutional means for ensuring more equitable development and usable rights to employment, social welfare, health, and education. Castro's leadership and the reorganization of politics via mass organizations and a single (Communist) party produced an atypical socialist centralization. In many important ways, class, race, gender, and rural-urban inequalities were resolved.

Dramatic improvements in basic living conditions reflect the successful pursuit of a more socially just Cuba. In 1995, 74.4 percent of a population of nearly 11 million was urban and nearly 20 percent lived in Havana. Yet thousands of kilometers of roads and highways now connect rural areas to urban ones, the number of dwellings has risen from 1.5 million to 2.75 million (and 85 percent of families own their homes), and sanitation and electricity have been provided to rural Cubans (*Hoy* 1992; *Informe* 1995). There were 281 hospitals and 442 polyclinics at the start of 1998, and more than 30,500 "family doctors" working as resident neighborhood physicians (*Trabajadores* 1997a: 4).

There have been numerous, more specific indicators of improvements in the well-being of infants and children after 1959. With regard to the former, there were 183 maternity homes in 1995; while only 20 percent of births were in hospitals in 1953, now virtually all are attended in institutions. In 1958, infant mortality was 33.4 per thousand live births. It rose to 46.7 in 1969, though it dropped to 9.9 by 1994. In 1997, it fell to a low of 7.2 per thousand live births (*Granma* 1998a: 1; *Informe* 1995; Mesa-Lago 1994).[3] Many diseases have been eliminated entirely. Because almost 97 percent of children under 2 have completed their immunization series, Cuba is ranked at the top of all nations by the World Health Organization (*Informe* 1995: 27; *Granma* 1998b: 8, citing a World Health Organization study reviewing immunization programs in 214 countries or territories). Majority begins at 18 (or with marriage); 17 is the age at which youth may work and are eligible for military service; and Cubans vote and may be elected to local office at age 16.

In 1993, 22.6 percent of the Cuban population was less than 15 years old and educational policy explains much about the changing circumstances of school-age children. Educational reforms were a vital part of the goals of the Cuban revolution (see Lutjens 1996). The swift expansion of formal schooling began in 1959; in 1961, education was nationalized, eliminating the private schools that supplemented the opportunities of middle- and upper-class children. The Literacy Campaign of that year mobilized the people—including students—for the islandwide elimination of illiteracy. The first decade of educational reform was marked by the tremendous growth in primary and secondary enrollment. It also introduced strategies that became distinctive elements of Cuban education, such as the combination of work and study and adult education. The qualitative improvement of the new system began in the 1970s. In 1958-1959, enrollments were 625,700 in primary, 88,100 in secondary, and 2,100 in higher education; by 1980-1981, they were 1,468,300, 1,146,400, and 200,000, respectively (DIPLAN 1988).

Formal schooling included more than the basic, obligatory 9 years of education, however. Efforts to provide formal preschool education began in 1961. There were 38 municipal crêches in 1958—charity institutions that cared for some 1,600 children under 6; in 1960 the FMC undertook the organization of new *círculos infantiles,* day care centers for working mothers, raising more than $100,000 in 3 months to finance them ("Los círculos infantiles" n.d.). Responsibility for the *círculos* was transferred to a national Children's Institute in 1971 and later to the Ministry of Education (MINED). In 1960-1961, there were 37 daycare centers with 108,729 children enrolled; in 1970, there were 606 *círculos* and in 1990-1991, there were 1,116 (Varela Hernández et al. 1995). Special education was also prioritized. In 1958, there was but one center for children with physiological or developmental problems. In 1960-1961, there were 964 students enrolled in special education; in 1962, a department of differential education was created in the Ministry of Education, and by 1970-1971, there were 7,880 students in 129 centers of special education. In 1990-1991, there were 512 centers with 59,035 students (Varela Hernández et al. 1995).

Special education in Cuba has also included children with conduct problems, demonstrating the shift from a repressive approach to a focus on prevention and reeducation. According to Carreras, the first asylum in Cuba was established in 1839 by the Real Sociedad de Amigos del País. With the U.S. military occupation of Cuba at the start of the twentieth century, the asylums for boys and for girls were converted into correctional schools, renamed reform schools in 1909. Religious instruction for girls continued the colonial tradition, while the school for boys placed the orphaned and abandoned together with those who had committed crimes. Both institutions suffered from inadequate teaching (Carreras 1981).

The postrevolutionary approach to delinquency relied on education in several ways. The system for preventing juvenile delinquency was first located in the new Ministry of Social Welfare; a law supporting reeducation and rehabilitation of delinquent minors was passed in 1959, as was one authorizing Casas de Observación, where individual cases would be studied and then reported to judicial authorities. Transition Homes were created, as were Training Homes where minors learned trades (Kautzman Torres 1988). Also typical of this early period of reform, mobilization was used in reeducating youth scarred by the neglect of the prerevolutionary state. In 1960, Fidel Castro called for the creation of Youth Brigades for Revolutionary Work. Thousands of young men participated in a movement that quickly became known as the Cinco Picos because they were asked to scale the Turquino peak five times as a symbol of their commitment. In a similar vein, the Clodomira educational center was created for teenage girls from the poorer neighborhoods in Havana. Both the Cinco Picos and the Clodomiras were managed at first by the political organization for youth (*La Asociación* 1986). The role of workshop or trade schools, apprenticeship programs, and youth movements has continued.

Subsequent reforms centralized the administration of the system for treating delinquents while maintaining the basic strategies of these first steps. The Ministry of Social Welfare was dissolved in 1961, and the new Ministry of Interior assumed responsibility. A Commission for Social Prevention of Juvenile Delinquency was created, its participants including the Ministries of Interior, Education, and Health, the National Institute of Sports and Recreation, the National Council of Culture, the attorney general, and representatives of the mass organizations. MINED opened the first schools for children with conduct problems, the emphasis being on smaller centers with care provided by the FMC (Arias Beatón et al. n.d.). Both the Ministry of the Interior and MINED maintained centers for studying problem children as a means to collective decision making about each case. In 1982, Decree-Law 64 established the current System for Attention to Minors with Conduct Disorders, implemented still by the two ministries, and in 1987, Decree-Law 95 created a new hierarchy of Commissions for Prevention and Social Welfare. The system removes minors under 16 from the court system—surpassing UN minimums, according to the 1995 Cuban Report on the Rights of Children (*Informe* 1995).

The system recognizes multiple levels of conduct problems. State responses to the more serious ones are special education in schools administered by the Ministry of Education and reeducation centers under the Ministry of Interior. A 1984 review of existing studies showed that 90–100 percent of delinquents were boys, that 10–16 was the most common age group, and that incident factors included personality and family background and difficulties—including young mothers, education, and social influences (Arias Beatón et al. n.d.). In 1986–1987, enrollments in schools for conduct amounted to 0.4 percent of the 9–16 age group, and in 1990–1991, 0.3 percent (Arias Beatón et al. n.d.). According to the 1995 *Report,* institutional internment occurs only in severe cases—0.04 percent of the population 10–16 years old (*Informe* 1995).

Special schools for conduct Cubans label as antisocial are thus only one of several state responses. It is in this context that the category of problem children has been transformed. Indeed, they appear to be children who do not—or cannot—take advantage of what the system has to offer, rather than being systematically excluded from the exercise of their rights by virtue of class, color, or location. "The problem of 'street children' doesn't exist in Cuba, nor that of 'child labor,'" explained the 1995 *Report,* "but there is a low figure of minors that have not linked to the Regular System of Education due to disorders of health or conduct" (*Informe* 1995: 44). The retention of students thus serves as an important indicator of real or potential problems. In 1988, the dropout rate was 4.1 percent in junior high, 7.0 in preuniversity, and 8.7 in technical and professional education (secondary level) (Valdés et al. 1992). In 1989–1990, 0.7 percent of children aged 6–11 and 5.7 percent of those aged 12–14 were not enrolled, though the percentages were higher for 15- and 16-year-olds (18 and 33 percent, respectively) (calculated from Arias Beatón et al. n.d.: 73).

The crisis conditions of the Special Period in Cuba have raised new challenges to state policies and educational practices. Not all problems had been solved before the crisis erupted, of course, but both change and continuity have new meaning in the 1990s. There were some 60,000 doctors in 1996, for example, 20 times more than in 1960, and the accomplishments of the health care system are widely acknowledged. Yet the U.S. embargo was tightened with the Cuban Democracy Act of 1992 and the Helms-Burton Amendment in 1996, coinciding viciously with the collapse of Cuba's socialist trade. Health-related dollar imports declined—for example, from $134 million for medicines in 1989 to $66 million in 1993 (recuperating to $126 million in 1996)—with consequences ranging from a rise in waterborne disease to a new reliance on "green medicine" (CEPAL 1997; *Los Angeles Times* 1997: A4 cites the report of a study conducted by physicians for the American Association for World Health). The dilemmas of austerity in the Special Period have affected education, too, though accomplishments—including the highest teacher/inhabitant ratio in the world: 1/42 inhabitants (*Granma* 1998c: 3)—remain a source of pride in official discussion of what the revolution has achieved and promises to sustain as adjustment continues in the Special Period.

THE SPECIAL PERIOD AND CUBAN CHILDREN

The current economic crisis has affected Cuban children, though the state has maintained its commitment to their education and welfare as it faces the difficulties of the 1990s. These difficulties have multiple causes and far-reaching consequences. The recognition of serious problems with Cuba's model of economic development began in the mid-1980s, prompting a reform program called "rectification." With the subsequent disintegration of the socialist bloc, Cuba's preferential—and increasingly concentrated—eastward trade disappeared, precipitating a 70 percent decline in imports and a related 34.8 percent drop in gross national product between 1989 and 1993, (CEPAL 1997; González Gutiérrez 1998). Production slowed dramatically with the loss of imported oil and other industrial and agricultural inputs; the contraction of agricultural production accentuated the absence of previously imported foodstuffs. Capital formation plummeted, as did real salaries; the fiscal deficit increased from 6.7 to 30.4 percent of GDP and unemployment rose to 8 percent nationwide in 1995 (10 percent in Havana) (CEPAL 1997; Martín and Capote González 1998). Changes related to the desired reinsertion in the global economy promote old and newer exports, invite foreign investment (there were 20 mixed associations with foreign capital in 1990 and 260 in 1996), and prioritize tourism. Others include a necessary alteration of property structures, the legalization of dollars, new agricultural markets, the creation of a self-employment sector (counting 7.4 percent of those employed in 1995 [Núñez Moreno 1998]), and fiscal reforms.

Economic growth resumed in 1994, though constraints on recovery include U.S. policy that exacerbates the crisis and its costs to the Cuban people. In 1996, the economy grew 7.8 percent, exports equaled 64 percent of the 1989 figure, and imports 45.3 percent; unemployment in 1996 declined to 6.8 percent (CEPAL 1997). Yet fuel shortages still require blackouts, public transportation remains insufficient, and though the new agricultural markets have improved food distribution and curbed the black-market dynamics associated with scarcities, only half the population has access to the dollars needed to augment effectively the ration book (remittances were an estimated $600 million in 1995). Cuban studies reveal new inequalities of income, with some 15 percent of the population classified as precarious because their incomes can't secure the basic basket of goods (Espina Prieto 1998; on remittances, see CEPAL 1997). Although the worst moment may have passed, recovery is hindered by the escalation of the U.S. embargo of the Cuban economy. According to 1997 Cuban estimates, the cumulative damages inflicted by U.S. policy total some $60 billion. For example, new barriers to third-country subsidiary trade raise the cost of medical imports by 30 percent (*Granma* 1997: 3; Ferriol Muruaga 1998). Yet some costs are deeper than dollars can measure. Health problems and a rise in the percentage of low-birthweight babies are surely related to matters of adequate food and medical supplies. The latter problem has been reversed, however, and social transfers rose 21 percent in 1989–1996 (CEPAL 1997). Economic health, moreover, still hinges in crucial ways on sugar production and international prices. Growth slowed to 2.5 percent in 1997 and less than 1 percent for 1998 ("Economía Cubana" 1998).

Structural adjustment and austerity have created new challenges for an educational system expected to both prepare and protect children. There were 2,199,200 students in the Cuban schools at the start of the 1997–1998 term, with even higher enrollments estimated for 1998–1999 (DIPLAN 1998). The education budget contracted 46 percent in the 1989–1996 period, though current expenditures' relation to GNP grew between 1990 and 1996 (CEPAL 1997). Educational planning can no longer assume full employment, nor offer unlimited training of professionals; university enrollments declined by more than 50 percent between 1987 and 1997. Secondary education, in turn, has been redirected toward agricultural and other vocational specialties that better serve economic needs, thus reducing enrollments in university-track secondary schools. Maintaining and repairing schools is a problem—one measured in both pesos and dollars, as are adequately rewarding teaching personnel and supplying millions of notebooks and pencils, school uniforms, and the requisites of life in Cuba's many boarding schools. Shortages of once-imported chemicals and medicines affect education; in the 1995–1996 term there were outbreaks of contagious conditions, for example (*Granma* 1996b: 2). Yet there were also 87 hospital classrooms in Cuba, with 250 teachers working with more than 500 children, and 1,107 day care centers served by 801 doctors and 1,552 nurses (*Granma* 1996c: 24; *Trabajadores* 1996: 8). And nonformal preschool education has been extended throughout the island.

Change is not easy given the high expectations of parents and the state, and concerns about children and the streets resurfaced in the 1990s. Ministry figures for 1994–1995 show a dropout rate of 0.8 percent at the primary level and 3.3 percent at the junior high level; 98.2 percent continued their studies after graduating 6th grade, while 92.8 percent continued after 9th grade (*Cuba: Organization of Education* 1996). In 1996–1997, the percentage of dropouts in primary was 0.6, in basic secondary 1.5, and in preuniversity 5.6; in 1997–1998, 2.7 percent of 9th-grade graduates did not continue their studies (down from 7.2 percent in 1995–1996) (DIPLAN 1998). Although the female share of enrollments in trade schools has increased, one Cuban sociologist notes a considerable group of girls who are not interested in vocational education after 9th grade (and are too young to work) (Domínguez 1996).[4] In Havana, retention improved in 1995–1996, with a overall rate of 98.3 percent (0.7 percent higher than 1994–1995), and 92.3 and 90.6 percent in polytechnical and trade schools, respectively. There were 2,380

Figure 3.1   Cuban schoolchildren from Estado de Cambodia elementary school parade through their Havana neighborhood in celebration of Jose Martí's birthday. (Photo: R. A. Mickelson)

minors *desvinculados* (neither studying or working) at the end of the 1995–1996 term, 1,669 of whom were "relinked" to the institutional network ("Estado Actual" 1996).

THE REEMERGENCE OF STREET CHILDREN

The ill effects of the Special Period have altered social conditions and placed pressure on families. The material conditions of daily life inside the home are difficult, and one result is greater instability of families. Outside the home—in *la calle* (the street)—a new mercantilism has created other problems. Expanding tourism (there were 1,001,739 visitors in 1996—a 30 percent rise over 1995, while average annual growth in the number of visitors during the 1990–1997 period was 20 percent; *Granma* 1996e: 1; *Trabajadores* 1997b: 6) has contributed to the resurgence of illicit street life in Havana and other tourist enclaves. One oft-noted example is prostitution. The prostitution inherited by the revolution was remedied, for the most part, with the closing of bordellos, sanctions, and opportunities for education, health care, and work; what remained through the years was not significant in the Cuban view. In fact, prostitution was not included in the penal code though both it and procuring were included in the index of "precriminal dangerousness" and antisocial conduct. According to Díaz and González, there are three types of prostitutes in the 1990s: those who search out tourists; those who frequent major thoroughfares; and those who work as dancers, artists, or models (1997; see also Díaz Canals and González Olmedo 1995). The findings of one small-scale study showed that typically, these are women under 25, single, without children, and mulatta (cited in Díaz Canals and González Olmedo 1997).[5]

The state has officially acknowledged new concern about life in the streets, although prostitution is not seen as the central issue. The official discussion of the growing presence of children in the streets names three problems. First is the phenomenon of begging that has increased with the growing number of foreign tourists. There are kids who besiege (*asedían*) tourists, according to a recent media report that commented that "seldom is a verb used with such efficacy" (*Juventud Rebelde* 1996b: 5). A second problem that has surfaced is children who work, offering their services as tour guides, windshield washers, car sitters, and in *paladares* (restaurants opened in private homes) or other commercial activities in the new self-employment sector. A third problem, of much less scale, is sexual activity, including homosexual activity, that involves Cuban minors (see, for example, the story in *Granma* 1996d: 2).

The official discussion identifies causal factors and the difficulties of resolving emergent problems. At the VI Congress of the FMC in March 1995, for instance, there was ample attention to the issues of children and the streets. Tourism and parents were both targeted. Coronel Cecilia Andrés, head of the Commission for Attention to Minors, explained a "subtle enemy" that had not existed at the start of the 1990s; rather than tourism or foreign investment, the enemy was "conduct and attitudes that are an outrage against our dignity and our tradition." She called for preventive work, not repression (*Granma* 1995: 4). The dilemmas of preventing the return of children to the streets are captured by one of many recent media accounts. "These children shouldn't be rejected. Those that don't have big problems, with stable homes and no great needs, can put themselves in the place of these kids, understand them, and help them" (*Juventud Rebelde* 1996a: 8–9). Another 1996 commentary counseled a proactive position:

> Eradicating the presence of these minors will not be easy. There are numerous causes of the phenomenon and that are not eliminated by decree or with wishes. The evil has to be attacked in its manifestations and not in its origins, which in my view is an inevitable and essential contradiction. Without discounting what the country, the society, in the midst of economic crisis, might do and is doing to eliminate the causes. (*Juventud Rebelde* 1996b: 5)

How extensive is the presence of children in the streets? In Old Havana, the *casco histórico* of the city that sees 5,000 tourists each day, the Commission for Social Prevention identified 2,233 cases in the first 6 months of 1996, compared to 2,027 in the first half of 1995 (Acosta 1996). About 40 children from the municipality were detected each week and another 20 from other parts of Havana. The article cites a study finding that the majority were boys between 5 and 11 years old—"although now there are recorded cases of mothers who carry their nursing babies with them to 'make an impression' and ask for dollars or other things"—and that work is a second choice because they prefer activities with tourists. The article deposits blame with the family; many of the parents are divorced, don't know the whereabouts of their children, don't work, are absent from the home, and tolerate or even promote the attitudes of their children. Still, the article explained that more than half the respondents in one study placed responsibility with the schools; and 80.9 percent of the children detected are behind in school or attend conduct schools. Inappropriate parental attitudes are criticized in a newspaper story about "Ivan," who went from begging to purse snatching and theft, using statements attributed to his mother: "the 'macho' belongs in the streets"; "asking for things is not a crime"; "figure it out, what I earn isn't enough to survive"; "he should learn to defend himself starting as a small child." Ivan (one of six children by different fathers) ended up in the Habana del Este reeducation center (*Granma* 1996a: 3).

While parents or guardians can be fined or taken to court, efforts to improve the system for children with conduct problems are informed by the preventive strategy. Areas stressed in the 1995 Report on the Rights of Children included early detection, full coverage of children needing attention, improving the knowledge base in order to provide treatment that is better in both technical and practical terms, and more vocational training—something that has been limited by lack of workshops, equipment, and primary materials (*Informe* 1995). Indeed, while the report cited 2,125 children in situations of social disadvantage, a September 1996 summary of conditions in education in Havana stated that 20,374 such minors had been identified; family conditions were the most important factor, it explained, with 32.7 percent lacking care, 15 percent abandoned, and 17.8 percent with families that had inadequate conduct ("Estado Actual" 1996; *Informe* 1995). Family was cited as the primary cause for the 1,000 children aged 12–16 in reeducation centers nationwide in 1996 (*Granma* 1996a: 3). Enforcing Decree-Law 64 is not the only means for responding to the needs of at-risk children; the criminal code was modified in 1997 to include procuring and sexual trade, pornography, and the corruption of minors.

Education still has a central role in keeping Cuban streets clean. The schools work with commissions and other local authorities, they monitor absenteeism, and they investigate the cases identified. Local governments in Havana have helped in establishing special recreation programs for weekends and after-school hours. Other special programs have been developed in tourist zones, including the Children and Tourism Project begun by an academic researcher and a museum technician in Old Havana in 1993. Implemented with the help of the FMC and other community participants, the program strives to integrate students with their own heritage in a municipality where economic conditions are "*nada féliz* [far from happy]" (*Tribuna* 1996: 5).

CONCLUSION

The Cuban state does not ignore the circumstances of children and their families in the 1990s. The reforms pursued since the onset of the Special Period in Cuba have been catalyzed by dire conditions, a commitment to survival, and the socialist goals defined during 40 years of postrevolutionary experience. Constraints on Cuban choices persist, ranging from the uncontrollable effects of weather on an agricultural economy to the U.S. embargo and the very outcomes of adjustments and reform. Indeed, the unforeseen consequences of change, including the growth of new social groups and inequalities, challenge past accomplishments and future possibilities. Yet Cuban policies still privilege social justice in general, and child welfare in particular. In addressing the matter of children who have taken to the streets, the state has not resurrected the repressive treatment typical of its capitalist past, nor lessened its commitment to education as key to the futures of Cuban children.

NOTES

1. I gratefully acknowledge the critical comments on previous versions of this chapter by Justo Chávez Rodríguez and Juan Félix García Santa, both of the Ministry of Education in Cuba.
2. Translations from Spanish here and below are the author's.
3. The mortality rate of children under 5 is 10.7 per 1,000 live births, accidents being the chief cause.
4. In 1985–1986, female enrollments in trade schools were 15.6 percent of the total, increasing to 29.3 percent in 1993–1994 (Varela Hernández et al. 1995: 106).

5. According to Diaz Canals and González Olmedo (1995), in a study conducted by *Juventud Rebelde* and reported in the press on January 23, 1994, 33 women were interviewed; more than 60 percent either worked or studied.

REFERENCES

Acosta, Dalia. 1996. "Cuba: niños que trabajan o mendigan en la calle son cada vez mas." Internet at cuba-l@unm.edu; Saturday, 19 Oct.

Arias Beatón, Guillermo et al. N.d. *Care for Children with Conduct Problems in Cuba.* Santa Fe de Bogotá: UNICEF.

Asociación de Jóvenes Rebeldes, La. 1986. Havana: Centro de Estudios sobre la Juventud.

Berges, Célia. 1995. Interview by author, National Headquarters, Federación de Mujeres Cubanas, Havana, 21 Feb.

Carreras, Julió A. 1981. "Los reformatorios de menores." *Santiago* 41 (March): 148–64.

"Círculos infantiles: una hermosa tarea de la FMC, Los." N.d. Typed manuscript, Centro de Documentación de la Mujer, Havana.

Comisión Económica para América Latina y el Caribe (CEPAL). 1997. *La economía cubana reformas estructurales y desempeño en los noventa.* Mexico City: CEPAL and Fondo de Cultura Económica.

Cuba: Organization of Education 1985-1987; Report of the Republic of Cuba to the 41st International Conference on Public Education. 1988. Havana: Ministry of Education (MINED).

Cuba: Organization of Education 1994-1996; Report of the Republic of Cuba to the 45th International Conference on Public Education. 1996. Havana: Ministry of Education (MINED).

Díaz Canals, Teresa, and Graciela González Olmedo. 1995. "Algunas reflexiones sobre la prostitución en Cuba." Paper presented at Taller Internacional Mujeres en el Umbral del Siglo XX, Cátedra de la Mujer, Universidad de La Habana, 22 Nov.

———. 1997. "Cultura y prostitución: una solución posible." *Papers: Revista de Sociologia* 52: 167–175.

Dirección de Planificación (DIPLAN), Ministerio de Educación. 1998. "Libreta no. 2: datos estadísticos de la educación." Photocopied.

Domínguez, María Isabel. 1996. "La mujer joven en los 90." *Temas* 5: 31–37.

"Economía cubana tendrá su más bajo crecimiento en cuatro años." 1998. *Cuba-L Direct,* 18 Nov.

Espina Prieto, Mayra Paula. 1998. "Panorama de los efectos de la reforma sobre la estructura social Cubana: grupos tradicionales y emergentes." XXI Congress, Latin American Studies Association, Chicago, 24–27 Sept.

"Estado Actual de la Educación en Ciudad de La Habana." 1996. *Documentación para la X Sesión Ordinaria del VII Período de Mandato, Asamblea Provincial Poder Popular, Ciudad de La Habana, 26 de septiembre de 1996.* Ciudad de La Habana: Asamblea Provincial.

Ferriol Muruaga, Angela. 1998. "Política social cubana: situación y transformaciones." *Temas* 11: 88–98.

González Gutiérrez, Alfredo. 1998. "Economía y sociedad: los retos del módelo económico." *Temas* 11: 4–29.

Granma. 1995. "Comunidad, familia, mujer, un análisis la luz de estos tiempos." 3 Mar., 4.

———. 1996a. "Dos viejos pánicos." 13 July, 3.

———. 1996b. "Reparadas más de 200 escuelas para el próximo curso escolar." 24 Aug., 2.

———. 1996c. "Un aula de niños en pijama." 25 Sept., 4.

———. 1996d. "Cazadores de inocentes." 30 Oct., 2.

———. 1996e. "Sobrepasan 1 millón de visitantes en 1996." 31 Dec., 1.

———. 1997. "Ni ficción ni embargo: brutal guerra económica." 27 Nov., 3.

———. 1998a. "El impacto del bloqueo en la salud pública cubana es un acto criminal." 16 Jan., 1.

———. 1998b. "Erradicadas 10 enfermedades transmisibles en el país." 24 Jan., 8.

———. 1998c. "Educación: las venas de nuestra cultura revolucionaria." 17 June, 3.

Hardoy, Jorge. 1975. "Estructura espacial y propiedad." Pp. 274–311 in *Cuba: camino abierto,* 3d ed., edited by David Barkin and Nitza R. Manitzas. Mexico City: Siglo XXI.

Hoy; datos y referencias de una nación que resiste y se desarrolla. 1992. Havana: Editora Política.

Informe de la república de Cuba al comité de los derechos del niño por conducto del secretario general de las naciones unidas en relación con las medidas adoptadas para dar efecto a los derechos reconocidos en la convención sobre los derechos del niño. 1995. Havana, Aug.

Juventud Rebelde. 1996a. "No trocar infancia por monedas." 14 July, 8–9.

———. 1996b. "Eso niños siguen ahí." 8 Dec., 5.

Kautzman Torres, Victor L. 1988. *Prevención del delito y tratamiento al delincuente en Cuba revolucionaria.* Havana: Editorial de Ciencias Sociales.

Los Angeles Times. 1997. "Embargo of Cuba Exacts a 'Tragic Human Toll,' Health Report Charges." 3 Mar., A4.

Lutjens, Sheryl L. 1996. *The State, Bureaucracy, and the Cuban Schools: Power and Participation.* Boulder: Westview Press.

Martín, José Luís, and Armando Capote González. 1998. "Reajuste, empleo y sujetividad." *Temas* 11: 76–87.

Mesa-Lago, Carmelo. 1994. *Breve historia económica de la Cuba socialista: políticas, resultados y perspectivas.* Madrid: Alianza Editorial.

Núñez Moreno, Lilia. 1998. "Más allá del cuentapropismo en Cuba." *Temas* 11: 41–50.

Rodríguez, José Luis, and George Carriazo Moreno. 1990. *Erradicación de la pobreza en Cuba.* Havana: Editorial de Ciencias Sociales.

Trabajadores. 1996. "Círculos infantiles: queriendo a los que saben querer." 8 Apr., 8.

———. 1997a. "Presentación del proyecto de presupuesto del estado para 1998." 15 Dec., 4–5.

———. 1997b. "Ratifican incremento en recepción de viajeros." 15 Dec., 6.

Tribuna. 1996. "Los Niños son lo primero." 7 Apr., 5.

Valdés, Teresa, and Enrique Gomariz, with Ester Veliz and Carolina Aguilar. 1992. *Mujeres latino americanas en cifras: Cuba.* Madrid: Instituto de la Mujer; Santiago: Chile, FLACSO.

Varela Hernández, Miguel et al. 1995. *Cuba: sistemas educativos nacionales.* Havana: Ministerio de Educación; Madrid: Organización de Estados Iberoamericanos para la Educación, la Ciencia y la Cultura.

4

The Education of Homeless Children and Youth in the United States:
A Progress Report

James H. Stronge

Homeless children and youth are arguably the most at risk for failure, if not outright omission from school, of any identiable student population (Stronge 1993b).[1] On a daily basis, these students often face economic deprivation, family loss or separation, insecurity, social and emotional instability, and, in general, upheaval in their lives (Bassuk and Rosenberg 1988; Nuñez 1994; Rafferty 1995; Rafferty and Rollins 1989; Quint 1994; Shane 1996; Stronge 1992). "Against this backdrop, efforts to make education accessible and meaningful for them and their families is like swimming upstream against a swift current. These students deserve the opportunity to attend and succeed in school—an opportunity paramount to achieving success in life and thus breaking the hold of poverty and deprivation on their lives" (Stronge 1997: 14). If an opportunity to succeed is to be achieved, homeless students and their families need the concerted efforts of the educational community.

The purpose of this chapter is to provide background information relative to homelessness among school-age children and youth in the United States and to chronicle the progress made in recent years in the provision of an appropriate educational opportunity for homeless students. Particular areas of concern for improved access to and success in school are noted in the conclusion.

BACKGROUND

Definition of Homeless in the United States

Unless we can define the homeless population, it is not likely that we can craft policies or practices that effectively address the problems associated with educating homeless students. Thus, how we define the homeless becomes paramount to increasing awareness and, subsequently, to building successful intervention strategies. Defining homelessness seems simple enough: "Either a person does or does not have a place to call home" (Stronge 1992: 7). The reality, however, can be quite different, with definitions often caught in political crosswinds. The result is that definitions of homeless range from narrowly construed ones to broad-based descriptions, depending on the point of view or political perspective of the definer (Stronge 1993a). Narrowly focused definitions accentuate the literal nature of homelessness—individuals living on the street or those living temporarily in homeless shelters (see, for example, Kaufman 1984)—while more broad-based ones tend to include all individuals who lack a fixed residence (see, for example, National Coalition for the Homeless 1990).

The Stewart B. McKinney Homeless Assistance Act of 1987 (P.L. 100-77 and amended by P.L. 101-645 and P.L. 103-382), defines a homeless person as one who:

1. lacks a fixed, regular, and adequate nighttime residence, or
2. lives in (a) a shelter, (b) an institution (other than a prison or other institution-alized facility), or (c) a place not ordinarily used as a sleeping accommodation for human beings.

Since the McKinney Act is the applicable governing legislation in most American juris-dictions, it is this definition that educators should rely upon when developing and imple-menting educational programs for homeless students.

Extensiveness of Homelessness in America

Accurate counts (or even estimates) of homeless individuals in America are elusive. Due to a variety of problems—such as the transiency of homeless individuals, a preference among the homeless not to be identified, and a preference in some localities not to acknowledge the existence of a homeless population—determining how many homeless there are is difficult and far from an exact science. The National Coalition for the Home-less (1990) estimated there were at least 3 million homeless people in America. A 1996 estimate by the National Law Center on Homelessness and Poverty placed the number of homeless on any given day at approximately 760,000, with 1.2-2 million in the homeless ranks in the course of a year. Although estimates of the number of homeless individuals are provided, as in the examples above, caution should be exercised in interpreting these data:

> There is no easy answer to [the question of how many homeless people reside in the United States], and in fact, the question itself is misleading. In most cases, homelessness is a temporary circumstance—not a permanent condition. A more appropriate measure of the magnitude of homelessness is therefore the number of people who experience homelessness over time, not the number of "homeless people." (National Coalition for the Homeless 1998a: 1)

Determining how many school-age children and youth are homeless also is prob-lematic. However, it is clear that their numbers are significant and have not diminished in recent years (Burt 1991, 1997; National Coalition for the Homeless 1998b; Reed-Victor and Stronge 1999). Based on reports from the states and territories, the United States Department of Education in 1989 estimated there were approximately 272,000 school-age children in the homeless population. By 1997, there were 630,000 homeless stu-dents (U.S. Department of Education 1999). These estimates tend not to accurately reflect the 56 percent of homeless students who do not stay in shelters. Children who are below school age are not included in the counts (Nuñez 1995); additionally, adoles-cent homeless tend to be undercounted (Powers and Jaklitsch 1992, 1993).

There is a common misconception that homelessness is an urban issue despite the fact that approximately one-third of Americans who are homeless live in rural areas. Additionally, proportions of families in the homeless population is higher in rural areas than in cities and rural prevalence of single homeless women with children is double the urban rate (Vissing 1996).

Family and Youth Homelessness in the United States

While homelessness in American society has been well documented throughout our history (see, for example, Levitan and Schillmoeller 1991), the emergence of large numbers of homeless families and school-age homeless children and youth has resulted in a nagging and persistent problem (Stronge 1993b, 1995). For instance, a 1997 U.S. Conference of Mayors survey of selected United States cities found that 25 percent of the homeless population in the cities was composed of children with an additional 4 percent of unaccompanied youth (Waxman and Trupin 1997). There is general agreement that families with children are increasingly represented in poverty (Children's Defense Fund 1995; National Center for Children in Poverty 1990, 1996/97; Nuñez 1995; U.S. Census Bureau 1994) and in the growing homeless population (McChesney 1993; Nuñez 1994; Nuñez 1995).

Bassuk and Rosenberg (1988) found that more than three-fourths of homeless families were single-parent families headed by women. Further clarifying the makeup of family homelessness, Nuñez found the typical homeless family head-of-household to be "a young, single woman without a high school diploma or substantial work experience" (1994: 14). Undereducation, poverty, abuse, and abusive lifestyles in families translate directly to child poverty. For example, the National Center for Children in Poverty (1990) found that more than half of all poor children in America lived with single mothers. The National Center for Family Literacy (n.d.: 2) reported that children "whose parents are undereducated are at grave risk of continuing the cycle," and that fewer of their children are in preschool programs, while more are early school failures and high school dropouts than are the children of better-educated parents.

Nuñez, in describing what he called the "new American poverty," characterized the American homeless population as "composed of more families and children than ever before" (1995: 7). More specifically, homeless mothers were characterized as unmarried (91 percent), under age 25 (69 percent), with children under age 6 (80 percent); in addition, 36 percent of these young women had not graduated from high school (Nuñez 1997). "Homeless mothers' overall youth and relative inexperience in managing the day-to-day obligations of money, family and home complicate their route to self-sufficiency even further than does their lack of work experience" (Nuñez 1997: 95).

The U.S. Conference of Mayors reported an increase in the percentage of families with children within the homeless population from approximately 27 percent in 1985 to 38 percent in 1996. In this same study of 29 U.S. cities, 24 percent of the shelter requests by families were denied due to lack of resources (National Coalition for the Homeless 1997). Relatedly, the following findings summarize the emergence of families and, particularly, women with children in the homeless population (Reed-Victor and Stronge 1999):

- "17 percent of Americans, primarily women and young adults, believe that they could become homeless" (1995 Gallup poll, as cited in Lewit and Baker 1996).
- Single-parent households with income less than 51 percent of the poverty level were estimated to be 2.5 million in 1991 (Lewit and Baker 1996).
- "Domestic violence contributes to homelessness among families. When a woman leaves an abusive relationship, she often has nowhere to go. . . . Lack of affordable housing and long waiting lists for housing mean that many women are forced to choose between abuse and the street" (National Coalition for the Homeless 1997: 2).

- Families are often divided by homelessness. Because shelters frequently house either adult males or females, children are placed in foster homes or parents leave their children with relatives or friends (National Coalition for the Homeless 1997).
- Twenty-five percent of young children live in poverty; 12 percent of young children live in extreme poverty (below 50 percent of the poverty line) (National Center for Children in Poverty 1996/97).
- In the last two decades, increased rates of young child poverty have been noted in the suburbs and within the white population; the poverty rate for the elderly has decreased dramatically during the same period (by two-thirds) (National Center for Children in Poverty 1996/97).

CAUSES OF HOMELESSNESS

The causes of homelessness are complex, multidimensional, and defy simple explanation. However, there are identifiable factors that typically are closely related to homelessness, including housing, economic, personal, and family problems (Reed-Victor and Stronge 1999).

Affordable Housing

Of particular concern for families with school-age children is the obvious correlate of homelessness: insufficient affordable housing. McChesney analyzed the problem of family homelessness from the perspective of "the 'low-income housing ratio'—the number of households living below the poverty line divided by the number of affordable housing units available." When the number of poor households exceeds the number of low-income housing units, the families have three basic options: (a) those who can, pay more for housing; (b) those who cannot pay more double up with family or friends; and (c) those who cannot do either become homeless. Thus, "only those programs that reduce poverty or increase the supply of affordable housing will be effective in decreasing the total number of homeless families in the United States" (1990: 191).

Economic Difficulties

Economic challenges, particularly unemployment or inadequate employment opportunities, are directly tied to homelessness. In a study of self-reported reasons for homelessness, Hagen (1987) found that both men and women listed unemployment as the number-one reason for their homelessness. Moreover, even for those individuals who have jobs or who find work, underemployment may not bring housing within an affordable range (National Center for Children in Poverty 1990). "In 1994, 62 percent of poor young children lived with at least one parent or relative who worked part-time or full-time" (National Center for Children in Poverty 1996/97: 1).

Personal Problems

Personal problems reflect a significant role in homelessness. The diversity of homeless students' needs are influenced by "such factors as length of time without a home, reason for homelessness, availability of outside support systems, the environment of the shelter, and the age, sex and temperament of the child" (Linehan 1992: 62). While their reactions are varied, homeless children are more likely to experience health and nutrition, psychosocial, developmental, and educational problems than their housed peers (McChesney

1993). Many homeless children lack the "semblance of order and stability" in their lives and the results can be reduced sense of control and social behavior, which increases their alienation from potentially supportive school environments (Stronge and Tenhouse 1990: 16).

Family Problems

Family problems, such as spouse abuse, may cause a family to break up, creating a need for independent housing for both parties—a circumstance that leaves women and children especially vulnerable to homelessness. Bassuk and Rosenberg found in their study that "about two-thirds of the men with whom homeless women had their most recent relationships had poor work histories, substance abuse problems, battering tendencies, or other problems" and that 41 percent of the homeless mothers willing to respond to the question detailed a relationship in which they had been battered (1988: 785). Thus, when living conditions become intolerable, women and their children frequently are forced to move out of the house

BARRIERS TO EDUCATION FOR HOMELESS CHILDREN AND YOUTH

Barriers to school access for homeless students are created through educational bureaucratic procedures, including residency, school records, immunization, guardianship, and transportation policies (Anderson et al. 1995; Helm 1993). The McKinney Act established clear mandates to reduce these barriers. Although greater access is now provided for some homeless students, numerous local schools are still unaware of their legal responsibilities to provide educational support.

The primary barriers to educational access for homeless students have been legal ones—specifically, issues related to residency, guardianship, and student records. In surveys conducted since the mid-1980s, homeless shelters, consistently, have indicated their personal knowledge of situations in which residency has been used to deny educational access (National Law Center on Homelessness and Poverty 1990; Rafferty 1995), and their perceptions of residency as a substantial barrier to education for the homeless (Stronge and Helm 1991).

Guardianship, another potential educational barrier for homeless students, is mandated either statutorily or by policy in most states and localities. It requires that a parent or legal guardian be present to enroll a child in school. Homelessness, however, frequently separates families and, thus, runs counter to this requirement. As an example of this type of problem, children who are temporarily staying with friends or relatives and who are unable to meet school guardianship requirements may be denied permission to register for school if the requirement is strictly enforced.

A third major issue related to educational access for homeless students is the unavailability of appropriate student records, particularly medical records. Most schools, by state law, mandate proof of immunization as a precondition to enrollment. Helm (1992) noted that homeless students, depending largely on the length of time they have been homeless, may have difficulty meeting this requirement in that: (a) the parents may not know about the requirements; (b) the parents may not be able to afford immunization or be aware of public health immunization programs; (c) the parents may have difficulty contacting the appropriate physician or public health office for copies of immunization records; and (d) the schools where the children were previously enrolled may be slow in responding to requests for document transfer.

Barriers to Success

Mere admission to school is no guarantee of success (Stronge 1993a). Once homeless children are physically enrolled in school, a myriad of problems can inhibit both the school's ability to deliver an appropriate educational opportunity and the students' ability to benefit from it. Among potentially inhibiting factors are problems with educational placement and academic support, inadequate or inappropriate support services, and personal or familial socioemotional concerns.

Appropriate educational placement can be problematic for homeless students, especially if they are in need of special education services. Procedural due process rights that are embedded in special education regulations (P.L. 94-142; P.L. 101-476) result in service delivery timeliness that is incompatible with transient lifestyles. Even with maximum cooperation from school personnel and families, the referral and eligibility process is likely to take 3 to 4 months to complete, thus running counter to the immediate service needs of homeless students (Korinek et al. 1992).

A final area of concern in facilitating success for homeless students is the issue of the socioemotional well-being of the students. While academic success is fundamental to breaking the grip of poverty, educators may not be able to bring into focus academic goals for these students until pressing social and psychological needs have been addressed.

ON THE ROAD TO SUCCESS

In response to problems experienced by school-age homeless children and youth, Congress enacted the education portion of the Stewart B. McKinney Homeless Assistance Act in 1987 (P.L. 100-77) and, subsequently, reauthorized the act twice—in 1990 (P.L. 101-645) and in 1994 (P.L. 103-382). The McKinney Act was enacted as America's first comprehensive emergency aid program for homeless individuals. In an effort to clarify the right of homeless students to receive a free appropriate public education, specific academic and educational support services to which homeless students are entitled were identified in the act.

The concerted efforts by Congress, state education agencies, local school districts, shelter providers, and a host of other public and private agencies to assist homeless students and their families is beginning to yield dividends. One area of improvement in homeless education is increased accessibility through changes in state residency requirements for homeless students. Prior to the implementation of the McKinney Act, bona fide residency was a significant enrollment barrier, with attempts to enroll homeless students sometimes resulting in litigation (Rafferty 1995; Stronge and Helm 1991). A recent study commissioned by the U.S. Department of Education found that "with few exceptions, states have reviewed and revised their laws, regulations, and policies to remove obstacles to the education of homeless children and youth. They report a high level of success in identifying and eliminating those barriers once posed by policies on residency and school records" (Anderson et al. 1995: vi).

Despite the removal, generally, of residency as an enrollment barrier, other requirements related to enrollment (immunization and guardianship) persist and are not so easily modified. Moreover, even with improved access through removal of residency barriers, "homeless students in different districts within the same state often have uneven access to educational services. State policies exempting homeless students from enrollment requirements do not eliminate barriers unless schools and districts are aware of and enforce these policies" (Anderson et al. 1995: iii).

Figure 4.1   Homeless children in Charlotte, North Carolina, work with their teacher on computers in their transitional classroom located in Irwin Avenue Open Elementary School. The technology and resource-rich program is atypical of most U.S. programs for homeless students. (Photo: A Child's Place)

Another indicator of improved educational opportunity for homeless students can be found in school attendance rates. Anderson et al. (1995) found that the average school attendance rate for *identified* homeless students in elementary, middle, and high school was 86 percent. This contrasts with estimates from only a few years earlier of attendance rates of 69 percent for homeless students (U.S. Department of Education 1989). While this improvement in attendance is encouraging news, a closer look reveals significant concerns. For one, the 86 percent attendance rate is based upon *identified* homeless students. Since homeless counts frequently draw heavily upon stays in homeless shelters, nonsheltered homeless individuals may well not be included in these figures. In fact, fewer than half of all homeless children and youth live in shelters, with 56 percent living on the streets, doubling up with relatives or friends, and residing in a variety of other settings (Anderson et al. 1995).

Even if homeless children and youth were enrolled in and attending school regularly, there is no guarantee of their succeeding once in school. Getting children through the schoolhouse door isn't enough; they must enjoy success once there (Stronge 1993a). An emerging line of study for homeless students that points to success is building resiliency in children by emphasizing constructive strategies that enhance individual, family, school, and community protective factors (Reed-Victor and Stronge 1997). Resilience-oriented approaches strengthen students' coping skills through the development of their own capabilities in the context of caring relationships. Schools, community agencies, and families work together to become catalysts for success by providing:

(a) positive role models; (b) access to knowledge; (c) interest/talent development; (d) goal-oriented activities; and (e) expanded supports (Masten 1994).

CONCLUSION

Given the above indicators, we can point to improvements in the accessibility, appropriateness, and promise of education for homeless students. Consensus regarding the effectiveness of efforts to educate homeless students, generally, and the McKinney Act, specifically, is that progress has been made in recent years. There are fewer lawsuits required to secure enrollment of homeless students, fewer denials of access to public schools, and greater percentages of identified homeless students enrolled in school. Additionally, limited as it may be, funding for education through the McKinney Act is intact and is serving as a catalyst for states and local school districts to offer improved educational opportunities for homeless students.

Unfortunately, progress to date has been slow and, at best, uneven. In a summary of evaluation results to date, the National Association of State Coordinators for the Education of Homeless Children and Youth found results inconclusive:

> On the one hand, they indicate that state coordinators and their local counterparts have made measurable progress in reducing some of the institutional and procedural barriers to public school access that have historically prevented homeless children from enrolling and succeeding in school. On the other hand, they show that other barriers, some of which are new, continue to plague homeless students' ability to fully participate in and benefit from public education. (1997: 3)

For example, despite the fact that, on average, states awarded 71 percent of their 1993–1994 McKinney Act grant allocations directly to local school districts for services for homeless students, only 3 percent of local education authorities (LEAs) nationwide received any funding. Clearly, this fact suggests that "the absolute number of homeless children and youth who are benefiting from special programs and services under [McKinney Act] subgrants—as opposed to general statewide homeless advocacy efforts—is not very great" (Anderson et al. 1995: xiv).

Persistent barriers to improved educational opportunities for homeless students in America remain. Included among these are:

- a lack of awareness and misperceptions regarding the educational needs of homeless students;
- limited parental involvement and support;
- the need for greater early-childhood education opportunities;
- problems associated with special populations within the school-age homeless population;
- the need for greater interagency coordination and collaboration in service delivery for homeless students; and
- the need for comprehensive evaluations of homeless education efforts.

Homelessness in America among school-age children and youth isn't disappearing; indeed, since 1991 the number of homeless children and youth identified and reported has more than doubled (LeTendre 1995). There remain numerous obstacles to overcome if homeless students are to enjoy any significant degree of success in school and throughout their lives. We have traveled some distance since the education of homeless students became a discernible problem in America, but we haven't arrived at the destination. We have miles to go before we sleep.

NOTES

1. Earlier versions of this chapter were presented at the 1996 Annual Conference of the Comparative and International Educational Society and published in the *Journal of Children and Poverty* (1997) by James H. Stronge. Assistance by Evelyn Reed-Victor and Patricia Popp in updating this chapter is gratefully acknowledged.

REFERENCES

Anderson, L. M., M. I. Janger, and K. L. M. Panton. 1995. *An Evaluation of State and Local Efforts to Serve the Educational Needs of Homeless Children and Youth*. Washington, D.C.: U.S. Department of Education.

Bassuk, E., and L. Rosenberg. 1988. "Why Does Family Homelessness Occur?" *American Journal of Public Health* 78: 783–88.

Burt, M. 1991. *Developing the Estimate of 500,000–600,000 Homeless People in 1987*. Washington, D.C.: The Urban Institute.

———. 1997. *Causes of the Growth of Homelessness During the 1980s*. Washington, D.C.: The Urban Institute.

Children's Defense Fund. 1995. *The State of America's Children Yearbook*. Washington, D.C.: Author.

Hagen, J. L. 1987. "Gender and Homelessness." *Social Work* 32: 312–16.

Helm, V. M. 1993. "Legal Rights to Education of Homeless Children and Youth." *Education and Urban Society* 25: 323–39.

Kaufman, N. 1984. "Homeless: A Comprehensive Policy Approach." *Urban and Social Change Review* 17(1): 21–26.

Korinek, L., C. Walther-Thomas, and V. K. Laycock. 1992. "Educating Special Needs Homeless Children and Youth." Pp. 133–152 in *Educating Homeless Children and Adolescents: Evaluating Policy and Practice*, edited by J. H. Stronge. Newbury Park, Calif.: Sage.

LeTendre, M. J. 1995. *Memorandum to Education for Homeless Children and Youth State Coordinators*. 9 Aug. Washington, D.C.: U.S. Department of Education.

Levitan, S. A., and S. Schillmoeller. 1991. *The Paradox of Homelessness in America*. Washington, D.C.: George Washington University, Center for Social Policy Studies.

Lewit, E. M., and L. S. Baker. 1996. "Homeless Families and Children." *Future of Children* 6(2): 146–58.

Linehan, M. 1992. "Children Who Are Homeless: Educational Strategies for School Personnel." *Phi Delta Kappan* 74: 61–66.

Masten, A. S. 1994. "Resilience in Individual Development: Successful Adaptation Despite Risk and Adversity." Pp. 3–25 in *Educational Resilience in Inner-City America: Challenges and Prospects*, edited by M. Wang and E. Gordon. Hillsdale, N.J.: Lawrence Erlbaum.

McChesney, K. Y. 1990. "Family Homelessness: A Systemic Problem." *Journal of Social Issues* 46(4): 191–206.

———. 1993. "Homeless Families since 1980: Implications for Education." *Education and Urban Society* 25: 361–80.

National Association of State Coordinators for the Education of Homeless Children and Youth. 1997. *Making the Grade: Challenges and Successes in Providing Educational Opportunities for Homeless Children and Youth*. Atlanta: Author.

National Center for Children in Poverty. 1990. *Five Million Children: A Statistical Profile of Our Poorest Young Citizens*. New York: National Center for Children in Poverty, School of Public Health, Columbia University.

———. 1996/97. "One in Four: America's Youngest Poor." *National Center for Children in Poverty News and Issues* (Columbia University School of Public Health) 6(2): 1.

National Center for Family Literacy. N.d. *The Power of Family Literacy*. Louisville, Ky.: Author.

National Coalition for the Homeless. 1990. *Homelessness in America: A Summary*. Washington, D.C.: Author.

———. 1997. *Homeless Families with Children: Fact Sheet*. Washington, D.C.: Author.

———. 1998a. *How Many People Experience Homelessness? Fact Sheet #2.* Washington, D.C.: Author.

———. 1998b. *Education of Homeless Children and Youth: Fact Sheet #10.* Washington, D.C.: Author.

National Law Center on Homelessness and Poverty. 1990. *Shut Out: Denial of Education to Homeless Children.* Washington, D.C.: Author.

———. 1996. *Mean Sweeps: A Report on Anti-homeless Laws, Litigation and Alternatives in 50 United States Cities.* Washington, D.C.: Author.

Nuñez, R. D. 1994. *Hopes, Dreams, and Promise: The Future of Homeless Children in America.* New York: Homes for the Homeless, Inc.

———. 1995. "The New Poverty in Urban America: Family Homelessness." *Journal of Children and Poverty* 1(1):7-28.

———. 1997. "Common Sense: Why Jobs and Training Alone Won't End Welfare for Homeless Families." *Journal of Children in Poverty* 3(1): 93-101.

Powers, J. L., and B. Jaklitsch. 1992. "Adolescence and Homelessness: The Unique Challenge for Secondary Educators." Pp. 115-132 in *Educating Homeless Children and Adolescents: Evaluating Policy and Practice,* edited by J. H. Stronge. Newbury Park, Calif.: Sage.

———. 1993. "Reaching the Hard to Reach: Educating Homeless Adolescents in Urban Settings." *Education and Urban Society* 25: 394-409.

P.L. 94-142, The Education for all Handicapped Children Act, 1975. Codified at 20 U.S.C. 1401-1420 (1975, Nov. 29).

P.L. 100-77, Stewart B. McKinney Homeless Assistance Act of 1987. Codified at 42 U.S.C. 11301-11472 (1987, July 22).

P.L. 101-476, Individuals with Disabilities Education Act, 1990. Codified at 20 U.S.C. 1400-1476 (1990, Oct. 30).

P.L. 101-645, Stewart B. McKinney Homeless Assistance Amendment Act of 1990. (1990, Nov. 29).

P.L. 103-382, Improving America's Schools Act of 1994. (1994, Sept. 28).

Quint, S. 1994. *Schooling Homeless Children: A Working Model for America's Public Schools.* New York: Teachers College Press.

Rafferty, Y. 1995. "The Legal Rights and Educational Problems of Homeless Children and Youth." *Educational Evaluation and Policy Analysis* 17: 39-61.

Rafferty, Y., and N. Rollins. 1989. *Learning in Limbo: The Educational Deprivation of Homeless Children.* Long Island City, N.Y.: Advocates for Children. (ERIC Document Reproduction Service No. ED 312 363.)

Reed-Victor, E., and J. H. Stronge. 1997. "Building Resiliency: Constructive Directions for Homeless Education." *Journal of Children and Poverty* 3: 67-91.

———. 1999. *Educating Everybody's Children: Diverse Teaching Standards for Diverse Learners.* Vol. 2. Alexandria, Va.: Association for Supervision and Curriculum Development.

Shane, P. G. 1996. *What about America's Homeless Children?* Thousand Oaks, Calif.: Sage.

Stronge, J. H. 1992. "The Background: History and Problems of Schooling for the Homeless." Pp. 3-25 in *Educating Homeless Children and Adolescents: Evaluating Policy and Practice,* edited by J. H. Stronge. Newbury Park, Calif.: Sage.

———. 1993a. "From Access to Success: Public Policy for Educating Urban Homeless Students." *Education and Urban Society* 25: 340-60.

———. 1993b. "Emerging Service Delivery Models for Educating Homeless Children and Youth: Implications for Policy and Practice." *Educational Policy* 7: 447-65.

———. 1995. "Educating Homeless Students: How Can We Help?" *Journal for a Just and Caring Education* 1: 128-41.

———. 1997. "A Long Road Ahead: A Progress Report on Educating Homeless Children and Youth in America." *Journal of Children and Poverty* 3(2): 13-32.

Stronge, J. H., and V. M. Helm. 1991. "Legal Barriers to the Education of Homeless Children and Youth: Residency and Guardian Issues." *Journal of Law and Education* 20: 201-18.

Stronge, J. H., and C. Tenhouse. 1990. *Educating Homeless Children: Issues and Answers.* Bloomington, Ind.: Phi Delta Kappa Educational Foundation.

U.S. Census Bureau. 1994. *The Dynamics of Economic Well-being: Poverty, 1990–1992.* Washington, D.C.: Government Printing Office.

U.S. Department of Education. 1999. *Report to the Congress for the Stewart B. McKinney Homeless Assistance Act.* Washington, D.C.: Author.

———. 1989. *Report to Congress: Education of Homeless Children and Youth—State Grants.* 9 Aug. Washington, D.C.: Author.

Vissing, Y. M. 1996. *Out of Sight, Out of Mind: Homeless Children and Families in Small-Town America.* Lexington: University Press of Kentucky.

Waxman, L., and R. Trupin. 1997. *A Status Report on Hunger and Homelessness in America's Cities: 1997.* Washington, D.C.: U.S. Conference of Mayors.

Part III: Education and Social Policy for Children: The Role of the State

5

A New Paradigm for Social Change:
Social Movements and the Transformation of Policy for Street and Working Children in Brazil

Steven J. Klees, Irene Rizzini, and Anthony Dewees

The plight of young people who work, and sometimes even live, in the streets of Brazil's urban centers has been well documented and widely diffused by national and international media. Their situation is part of a much larger and complex problem in which vastly greater numbers of children in Brazil, and around the world, also suffer deprivation, exclusion from opportunities, and a very limited realization of their human rights. Most of these children must work to survive, some on the streets of cities, others in factories, on farms, in small and large businesses, and at home. Often the conditions of work are horrendous. Even when they are not, a changing global context has made this situation harmful to the well-being of these children. In an era of globalization, where schooling is the primary avenue to the skills and credentials necessary for better jobs and higher income, any activity that adversely affects school attendance and intellectual development is a threat to a child's future. All of these children who are growing up in circumstances that are severely detrimental to their human development and well-being are referred to here as *street and working children.*[1]

The dynamic driving these conditions extends worldwide. After decades of prolonged global economic crisis, the fundamental problem underlying the situation of so many children—poverty—grows worse. From 1970 to 1990 the number of chronically hungry people grew 20 percent, from 460 million to 500 million.[2] Currently, there are somewhere between 1 billion and 1.5 billion people living on the planet in a state of extreme poverty—20 percent to 25 percent of the world's population (UNDP 1998; Institute for Food and Development Policy 1992). This dire situation is embedded in one of extreme global inequality: the richest 20 percent of the world's people consume 86 percent of what is produced while the poorest 20 percent consume a minuscule 1.3 percent (UNDP 1998).[3] Any solution to the difficult array of problems facing street and working children must confront this context squarely.

While the problems facing street and working children are visible around the globe, Brazil is of special interest. In the 1980s, after almost 20 years of a dictatorial military regime, Brazil experienced a far-reaching social movement that mobilized the population in the defense of the rights of children. This movement led to one of the most progressive transformations of laws protecting children and youth seen anywhere in the world.

Figure 5.1　A street child in the Copacabana area of Rio de Janeiro cleans the window of a *carioca*'s car as she discusses his fee with him. (Photo: Luiz Caleffe)

The development and adoption in Brazil of the Child and Adolescent Statute, signed into law in 1990, reflects and is provoking profound changes in the roles of all public and private entities dealing with street and working children. The Child and Adolescent Statute has been characterized as a "sea change" in public policy toward children in Brazil.

　　This chapter examines the unusual transformation of national policy brought about by this social movement and its broader implications for social change. Understanding what has happened in Brazil is especially significant because it is about what we and others see as the only possible route for progressive social change—through the political action of social movements instead of, as the dominant wisdom has long contended, through a technically rational search for best solutions. We therefore begin our analysis by examining the inherent failure of a dominant paradigm that is wedded to a belief in the progressive nature of liberal democracy undergirded by the use of scientific analysis and evaluation to guide public policy.

Figure 5.2   An adolescent in São Paulo sells plants to his customers in a parking lot. (Photo: Fúlvia Rosemberg)

THE FAILURE OF TECHNICAL RATIONALITY

The poverty and problematic future facing street and working children is perhaps the worst manifestation of the persistent inequalities of a global capitalist economy—these children are the poorest of the poor and they are provided with few opportunities to improve their situation. The technically rational model through which we most commonly attempt to respond to these problems never comes close to resolving them, often serving more as an excuse for inaction, rather than change. To solve educational and other social problems, the logic of this approach calls for a research and evaluation effort to identify or develop the programs needed—for street children, for rural children, for increasing achievement, for dropout prevention, for drug education, for health promotion, and so forth. The assumption is that once a good pilot or model program exists, it can be replicated until the problem is solved.

Unfortunately, replications on a large scale rarely happen. Strong disagreements usually exist about the worth of any model program, with research and evaluation results supporting divergent conclusions. When programs are expanded, they often do not work as planned for a variety of reasons: they were never designed for an expanded, less controllable environment; expansions are usually underfunded; generic models cannot work well if solutions need to be contextually specific; and expanded programs are often co-opted so that they do not challenge dominant interests. There have been voluminous criticisms of this narrow technical logic with which applied social science has tried to direct policy choices.[4]

Believers in technical rationality often blame its failure on poor policy implementation. This is simply not credible, as Plank et al. argue regarding educational policy failure in Brazil: "Explanations of this type face the monumental task of accounting for *six decades* of consistent policy 'failure' in the Brazilian educational system. To attribute the persistence of Brazil's educational backwardness to problems in policy implementation is to impute an extraordinary low level of competence to a long line of Brazilian governments. It is simply implausible" (1994: 77). To the contrary, they argue that these 6 decades of educational policy were not "failures," but actually were successes in terms of furthering certain powerful interests. The debates about "ostensibly technical questions" masked a "struggle for control of resources" (1994: 78). What governs resource allocation is not some mythical technical search for best solutions: in Brazil, "the public purposes [of education] . . . are systematically subordinated to the service of private interests" (1994: 79) through a variety of mechanisms, from the more obvious political spoils system (*clientelismo*), in which government service considerations take a backseat to rewarding supporters with jobs, to more fundamental structuring and financing of education and other public services in ways that benefit the relatively wealthy.[5]

This situation is not, of course, particular to Brazil or to the South. Throughout the world technical rationality has offered us a profusion of educational solutions—the use of technologies such as radio, TV, and computers; learning process changes like distance education, open classrooms, and individualized instruction; governance changes like Program Planning Budgeting Systems (PPBS), decentralization, and privatization. Yet there is abundant evidence that none of these "innovations," even when blessed by some economist or evaluator priests as "cost-effective" or "efficient," ever does more than tinker with the fundamental educational and social problems in question. There is not necessarily anything fundamentally wrong with these innovations. The problem is that they ignore the political rationality that maintains, reproduces, and often exacerbates inequality.

Technical rationality does not fail because of poor implementation, corrupt governments, or even lack of good will or ideas. Educational and other social policies do very little to solve social problems, not because they cannot, but because there are interests that benefit from doing very little and structures—capitalist, patriarchal, racist, and more—that favor these interests. Public policy decisions follow the political rationality of these structures, and technical rationality has served as a cover-up to mask the biases behind the policy choices made, legitimating them as "best." As in Brazil, government expenditures in most countries favor the well-to-do in providing services, in creating jobs, in giving subsidies, and so forth. In recent years, the fact that government's role in society has been under attack by a neoliberal mythology of the efficiency of the market over government has placed solutions to any significant social problem even further out of policy reach. "Solutions" arising from technical rationality, under these circumstances, become endless exercises in futility.

A principal alternative for making significant social change follows a more "politically rational" model in which large social movements, giving voice and power to excluded groups, pressure the state for meaningful reform.[6] During the last several decades there has been a more explicit recognition of the role of such social movements worldwide, perhaps most especially in Latin America, and there is a growing literature on their role and efficacy (Adam 1993; Wolfe 1993; Melucci 1992). If the technically rational framework we have increasingly followed in all nations offers no real hope for educational and social progress, then it is important to learn more about the alternatives and the extent to which they can make a difference. The recent history of the social movement for the rights of children in Brazil provides some insight on these issues.

THE BRAZILIAN CONTEXT

Despite Brazil's being among the world's 10 largest economies, poverty is widespread due to very unequal income and wealth distributions. The World Bank (1997) reports that Brazil has the worst income distribution among more than 60 countries for which data is available. The richest 10 percent of the population effectively control 51.3 percent of total income, while the poorest 20 percent had access to just 2.1 percent of total income. As is the case in other contexts, children and youth in Brazil bear the burden of poverty disproportionately. It is estimated that some 40 percent of those 14 years and under survive precariously in households whose total monthly income is less than one-half Brazil's minimum salary (US$65) (IBGE 1997), with serious consequences for health and access to basic services. Infant mortality rates (44 per 1,000 live births) are much higher than for other countries at a comparable level of development (UNDP 1998).

The educational system reflects a history of inequality and neglect. About 30 percent of children never reach the 5th grade of primary schooling (UNDP 1998). Only 22 percent of 15-to-17-year-olds are in secondary school. Moreover, these indicators mask tremendous geographic differences. For example, in southern Brazil 30 percent of 15-to-17-year-olds are in secondary school while in the Northeast the figure is only 17 percent.

The overall economic situation offers few educational or work opportunities for vast numbers of children, youth, and adults. This lack of opportunities combined with an urban environment of disorienting and disordered growth and easy access to firearms and drugs has led to an explosion of violence where young people have again borne a heavy burden. The precarious social, psychological, and economic conditions of poor, marginalized youth and adolescents make them susceptible to involvement in crime. Involvement in petty crime, or even proximity to it, have too frequently made children victims of violence, especially by renegade police and vigilante groups. In São Paulo the number of violent incidents involving young people actually doubled between 1997 and 1998. Homicide has become the most common cause of death in São Paulo for young people between 10 and 14 years of age (Toledo 1998). In the state of Rio de Janeiro the consequences are similar, with almost 3,000 youths between 15 and 17 years of age being killed by firearms between 1991 and 1998. In the first half of 1998, 25 percent of the 247 deaths of youths (15–17) were the result of homicide (Antunes 1998).

Street and working children in Brazil have received international attention, in part because of the violence done to them. Estimates of the number of children living or working on the streets of Brazil reach as high as 17 million (Barker and Knaul 1991: 3). While there is controversy about the accuracy of such estimates, there is also considerable agreement that widespread poverty has had alarming effects on millions of children (see Rosemberg this volume and 1993). The lives of these children, raised in extreme deprivation, have long been desperate, and the response of society, in Brazil and elsewhere, has for too long been meager, if not actually harmful.

CHILD POLICY: FROM CORRECTION TO ASSISTANCE TO CHILD RIGHTS

That laws characterized by former UNICEF director James Grant as "the best child protection legislation in the world" (*O Globo* 1992: 27) would emerge from a country facing such severe economic and social straits is both ironic and hopeful. The poverty and violence suffered by children and youth has been increasingly seen as a national disgrace by Brazilians and has motivated many to raise their voices and demand an end to an intolerable situation. The adoption of a constitutional clause proclaiming the rights of the child and adolescent and the subsequent Child and Adolescent Statute mark significant points in an historic evolution of thinking about the place of children and adolescents in Brazilian society.

As a number of studies have pointed out, there has been a progressive change in the basic model underlying services for children—from one focused on the correction and control of delinquency to one centered on providing social assistance to needy children, and, more recently, to one that emphasizes, instead, the rights of the child and the need for special protections and guarantees to ensure those rights.[7]

The 1960s and 1970s: Assistance and Repression Intertwined

The first national institution to assist poor children, focusing on those abandoned or delinquent, was the Assistance Service to Minors (SAM) created in 1941. SAM was supposed to assess the needs of these minors, and to develop and administer institutions to provide assistance. From the beginning, a repressive penal approach was taken to abandoned and delinquent children who were seen as threats to social order. The correctional facilities that were created have been described as "branches of hell" (Costa 1990a: 82). Their conditions became a scandal in the press of the 1950s and early 1960s, with exposés of corruption and the awful and often violent treatment of children. In 1963, the democratically elected government of President João Goulart set up a commission to revise radically SAM, but the 1964 military coup ended, or at least, redirected that effort. The military regime did replace existing legislation with what it characterized as "anti-SAM" reforms, setting up the National Foundation for the Welfare of Minors (FUNABEM) directly under the president of the republic to administer the new system. While the rhetoric moved toward policies that provided assistance to marginalized youth, the reality was that the new system inherited the culture, institutions, staff, and punitive incarceration model of SAM. Moreover, under the military dictatorship the "problem of the minor" came to be seen as a question of national security, a view legally institutionalized in the Minor's Code of 1979 (Vogel and Rizzini 1995).

Under the new laws of the military regime, the government was empowered to intervene in the lives of children and adolescents in "irregular circumstances"—the term grouped together abandoned children and youth, children and youth who congregated in public places for recreation and informal commerce, as well as young people involved in criminal activities. The result of the policy was to criminalize the activities of millions of young people in "irregular circumstances" whether they had committed a crime or were in the streets seeking the means of survival.

Established under the direction of FUNABEM, state government child welfare institutions (State Foundations for the Welfare of Minors, FEBEMs) held young people deemed to be in irregular circumstances. These institutions housed both children who had committed crimes and those rounded up in actions to remove children from the streets. They quickly developed the same reputation as the earlier SAM "hellholes." The new system continued to be corrupt and violent, characterized by frequent instances of beating and torturing of children by police and others, horrible living conditions, and little in the way of actual "assistance."

Silva (1990), a public prosecutor well known for his participation in formulating the Child Statute, points out the almost Orwellian euphemisms that became an integral part of the structure: children were not prisoners, they were "interned"; they were not punished, they were "protected"; they were not accused, they were "guided." To many critics, the use of the word "minor" became indicative of this approach. Seeing street and working children as "minors" emphasized their inferior legal status as individuals with proscribed rights.

The Early 1980s: Organizing for Change

By the late 1970s and early 1980s, these conditions, combined with the political *abertura* (opening), led an increasing number of grassroots, nongovernmental organizations (NGOs) to seek alternative means of meeting the needs of children in "irregular circumstances." Proponents of the alternatives stressed that not the children themselves, but rather the conditions in which they were forced to seek their survival, should be seen as "irregular." While alternative programs developed with few resources and in isolation from each other, the recognition of the inadequacy of the correctional model grew. A number of those working in policy positions in the government also saw current policies as ineffective or counterproductive. In the early 1980s a group of government officials from FUNABEM, the Social Action Secretariat, the Ministry of the President and Social Assistance, and UNICEF in Brazil signed an agreement to study the problem of street and working children under the name of the Alternative Services for Street Children Project.

These groups began a nationwide examination of the dimensions of the problem of street children as well as of the alternative programs that had emerged. The explicit focus was on children living and working on the urban streets, recognizing that this was the "point of the lance" that might open up examination of the problems facing poor children throughout Brazil. One of the most important outcomes of what came to be called the "Alternative Project" was that individuals and programs who had worked for as long as a decade in isolation now had a channel for sharing their experiences and weaving together an informal network.

The project culminated in the First Latin American Seminar on Community Alternatives in Attention to Street Boys and Street Girls in November of 1984 in Brasília. This event, widely reported in the media, placed the Alternative Project, now openly critical of the intertwined assistance and repressive-correctional model of the state programs, in a recognized position of leadership within the entire movement of popular groups advocating alternative social policies.

One of the most significant activities of the Alternative Project was to bring together groups of street and working children and their advocates into a more visible national political movement. Local and state commissions were established and, in 1985, a directorate was elected for the National Movement of Street Boys and Street Girls.

The National Movement captured the attention of all Brazil when the First National Meeting of Street Boys and Street Girls was held in Brasília in May 1986. This national meeting was attended by some 500 street children delegates from all over Brazil and was conducted with considerable participation from the children themselves. It drew widespread attention to the conditions of their lives and the underlying forces that had driven them to the streets. The theme most constantly and vigorously denounced by the children was violence, and their testimony eventually led the Brazilian Congress to hold special hearings concerning organized violence against street children. The country, saturated with media coverage of the meeting, was astounded by the ability of these children to articulate their concerns and demands. This was an intensive learning experience both for the street and working children involved and for the nation as a whole.

The Mid-1980s: The Transition to Democracy and the Rights of the Child

The national movement to address the problems of street children coalesced during the mid-1980s, when Brazil was beginning a transition back to civilian democracy. The movement sought to tie the struggle for new policies for children to this transition by reframing the issues surrounding the lives of street and working children, switching from an assistance or charity model to a focus on children's "rights," explicitly building on the International Declaration of the Rights of Children promulgated by the UN. The convocation of a national assembly to draft a new national constitution presented a unique opportunity to incorporate the rights of children into the new legal system.

The National Movement of Street Boys and Girls was one of several organizations that evolved during the 1980s and took up the struggle to incorporate the needs of street and working children into the legal foundation of a new democratic government. The National Movement joined with the National Front for the Defense of Child and Adolescent Rights, the National Council of Brazilian Bishops, the National Order of Attorneys, and other organizations to mobilize public opinion in favor of constitutional language protecting children as well as to elect members to the Constitutional Assembly sympathetic to the cause. Universities were active participants in this process and research centers grew up to focus specifically on these issues.[8]

In the late 1980s, a variety of NGOs, government ministries, and other organizations joined in a process that led to the formation of the National Commission on the Child and the Constitution in order to coordinate the various related advocacy efforts and to help draft a constitutional clause on children's rights. The mobilization of interest, discussion, and support was massive. Drafts of the clause came in with petitions signed by more than 200,000 adults and 1,300,000 children. John Donahue, representative of UNICEF in Brazil at the time, describes how struck he was by the entire process when these petitions were finally presented to the national assembly. "We went into a hall with just over 400 people sitting in it and by the time we finished we realized we were sitting in a room with more than 1,600,000 Brazilians. For me that was a point in the process that made the clear statement that this was not just a repeat performance of a legislature writing out a constitutional text—the seventh in Brazil's history. This part of the text on children and adolescents had really involved people in ways that no one would have imagined possible even a year before" (Swift 1991: 19).

On November 20, 1989, Article 227 of the new Brazilian Constitution was approved. The article incorporates and extends the basic content of the International Convention on the Rights of the Child: "It is the duty of the family, the society, and the State to guarantee to the child and adolescent, with absolute priority, the right to life, health, nutrition, education, leisure, professional training, culture, dignity, respect, liberty, and community and family living, as well as protecting them from discrimination, exploitation, cruelty, and oppression" (Brazilian Constitution 1989: Art. 227).

With the battle for constitutional protection for children and adolescents won, the efforts of advocates now turned toward the elaboration of the detailed implementation of the legislation that would be necessary to put the constitutional principles into action. To help do so, many NGOs working in the areas of child protection and defense joined together in an umbrella organization, the Child and Adolescent Rights Forum (Forum–DCA). The forum held thousands of meetings and seminars throughout the country seeking input from the public into the new legislation. Despite considerable opposition from conservative forces, a broad coalition was able to push through very progressive legislation. On July 13, 1990, implementing legislation for the Child and Adolescent Statute was signed into law.

The Child and Adolescent Statute

The Child and Adolescent Statute replaced the Minors' Code as the organizing principle for the legal system, the social welfare system, and the policy-making process regarding children and adolescents. The simple change in terminology from "minors" to "child" and "adolescent" was meant to be indicative of the radical change in perspective embodied in the new law. The minor, an individual with proscribed rights, has been replaced by child and adolescent, terms that emphasize a particular stage in all human life. While the minor has limited rights, a child or adolescent is, by birth, endowed with basic human rights and entitled to special protection. The 267 articles of the statute form a new legal and institutional structure for issues related to children and youth, characterized by three areas of innovation: changes in content; methods; and decision making.

Content

The statute grants full human rights to the child and adolescent. These rights include: free movement and the right to use public spaces; free expression; freedom of religious beliefs; the rights to play, practice sports, and engage in leisure activities, to participate in family and community life, to participate in political life, and to find refuge and assistance; and physical inviolability. An extensive series of rights to education are spelled out, including: free, accessible basic education (8 years), with a similar right to secondary education to be progressively expanded; access to preschools, night schools, and special education services; and the right of students to organize.

In addition, the statute grants special protection and priorities to children and adolescents due to their "special stage of development." These protections, according to the statute, may not be implemented in a way that limits or infringes on their full human rights. These protections include being made the highest-priority group in any social welfare policy.

Methods

While the Minors' Code removed street and working children from their environment for "correctional" purposes, the Child and Adolescent Statute outlines a hierarchy of protective and socioeducative programs designed to assist and educate these young people in their environment. The statute establishes a hierarchy of "least restrictive alternative" interventions that includes family counseling and support, socioeducative support in an unrestricted environment, foster care, shelter, assisted liberty (regular reporting to an adult authority), semiliberty (confined weekdays only), and incarceration. Intervention that deprives adolescents of their liberty is discouraged, in all but the most severe cases, by closely regulating the facilities that can hold children and adolescents and making it difficult to hold any child less than 18 years of age.

"Socioeducative actions" are the principal interventions in this policy. The statute requires that these activities be implemented in such a way as to strengthen the relationship between the child or adolescent and the family and community. Possible activities outlined in the statute include counseling and temporary supervision, obligatory school attendance, integration in community programs of family assistance, facilitation of medical, psychological, or psychiatric treatment, integration into a community treatment program for alcohol or drug abuse, integration into a formal shelter, and foster care.

Decision Making

To implement these radical changes, the statute calls for new structures of decision making and control that are more locally based and participative. The new Constitution incorporates language in its opening article that generally sanctions the concept of more direct forms of citizen participation in government as an alternative to participation through elected representatives. The Child and Adolescent statute establishes a decision-making process that, in part, utilizes this direct representation by requiring that the decision-making bodies outlined in the statute be composed of representatives of nongovernmental advocacy groups or grassroots programs, as well as elected officials.

The statute shifts the responsibility for child and adolescent welfare, rights, and protection from the federal level to states and, most strongly, municipalities. Each municipality is required to write a municipal child rights law within guidelines established by the national legislation. For implementation, the statute stipulates the formation of two specific bodies with different functions, the Municipal Children's Rights Councils and the Guardianship Council. The Municipal Children's Rights Council is composed of elected municipal officials and representatives of NGOs that work with children and is charged with coordinating children's policy and funding at the municipal level. State Children's Rights Councils carry out the same function at the state level; and one Federal Children's Rights Council oversees both state and municipal councils (Rizzini et al. 1998).

The other major implementation component of this new decentralized institutional framework called for by the statute are the Guardianship Councils. These are established at the municipal level for responding to individual cases of children in need and for ensuring that children receive the best possible assistance. The councils do not provide services, but rather act as points of entry into the children's services system and as an advocate for children and families within the state and nongovernmental service system. Members are directly elected by the communities, and the number of Guardianship Councils depends on the size of the municipality. These councils replace many of the social welfare functions previously held by the judicial powers. Guardianship Councils have direct contact with children and adolescents who need assistance in receiving the rights and protections guaranteed in the statute. The Guardianship Councils have the authority to take protective actions for children threatened by lack of attention from municipal authorities, by abuse from parents, or by the consequences of the child's or adolescent's own conduct. Possible interventions include the full variety of community-based social and educational initiatives previously mentioned. The councils also have the authority to require parents to participate in counseling, education, or substance abuse programs. In addition, the councils represent children and adolescents before those agencies with responsibilities for fulfilling the services guaranteed by the statute (police, judicial, education, health, and so on).

"The Statute Is There—All That's Left Is to Comply"

This 1992 slogan of the National Movement for Street Boys and Street Girls still sums up the post-statute situation well: an unusual, very progressive set of legislation was passed into law, yet real implementation is very slow in coming. The institutional infrastructure

itself is far from completely created. By 1997, only about 55 percent of Brazil's approximately 5,500 municipalities had created a Municipal Children's Rights Council, and
many of these are only partially implemented. Guardianship Councils, the direct links to
children and youth, have even further to go; in 1997, there were only about 2,050 initiated (IBAM 1997/1998). Moreover, even when these newer institutions are established,
they still face the same "inheritance" problem noted in the previous policy changes; at
the local level, often it is still the same people and infrastructure that are responsible for
dealing with children.

The coexistence of new legislation and old structures has set up many conflicts,
especially concerning police and judicial authority. One of the most controversial issues
is posed by critics who charge that dangerous criminals are not being arrested or are
released because the statute makes it difficult (some say impossible) to detain anyone
under 18 years of age. Defenders of the statute argue that young criminals can be
detained as long as their rights are respected, which means that they must be separated
from adult criminals and given access to a variety of services.

This situation has created conflicts within the judiciary and police establishment.
Judges often disagree with the police, as well as with each other. For example, in Rio de
Janeiro there have been attempts to remove Judge Siro Darlan, who has angered some by
his application of the statute. He enforces the provision requiring that a child or adolescent be brought before him the same day as the arrest. Many also criticize his extensive
use of probation and community service (O Globo 1992).

In response, Judge Darlan cites Article 122 of the statute: "In no circumstance will
incarceration be applied when there exists an adequate alternative." He points out that
few of the children and adolescents brought before him have committed serious crimes.
He also cites the penal code's provision that "there is no crime when the agent acts out
of a state of necessity or legitimate self defense." Judge Darlan adds, "When these children say they robbed because they were hungry, they are not lying." Even in the cases of
more serious crimes, he argues, there are often alternatives. "The Public Ministry
demanded the incarceration of a young girl who participated in a kidnapping. I gave her
a sentence of community service. In two months she had organized all of the medical
files in a hospital, for nothing. She is seventeen years old, is going to high school, works,
and maintains her two smaller brothers. If I had given her a prison sentence, what would
have happened? She would have become involved with other, more serious offenders,
and stopped studying and working. The objective of the Statute is to lift up a person, not
step on them" (O Globo 1992: 14).

In the post-statute era, the violence surrounding street children is still apparent,
most flagrantly exhibited in 1993 when an incident in Rio de Janeiro captured headlines
worldwide. Around 1:00 A.M. on July 23, eight street children (seven of whom were
between 10 and 17 years old, and one was 22) were sleeping beside Candelaria Church
in the center of the city. A group of gunmen, some of them hooded, drove up and
opened fire on the children. Four boys died instantly, two more died in the hospital, and
two more had been shot in the head, moments before, in the gardens of the nearby
Museum of Modern Art. Other children were wounded. A conflict between some street
children and police the day before supposedly gave rise to death threats by the police
and the massacre. Members of the military police were arrested for the crime. Yet
despite many years of judicial procedures that were watched closely throughout Brazil,
the perpetrators have received little or no punishment. Unfortunately, this is not an isolated incident. Explicit violence against children and adolescents continues in institutions and on the streets, as does the less explicit daily violence in the form of a constant

violation of their rights and the perpetuation of the inhuman conditions under which a large part of the population lives (Rizzini 1994).

Yet, despite continued deprivation and violence, there have been a number of instances of progressive change. For example, public prosecutors, who were usually allied with a correctional-repressive perspective in the past, are increasingly allies of the statute. There is also some support in the judiciary, and not just in the criminal justice arena. One judge was confronted with a case involving a seriously deficient school and a municipality that claimed it had no resources available to remedy the situation. The judge used the statute to argue that the "absolute priority" accorded to the rights of children demanded a remedy; he then halted an unrelated municipal construction project until the money was "found" for the school.

Much of the eventual success of the statute will depend on the operation of the local level council structures. There are already good examples of strong new municipal laws. Activist communities have required that those serving on Guardianship Councils possess relevant background and experience and have enabled some Municipal and Guardianship Councils to push traditional municipal power structures toward enforcement of the statute.

In many ways, the council structure is an experiment in the unknown, and one that faces many obstacles. The councils are part of the transition to democracy in what has heretofore been a very authoritarian system, especially at the local level. For the council system to be effective in defending the rights of children, it must often challenge the local powers. Council members usually have neither the political sophistication nor the independence and skills to do so. Funding is also a problem. Municipal councils have a small independent operating budget, but that may be more hindrance than help. It may make it easier to avoid getting engaged in their central task of defending children's rights in the jugular politics of municipal patronage and budget allocation. Of course, the larger context plays an important role here, since one of the biggest problems in fulfilling the rights of children and adolescents is that municipalities do not have funds to provide even bare minimum necessities.

Thus, while the ideas contained in the Brazilian statute may constitute a progressive change, their effective implementation will be a long and slow process at best. For several years, the national legislature has been talking about passing a fiscal reform bill that would get money to municipalities in order to move beyond the decentralization-without-any-resources strategy—a strategy that is too common worldwide as a way of passing on responsibility without the resources to fulfill them. Some training courses have been set up to help council members do a better job in their new function. A number of NGOs are working to educate community groups about the statute and how they can press for its enforcement. But even with better funding, training, and community involvement, change will be difficult. The meaning of the statute, so sweeping in its language, will be spelled out in legal disputes for many years to come. Some believe that the "absolute priority" language should legally signify the redistribution of wealth to eliminate poverty while others fight to limit the statute, for example, by lowering the age to which criminal statues apply from 18 to 16. Clearly, the conflict today is a continuation of a historical struggle for all citizens to be included in the exercise of their full rights to political and social participation.

DISCUSSION

Brazil has long had many excellent programs for helping street and working children. Even during the military dictatorship, when repression made it difficult and sometimes even dangerous to work with marginalized groups, grassroots NGOs began to develop alternative programs. Although isolated from each other, these programs frequently had characteristics in common. Faced with children who were often a little wild, very competent in many ways, very scarred, and very wary of adults, these programs evolved some similar strategies, which parallel in a striking manner the approach of successful programs in places as diverse as India, the Philippines, and Kenya. Children were treated with respect; it was the adults who had to prove they were trustworthy to the children. These programs imposed little on the child, but tried to begin from the child's reality and jointly construct directions, applying principles from critical adult education. This orientation permeated all aspects of successful programs, from curriculum to organization to governance (Easton et al. 1994).

As others have pointed out, however, although these programs may be "jewel boxes"—beautifully crafted efforts that really help some children—taken together, they do not begin to address the magnitude of the problem (Myers 1991: 6). The failure of technical rationality as an educational and social paradigm is embodied in our continuing failure to go beyond these "jewel boxes," in Brazil and elsewhere, as discussed at the outset.[9] A technically and economically rational framework is used by governments and international agencies throughout the world to talk a good game but never to commit to the changes and resources needed. The utter failure to improve the lives of the vast majority of the world's street and working children is, in part, a consequence of adhering to this bankrupt model.

In the Brazil of the 1970s and 1980s, radicalized by an oppressive military government, there was widespread recognition of the criticisms above. Program developers understood how small their efforts were relative to the size of the problem. Reformers talked about how attention to "alternative" programs was (and is) used as a substitute for the type of sweeping "alterative" changes that are really needed to effect large-scale change (Costa 1990a: 92). The military government's illegitimacy and its neglect of the poor majority made it apparent that solutions to social problems were not forthcoming. As a consequence, Brazil experienced a growing political activism that fueled an expanding social movement. The key question for social change in today's world is whether and how social movements like the one in Brazil can promote progressive social change in practice. Addressing this question depends critically on our understanding of the nature of poverty and inequality.

POVERTY, INEQUALITY, AND SOCIAL CHANGE

Has this Brazilian story about street and working children been one of progressive social change? Can the political rationality of social movements offer an alternative to a model based on a supposed technically rational search for optimal solutions to social problems? Responding to these questions depends on how these social problems are understood. The most fundamental problem facing street and working children and their families is poverty, which underlies so many educational and social problems. It has become widely accepted that poverty should be eliminated, and increases in global productivity and wealth have made this technically feasible. However, the pervasiveness and persistence of global inequality and poverty—perhaps one-quarter or more of the citizens of the planet do not have the resources to sustain a minimally decent life—make it hard to believe in the effectiveness of standard remedies (charity, poverty programs, education, economic growth).

Globalization and neoliberalism have exacerbated these problems. From a political economy perspective, poverty and inequality are pervasive and persistent because they are a necessary part of a capitalist economy.[10] In some ways, this is recognized even by mainstream policy analysts, who argue that poverty is a necessary spur to initiative or that government "safety net" programs are needed to soften the blow of poverty. The nations that have done the most to combat poverty and inequality are not capitalist. While the failure of state socialist regimes showed the flaws of large-scale government planning and control of an economy, and the horror of the repression this too often entailed, many of these same countries showed the successes that government action could have against poverty and inequality (Carnoy et al. 1990).

The Russian, Chinese, and Cuban revolutions all led to societies where, in contrast to similar capitalist countries, starvation and absolute poverty were virtually eliminated and street children hardly existed. Not surprisingly, in the "transition" to capitalism in Eastern Europe and the Soviet Union, street children have been a growing problem, as is poverty (Cornia and Sipos 1991). Horst Hebenicht, the head of the International Labor Organization's (ILO) Program on the Elimination of Child Labor, explained, "In socialist systems, the state organized work and excluded children. Now, free markets and private employers try to get the cheapest labor. With the state's role diminished, and no social protection or legislation in place, child labor is growing" (Wright 1994: 1a). Similarly, in newly industrializing Third World countries, human rights and a longer-run economic investment perspective are often secondary to immediate development needs, as was pointed out by Chira Hongladaram, the executive director of Bangkok's Human Resource Institute. "Economic growth over the past seven years has had a negative impact on the social system, particularly family structure. Children, now part of the productivity process, are treated as [short-run] economic goods rather than society's future" (Wright 1994: 1a). Rotjana Phraesrithong, who works with slum children for an NGO in Bangkok, puts it more vividly: "Becoming an NIC (newly industrializing country) is destroying the social fabric of this society. And the kids are paying the highest price" (Wright 1994: 7a).

If poverty is an inherent part of capitalist economic organization, then the inadequacy of a technical response to it and associated problems is clear. The endless technical responses have actually provided a way to avoid committing sufficient resources and making necessary structural changes. To obtain sufficient resources and to change key structures becomes a political task, but one that threatens dominant interests. The extent to which even a large-scale social movement, like the one mobilized in Brazil, can successfully challenge such interests, especially over the long term, is unclear.

During the last several decades in Brazil, there has been a wide diffusion of a highly critical, political economy view of the capitalist state. The misery of widespread poverty, its effects on street and working children, and its roots in capitalism were explicitly recognized by many who were part of the Alternative Project network in the 1980s. Children's rights were seen by many to imply the necessity of moving from capitalism to some sort of democratic socialism that would allow the redistribution necessary to realize these rights. Such a critical perspective was also a significant part of the larger social movement struggling to end 20 years of military dictatorship (Rizzini 1993; Fausto and Cervini 1991; Swift 1991).

BRAZIL'S REFORM: PROGRESSIVE TRANSFORMATION OR RETROGRADE RETRENCHMENT?

Of course, this Brazilian social movement was composed of individuals and organizations with a variety of political perspectives. Sharing a common enemy—a military dictatorship with a poor economic performance and repressive tactics—forged a strong alliance.

With the success of initiating a new constitution and the election of a civilian government, this alliance fell apart. The movement that remains has more internal conflict and
less active popular support than it once had, even for that part of the movement that
focuses on children. Some say that there is too much politicizing of street children
instead of pursuing reforms to make their life better. Others argue that government agencies and NGOs are not really interested in radical changes, and NGOs have even been
publicly attacked (although most would say unfairly) as benefiting from caring for street
children.

Such different points of view are reflected in different assessments of what this
social movement has accomplished. Many observers agree that this recent history of
social activism in Brazil has led to a "sea change" in law, policy, and the underlying philosophy toward children, from one of the most oppressive orientations in the world to
one of the most progressive. The legal relationship between street and working children
and the public authority has been turned completely around. The legal system, once the
force that proscribed the rights of children and adolescents, is now the guarantor of their
liberty. A legal system that once represented and exercised the rights of the society to
intervene in the lives of young people, to remove them from public spaces, and to "correct" their "irregular circumstances" is now supposed to represent and protect the rights
of children and adolescents as full members of the community.

An integral part of this transformation was the development of more positive public
attitudes toward street and working children. Public attitudes changed for many reasons:
the visibility and articulate statements of some of these children, the media attention to
their circumstances and to the violence directed against them, and the public education
campaigns by NGOs and governments. Many consider these changes in attitudes essential to the legislative success that has been achieved.

Another interesting and potentially progressive feature of this recent period in
Brazil has been the changing role of civil society, especially in the interplay between
NGOs and government.[11] NGOs, which had been principally occupied with delivering
services to street and working children, began to take on new roles as advocates,
defenders of children's rights, and lobbyists for policies. Some began working exclu-
sively as advocates. A UNICEF staff member involved in this movement commented that
the law itself—the provisions in the Constitution and statute safeguarding children and
adolescents—would never have been written by legislators. The provisions are too
sweeping, ambiguous, and politically dangerous for legislators. They were almost literally written by a social movement at a time of democratic transformation during which
the distinction between being inside and outside the government became blurred. This
ambiguity continues in the controlling role NGOs are given within the newly created
Municipal Councils. The legislation can be seen as creating a parallel municipal government run by NGOs. Although how this situation will evolve is unclear, it can be argued
that politics and governance may be changing in ways that offer greater possibilities for
more open, democratic, locally determined, participative, and successful processes to
help street and working children.

On the other hand, it is easy to romanticize and exaggerate the successes Brazil has
achieved. Public attitudes may have changed some, but violence against children continues at alarming rates; laws have changed, but practice is very slow to do so. Government enforcement of the statute remains weak, with little political or fiscal power being
brought to encourage implementation. NGOs sometimes compete destructively with
each other and with government bodies for the same meager resources. When alternative program practices are occasionally incorporated into government programs, the

elements that made them successful to begin with, such as small-scale and local control, rarely survive.

It is even possible that this Brazilian "transformation" has actually exacerbated the problem more than helped remedy it. Rosemberg (this volume and 1993), for example, argues that international support for the movement for street and working children in Brazil during the past decade has too often defined the children's needs as welfare assistance—trivializing the problem, neglecting its structural roots in poverty and inequality, mistaking priorities, and stigmatizing the children and their families (also see Ennew 1995). Even the end of the military government does not have to be seen as progressive. The military wanted out and, in some ways, their departure left the state even more firmly controlled by economic interests.

In theory, the legal change in Brazil from a centrally planned welfare assistance model to a child rights model, combined with a locally determined, participative, advocacy-oriented implementation process, could lead to substantial, progressive change. In practice, however, evidence of legal progress can become an excuse for the Brazilian government to do nothing more, neglecting enforcement of existing legislation. Decentralized implementation responsibilities make it easier to avoid action, allowing educational decline, violence, and poverty to continue unchecked.

CONCLUSIONS: SOCIAL MOVEMENTS AND SOCIAL CHANGE

During the last several decades, numerous social movements have developed worldwide in response to social problems, and a growing research literature has examined them (Melucci 1992; Touraine 1985). Much of this literature explicitly departs from a critical political economy perspective, emphasizing the agency of workers and other social actors (Adam 1993; Wolfe 1993; Soto 1989). Rather than seeing class struggle as deus ex machina,[12] social change is seen as subject to individual and collective action. Recognizing the limits to making a "revolutionary break" by overthrowing the State, social movements are instead seen as one of the main avenues for pursuing progressive social change.[13] There is hope that social movements can, as Bowles and Gintis (1986: 177) put it, "continue the expansion of personal rights and thus . . . render the exercise of both property rights and state power democratically accountable."[13]

This literature, of course, recognizes that social movements can fail, or even lead to a worsening of the problem. In Brazil, many of the social movements of this century were soundly defeated by the military and political power of the state (Wolfe 1993). The alliances and accommodations that movements must make may prevent radical reform, sometimes yielding changes that reinforce the very structures that maintain the problem. This is especially true when the problem, like poverty, stems from the basic inequalities of capitalist economic organization. As Adam argues, the fundamental question is "whether the new social movements represent . . . [a way of] . . . circumventing capitalist hegemony with a potential of making 'end runs' in the name of democracy, or whether they will necessarily leave the deep structure of capitalism untouched and avoid taking on the prevailing distribution of wealth and power" (1993: 331).

We believe, along with many in Brazil, that the changes brought about by Brazil's social movement for children's rights and democracy, despite their limitations and unclear future, do represent challenges to the prevailing distribution of wealth and power. While debates about the progressivity of these changes are valuable, they should not be seen as demanding an all-or-nothing answer. This social movement helped give children and adolescents very strong legal rights, set up participative and decentralized mechanisms to enforce these rights, and included NGO child advocates in the monitoring and control of these mechanisms. It challenged prevailing assumptions and knowledge, legitimating the voices of heretofore powerless groups like street children. Most broadly, this social movement helped end the overt repression of the military and changed public attitudes and consciousness about social problems and reforms.

The key question, of course, is how these changes will play out over the longer run, in Brazil and elsewhere. In Brazil, some would say that some of the impetus to fight for social transformation has been lost, perhaps similar to how some view post-apartheid South Africa. Nonetheless, as social movements throughout the world have begun seriously to challenge existing structures of power, successes, even very partial ones, are important to examine. This is especially so because these movements may offer the only hope for resolving our most serious social problems. As we argued in the beginning, the alternative of emphasizing "technical" approaches to "rational" social decision making within a liberal democratic framework has no chance of success. Instead, in the guise of looking for best alternatives, a technical, science-based model of social change has become a bulwark for retaining privilege.

It is not lack of knowledge or lack of means that is at the root of social problems. We basically know what to do and how to do it. What is lacking is the power to effect change. Social movements appear to be the only viable means of generating the power to pressure the state to make progressive social change. Clearly, this has not been and will not be easy. Social movements that challenge fundamental structures of privilege and power are subject to repression. Simply working with poor children in Brazil under the military dictatorship was dangerous, and the violence continues. Nonetheless, an important lesson from Brazil is that potentially far-reaching changes can be made. And, clearly, this is not only a lesson for Brazil. Brazil is, in many ways, more advanced than countries in the North, like the United States, and there is much that can be learned from the laws and programs for street and working children that have been developed in Brazil and other countries.

Much of the success of social movements has been in advancing the discourse of rights of children, women, minorities, and human beings as a whole. Yet the limits of this discourse are well recognized and highly visible in the continuing marginalization and exclusion of so many from exercising these rights in practice (Rizzini et al. 1998; Ennew 1995). The struggle now is for real inclusion in the practice of these rights, which will require major changes in how society operates globally. Fundamentally, this means reorganizing our world so every individual is guaranteed a right to a sustainable and rewarding livelihood, without which other rights cannot be achieved in practice. There is nothing utopian about such visions. The challenge is for people to realize they can make this so and to develop a global social movement that demands needed changes. Although there are no guarantees of its success, without that effort the fate of generations of street and working children, in Brazil and every other country in the world, will not improve.

NOTES

1. As discussed in various chapters in this volume, the term *street children* has been used in very different ways, sometimes causing confusion, arguments, and even the further stigmatization of these children (also see Rizzini et al. 1998). In this chapter, as indicated above, we use the term *street and working children* in a much broader sense to include urban and rural children living and working in exceptionally difficult circumstances.

2. World Food Council figures reported in "People Are Hungry Despite the Cornucopia" (*Tallahassee Democrat* 1992).
3. The inequality of the global distribution of wealth is even more shocking: Barnet and Cavanaugh (1995) reported that the combined net worth of the world's 358 billionaires was equal to the combined net worth of the poorest 45 percent of the world's population, about 2.5 billion people.
4. These criticisms have come from a variety of perspectives. See, e.g., Samoff 1996; Welch 1991; Guba and Lincoln 1989; Torres 1989; Saul 1988; Morgan 1983; Schon 1983; Papagiannis et al. 1982; Stanley 1978; and Habermas 1970.
5. For an historical examination of the misdirection of public policy and resources for children in Brazil, see Rizzini 1997; and Plank 1996.
6. "Popular rationality" might be a better label for this social-movement-driven logic of social change than "political rationality." The former, similar to ideas about "popular education" and "popular economy" in Latin America, better connotes that this logic is in significant part generated from the activities of the poor and working classes and explicitly tries to act in their interests.
7. For a greater elaboration of this history see Rizzini 1997, 1993; Pilotti and Rizzini 1995; Costa et al. 1991; Mendez 1991; Swift 1991; and Costa 1990a, 1990b.
8. The two earliest university research centers to work in this area began in Rio de Janeiro: in 1982, the Núcleo de Estudos e Ação do Menor at the Catholic University (PUC); and, in 1984, the Center for Research on Childhood (CESPI) at the University of Santa Ursula, directed by one of the authors, Irene Rizzini.
9. This is not to argue that "the solution" is simply massive creation of alternative programs, unless they formed part of an integrated strategy based on a very different set of societal assumptions and practices than those that currently dominate, as discussed below.
10. Patriarchal and racist structures are inseparably entwined with a global capitalist economy, so that women, people of color, and many minority groups bear the brunt of this persistent and pervasive poverty.
11. See Klees (1998) for a discussion of NGOs, contradictory role as a progressive force and as a neoliberal tool (for more on the topic, see the entire issue of the *Current Issues in Comparative Education* electronic journal in which this article appears).
12. As they are sometimes caricatured, e.g., see Melucci 1992: 45.
13. For Bowles and Gintis (1986), the potential efficacy of social movements follows, in part, from a belief that the democratic state, despite being embedded in capitalism, may have space to institute reforms that challenge capitalist hegemony (also see, e.g., Carnoy and Levin 1985).

REFERENCES

Adam, Barry D. 1993. "Post-Marxism and the New Social Movements." *Canadian Review of Sociology and Anthropology* 30(3): 316–36.
Antunes, Laura. 1998. "Miséria fotografada e cadastrada: meninos de rua do Rio ganham uma carteira de identificação do juizado de menores." *O Globo,* 11 Sept.
Barker, Gary, and Felicia Knaul. 1991. *Exploited Entrepreneurs: Street and Working Children in Developing Countries* (Working Paper No.1). New York: Childhope.
Barnett, Richard J., and John Cavanaugh. 1995. *Global Dreams: Imperial Corporations and the New World Order,* New York: Simon and Schuster.
Bowles, Samuel, and Herbert Gintis. 1986. *Democracy and Capitalism.* New York: Basic.
Brazil Constitution. (Constituição do Brasil). 1988. 8 Oct.
Carnoy, Martin, and Henry Levin. 1985. *Schooling and Work in the Democratic State.* Stanford, Calif.: Stanford University Press.
Carnoy, Martin, Joel Samoff, Mary Ann Burris, Anton Johnson, and Carlos Alberto Torres. 1990. *Education and Social Transition in the Third World.* Princeton: Princeton University Press.
Cornia, G., and S. Sipos. 1991. *Children and the Transition to the Market Economy: Safety Nets and Social Policies in Central and Eastern Europe.* New York: UNICEF.

Costa, Antonio Carlos Gomes da. 1990b. "Infância juventude e política social no Brasil." Pp. 20 in *Brasil criança urgente: A lei 8060/90,* edited by Antonio Carlos Gomes da Costa and Deodato Rivera. São Paulo: Columbus Cultural.

———. 1990a. "A mutação social." Pp. 8 in *Brasil criança urgente: A lei 8060/90,* edited by Antonio Carlos Gomes da Costa and Deodato Rivera. São Paulo: Columbus Cultural.

Costa, Antonio Carlos Gomes da, Agop Kayayan, and Ayrton Fausto 1991. "Do avesso ao direito, de menor a cidadão." Pp. 9-14 In *O trabalho e a rua: crianças e adolescentes no Brasil urbano dos anos 80,* edited by Ayrton Fausto and Ruben Cervini. São Paulo: FLACSO/UNICEF.

Easton, Peter, Steve Klees, Sande Milton, George Papagiannis, Art Clawson, Anthony Dewees, Hartley Hobson, Bayard Lyons, and Judy Munter. 1994. *Education for Street and Working Children: From Practice to Policy.* New York: UNICEF.

Ennew, Judith 1995. "Outside Childhood: Street Children's Rights." In *The Handbook of Children's Rights: Comparative Policy and Practice.* London: Routledge.

Fausto Ayrton, and Ruben Cervini, eds. 1991 *O trabalho e a rua: crianças e adolescentes no Brasil urbano dos anos 80.* São Paulo: FLACSO/UNICEF.

Guba, Egon, and Yvonna Lincoln. 1989. *Fourth Generation Evaluation.* Newberry Park, Calif.: Sage.

Habermas, Jürgen. 1970. *Toward a Rational Society.* Boston: Beacon.

Instituto Brasileiro de Administração Municipal (IBAM). 1997/1998. *Os conselhos de direitos da criança e do adolescente e os conselhos tutelares no Brasil: dados da pesquisa national.* Rio de Janeiro: Author.

Institute for Food and Development Policy. 1992. *Why Should Children Starve in a World of Plenty?* San Francisco: Author.

Instituto Brasileiro de Geografia Estatística (IBGE). 1997. *Indicadores sociais.* Rio de Janeiro: Author.

Klees, Steven J. 1994. "The Economics of Educational Technology." Pp. 1903-1911 in *The International Encyclopedia of Education,* 2d ed., edited by Torsten Husen and T. Neville Postlethwaite. Oxford: Pergamon.

———. 1998 "NGOs: Progressive Force or Neoliberal Tool?" *Current Issues in Comparative Education* 1 (Nov.).

Melucci, Alberto. 1992. "Liberation or Meaning? Social Movements, Culture and Democracy." *Development and Change* 3: 43-77.

Mendez, Emilio G. 1991. *Liberdade, respeito, dignidade: notas sobre a condição sócio-jurídica da infância—adolescência na américa latina.* Brasilia: Brazilian Goverment. Mimeograph.

Morgan, Gareth, ed. 1983. *Beyond Method: Strategies for Social Research.* Newberry Park, Calif.: Sage.

Myers, William, ed. 1991. *Protecting Working Children.* London: Zed Books/UNICEF.

O Globo. 1992. "Diretor da UNICEF elogia estatuto da criança brasileira." 6 Sept., 27.

Papagiannis, George, Steve Klees, and Robert Bickel. 1982. "Toward a Political Economy of Educational Innovation." *Review of Educational Research* 52: 245-90.

Pilotti Francisco, and Irene Rizzini, eds. 1995. *A arte de governar crianças. A história das políticas sociais, da legislação e da assistência à infância no Brasil.* Rio de Janeiro: IIN, EDUSU, AMAIS.

Plank, David. 1996. *The Means of Our Salvation: Public Education in Brazil.* Boulder: Westview.

Plank, David, José Amaral Sobrinho, and Antonio Carlos da Ressurreição Xavier. 1994. "Obstacles to Educational Reform in Brazil." *La Educación* 117: 70-85.

Rizzini, Irene. 1993. *A criança hoje no Brasil: Desafio para o terceiro milênio.* Rio de Janeiro: Editora Universitária Santa Ursula.

———. 1994. "Children in the City of Violence: The Case of Brazil." Pp 257-275 in *The Culture of Violence,* edited by K. Rupesinghe and M. Rubio. New York: United Nations University.

———. 1997. *O século perdido: raízes históricas das políticas públicas para a infância no Brasil.* Rio de Janeiro: EDUSU/AMAIS.

Rizzini, Irene, Gary Barker, and Neida Cassaniga. 1998. "From Street Children to All Children: Improving the Opportunities of Low Income Urban Children and Youth in Brazil." Paper presented at

The Johann Jacobs Foundation Conference, Youth in Cities: Successful Mediators of Normative Development. Germany, Oct. 25.

Rosemberg, Fúlvia. 1993. "O discurso sobre a criança de rua na década de 80." São Paulo: Fundação Carlos Chagas.

Samoff, Joel. 1996. "Chaos and Uncertainty in Development." *World Development* 24(4): 611-633.

Saul, Ana Maria. 1988. *Avaliação emancipatória.* São Paulo: Cortez.

Schon, Donald. 1983. *The Reflective Practitioner: How Professionals Think in Action.* New York: Basic.

Silva, Antonio Fernando do Amaral e. 1990. "Mutação judicial." Pp. 46-53 in *Brasil criança urgente: a lei 8060/90,* edited by Antonio Carlos Gomes da Costa and Deodato Rivera. São Paulo: Columbus Cultural.

Soto, Orlando Nunez. 1989. "Social Movements in the Struggle for Democracy, Revolution, and Socialism." *Rethinking Marxism* 2(1): 7-22.

Stanley, Manfred. 1978. *The Technological Conscience: Survival and Dignity in an Age of Expertise.* Chicago: University of Chicago Press.

Swift, Anthony. 1991. *The Fight for Childhood in the City.* Florence, Italy: Innocenti Center.

Tallahassee Democrat. 1992. "People Are Hungry Despite Cornucopia." 31 May, 9A.

Toledo, José Roberto de. 1998. "Mapa da exclusão: crise financeira mundial agrava condições de vida." *Folha de São Paulo,* 2 July.

Torres, Carlos Alberto. 1989. "The Capitalist State and Public Policy Formation: A Framework for a Political Sociology of Educational Policy-Making." *British Journal of the Sociology of Education* 10: 81-102.

Touraine, Alain. 1985. "An Introduction to the Study of Social Movements." *Social Research* 52: 4.

United Nations Development Program (UNDP). 1998. *Human Development Report.* New York: United Nations.

Vogel, Arno, and Irma Rizzini. 1995. "O menor filho do estado: pontos de partida para uma história da assistência à infância no Brasil." Pp. 237-346 in *A arte de governar crianças. A história das políticas sociais, da legislação e da assistência à infância no Brasil,* edited by Francisco Pilotti and Irene Rizzini. Rio de Janeiro: IIN, EDUSU, AMAIS.

Welch, Anthony. 1991. "Knowledge and Legitimization in Comparative Education." *Comparative Education Review* 35: 508-31.

Wolfe, Joel. 1993. "Social Movements and the state of Brazil." *Latin American Research Review* 28(1): 248-58.

World Bank. 1997. *World Development Report 1997: The State of a Changing World.* New York: Oxford.

Wright, R. 1994. "Nations Selling Their Futures into Economic Slavery." *Los Angeles Times,* 16 Jan., 1A-7A.

6

Dependency Served:
Rhetorical Assumptions Governing the Education of Homeless Children and Youth in the United States

Irving Epstein

Although it can be convincingly argued that in recent years, the legitimacy of the welfare state in the United States has been subjected to an unrelenting attack, it is clear that social policy toward homeless people, generally, and homeless children and youth, specifically, reflects larger contradictions intrinsic to the nature of that entity. It is clear that the state has an expressed interest in limiting the political and economic costs of alleviating poverty so as to protect those market forces that contribute to its creation, since those forces concurrently allow privileged elites to maintain and perpetuate their economic position. On the other hand, until recently, the state has also viewed it beneficial to claim some responsibility for reducing the effects of poverty and in so doing, communicate a sense of mission that masks its other inherently coercive policies. The contradiction has usually been resolved through protecting market forces by proposing short-term solutions that do little to threaten status quo practice (Blau 1992). While even short-term solutions are now being rejected by the political right, the justification for abandoning those in need remains the same.

As an alternative to active government involvement in social policy, the state promotes an ideology of self-reliance that implies that the homeless are to blame for the predicament they confront. Accordingly, the homeless should be held directly responsible for ameliorating their harsh living situations, and in any event, they already have adequate resources available to resolve their dilemmas. This stance serves the interests of the state quite well, for it minimizes the state's responsibility to initiate structural reform by posing the issue as one of individual competence and will.

In conceiving of the state, it is useful to examine the discursive function of its institutional components. State institutions are responsible not only for forming and implementing policies but also for legitimizing them. They consistently attempt to make the case that it is the general will rather than that of specific interests that is well served when policy formation and implementation occurs. As Bob Jessup notes:

> Any general definition of the state would need to refer to state discourse as well as state institutions. . . .The core of the state apparatus comprises a distinct ensemble of institutions and organizations whose socially accepted function is to define and

99

enforce collectively binding decisions on the members of a society in the name of their common interest or general will. (1990: 341)

Schools are particularly important, as they employ curricular and instructional mechanisms that reify exclusionary practices in the name of inclusivity. Following Bourdieu (1977; Bourdieu and Passeron 1977), the formation and dissemination of the formal curriculum contributes to the acquisition of cultural capital, whose possession is valued by privileged elites. By including and excluding certain knowledge domains deemed worthy of mastery, often according to the degree to which these domains are abstracted from common working- and lower-middle-class experience, schools promote a particular form of symbolic violence even as they present themselves as inclusive organizations.

Common socialization tendencies within the classroom further perpetuate an achievement ideology that views individual competition as intrinsically worthwhile and demands that those who do not succeed internalize their sense of failure. This ideology shields school practice from criticism and critique. As a result, individualism and self-reliance are continually reified as commonsense positive virtues. Ultimately, schools mask their own sorting and selection functions through asserting that, both in form and content, that which is taught to students is value-neutral and can stand the test of objective evaluation. As a result, schools also reinforce broader social messages concerning the limited responsibility all mechanisms of the state possess to minimize social inequality.

An analysis of how schools teach children who are homeless as well as how they teach about homelessness is useful. Homelessness and street life share important features that often directly challenge those mainstreamed values enunciated in school settings. For example, life on the street usually demands public disclosure of personal destitution. One's poverty is made so visible that there is no escape from confronting its existence for the external observer as well as victim. One's uniqueness becomes difficult to mask. Second, survival on the street necessitates the abandonment of a futuristic time orientation as survival becomes a moment-to-moment preoccupation. For those in such a situation, the ability to divide and order time so as to contemplate, let alone plan for, a future is an unfamiliar luxury. Third, street life demands ceding one's entitlement to personal and private space. As a result, trust in the ability to achieve a sense of permanence regarding personal and social relationships is easily compromised.

Schools, as rule-governing institutions that promote the virtues of individual achievement, acquired through competition for the delayed gratification of receiving good grades, find it difficult to address these cultural characteristics unique to homelessness. To be sure, part of the mandate of compulsory schooling is to provide an inclusive education for all children while addressing their specific needs. Truancy and poor school attendance, behaviors that can be logically associated with homelessness, communicate a form of resistance that directly threatens that mandate (Enomoto 1994). Indeed, the clash of values that occurs between generic classroom expectations and negative educational experiences encountered by generations of children and parents in poverty makes the decision to drop out a logical resolution of such conflict (Okey and Cusik 1995). Of course, homelessness represents a particular form of destitution whose effects are sudden, comprehensive, and immediate. The intensive monitoring of personal and social relations within classroom environments and the enforcement of general rules of behavior for all students regardless of their background present a stark contrast to life on the streets or in shelters, where one's survival demands more flexible and immediate responses to life-threatening situations. The curricular and instructional practices that schools employ to teach to and about homeless youth are therefore of interest, not only because they reiterate mainstream educational values in a specific context but also because they define the limits upon which those values maintain their salience in particularly tragic circumstances.

HOMELESSNESS AS A CATEGORY OF "AT-RISK" BEHAVIOR

Homeless children and youth are often characterized by educators as *at-risk students.* The term is borrowed from a medical metaphor, whereby it is assumed that potential illness can be identified and treated in preventive fashion, before being allowed to fester fully. Through analogy, it is argued that by successfully addressing the needs of at-risk students, long-term harmful behaviors such as dropout, delinquency, and criminal activity can also be prevented. It is important to note that when applied to homelessness, the term *at-risk* is quite ambiguously defined to include cognitive and motor function and development, psychosocial and emotional development, and socioeconomic circumstance, as well as particular learned behaviors judged to be unhealthy. The attributes associated with children and youth reiterate this pattern. At the same time, as Gartner and Lipsky note:

> The medical model views disability as located within the individual, and, thus, primary emphasis is devoted to the etiology or causes of conditions and the placement of persons in separate diagnostic categories. From this perspective, efforts to improve the functional capabilities of individuals are regarded as the exclusive solution to disability. (1987: 390, n.6)

Natriello and his colleagues argue that the at-risk term evolved from cultural deprivation and cultural deficit models. The advantage to its use lay in the assumption that educational as well as environmental factors including the quality of community and family relationships shared equal responsibility for guaranteeing a student's future school success or failure. In addition, the ability to identify, early on, those who were in potential harm could prove beneficial in preventing later dysfunction (Natriello et al. 1990). Its use within the context of homelessness shows few of these potential advantages, though. Unlike specific special education designations (communicative disorder, visual or auditory impairment, for example) that at least pay a half-hearted attempt formally to define disabilities with a certain degree of specificity, the nature of homelessness is so global as to make the term easily susceptible to blanket stigmatization. And the fact that children are viewed as sharing the unfortunate condition with their parents is likely to result in the gross labeling of both parties in pejorative terms. There simply is no reason for educators to make a shared commitment with community members and parents to alleviate its negative effects if those parties are characterized as sharing the inherently dysfunctional attributes associated with their children and can therefore be held directly responsible for their perpetuation.

In analyzing the assumptions that form the basis for our impressions of homelessness and its effect upon children and youth, it is clear that functionalist principles of cognitive and psychosocial development are continually reinforced. Those assumptions view development as unilaterally progressive, deterministic, generalizable, and decontextualized. Historically, these assumptions, when applied to curricular issues, justified the move toward increasing reliance upon social control, bureaucratic hierarchy, and efficiency within school walls (Popkewitz 1987). But their effect upon perceptions of homeless children has been quite specific. It is widely assumed that the characteristics homeless children exhibit separate them from the norm. If these characteristics are addressed successfully, then students presumably reacquire normalcy. If unsuccessfully addressed, then their exceptionality legitimizes further exclusionary practices and policies, since there is a real danger of those difficulties becoming permanently disabling.

As is true of the at-risk label generally, the homeless label serves as a social marker, defining normalcy for the majority population, rather than enhancing our understanding of a group in need. But in the case of homeless children, the at-risk label can be even more pernicious. Not only is the courage and strength that many of these children display minimized, but their inventive use of survival strategies, their enhanced flexibility in making quick decisions, their heightened awareness of external threats and influences, and their willingness to take risks are all deprecated. Instead, it is their dependency that is stressed.

THE AMBIGUITY OF EDUCATIONAL INSTITUTIONAL RESPONSE

It is not surprising that ambivalent policy leads to ambiguous practice. Several years after the passage of the McKinney Act, Maria Yon surveyed 184 school districts regarding homeless students. Of the 101 districts (55 percent of the sample) that responded, 69 percent of the reporting districts described the number of homeless children within their boundaries as being nonexistent or of small size. Forty-eight percent reported that they had not made any plans to educate homeless children, and of the 52 percent who made such plans, only 7 percent received grants for the expressed purpose of educating them. While 22 percent of those districts that acknowledged homelessness to be a problem offered in-service training to their teachers, only one district actually provided a course on the topic for their staff. Yon concluded that homelessness is more likely to be perceived to be a significant problem among larger, rather than smaller, districts, but the growing problem of hidden homelessness, which probably affects districts of all sizes, remains unaddressed (Yon 1995).

Given this degree of general institutional ambivalence, it is not surprising that curricular and instructional policies at the local level are ambiguous and contradictory. Educators are asked to participate in practices that both identify and ignore situations related to homelessness, empathize with as well as objectify conditions of homelessness, and assimilate as well as separate homeless children from the normal school population.

IGNORANCE/IDENTIFICATION

One of the major complaints of school districts involves the difficulties their staff confront in obtaining adequate records of transient population groups such as homeless children. How does one secure and evaluate their previous academic records? At what level should they be placed? In what areas are they in need of remediation or special assistance, if any? Have they been fully immunized and do they suffer from specific health problems that warrant immediate attention before entering school premises? And, in the absence of such information, what can one expect schools to reasonably do in offering assistance to homeless children? As has been noted, the McKinney Act both places pressure upon school districts to keep and maintain adequate records and yet asks that their personnel implement policies flexibly, so that the absence of specific information does not become an impediment to the delivery of appropriate educational services.

Discovering appropriate answers to these questions is made even more difficult because of the potential harm that can result regardless of the specific solution that is employed. We are acutely aware of the negative effects of labeling that result from an insensitive reliance upon school records, particularly those that are constructed anecdotally. Yet anecdotal information is the first type and in some ways the most crucial of the information that will be gathered when a homeless student is initially placed in a new school, as it allows educators to contextualize other raw data that usually arrives later. At the same time, the willingness to ignore homeless student needs in the absence of available information is a serious danger that is also present. Of course, of greater importance than the type, quality, or quantity of information gathered about homeless children is how that information is used or misused. But given the general tendency of school districts to ignore the existence of the homelessness, one can reasonably question the contention that it is inadequate record keeping and inaccessibility to background information that are the primary reasons for the failure of schools to address the needs of these children.

EMPATHY/OBJECTIFICATION

To the extent that staff and teacher in-servicing does occur, it focuses upon enhancing general awareness of homelessness as a social phenomenon. That awareness is reinforced through offering information about its prevalence and its effects upon student behavior and performance, and providing the names and addresses of neighborhood shelters and/or social service agencies that might offer assistance to the children and their families. Such understanding, however, is rarely translated into unique instructional classroom practice.

The Massachusetts Department of Education, for example, has created a specific unit responsible for providing educational services for homeless children and youth within the state. Of the five issues its in-service workshop on homeless children attempts to address, only one directly involves instruction, "Ways school personnel can support children during this time of transition [What specific strategies can teachers, counselors, and administrators implement to overcome barriers homeless children face as they attempt to stay and succeed in school?]" (Douglas 1992). The fact that classroom instructional strategies are linked with those addressed by counselors and administrators reflects the lack of instructional focus directed toward the issue.

Indeed, among the six priorities the U.S. Department of Education lists for educators as meeting the specific needs of homeless children and youth (remediation and tutoring; support services including social work and counseling; after-school and extended day services; awareness training for personnel; assessment, screening, and placement; and program continuity and stability), not one directly involves special classroom instruction (Heflin and Rudy 1991). These responses create what I call an appeal to empathy based upon objectification. It is assumed that a global, objectified awareness of homelessness will lead to increased staff and instructor sensitivity that will further expedite the development of coping skills for children who are adversely affected.

Why is it assumed that once such awareness is enhanced, progressive action on the part of teachers and school officials will necessarily follow? There is the presumption that empathy, resulting from this heightened understanding, will create the motivation that is a prerequisite for further action. But, as long as specific instructional responses are generically defined in the most global of terms (tutoring, remediation, after-school servicing), the framing of policy toward homeless children allows those school personnel responsible for implementing policy to distance themselves from the specific needs of the children. Cognizance of the objective conditions of homelessness may legitimize empathetic attitudes, but it does little to guarantee concrete responses. As a result, the prerogative for action is defined in conditional terms. The message that is being sent communicates the view that one *should* respond to the needs of homeless children in such and such a way, rather than that one is responsible and will be held directly accountable for enacting a set of concrete policies that are designed to produce beneficial results.

Andy Hargreaves has commented upon the role of persecutory and depressive guilt that teachers experience. Persecutory guilt occurs when one fails to comply with bureaucratic controls and accountability standards. Depressive guilt occurs with the realization that through neglect or inattention, we inflict harm upon those for whom we care (1994). The failure to create instructional approaches designed specifically for homeless children obviously enhances feelings that exacerbate both forms of guilt on the part of teachers.

ASSIMILATION/SEPARATION

The range of policy options created to address issues affecting homeless youth incorporate both assimilationist and separationist strategies, even though the McKinney Act specifically argues in favor of an assimilationist perspective. In a few large school districts, for example, specific facilities have been specially designated as schools for homeless children. All of the children within district boundaries who are homeless will attend the designated schools, often established within a shelter or near shelter premises.

But if this type of policy invokes separation at its most extreme, other approaches are in evidence too. The identification of a single staff member as coordinator of services for homeless children within the regular school complies with the intent of the McKinney Act but also defines responsibility in individual and separate, rather than collective and shared terms. This is the case in New York City, where under the Fair Share system, no one school is given responsibility for the education of homeless children, but one staff person per school is appointed as a homeless advocate (U.S. Department of Education 1992).

With respect to classroom instruction and practice, assimilationist tendencies are more popular. Teachers are encouraged to use a buddy system for homeless students, so that a peer will give needed attention to the newly enrolled student. However, it is also recognized that such a system should be established for *all* new students, regardless of whether they are homeless. The creation of after-school tutoring and extracurricular activities on school premises as well as within shelters is widely applauded, particularly for adolescents in need of GED training and vocational counseling. Yet it is acknowledged that such services should be made available for all interested students, not simply those who are homeless.

We have already noted that the placement of homeless children in special education programs, generically designed for those who are "at risk," may have separationist outcomes, but its implementation is conducted in assimilationist terms, where little distinction is made between homeless as opposed to nonhomeless special education students. There is little specific guidance that is offered to educators that would encourage decision making based upon the children's best interests, since those interests are rarely recognized as being unique.

Staff connections between the disparate environments of shelter and school are initiated in a number of ways. As has been noted, some schools employ social workers who will work directly with homeless children and their families on the school site; occasionally guidance counselors and school personnel will visit the shelters themselves. There are some classroom teachers who will both teach in or visit shelters on a regular basis, although their numbers are less prevalent. Among the most successful programs to receive national publicity is the KOOL-IS (Kids Organized on Learning in School) initiative established at the Benjamin Franklin Day Elementary School in Seattle. The program uses teachers, volunteers, homeless parents, corporate, church, and community sponsorship, and professional case workers to serve the needs of its students, of whom a disproportionate number are homeless. Its success is a testament to the power of networking and the potential effectiveness of caring, intelligent, and energetic school administrators, such as Carole Williams, the school principal described by Sharon Quint (1994).

EDUCATIONAL PROGRAMS OUTSIDE OF SCHOOL

After-school and shelter tutoring are important activities that supplement formal instruction within schools. Model programs, such as those implemented in Seattle, create student assistance teams that offer students transitional assistance, troubleshoot, and coordinate tutorial services and individual plans of action for children and their families. Student assistance teams consist of eight members including the school principal, case manager, family support worker, school psychologist, the school's coordinator of volunteer services, a volunteer worker, a tutor, and a program coordinator, who meet once a week to review their clients' progress. A program with similar intent in Madison, Wisconsin, the Transitional Education Program, provides the same services: counseling, school and personal supplies, and food, to both children and their parents. In New York City, the board of education has initiated a program titled "Students Living in Temporary Housing," where family assistants provide educational programs for parents and children at shelters, while social workers and guidance counselors are used as complementary staff. For older children, Career Education Centers have been established to work with adolescent homeless at 25 shelters, creating educational programs at each site. These programs include academic instruction, counseling services, and enrichment activities that consist of networking with community arts groups, business partnerships that give financial aid to students, and general mentoring. Together, these programs emphasize the importance of using a holistic approach to attack the effects of homelessness (U.S. Department of Education 1992).

Yet there are pervasive policies and structural decisions that limit the potential impact of educational efforts within shelter walls. In the first place, most shelters restrict the clientele they serve. It is obvious that large numbers of homeless children do not have their educational needs served as a result of their direct or indirect association with parents who fail to meet shelter selection criteria or, in certain cases, their own adolescence.

A second set of policies involves length of stay and conditions of residence. Seventy-five percent of all shelters place restrictions upon one's length of stay; most require residents to sign contractual agreements enunciating shelter rules and responsibilities that may include compulsory parent education and counseling sessions, housekeeping chores, prohibitions against vulgar language use, alcohol and drug use, and the physical disciplining of one's children, and so forth (Weinreb and Rossi 1995). Children whose parents fail to comply with these restrictions are obviously adversely affected. Although shelters provide many services to their clients, they are more likely to assess the needs of adults, rather than children, and while they report high percentages of children with learning, behavioral, physical, and developmental problems, only about 50 percent of the shelters surveyed in the Weinreb and Rossi study offer specific assessments of children's needs in these areas (1995).

Restrictive selection criteria, limited lengths of stay, and an insistence upon operating potentially stigmatizing parent education programs are indicative of the pervasive degree of institutional mistrust that accompanies aid to the homeless within shelter

environments. An unwritten message that seems quite clear is that the quantity and quality of such assistance must never be perceived by their clients as being so high so as to
foster their dependency or compromise their ability to make a commitment to individual
self-reliance. As a result, the smell of coercion, even if communicated informally,
becomes an intrinsic part of the shelter experience. Therefore, the potential success of
educational programs that operate within such an environment must be viewed with a
certain degree of skepticism.

There are success stories, though. One is the Jump Start program created by The
Homes for Homeless (HFH) organization. It utilizes a variation of the *High/Scope* curriculum, a reading program for preschool students that encourages direct student participation and involvement in the selection of appropriate instructional activities. HFH
also developed the Brownstone School, an after-school program offering accelerated,
rather than remedial, instruction to elementary students aged 5–13 (Nuñez 1994). Its
activities are discussed more fully in Nuñez's chapter in this volume.

Efforts to motivate children through encouraging their engagement with empowering activities would seem to stand out given the typical shelter environment to which
many are accustomed. Nonetheless, that environment will always differ significantly
from that of the classroom due to the continued turnover of its population, severely
overcrowded living conditions, and, in large transitional shelters, overt surveillance of
client activities and a direct dependence upon the threat of coercion so as to ensure the
physical protection of clients.

CONCLUSION: WHOSE DEPENDENCY?

Throughout this chapter, I have argued that educational policy and practice reflect the
ideological ambivalence of the reluctant welfare state, which is unwilling to address
directly issues of homelessness lest the short-term interests of those who are privileged
be compromised. Yet the state is equally unwilling to admit to the coercive implications of such a stance. When educational efforts are forthcoming, they fail to speak
directly to the unique characteristics of the culture of homelessness. Instead, educators are encouraged to rely upon global "at-risk" categorizations as they design their
courses of action. Educators are given contradictory messages with respect to the
amount of background information that should be used in making instructional decisions, the extent to which they are responsible for creating specific instructional and
curricular initiatives that directly speak to the needs of homeless children, and the
degree to which homeless children and youth should be segregated from or assimilated into mainstream groups.

In spite of some outstanding efforts on the part of selected educators to go beyond
school walls and directly confront issues affecting homeless children who reside within
shelters or on the streets, comprehensive action of this sort is the exception, rather than
the norm. Instead, it is the generic tutorial, remedial, and special-education program that
is most often utilized; the effect is one of treating homelessness as one of the many types
of disability with which we are more familiar. Coupled with a lack of understanding of
the uniqueness of the culture of the street and the institutional culture of the shelter is
the tendency to objectify homeless children and youth into the roles of psychological
and socioeconomic dependents.

Given the role schools have traditionally played in legitimizing the contradictions of
the reluctant welfare state, these responses are not surprising. They are made even more
understandable when one recognizes the fact that the culture of homelessness is more

diametrically opposed to the culture of the school than those typical social class differences with which we are more familiar. Nonetheless, in equating homelessness with generic dependency and at-risk behavior, while maintaining adherence to an achievement ideology with its claims of inclusivity in the midst of exclusionary practice, schools express their own form of ideological dependency. This dependency is fostered by an unwillingness of a middle class to admit directly to the existence of class conflict and confront its own fears of facing potential homelessness. Given such a climate, the curricular and instructional activities that are utilized by caring and dedicated educators are even more remarkable, although it is difficult to conclude that they will ever become widespread. In acknowledging the presence of social pressures that limit the range of options available to those engaged in curricular and instructional practice, we are able to obtain a clearer perspective regarding the limitations and possibilities for curricular change and reform on a broader scale. If the treatment of homelessness is indicative, then those possibilities are indeed circumscribed.

REFERENCES

Blau, Joel. 1992. *The Visible Poor: Homeless in the United States.* New York: Oxford University Press.

Bourdieu, Pierre. 1977. *Outline of a Theory of Practice.* Cambridge: Cambridge University Press.

Bourdieu, Pierre, and Jean-Claude Passeron. 1977. *Reproduction in Education, Society and Culture.* Beverly Hills, Calif.: Sage.

Douglas, Ann. 1992. *Homeless Children and Their Families: A Resource Booklet for School Personnel.* Malden, Mass.: Massachusetts Department of Education, Office for the Education of Homeless Children and Youth.

Enomoto, Ernestine K. 1994. "The Meaning of Truancy: Organizational Culture as Multicultures." *Urban Review* 26: 187–207.

Gartner, Alan, and Dorothy Kerzner Lipsky. 1987. "Toward a Quality System for All Students." *Harvard Educational Review* 57: 367–93.

Hargreaves, Andy. 1994. *Changing Teachers, Changing Times.* London: Cassell.

Heflin, L. Juane, and Kathryn Rudy. 1991. *Homeless and in Need of Special Education: Exceptional Children at Risk.* Reston, Va.: Council for Exceptional Children. (ERIC Document no. ED 339-167.)

Jessup, Bob. 1990. *State Theory: Placing Capitalist States in Their Place.* University Park: Pennsylvania State University.

Natriello, Gary, Edward L. McDill, and Aaron M. Pallas. 1990. *Schooling Disadvantaged Children: Racing against Catastrophe.* New York: Teachers College Press.

Nuñez, Ralph da Costa. 1994. "Access to Success: Meeting the Educational Needs of Homeless Children and Families." *Social Work in Education* 16: 21–30.

Okey, Ted N., and Philip A. Cusick. 1995. "Dropping Out: Another Side of the Story." *Educational Administration Quarterly* 31: 244–67.

Popkewitz, Thomas S. 1987. "The Formation of School Subjects and the Political Context of Schooling." Pp. 1–24 in *The Formation of the School Subjects,* edited by Thomas S. Popkewitz. New York: Falmer Press.

Quint, Sharon. 1994. *Schooling Homeless Children: A Working Model for America's Public Schools.* New York: Teachers College Press.

U.S. Department of Education. 1992. *Serving Homeless Children: The Responsibilities of Educators.* Washington, D.C.: Author.

Weinreb, Linda, and Peter H. Rossi. 1995. "The American Homeless Family Shelter System." *Social Service Review* 69: 86–101.

Yon, Maria G. 1995. "Educating Homeless Children in the United States." *Equity and Excellence in Education* 28: 58–62.

7

Educating Homeless Children in the United States:
An Overview of Legal Entitlements
and Federal Protections

Yvonne Rafferty

A cross the United States, homeless children's opportunities to experience school success are severely compromised by their high rates of residential and school mobility, poor school attendance, shelter policies that jeopardize their physical and psychological well-being, and barriers to accessing both schooling and appropriate educational services once they are in school. Federal legislation, specifically the Stewart B. McKinney Homeless Assistance Act and its subsequent amendments, mandates that state educational authorities (SEAs) review and revise all policies, practices, laws, and regulations that may act as a barrier to enrollment, attendance, and school success of homeless students. This chapter provides an overview of federal mandates and describes persistent obstacles that continue to jeopardize the school success of homeless children and youth in the United States.

THE STEWART B. MCKINNEY HOMELESS ASSISTANCE ACT

The threat to school success as a result of homelessness was recognized by the U.S. Congress more than 10 years ago when it passed the first comprehensive legislation to aid the homeless. The 1987 Stewart B. McKinney Homeless Assistance Act, and its subsequent amendments in 1990 and 1994, provided considerable protection for the educational needs of homeless children and youth. It also provided formula grants to SEAs to carry out the Education for Homeless Children and Youth Program created by the act.

Equal Access to Public School Education

One of the most important provisions of the Education for Homeless Children and Youth Program is the requirement that SEAs ensure that local educational agencies (LEAs) do not create a separate education system for homeless children: "Homelessness alone should not be sufficient reason to separate students from the mainstream school environment" [Sec. 721(3)]. State and local educational agencies must "adopt policies and practices to ensure that homeless children and youth are not isolated or stigmatized" [Sec. 711(g)(1)(H)]. Homeless children must get the same access to education that children with established residences receive: "Each state educational agency shall ensure that each child of a homeless individual and each homeless youth has equal access to the same free, appropriate public education, including a public preschool education, as provided to other children and youth" [Sec. 721(1)].

Prior to the 1994 reauthorization, homeless preschoolers were not explicitly mentioned in the legislation, although they were covered by the definition of "school-age." As a result, these youngsters were routinely excluded from available programs. SEAs are now required to ensure that homeless preschool children "have equal access to the same public preschool programs, administered by the state agency, as provided to other children" [Sec. 722(g)(1)(D)].

Choice of School Placement

Homeless children may attend (a) their "school of origin" (through the end of the current school year, or if the child becomes homeless between academic years, for the following academic year), or (b) transfer into "any school that nonhomeless students who live in the attendance area in which the child or youth is actually living are eligible to attend." *School of origin* is defined as the school they had been attending when permanently housed, or the school in which the child or youth was last enrolled, regardless of where the family is temporarily staying [Sec. 722(g)(3)(A)].

The choice regarding school placement must be made "in the child's or youth's best interest" [Sec. 722(g)(3)(A)]. Congress recognized the importance of parent involvement in the education of their children by mandating that LEAs "shall comply, to the extent feasible, with the request made by the parent or guardian regarding school selection" [Sec. 722(3)(B)]. SEAs must have procedures in place to resolve disputes regarding placement determinations [Sec. 722(g)(1)(A)].

Access Barriers

SEAs must remove barriers to the enrollment, attendance, and success in school of homeless children:

> In any state that has a compulsory residency requirement as a component of the state's compulsory school attendance laws or other laws, regulations, practices, or policies that may act as a barrier to the enrollment, attendance, or success in school of homeless children and homeless youth, the state will review and undertake steps to revise such laws, regulations, practices, or policies to ensure that homeless children and youth are afforded the same free, appropriate public education as provided to other children and youth [Sec. 721 (2)].

For children who are transferring into new schools, LEAs are mandated to transfer their records in a timely manner. Records include "any record ordinarily kept by the school, including immunization records, academic records, birth certificates, guardianship records, and evaluations for special services or programs" [Sec. 722(e)(5)].

Equal Access to School Programs and Services

Some homeless children require additional educational services such as special education or bilingual education. SEAs must ensure that homeless children (including preschoolers) have the same access as their housed peers to special education, as well as all other educational programs and services for which they are eligible:

> Each homeless child . . . shall be provided services comparable to services offered to other students in the school, including (a) transportation services; (b) educational services for which the child or youth meets the eligibility criteria, such as services provided under

Title 1 of the Elementary and Secondary Education Act of 1965 or similar state or local programs, educational programs for children with disabilities, and educational programs for
students with limited English proficiency; (c) programs in vocational education; (d) programs for gifted and talented students; and (e) school meals programs [Sec. 722(g)(4)].

In addition to school-based programs and services, children who are permanently
housed often access other federal, state, or local programs. SEAs must ensure that homeless children who meet the relevant eligibility criteria for such programs are "able to participate in Federal, State, or local food programs . . . have equal access to the same public
preschool programs, administered by the State agency, as provided to other children . . . before-and after-school care programs" [Sec. 722(g)(1)(C) and (D)].

Direct Services

The 1990 amendments moved beyond access barriers and recognized the need for services once children are enrolled in school. The amendments increased appropriations
significantly from the 1987 levels, and explicitly mandated SEAs to use 95 percent of
their McKinney funds to provide grants to LEAs for the purpose of "facilitating the enrollment, attendance, and success in school of homeless children and youth" [Sec.
723(a)(1)]. Schools may use the funds to provide before- and after-school programs,
tutoring programs, referrals for medical and mental health services, preschool programs,
parent education, counseling, social work services, transportation, and other services
that may not otherwise be provided by public schools. LEAs that receive assistance must
also coordinate with other agencies and designate a liaison to ensure that homeless children "receive educational services for which such families, children, and youth are eligible, including Head Start and Even Start programs and preschool programs administered
by the local educational agency, and referrals to health care services, dental services,
mental health services, and other appropriate services" [Sec. 722(7)(A)].

Interagency Coordination and Communication

SEAs are required to facilitate collaboration between the SEA, the state social services
agency, and other relevant programs and service providers (including programs for
preschoolers and runaway and homeless youth) in order to improve the provision of
comprehensive services [Sec. 722(f)(5) and (6)]. They must also work to improve the
provision of comprehensive services to these children and youth and their families
through the development of relationships and coordination with other education, child
development, and preschool programs, and services providers. Comprehensive services
include health care, nutrition, and other social services.

Coordination with Emergency Shelter/Housing Providers

The McKinney Act also mandated coordination with emergency shelters or housing
providers.

Where applicable, each state and local educational agency that receives assistance under
this subtitle shall coordinate with state and local housing agencies responsible for developing the comprehensive housing affordability strategy described in Section 1005 of the
Cranston-Gonzalez National Affordable Housing Act to minimize educational disruption
of children who become homeless [Sec. 722(g)9].

The U.S. Department of Education (ED) in its guidance to the states is more specific
with regard to the nature of this coordination.

State coordinators, LEAs, and liaisons should coordinate with state and local housing authorities to develop a process whereby homeless families with school-age children are placed in housing that is accessible to transportation facilities and schools determined to be in the best interests of the children and youth. (1995: 13)

PROGRAM IMPLEMENTATION AND OVERSIGHT

The U.S. Department of Education is authorized to make grants available to SEAs for implementing the Education for Homeless Children and Youth Program. To receive funding, SEAs are required to establish an Office of Coordinator of Education of Homeless Children and Youth. Coordinators must estimate and report to ED the number of homeless children, document the problems they experience gaining access to schools/preschools, progress made in addressing access barriers, and the success of the state's Education for Homeless Children and Youth Program in facilitating school enrollment, attendance, and success [Sec. 722(f)(2)]. Coordinators must also develop and carry out a state plan, which explains how the SEA will provide for the education of homeless children and youth. State plans must contain provisions designed (a) to authorize personnel to make school placement determinations in the best interests of each homeless child; (b) to provide procedures for the prompt resolutions of disputes; (c) to develop programs for school personnel; (d) to ensure participation in both before- and after-school programs; (e) to address problems of access to, and placement of, children in schools, including transportation issues and enrollment delays; and (f) to demonstrate that state and local education agencies have developed policies to remove barriers to the enrollment and retention of homeless children in schools and have adopted policies that ensure that homeless children and youth are not isolated or stigmatized [Sec. 722(e)].

Although ED is required to oversee implementation of the program, it took a federal lawsuit, filed by advocates for homeless children, to get the department to implement the Education for Homeless Children and Youth Program after it was signed into law in 1987 (National Coalition for the Homeless 1989). Program funds were not made available to states in a timely manner until 1991, when a law mandated that ED award funds within 120 days. While the grant application process has improved in recent years, some delays in awarding funds have persisted (Rafferty 1995).

ED has been criticized for its leadership in reviewing and approving state plans and ensuring that SEAs remove the barriers to education. Studies that examined ED's compliance with the act indicate that state plans routinely omit provisions mandated by the act (Rafferty 1995). Anderson et al. (1995), under contract from ED, examined state plans and progress reports of 55 states and territories submitted to ED between 1988 and 1992. They focused on five areas emphasized in the McKinney Act: access to school; access to educational programs and services; awareness-raising activities; coordination and collaboration; and support to local school districts. They concluded:

> We found state plans and progress reports to be vague about the actual level of implementation, support, and resources channeled into activities for the education of homeless children and youth. In many cases, individual states did not include any detailed information on their activities in one of more of these five areas of interest, or references to activities in these areas were ambiguous. In some of their early reports, several states described specific programs that were being considered for future implementation. Later progress reports, however, made no reference to the proposed programs, so it was unclear whether the proposed programs had actually been implemented. (Anderson et al. 1995: 5)

The 1994 reauthorization of the Education for Homeless Children and Youth Program addressed these limitations by mandating SEAs to describe the various procedures and programs adopted by the state to comply with the act's requirements. SEAs were given the option to combine plans from several educational programs into a single plan to promote greater cross-program coordination, planning, and service delivery, and enhanced integration of programs (ED 1995).

Overall, 41 states chose to include the Education for Homeless Children and Youth Program in a consolidated state plan. The National Law Center on Homelessness and Poverty [NLC] reviewed the consolidated state plans and found that very few of the plans addressed any of the key requirements for state planning under the McKinney Act. For example, 75 percent (32) made no mention of homeless children, 85 percent (35) did not describe how consolidation would contribute to more effective use of funds, and 27 percent (11) contained no details on how funds would be used. The NLC concluded that the omission of individual program requirements "produced documents so general that they are meaningless" (1995: 53). The 9 states that submitted individual plans, in contrast, addressed the educational needs of homeless children adequately.

One major reason for inadequate state plans has to do with the technical assistance provided by ED. For example, ED's guidance to states did not reflect the mandate for plans to identify particular information from "each program" for inclusion in a consolidated plan (NLC 1995). The limited content requirements established by ED for approval of a state's plan, and the complete omission of application and plan requirements under the McKinney Act, misconstrue provisions of the federal laws governing consolidation (Center for Law and Education 1995).

A third issue pertains to compliance by ED with regard to program reporting requirements (NLC 1990). ED is required to issue a report to Congress within 45 days of state reports. Data for the previous published report was to be based on state data received no later than December 31, 1993. ED did not issue their report until July 1995—15 months late (NLC 1995). The department's report based on 1997 data was issued in early 1999—again, almost a year and one-half late! ED has also been lax in including the required information in reports. For example, reported attendance rates are meaningless because of inconsistencies in how states define "homeless"; whether or not preschoolers are counted as required; and the persistent inability of some SEAs (New York in particular) to calculate attendance rates for children who are homeless, as is required by federal law.

REMAINING BARRIERS

The Department of Education has been negligent in monitoring compliance and ensuring that SEAs remove the barriers to education that are still in existence in some school districts. The following section highlights three persistent barriers to school success: school access barriers; shelter policies; and high rates of school mobility.

School Access Barriers

Before the passage of the McKinney Act in 1987, homeless children faced many barriers to accessing education. Residency requirements were the most significant barrier, since homeless students are, by definition, without a residence. When parents attempted to enroll their child in the school district where they were temporarily staying, admission was frequently denied because they were not residents of the district. Even when children were allowed to register, many experienced substantial delays associated with a lack of records. Children who were not transferring into other schools also confronted barriers posed by residency requirements: some schools argued they were no longer eligible to attend the same school because they no longer lived in the school district. In many cases, continued attendance at their current school was made impossible because of inadequate transportation. School access barriers also confronted homeless children who were not currently staying with their family because of either discriminatory shelter policies against males (particularly those over the age of 12) or their temporary placement with relatives or friends. Some schools routinely denied or delayed the enrollment of children who did not reside with a parent or legal guardian in the school district.

In response to federal mandates, many states have undertaken legislation and regulatory reform to remove residency obstacles. The impact has been substantial. For example, residency requirements were identified as a major barrier by 64 percent (12) of the 20 states surveyed by the NLC in 1990. In a follow-up survey, conducted in 1995, residency barriers were identified as a major barrier by 30 percent of shelter providers in 20 states (NLC 1995). In addition, only 4 of the 52 state coordinators nationwide who were surveyed in 1994 reported that residency requirements continued to serve as a barrier in their state (Anderson et al. 1995).

Substantial progress has also been made with regard to guardianship and immunization requirements, although they remain persistent barriers in some states. For example, 20 percent of the shelter providers surveyed by the NLC in 1995 and 15 of the state coordinators surveyed in 1994 reported that guardianship requirements remained a hindrance to school enrollment (Anderson et al. 1995; NLC 1995). Immunization barriers were also identified by 15 state coordinators, and for elementary students by 35 percent of shelter providers. The transfer of school records was identified as a persistent barrier by 5 state coordinators and 51 percent of the shelter providers. Less progress has been made in removing the barriers to education caused by transportation. Transportation remains among the major obstacles to education, especially limiting placement options for children. Overall, 71 percent of service providers reported that transportation was the most significant barrier that prevents children from being able to continue attending their current schools (NLC 1995). Transportation was also identified as a persistent barrier by 30 state coordinators nationwide (Anderson et al. 1995).

Little progress has been made with regard to involving parents in the determination of school placement as mandated by federal law. For example, none of the 142 homeless parents in Chicago, representing 319 school-age children, had been informed of their rights with regard to the determination of school placement. Consequently, all of the children had been transferred into new schools (Dohrn 1991). In addition, 33 percent of 363 school-age children in New York City had been transferred into new schools without their parents being informed of their rights (Rafferty and Rollins 1989). More recently, 50 percent of the shelter providers surveyed by the NLC (1995) reported that parents are not being informed about the educational rights of their children and that school officials generally make the decision. Anderson and colleagues concur:

> Despite State changes in residency requirements, it is not clear how much choice homeless children and youth have in selecting a school to attend. Although the McKinney Act states that the best interest of the child must be considered in making school placement decisions, site-visit data suggest that determining what is in the best interest of the child rarely results in returning homeless children and youth to their school of origin. (1995: 15)

Sadly, an increasing number of homeless children are being required to attend a school at or near the emergency shelter where they are temporarily staying. In some cases, children with disabilities who were receiving special education services prior to becoming homeless are also placed in these separate schools, without receiving the services to which they are legally entitled. The existence of separate schools for homeless children violates not only the McKinney Act but also the practice of systematic denial of services to children with disabilities also violates the Individuals with Disabilities Education Act (IDEA) [P.L. 105–17].

Homeless students are still not receiving the same educational services that are available to their permanently housed peers. Participation in after-school programs, for example, is often not possible because the programs have been filled at the beginning of the school year. Homeless children, who frequently transfer from one school to another, often in the middle of the school year, are thus more likely to be excluded. Even when space is available, the lack of transportation back to the shelter prevents children from taking part. According to the NLC (1995) shelter providers considered it to be a problem for homeless children to be evaluated for special education services (56 percent), to participate in after-school events and extracurricular activities (58 percent), and to access before- and after-school programs (55 percent). Anderson and colleagues (1995) reported that a large proportion of homeless children still experience difficulty gaining access to needed educational services such as special education, Title 1 remedial programs, and Head Start.

Finally, some children are not afforded their legal protections under the McKinney Act because their SEA does not comply with the act's definition of "homelessness" (e.g., temporarily staying with relatives or friends, living in domestic violence shelters). Some SEAs also exclude children who are eligible for kindergarten, preschoolers, and preschoolers with disabilities (Rafferty 1995).

Shelter Policies in the United States

While affordable permanent housing is the fundamental issue of homelessness, it is not the sole need of homeless children and their families. One immediate need is for emergency transitional shelter. Sadly, there is no right to shelter in the United States. The right to shelter has been established by legislation only in West Virginia and New York City, although in both places there has been frequent noncompliance. Consequently, the emergency shelter needs of homeless families are frequently disregarded in every state of the richest nation in the world. Even when families obtain shelter, other obstacles prevent children from achieving regular school attendance and academic success. Placements in shelters and hotels are often made without regard to community ties or educational continuity. Unstable shelter placements create havoc for children's education. In many cases, each transfer to a different shelter requires children to transfer to a new school. With each transfer to a new facility, valuable school days are lost. Sometimes, shelter stays are too short to make enrollment worthwhile. Not surprising, unstable shelter placements are consistently identified as a major barrier to the education of homeless children (Rafferty 1997).

Shelter policies also affect children's ability to be educated by jeopardizing their physical and psychological well-being. Research on residential stability indicates that children who move frequently are at increased risk for physical and mental health problems, especially depression and low self-esteem. Shuffling children between short-term placements results in nutritional deprivation and exhaustion and contributes to both physical ill health and emotional instability. Every education coordinator in New York City cited fatigue and sleep deprivation resulting from unsuitable sleeping accommodations, frequent moves, and erratic schedules as a major barrier to school attendance and academic achievement (Rafferty 1991). Such social stressors as the noise level present when many individuals share the same room, as well as the constant flow of traffic, make it difficult for children to do their homework or get a sufficient amount of sleep.

High Rates of School Mobility

Multiple movements between schools are one of the major barriers to school success for homeless children (Rafferty 1997). Entry into the emergency shelter system and the subsequent bouncing from one facility to another results in numerous school transitions for homeless children. For example, 76 percent of 390 school-age children in New York City had transferred to a different school at least once since becoming homeless, 33 percent at least twice, and 11 percent three or more times (Rafferty and Rollins 1989). In addition, 75 percent of 319 homeless school-age children in Chicago had attended three or more schools during the prior year (Dohrn 1991). Finally, 40 percent of 169 school-age homeless children in California had been in two or more schools during the prior year (Zima et al. 1997).

Higher rates of school mobility are also associated with school failure and a higher rate of dropping out of school. The transition from one school to another is a stressful experience for children. When both home and school disappear simultaneously, children are especially unanchored. They lose their friends and must make new ones. At the same time, they have to get used to a new school, new teacher, and new schoolwork that is often discontinuous with the work they were previously doing. Children who enter classrooms in midsemester are also more likely to be held to lower expectations by their teachers. Besides the emotional and educational impact on children, high student mobility also makes it more difficult for schools to provide meaningful services. The way schools are organized assumes continuity. When rosters change from week to week, continuity of instruction is virtually impossible. When children remain in a school for only a short period of time, it is difficult to provide any educational services of lasting value, or to begin to repair the damage done by the combination of instability, homelessness, and poverty.

CONCLUSION

For almost 12 years now, the McKinney Act has mandated SEAs to respond to the educational needs of homeless children and to remove all barriers to their school enrollment, attendance, and success. SEAs must ensure that all homeless children between the ages of 3 and 21 receive access to the same education as their permanently housed peers. They must receive comparable educational services and the same access to other school programs including tutoring, counseling, before- and after-school programs, and state and local food programs. Finally, schools must collaborate with LEAs in designing and implementing local programs.

Despite noteworthy progress in recent years in removing some major barriers to education for homeless children and youth, obstacles continue to prevent them from achieving regular school attendance and academic success. Consequently, many homeless children do not receive the educational services that were mandated more than a decade ago. At the very least, the mandates set forth in the McKinney Act need to be enforced if continuity of educational services is to be achieved. Homeless children should not have to experience additional instability in their lives by being forced to shift from school to school during the academic year. Instead, the goal should be for them to remain in their original schools, with familiar teachers, curricula, and peers. Parents need to be informed of the educational rights of their children, and be involved in the decision of which school their children will attend. The practice of requiring homeless children to attend a school at or near their shelter with only other homeless students must cease.

LEAs must also provide outreach services to locate and identify homeless children and thus minimize the disruption to their education. For children who continue to attend their original schools, transportation problems need to be expeditiously resolved, attendance to be monitored, and follow-up services to be provided if attendance is not satisfactory. For children who transfer to new schools, placement in appropriate educational settings must be made with a minimum of delay, and every effort made to ensure that students receive services comparable to those given their permanently housed peers. There must be efficient procedures for transferring student records. Special attention must be paid to bilingual students and students who need special education services.

Schools and communities have a vital role to play in meeting the educational needs of homeless children and youth and in mitigating the potentially harmful effects of homelessness. Because the educational needs and problems of homeless children are many and the solutions are complex, no agency or school can solve these problems alone. These needs can be best met through support, coordination, cooperation, and collaboration among the various agencies that work with homeless families, as well as communication among agencies at the state and local level. A coordinated model of service delivery would enhance the provision of programs and services to homeless children and their families.

Ultimately, however, broader issues will have to be addressed. The United States must achieve a coherent and comprehensive national family policy with a strong concern for the social problems confronting children in poverty. There must be a shift of responsibility from state and local governments toward a more serious and sustained investment in children by the federal government if we are to help secure promising futures for our children. The federal government must recognize that programs for the reduction or elimination of poverty would, in the long term, cost our society less than the persistence of current levels of poverty and its consequences. Whatever vulnerabilities to homelessness may exist, an abundance of research continues to indicate that homelessness is associated with deficiencies in (a) the availability of affordable permanent housing; (b) the opportunity to earn an adequate income; (c) education to prepare people to be productive; (d) safe communities; (e) a supportive and stable childhood environment; and (f) accessible health care. Policies must be developed to meet the needs of families as a whole and, at the same time, the needs of children within them. In view of the continuing crisis in the nation's housing system, and the great suffering that vulnerable children who lack permanent housing continue to endure each night, there is an urgent need for action. The time for action is now.

REFERENCES

Anderson, L., M. Janger, and K. Panton. 1995. *An Evaluation of State and Local Efforts to Serve the Educational Needs of Homeless Children and Youth.* Washington, D.C.: U.S. Department of Education. Prepared by Policy Studies Associates, Inc.

Center for Law and Education. 1995. *Department of Education on the Verge of Releasing Schools and States from Key Legal Requirements: Comments Concerning the Department of Education's Proposed Criteria for Consolidated State Plans.* Cambridge, Mass: Author.

Dohrn, B. 1991. *A Long Way from Home: Chicago's Homeless Children and the Schools.* Chicago: Legal Assistance Foundation of Chicago.

Individuals with Disabilities Education Act (IDEA). 1990, 1995, 1997. Codified as amended at 20 U.S.C. Sections 1400–1476. Code of Federal Regulations, Title 34, C.F.R. Section 300.532(b).

National Coalition for the Homeless. 1989. *Federal Lawsuits Involving the National Coalition for the Homeless.* Washington, D.C.: Author.

National Law Center on Homelessness and Poverty (NLC). 1990. *Shut Out: Denial of Education to Homeless Children.* Washington, D.C.: Author.

———. 1995. *A Foot in the Schoolhouse Door: Progress and Barriers to the Education of Homeless Children.* Washington, D.C.: Author.

Rafferty, Y. 1991. *And Miles to Go . . . : Barriers to Academic Achievement and Innovative Strategies for the Delivery of Educational Services.* New York: Advocates for Children. (ERIC Document Reproduction Service, No. ED 343–968/UD028–585.)

———. 1995. "The Legal Rights and Educational Problems of Homeless Children and Youth." *Educational Evaluation and Policy Analysis* 17(1): 39–61.

———. 1997. "Meeting the Educational Needs of Homeless Children." *Educational Leadership* 55(4): 48–52.

Rafferty, Y., and N. Rollins. 1989. *Learning in Limbo: The Educational Deprivation of Homeless Children.* New York: Advocates for Children. (ERIC Document Reproduction No. Ed 312 363.)

Stewart B. McKinney Homeless Assistance Act. 1994. Pub. L. No 100–77, Title VII(B), 101 Stat 482, 525 (1987), amended by the Stewart B. McKinney Homeless Assistance Amendments Act of 1990, Pub. L. No. 101–645, 104 Stat. 4673, 4735, and the Improving America's Schools Act of 1994, Pub. L. No. 103–382, 108 Stat. 3519, 3957 (codified as amended at 42 U.S.C. Sections 11431–35).

U.S Department of Education (ED). 1995. *Preliminary Guidance for the Education of Homeless Children and Youth Program.* Washington, D.C.: Author, Office of Elementary and Secondary Education.

Zima, B. T., R. Bussing, S. R. Forness, and B. Benjamin. 1997. "Sheltered Homeless Children: Their Eligibility and Unmet Need for Special Education Evaluation." *American Journal Public Health* 87(2): 236–40.

8

From Discourse to Reality:
A Profile of the Lives and an Estimate of the Number of Street Children and Adolescents in Brazil

Fúlvia Rosemberg

Ever since the 1979 International Year of the Child, there has been worldwide concern about children and adolescents who use the streets of urban centers as their
principal or secondary living space. Some of the initiatives taken in recent decades on
behalf of street children include campaigns appealing for international solidarity; experiments with new educational strategies compatible with conditions on the street; establishment of special organizations to assist these youngsters; media reports lamenting
their deplorable living conditions; seminars and national and international conferences;
and research studies on their demographic profile, ways of dealing with life on the
streets, or their family history and educational background. The matter of street children
has transcended national borders and cuts across the boundaries of academic disciplines
and professional specializations.

In the course of this activity, a body of rhetoric developed about this population
group that has captured the imagination of the general public: the world is said to be
overrun by millions of street children who represent the poverty of the underdeveloped
world. During the 1980s, many disparate and inflated estimates circulated about the
number of children and adolescents surviving on the streets of Third World metropo-
lises. These estimates were usually developed using deductive reasoning that assumed a
linear relationship between poverty and whether a child does or does not live on the
street. In most instances, they were produced with the aim of denouncing the poverty
of urban underdevelopment. The basic assumptions were: poor families inevitably abandon, expel, or alienate their children; their exclusion from access to social goods and
institutions (school, especially) also inexorably leads to a search for survival on the
street; poor families do not control their children and so produce the street urchins
today who are the criminals of tomorrow—and, in the case of girls, today's prostitutes
and the mothers of tomorrow's street children.

Like other researchers and activists involved with the rights of children and adolescents, during the 1980s I analyzed and criticized this approach because I considered
it to be: (a) stigmatizing to poor families at a time when a growing number of studies,
mainly anthropological, were demonstrating the centrality of the family, real or represented, in the formation of identity among the Brazilian poor (Sarti 1994); (b) the wrong

foundation for the development of social policies that would guide "omnibus" policies in light of the specific needs of a particular population segment; (c) restrictive of knowledge, since if poverty by itself inevitably produces street children (whether or not family disintegration is involved), any psychosocial reflection on the nature of this phenomenon is futile.

It was in the context of this rhetoric and for these reasons that I coordinated a research project entitled Contagem de Crianças e Adolescentes em Situação de Rua (Census of Children and Adolescents in Street Situation), which was conducted in the city of São Paulo, Brazil, in October 1993, by the Department of Children, Families, and Social Welfare of the State of São Paulo. This project became 1 of 17 such studies that have been done in Brazil since 1986. The source of the interest in publicizing the census taken in São Paulo was twofold: (a) the extent and population density of the city (9.8 million people living on 1,493 square kilometers) offer parameters for rethinking estimates made elsewhere in the world; and (b) the complexity of the city and the support afforded by the counting experiences in other Brazilian cities. Additionally, the backing of a state government department in the field of open-environment education (the Casas Abertas, or Open Houses) made possible a refinement of the strategies used in the São Paulo research.

This chapter, therefore, is composed of three parts: an analysis of the discourse about street children disseminated by the academic press, or popularized internationally and in Brazil during the 1980s; a description and analysis of the censuses made of street children in Brazilian cities; and a report on the census of street children and adolescents in the city of São Paulo.

THE ACCUSATORY DISCOURSE

This analysis of the discourse on the subject of street children will center primarily on the "estimates" that constitute the touchstone of a rhetoric of denunciation stigmatizing poor families in the Third World.[1] The dissemination of a discourse on street children found one of its principal emissaries in the United Nations Children's Fund (UNICEF) during the 1980s. In 1981, Peter Taçon, then the UNICEF advisor on issues related to abandoned and orphaned children, announced what was perhaps the first estimate of the world's population of street children.

> Perhaps no children have been more intensely exploited and abused in today's world than those who are forced to survive on city streets—the descendants of economic miracles and human tragedies. Any reasonable estimate would put their numbers at about 100 million—and it's possible that half of these live in Latin America. (Taçon 1981a: 13)

Two components of that statement deserve emphasis: the exorbitance of the figure; and the identification of the role of economic and familial factors.

Taçon's estimate of 100 million falls to 70 million in the "underdeveloped world" in Maggie Black's study (1986) on the history of UNICEF. Black made the category of "street children" more complex when the condition of "irregular family situation" was defined. She argued that 40 million of the world's 70 million street children live in Latin America.

Two years later, Cassie Landers, in her 1988 article "A Cry for Help: UNICEF's Response to Street Children in the Third World," after discussing the inconsistency among definitions of street children and the difficulties of keeping track of them statistically, cites an estimate made by the Anti-Slavery Society in 1985, in which the figure drops to 30 million. She maintains the claim that half the street children live in Latin

America. The countries most affected are societies with moderate incomes, such as Brazil, Colombia, and Mexico (1988: 37).

Some years later, in the widely circulated publication *As crianças das Américas* (*The Children of the Americas*) the estimates remained at 15 million for Latin America on page 7 (UNICEF 1992), but dropped to 8 million several pages later (UNICEF 1992: 18, Chart 6). The strange thing about these figures in publications edited and published by professionals who have ties with UNICEF is that none of them discuss or analyze the earlier ones. Very often, they do not even mention sources, data collection procedures, or justifications for the calculations made.

The legitimacy that UNICEF enjoys in the eyes of the public, its access to the international media, and Taçon's charismatic personality (according to people who knew him) were sufficient to guarantee unquestioned faith in his figures, which soon made headlines in major newspapers: "UNICEF is doing what it can to help the 40 million abandoned Latin American children," wrote the *New York Times* on September 7, 1983 (quoted in Lusk 1989: 75); citations in academic theses in the United States (Apteker 1988: xiv), or in books circulated in Europe (Engelmann 1986: 42). Academic journals, such as the U.S. publication *Anthropology & Education Quarterly,* did not hesitate to publish articles citing estimates that do not withstand close inspection, or even the application of common sense. After mentioning the 40 million figure released by Taçon in 1981 and 1983, Lewis Apteker commented: "Although Latin America has only 10 percent of the world's population of children, it accounts for approximately 50 percent of the street children. The number of street children in Latin America is equal to the total population of Colombia, plus all of Central America" (Apteker 1988: 326).

Simultaneously with the estimates of figures for the world and for Latin America, Brazilian and foreign individuals and institutions hazarded estimates on the number of abandoned children in Brazil. Very often, these were also identified as "needy" children and "street" children and, more recently "child laborers," terms that many used indiscriminately during the 1980s, thereby consolidating under the same simplistic label the diversity of situations in which impoverished children and adolescents find themselves, whether or not they are actually on the street. In this context of conceptual imprecision, the estimates (always indirect) of street children in Brazil ranged from 49.6 million to 1 million during the period between 1982 and 1993.

UNICEF also became the international institution most frequently mentioned as the original source of the figures on street children in Brazil, either in reports that UNICEF itself (or professionals working for it) published or that were disseminated by popular media; "according to [Peter Taçon], there are about 40 million abandoned minors in all of Latin America, some 20 million of whom are in Brazil" (*O Globo* 1982: 9). Four months later—still in 1982—the newspaper *O Estado de São Paulo* published, on what it said was an exclusive basis, a summary of the report of research done by UNICEF in which it was stated: "More than one-fifth of Brazilian youngsters age 7 to 17 are 'street children': they are neither working nor attending school."

This article deserves extra attention. The report attributed to UNICEF specifically mentioned one of the methodologies used for calculation: "street children" are considered to be children and adolescents in the 7-to-17-year age bracket who are declared to be neither working nor attending school. Anyone who has even a casual knowledge of Brazil would immediately raise an objection that would cut the figure approximately in half at the outset: for female Brazilian children and adolescents, at least, being occupied with "household tasks," i.e., staying at home (and not in the street) constitutes a fairly widespread cultural practice.

Despite numerous methodological flaws in the UNICEF report, Brazilian officials extrapolated it and arrived at 1.9 million *abandoned* and 13.5 million *needy*—in other words, 15.4 million "children severely at risk" (UNICEF/Brasília 1984: Appendix A, 1). According to the report, the Brazilian Ministry of Justice estimated that an increase of 3 million had occurred between 1975 and 1980. The UNICEF report (1984: 2) added another 5 million between 1980 and 1984 "as a result of both demographic and economic factors." Thus did UNICEF arrive at the figure of 24 million "desperately poor children, who by definition do not have their basic needs met at home" (1984: 21). And the report ends by stating that inasmuch as "many have observed that, because primarily the smaller municipalities reported, the congressional investigating committee seriously undercounted the actual number of abandoned and needy children. In this view, the estimate of 10 million children out looking for income seems quite prudent indeed" (1984: Appendix A, 2). Thus were conjectures, hypotheses, and guesstimates transformed into "hard data."

Other highly regarded international institutions, such as Amnesty International, reported the same astronomical figures without the kind of concern for citing sources that it typically displays in its reports on other fields to ensure its prestige and credibility: "It is estimated that seven million children are living and working on the streets of Brazil. Some of them are dragged into a life of crime and are thieves or drug dealers (the Spanish word *correo* was used) in gangs of delinquents; others scratch out a living by begging, selling things on the streets, or scavenging through the trash dumps" (*Enfoque* 1990: 3–6).

Besides its conceptual imprecision and overestimates (characteristics that are interrelated), the rhetoric of the 1980s stigmatized poor families and poor children and adolescents. To the epidemic dimensions of the situation (as we have seen, they were talking in terms of millions) was added an anecdotal description of what was assumed to be the typical behavior of these children and their families. It comes from a report by a delegation sent to Brazil by the International Federation of Human Rights and the International Association of Democratic Lawyers, with backing from the International Movement of Catholic Jurists, sponsorship by the Swedish agency Redda Barna, and official support from the Norwegian Ministry of Justice.

> Many personalities have already described what happens to abandoned children in Brazil. Some say there are 30 million, others 32 to 36 million. The boys *naturally* become delinquents (they steal and mug, attack the elderly, etc.) and the girls become prostitutes at an early age. (FIDH 1986: 106 [emphasis mine])

It is not surprising, then, that estimates on child prostitution in Brazil began to appear in the late 1980s: 5 million, according to the report by the delegation from the International Association of Democratic Lawyers and the International Federation of Human Rights (AIJD 1986: 29);[2] 2 million, announced by the periodical *Mulherio* in 1987, citing UNICEF as its source (Castilho 1987). The figure of 500,000 child prostitutes, the most widely published in recent years, is attributed to various sources: sometimes the Brazilian Center for Childhood and Adolescence (CBIA), sometimes UNICEF, and in most cases with no precise bibliographic reference. As far as I have been able to determine, there is no trace of that particular survey or any other research project that has arrived at this or any other figure for child and adolescent prostitution in Brazil, except for the survey done by the Casa de Passagem in Recife about girls and young women (up to age 20) living in the streets, which arrived at significantly lower figures.

The estimates of child prostitution, which I mention merely in passing in this chapter, exhibit similar vagueness in their base of calculation.

According to an estimate by the National Conference of Brazilian Bishops (CNBB), there are about ten million working prostitutes in this country. UNICEF estimates at two million the number of girls between the ages of 10 and 15 that have gone into prostitution. . . . If the UNICEF estimate is close to the truth, then approximately 20 percent of Brazilian girls age 10 to 15 are engaged in prostitution. (Castilho 1987:9)

These estimates were published late in the 1980s, at the same time that censuses were being taken of children and adolescents living on the street in certain Latin American capitals and Brazilian cities. These surveys arrived at rather low estimates, but they were not given the same publicity as were the astronomical figures. The following sections discuss one of these studies.

RESEARCHING THE REALITY OF STREET CHILDREN

Since the second half of the 1980s, certain researchers have timidly begun to question the social construction of the rhetoric about street children. Those of us who work frequently with population data on childhood and adolescence in Brazil on subjects such as education and labor have perhaps gained a different perception of the significance of these estimates. Furthermore, while analyzing and collecting data, we encountered a plurality of ways in which poor families organized themselves and a variety of relationships between parents and children in impoverished families (Gomes 1988; Sarti 1994). These showed the irrationality of the dominant model that identified street children and adolescents with abandonment by a poor family or sexual promiscuity. We were bothered by the absurdity of the syllogism: all street children are poor, therefore all poor children are (or will be) on the street.

The first research study known in Brazil to have attempted, inter alia, to assess the extent of the phenomenon was done by Zalua Gonçalves and published in 1979. This study, based on the theory of marginality and conducted to establish a profile of poor children and adolescents, registered the children and adolescents who lived or worked on the streets of the city of Belém do Pará (north region). Although few details were given about the methodology employed to identify and register these children and adolescents, the project registered about 3,000 people identifiable as " street children." Although this research was quoted in various papers in the very early 1980s (even by Peter Taçon), no attention was paid to the fact that it contained the first direct estimate of the extent of the street children phenomenon.

When the topic of street children had already won publicity, IBGE, the agency responsible for conducting the national census every 10 years as well as the annual National Surveys of Sample Households (PNAD), included in its basic questionnaire for the 1985 PNAD a supplement to investigate the living conditions of children and adolescents up to the age of 17 who lived in metropolitan areas.

Since this was a survey based on a sample of households, the information gathered by PNAD 85 supplied only indirect indicators of the extent of the condition known as "abandonment of children and adolescents" and, obviously, no direct data on street children. But 1985 was an era when both foreign and Brazilian writers still considered street children to be abandoned children. No distinction would be drawn until later in the decade, when differences of meaning were introduced into the terms *children on the street* (those who are temporarily on the street and retain some family ties) and *street children* (those who remain on the street and who have partly or completely lost their family ties).

The Children's Supplement to PNAD 85, which was not published until many years later, revealed—to the astonishment of some—that few children and adolescents in metropolitan areas lacked any family tie: 4.2 percent of children and adolescents were living far from their mothers, but an impressive number of them (85.5 percent of the 4.2 percent) were living with their fathers or other relatives (Ribeiro 1988: 18).

Other research studies were produced at the end of the 1980s, and now they counted children and adolescents "in a street status/situation" in various Brazilian and Latin American cities. These revealed fairly low numbers, usually not higher than the tens of thousands. These counts, sometimes called "censuses," were begun in 1986 in Rio de Janeiro by the Brazilian Institute of Social and Economic Analysis (IBASE). Since then, we have been able to identify 17 research studies that conducted counts of children and adolescents found living on the streets during the day or nighttime hours.

Two very similar procedures were adopted in these research studies. The first performs the count by simultaneous observation, a sort of "blitz" in a very short space of time. The second identifies street children and adolescents via interviews conducted by researchers who remained on-site for longer periods of time. These procedures, which literature in the field has called *direct estimates* (Breakey and Fisher 1990: 32), have also been used in the United States to estimate the number of homeless (Rossi et al. 1987) and were the basis of Operation S-Night ("S" for street and for shelter) conducted 10 days prior to the date of the 1990 census (Martin 1991).

The procedure most frequently used in Brazilian surveys has been identification by observation, without contact. Essentially, this involves dividing the surveyed urban space into zones and assigning teams of enumerators to traverse them, at the same time of day or night, following predetermined routes. The surveyors count the street children and adolescents whom they identify during their circuit. The effect is a simultaneous snapshot of children and adolescents who were using the streets (and other public places) as a place to generate income and socialize on a specific day of the year, at a specific time (Pereira Júnior and Drska 1992: 88). The basic theory behind this procedure is that space on the streets is not occupied in a random fashion and that street children and adolescents tend to gather or circulate in areas that afford opportunities for income, shelter, and amusement.

This method makes it possible to estimate the number of street children and adolescents on a given day, at a certain time, for purposes of public policy planning. It is an estimate since, in addition to the limitations inherent in any survey, "being in street status" is for many children and adolescents a temporary condition, not a permanent one. It results from an interaction between their needs and what the public spaces offer to satisfy them. Latin American and Brazilian literature reports another counting procedure in which researchers, after identifying the points where street children and adolescents gather, remain there for a relatively long period until they are able to identify who these young people are and, therefore, how many of them there are.

These procedures chiefly differ, not on the basis of whether or not people are contacted and identified during the count, but mainly in the time slice they focus on. Although all of them are cross-section surveys—i.e., they do not monitor the use of the street in the life histories of the individuals in order to understand its dynamics—the procedures differ in the length of time during which use of the street is observed. However, the length of time spent in the streets to observe their use determines, in part, the figure one arrives at because, as we have said, the use of the street for survival is not an attribute of the person, but a condition in which some people find themselves at some points in their lives (Blasi 1990). Not all children and adolescents use the space on the streets for survival every day of the year or every hour of the day, and the term "being in street status" hides a wide variety of situations.

When the 1992 nighttime count in Rio de Janeiro was announced, the press published a series of articles and statements challenging the estimated figures. Their authors claimed to know that more children and adolescents than cited by the researcher were in fact spending the night at certain sites. Well, the Rio survey did not plan to estimate the number of children/adolescents who spend every night, or who have ever spent a night, on the streets of Rio de Janeiro. It simply tried to estimate how many were there on a typical night. The purpose was to determine how many beds would be necessary to shelter them.

DISTINGUISHING AMONG STREET CHILDREN

Direct observation of children's lifestyles and surveys of social programs carried out in the first half of the 1980s fractured the concept of street children as abandoned. Very early on, researchers observed that a significant number of the children/adolescents seen on the streets maintained ties with their parents and returned periodically (many of them, daily) to their family homes (Rizzini 1986). So two concepts resulted from this fracture: children/adolescents *of* the street, for whom the street is their home and fundamental site of socialization; and children/adolescents *on* the street, for whom the street was merely a place to generate income, while maintaining family ties and returning routinely to their homes.

The empirical knowledge that has developed during the 1980s about this population has shown its temporal dimension and highlighted the diversity of family and residential conditions that apply to children and adolescents who use the street space for purposes beyond just getting around (Lucchini 1996). So it has been possible to identify a variety of combinations of family ties, residence, and work. There are children/adolescents who live with their families on the streets (residents of the street). There are some who accompany their parents who earn income on the street and who may or may not assist in earning that income; they live in houses. There are some who maintain family ties and, from time to time, earn income on a street near their homes (occasionally working at the open-air market, for example). There are children/adolescents who maintain family ties and regularly and continuously work on the street. Then there are those who live with their families in a home, attend school, and work on the street sporadically (for example, distributing leaflets at traffic lights on the weekends). There are some who maintain family ties, work on the street, and occasionally sleep there. There are those who live on the street during a short period of their childhood and/or adolescence. Others spend most of their childhood and adolescent life on the street.

Given this diversity of conditions, the Children's Affairs Office of the State of São Paulo has been using the term "children and adolescents in street situation [*em situação de rua*]" to refer to individuals up to age 17 for whom the street constitutes the "primary or secondary everyday space in guaranteeing survival and leisure, or both simultaneously" (State of São Paulo 1992: 19). This terminology/concept, used in the São Paulo survey, needs a fourfold explanation:

- it makes it clear that adolescents are also present, an important fact in Brazil where young people may legally work at age 14, which is also the age when they may legally stop attending school;
- it is a descriptive term that does not presuppose causes or make determinations about "being in street status" beyond the one that situates the social origin of this population in the poorer strata of the population;

- it considers, as other surveys demonstrated, that being on the street is not an attribute of the individual, but a contingent response by certain poor children, adolescents, and families to the pressures of family life (human relations, economic status), conditions at home, the dynamics of the schools, the job market, and the street itself; and
- it assumes that this population uses the street for more than just getting around, it uses it for activities that one would prefer not to see pursued there.

THE SÃO PAULO STUDY

The survey that attempted to estimate the number of street children/adolescents in the city of São Paulo was conducted by the Office of Children, Families, and Social Welfare, which was established in 1987 (then called the Office of Minors' Affairs). Since its founding, the office has been carrying out a specific program of "open education" for this population. This program, which obtained logistical support from the so-called Open Houses, was the first Brazilian government initiative to serve street children in an open environment.

The Open Houses were set up at strategic locations that seemed most likely to interrupt the flow of children/adolescents toward the center of the city. They were single-story buildings containing at least one big room and two smaller ones, used for group recreational and educational activities or for individualized attention. There was also a small yard with an outdoor sink, bathrooms with showers, and a kitchen. The facilities were open only during the day (at first they were open at night, but the conflicts were more than the available human and physical resources could handle) and they occasionally served snacks. An agreement between the Office of Children and the Secretariat of Public Safety (police) provided that the Open Houses were to be neutral territory that the police were forbidden to enter.

The primary objective of the program was to make it possible for children and adolescents to access the available community resources, especially education, health care, basic documentation, safety, and emotional and psychological support. The program called for providing occupational guidance to young people older than 14. Another goal of the Open Houses was to try to reestablish the link between the child and his or her family when it had been broken. It is not always possible to accomplish this, given the desires/needs on both sides.

The work at the Open Houses was carried out mainly by "street instructors," young college-educated adults (not necessarily educated in the specific field) trained and supervised by the Office of Children. The instructors worked primarily in the street, and the philosophy behind the "school without walls" envisioned that children and adolescents would commit themselves to their own development.

The activities of the Open Houses and the availability of a large staff of instructors who were used to working in an open environment made it possible to undertake the survey that counted street children/adolescents in the city of São Paulo. The field work was done in October 1993, after a long period of planning. The defined objectives of the survey were: (a) to estimate the number of children/adolescents found in street situation in the city of São Paulo during the daytime and nighttime hours, with a view to redirecting the planning of actions by the office with respect to this population; (b) to assess the capabilities and actual occupancy rate of institutions that accept street children/adolescents for shelter at night.

Procedures

The procedures used in this survey were inspired by the "blitz" methodology used by IBASE. This apparently simple counting strategy conceals a multiplicity of details, as well as precautions to be taken so as not to either overestimate or underestimate the number of children and adolescents who use the streets of the city as their primary space for socialization. In general, the procedure involves five steps: (a) compiling a list of the points where street children and adolescents gather and circulate; (b) dividing the city into sectors within which these points are found; (c) marking routes through those sectors so they can be traversed quickly so as to control the effect of spatial mobility and thus avoid double counting; (d) sending trained teams into the field who simultaneously travel the stipulated route by car and on foot and to start to identify and count the children and adolescents— again, attempting to avoid double-counting; (e) recording observed data on a worksheet with only a few variables: usually gender and activity, sometimes age and race as well.

The field work (usually brief, lasting not more than 3 hours per shift) is preceded by a period of intense planning that involves decisions about the time and space where the count is to be done, and the training of the survey workers (and the drivers and security personnel who will accompany them) in research procedures. Particularly, they must assimilate the operational definition of "child/adolescent in street situation" and learn how to use the instruments provided for recording their observations.

- The *time* dimension involved decisions about the hour, day of the week, and duration of the census. The use of streets by children/adolescents is not anarchic; one can see that there is a time flow. In the São Paulo survey, the choice of the day of the week and the hour was designed to take a snapshot of the street during a peak period of its use by children and adolescents. It was decided to send the teams out for the daytime census from 4:00 P.M. to 7:00 P.M. on a Thursday, and then send them back out from 2:00 A.M. to 5:00 A.M. on a Friday for the nighttime count. The experience of the Office of Children's street instructors influenced this decision.

- The *space* dimension involved listing the points where street children and adolescents gather and circulate, dividing the city into sectors that encompass those points, outlining the routes to be traveled by the survey teams, and projecting those routes onto maps. To start with, "well-informed sources" reported on the sites of which they were aware. In the São Paulo survey, instructors from the Office of Children's "schools without walls" (located in nine different parts of the city) were consulted, as were the civilian and military police. Informants described 1,386 points of circulation, wandering, or concentration of children/ adolescents "in street situation" in the city of São Paulo. After an intense period of presectorization, the city was divided into 39 zones for the daytime census (including three routes covering subway lines) and 19 for the nighttime count. The route for each sector was laid out in great detail. In all, the routes through the daytime sectors passed through 1,783 public places (streets, parks, subway stations, trains, buses, gardens, and so on), covering a total of 1,530 kilometers; the nighttime sectors included 775 public places, covering a total of 788 kilometers. The itineraries were studied by the drivers and instructors, and they made a dry run through the established areas prior to the count.

- The identification of street children/adolescents during this survey was made by observation. None of the young people were contacted or interviewed; the survey teams traveled the sectors using an operational definition that covered three aspects: the appearance of the child/adolescent; the space where he/she was seen; the activity in which he/she was engaged. In most cases, the *appearance* in terms of apparel and hygiene was that of a poor person. This was especially true of the younger children. Children and adolescents may depart from this pattern, for example, when distributing advertising leaflets at traffic lights. Such children/adolescents were also counted as being in street situation.

- For purposes of the operational definition, the "street" was considered to be any *outdoor* public way or area: plazas, bridges, parking lots, landfills, entrances to various kinds of buildings (churches, universities, restaurants, and so forth). Surveyors did not enter any indoor spaces (except subway trains and stations). This decision, adopted in several Brazilian surveys (in Aracajú or Salvador, for example), was made to ensure the safety of both the children/adolescents and the researchers. Children/adolescents were identified as being in "street situation" when they used those spaces as their primary or secondary space for working, begging, sleeping, wandering, and playing—in other words, activities other than just "getting around." Therefore, children/adolescents walking or playing near their houses (which is normal in Brazil and other warm-weather countries) were not classified as being in street situation unless they were working or begging. However, children/adolescents found in outdoor spaces near "street dwellings" (shacks, tents) were classified as being in street situation.

- In addition to appearance and location, the *activity* engaged in is of fundamental importance in identifying children/adolescents in street situation. Activities included in the operational definition were: working, begging, wandering, sleeping, and playing. Many adolescents of different social classes circulate through the city, yet they would not be identified as being in street situation, for example delivery boys, messengers, students getting out of school, or people going shopping or engaged in recreation. These activities would not put them "in street situation" because they do not fit the definition that prescribes that the street be their principal or secondary space for socialization.

The categories pertaining to the selected variables (activity and gender), as well as general information about the itinerary followed by the field workers in their tour, were diagrammed on a survey worksheet (a tool for recording the observed data).

Each survey team consisted of two instructors and/or technical staffers and one driver, all of whom were working for the Office of Children. Some of the teams also included observers from invited institutions and the media. At night, each team was accompanied by two detectives from the civil police. The survey teams, who already had experience working in open environments, received special training, both in identifying children/adolescents in street situation (through written materials and videotape) and in the procedure for traveling the preestablished route.

We would not have enough human and physical resources to verify the consistency of the work of the observers as thoroughly as the researchers of American Operations Night were able to do. However, we employed four techniques to help control for possible distortions: one week prior to the census we did a pretest in five sectors that are densely occupied by children/adolescents in street situation; we tested the survey workers and drivers on their ability to gauge the age of adolescents and young adults; we had one of the sectors recounted by another team, unbeknownst to the main team, 15 minutes after the start of the official count; we invited several well-known Brazilian and international institutions, mainly those who had prepared deductive estimates, to be present during the entire survey process (discussion of the project, the field work itself, data processing, and the announcement of results at a press conference). An analysis of the results obtained from these strategies demonstrated that the procedures were satisfactorily consistent (State of São Paulo 1993).

The technical team responsible for the survey was always mindful of the complexity of taking a daytime census in São Paulo because of its vast area, high population density, and very heavy traffic of persons and vehicles. In this ecological context, we sought to channel our efforts toward the primary purpose of this project, which was to estimate as carefully as possible the number of children/adolescents in street situation found during the late afternoon and nighttime hours in the city of São Paulo. We felt that introducing additional variables into the survey worksheet would greatly increase the complexity of the task of the survey workers and impair the quality of the observation function.

Furthermore, we questioned the validity of having the survey workers assess the age or racial origin of the child or adolescent on the basis of their personal impressions. Certainly if we could have this data on age, and if it were minimally reliable as regards uniformity in the manner it was gathered, it would be extremely valuable. But the indicators available to us suggested that individuals vary greatly in their ability to assess age. Such data also reflect the subjective impressions of the observer that could be interpreted as attributes of the subject being observed, which, of course, would be inappropriate.

Moreover, as regards racial origin, we would be violating an ethical principle by imposing a racial classification on another party without considering his/her own sense of racial identity. In this regard, we opted to prepare a questionnaire to be completed by the instructors after they returned from the field, concerning their impressions with respect to characteristics of the population and the conditions under which the survey was taken. In other words, we preferred to treat impressions as just that—impressions.

RESULTS OF THE SÃO PAULO COUNT

The data gathered and recorded by the instructors went far beyond a mere enumeration of how many children/adolescents were encountered in street situation during 3-hour periods in late afternoon or nighttime. They enabled us to sketch a profile of the population of poor children and youth who survive on the streets of the city.

How many are there, and where are they?

We counted 4,520 children/adolescents in street situation during the day and 895 at night, in addition to 468 who were spending the night in some sort of shelter.

Two initial findings based on these first figures: the number of children/adolescents in street situation in the city of São Paulo is significantly lower than the estimates that were making the rounds during the 1980s; the number of children/adolescents being assisted by special programs, particularly those offering overnight shelter, is very small. One important observation: although the capacity of overnight shelters for children/adolescents and families in the city of São Paulo is very limited, since the number of beds is less than the number of children/adolescents who spend the night on the streets, the shelters were underutilized (55.9 percent of the beds were occupied).

An interpretation of this figure on unused shelter capacity must take into account various aspects: shelter locations are not always near the places where street children/adolescents spend the night; their objectives and regulations are often incompatible with the usage and customs of their intended clientele; features of the shelter itself (cleanliness, availability of bathrooms) can discourage its use; and, finally, specific decisions by the children/adolescents themselves come into play (hostilities and dislikes between subgroups, for example).

An analysis of the geographical distribution of the city's shelters shows that the sectors where the largest number of children/adolescents in street situation can be found are not the downtown areas—the ones most frequently portrayed in the media—but two regions in neighborhoods that could almost be called peripheral. These are zones where income can be earned closer to where the young people live: the large wholesale market in São Paulo (where 9.6 percent of the children/adolescents were found in the daytime census) and a large city bus terminal from which buses depart for the eastern suburbs of the city (8.3 percent of the children in the daytime census).

Who are they?

As is true in all the other Brazilian state capital cities, so in São Paulo, the children/adolescents observed in both the daytime and nighttime surveys were overwhelmingly male. The distribution of genders by geographical sector was not homogeneous, making it difficult to find a single valid explanation for all the situations. In some sectors that include red-light districts, a larger contingent of female children/adolescents were observed. However, other neighborhoods that also evidenced a high percentage of females do not fit into that category. Some tendency was noted, however, for the more central regions and entertainment districts to receive more girls and young women than the more peripheral ones. Each zone afforded different specific opportunities for earning income (flower sales and prostitution in the entertainment districts, parcel carrying and the sale of merchandise in the outlying areas).

The responses by the survey workers to the questionnaire on their *impressions* furnished supplementary data on the age bracket and racial origin profile of children and adolescents found in street situation in the city of São Paulo. Despite the variation in the impressions expressed by the survey workers as to the frequency of occurrence of the different age brackets (which may reflect an actual diversity among the sectors), the two categories at either end of the scales (first and last positions) suggest that in most sectors, young people between the ages of 10 and 15 predominate, and that infants are rarely seen on the streets.

The predominance of preteens and younger teens on the streets has often been mentioned in literature on the subject (Rizzini and Rizzini 1991), which suggests that we need to find less simplistic interpretations of the use of the street by adolescents than those based solely on determinative economic factors. It is possible that the street affords better opportunities for earning income and more recreational alternatives for this age group; it is possible that adolescents and young adults have more confrontations with the police (and vice versa). We must remember that young people in Brazil may legally work when they reach the age of 14, and that mandatory school attendance ends at that age. However, we should also consider whether some of these preteens and younger teens may be working out "more elaborate" responses, that they are using the street to challenge adult authority (both male and female) at home and in school in a dynamic of accommodation and resistance to the intergenerational conflicts they face.

The position of prominence assumed by the 10–15 age group also held true in the survey of the nighttime hours, but older adolescents ranked a close second. The "aging" of adolescents who spend the night on the street when compared with those found there during the day, and the presence of fewer small children on the streets, suggest two interconnected orders of interpretation that need further consideration: the dynamic of the street discriminates by age just as it does by gender. One might assume that families and children/adolescents in street situation appear to consider this space inappropriate for women and younger children. In other words, one may presume that a code of values and hierarchy of choices appear to orient the lives of these families and their children, situating them above and beyond the stigma of anarchic promiscuity that surrounded them during the 1980s.

The survey workers also recorded their impressions of the racial origin of the children/adolescents in street situation; they more often identified the street children/ adolescents as blacks than as whites. The impression that black children/adolescents predominated among those found in street situation is associated with the economic and educational status of this racial group in Brazil. In fact, recent Brazilian literature on race relations has demonstrated that the poor population group is predominantly black (Silva 1992), and that they have more trouble gaining access to and staying in school (Rosemberg et al. 1987; Barcelos 1993). Inasmuch as every care was taken not to reinforce the stigma, the interpretation of this predominance of black male preteens and younger teens must admit not only explanations related to opportunities for earning income on the streets and elsewhere but also symbolic, cultural, and historical dimensions.

What are they doing?

Considered as a whole, a significant number of children/adolescents found during the daytime count were working; at night they were wandering (42.9 percent) or sleeping (35.1 percent). Even during the wee hours of the morning, a sizable proportion (15.4 percent) of children/adolescents were working. The high frequency with which the young people were reported as "wandering" can be ascribed partly to the dynamics of the use of the street and partly to the instructions given the field workers, which favored the observation of the moment and discouraged them from making inferences during the actual data collection. If the youngsters were workers who weren't carrying merchandise, or were walking around waiting for a potential customer or an opportunity to beg, they were classified as "wandering." However, children and adolescents who use the streets to survive do indeed simply "move around," traveling on foot from one place to the next. In other words, "wandering" can mean circulating through the streets just like any other transient does, or an activity pursued in intervals between a succession of activities. "Wandering" can also mean exploiting the street or working as a prostitute. Given this multiplicity of meanings, the night offers a greater opportunity to observe children/adolescents wandering, especially in the evening entertainment districts.

Men and women do not engage in the same activities with the same frequency: boys and young men tend to work and play more than do girls and young women, who, in turn, spend more time begging and, at night, wandering. This sexual division of activities pursued in the street can just as well be interpreted as an adaptation by children/adolescents to the possibilities for earning money—a girl is more likely to be successful in begging than is a boy (the street, as a closed space, is also governed by the laws of marketing)—as an expression of the defense of the work space by stronger individuals/groups (young men), or of physical protection (certain income-generating spaces are more dangerous for women).

The frequency with which, in some parts of the city, street children/adolescents were observed working in the predawn hours is remarkable. The kind of work most frequently noted by the instructors was selling, followed by scavenging for recyclable material and "guarding" cars. In contrast with the images popularized by the media, the survey workers who traveled the streets of the city seldom observed children and adolescents using drugs, working as prostitutes, or committing crimes. We must emphasize the significance of these data: they merely report that during their tour of the sector, the instructors observed few situations where children/adolescents were so occupied (using drugs, engaged in prostitution, or committing a crime). The survey workers/instructors also noted that not only was the incidence of such situations low, only a few children and adolescents were involved in each.

Street children/adolescents tend to live out their experiences in groups. Sleeping, begging, wandering, or working are activities that are carried out mainly in groups of peers, the survey workers found. During the nighttime hours, the data recorded on the survey worksheets showed children/adolescents in street situation seeking protection in the group; they avoided having to sleep by themselves. With a certain frequency, children and adolescents were also seen to be accompanied by adults.

To sum up, the snapshot of the children and adolescents observed on the streets of the city of São Paulo during the 3-hour survey period appeared to diverge markedly from the stereotype that has captured the imagination of the public in recent decades. During the day, it is work that characterizes their daily life: they work more than they beg. They look for ways to survive on the streets, and they engage in a variety of activities. For example, they stand in line for food distributed by the Anti-Hunger Campaign; they help unload trucks, they help sell things, they guard cars, they carry packages, beg, collect food.

At the traffic lights and on trains they sell hard candies, chocolates, and dust cloths. On street corners they wash windshields, guard cars, and beg. As they travel the streets, they look for recyclable materials, thus preserving the environment out of a practical need to survive, rather than in response to an abstract guiding principle. At bus and train stations, they sell things and commit petty crimes. Some work as prostitutes. Families of street vendors bring their children to work with them on the street: small children play near their parents, sell a few things, earn a little money, are close by. They are cared for in the street, not abandoned there. Other children are used by adult beggars as decoys for begging, to boost the sale of products, or to commit crimes. Children and adolescents play. At night and in the predawn hours, some of them are working: the São Paulo wholesale market is the principal source of night work. At night, the rhythm of the city varies from neighborhood to neighborhood, and each hosts different groups. While the downtown area is one big bedroom, in the entertainment and wholesale market districts children and adolescents are at work in the wee hours.

CONCLUSION

In this world where there are no more lands to be conquered, the poor child from the poor world represents the exotic, the other, the far-off. The street child, a unique and circumscribed experience of underdevelopment, is made "larger than life" in order to serve not as a symbol or metaphor of underdevelopment, but as its identity.

What kind of impact does this rhetoric have on street children and adolescents? I can only begin to suggest some repercussions: (a) the waste of domestic and foreign appropriated funds that are allocated to programs for street children, and the misrepresentation of the extent of the problem to the detriment of more comprehensive projects for poor children and adolescents (there are innumerable examples of this); and (b) national mistakes in developing public policy that, by identifying any and all poor children and adolescents as being street children, either proposes programs for all in light of a specific population group and/or fails to propose and adopt specific measures that would truly assist this contingent of children and adolescents.

One might also point out the constraints that this rhetoric may impose on the search for concrete and immediate solutions for children and adolescents who remain in the street. The rhetoric maintains that the problem is so huge that it has no solution and so widespread that it can be solved only by general structural transformations of Brazilian society, something like a revolution to end misery. The identification of poverty with street children ignores the fact that children and adolescents in street situation constitute only one of the forms of expression of urban poverty, an expression that in many cases is temporary, and about which little is known.

Asking herself whether it was legitimate to exaggerate the extent of hunger in the world, Brunel (1991: 50) concluded: "Exaggeration produces an opposite effect, by discouraging those who, sincerely, would do anything to combat hunger. Many are ready to help on an *ad hoc* basis, when they think their actions would be useful. On the contrary, few are willing to dedicate their lives, their energies, or even just their leisure time to a cause—like hunger—that after having been battled, seems to resurge time and time again, like the heads of the hydra serpent" (50).

The pictures of poor adolescents that have fed our imaginations have the dangerous tendency to associate men with violence, crime, drug addiction, and sexual abuse and women with sexual promiscuity, prostitution, and child abandonment.[3] However, perhaps the most insidious effect is that this rhetoric trivializes violence, stigmatizes poor families, children, and adolescents, and may interfere with the very living conditions of street children/adolescents.

Setting the rhetoric of the 1980s against the data accumulated in the census research, I would like to emphasize four points:

1. the relatively small number of street children/adolescents when compared with the extent of poverty in the city of São Paulo and the surrounding metropolitan areas, and the absence of programs and proposals that would, nevertheless, meet the needs of this population;

2. the configuration of a pattern of use of the street by children and adolescents, evidenced both by the demographic composition of the group (predominantly black male preteens and younger teens) and the gender-based division of activities pursued there;

3. the diversity of situations (and, possibly, determinations) in which street children/adolescents find themselves, with work predominating and only residual unlawful activity, which takes them out of the stereotyped portrait that has captured the imagination of society; and

4. the presence on the street of a small contingent of sons and daughters of poor families, which suggests that we should be very careful in making exaggerated generalizations about the neglect, abandonment, or *anomie* of such families.

On the basis of the foregoing, I would like to outline some suggestions for action. First, we must invest in the production of knowledge that explains not only the structural but also the cultural and psychosocial determinations that foster the permanence of children/adolescents in the streets of the city where they earn income and socialize. Next, we must avoid being trapped by the search for a single understanding of the phenomenon and, instead, attempt to identify the multiplicity of determinations that cause different children and adolescents to use the streets as their primary space for survival and leisure. We need initiatives that will destroy the stereotypes that make the living conditions on the street even tougher.[4] Finally, we need programs that will respond now to the needs of these children and adolescents who are working, eating, playing, and begging on the streets. It is unacceptable that a city like São Paulo does not have enough beds in suitable shelters to house the children and adolescents who spend their nights on the streets.

NOTES

1. I gathered the documents analyzed here during the 1980s. They include reports and documents prepared by intergovernmental and Brazilian government agencies, and by Brazilian and foreign NGOs; master's theses and doctoral dissertations defended in Brazil and elsewhere; books published in Brazil and abroad; and newspaper clippings (especially from two major São Paulo newspapers, *O Estado de São Paulo* and *Folha de São Paulo*). These documents were found at various documentation centers and offices, or at internal libraries maintained by the aforementioned institutions, namely: libraries at UNICEF offices in Brazil, Colombia, and New York; the library at the Centre International d'Enfance (Paris); a bibliography developed by the Centro Interamericano del Niño (Montevideo); the Ana Maria Poppovic Library at the Carlos Chagas Foundation (São Paulo); a bibliography developed by the Santa Ursula University (Rio de Janeiro); the Documentation Center at the National Movement of Street Boys and Girls in São Paulo; and the library of the Center for Studies of Violence at the University of São Paulo.
2. This report states: "According to the report, the number of child prostitutes in Brazil would be about five million. These are, essentially, girls age 12 to 14" (AIJD 1986: 29). For more information about rhetoric on child and youth prostitution in Brazil, see Rosemberg and Andrade (1999).
3. The estimates of 5 million, 2 million, or even 500,000 child prostitutes inevitably suggest an unimaginably high number of adult Brazilian males and male foreign tourists who are disposed to sexual abuse of girls and adolescents. If the logic that was directed toward the construction of these estimates on child prostitution were applied to the ones who solicit those acts, possibly the Brazilian adult male population and an incalculable number of foreign tourists would be suspected of "sexual abuse of minors" at least once in their lives. In the public policy arena, this would entail expansion of the court system, the development of programs to "reeducate Brazilian men," or a tremendous increase in prison capacity.
4. In a forthcoming report, we elaborate on a code of ethics designed to protect vulnerable children and adolescents from media abuse.

REFERENCES

Aptekar, Lewis. 1988. *Street Children of Cali.* Durham, N.C.: Duke University Press.

Association Internacionale des Juristes Democrates (AIJD). 1986. *Bulletin d'Information sur les Activités de l'AIJD en 1986.* Pp. 29–30. Brussels: Author.

Barcelos, Luiz Claudio. 1993. "Educação e desigualdades raciais no Brasil." *Cadernos de Pesquisa* 86 (Aug.): 15–24.

Belém, City of. The Pope John XXIII Foundation. 1993. *Crianças e adolescentes em situação de rua na cidade de Belém.* Belém: FUNPAPA.

Belo Horizonte, City of. Municipal Social Development Secretariat. 1993. *Programa emergencial para meninos e meninas de rua.* Seminar on Social Policy, 16 Mar. 1993. Belo Horizonte: Secretaria Municipal do Desenvolvimento Social.

Black, Maggie. 1986. *The Children and the Nations: The Story of UNICEF.* New York: UNICEF.

Blasi, Cary L. 1990. "Social Policy and Social Science Research on Homelessness." *Journal of Social Issues* 40(4): 207–19.

Breakey, W. R., and P. J. Fisher. 1990. "Homelessness: The Extent of the Problem." *Journal of Social Issues* 40(4): 31–45.

Brunel, Sylvie. 1991. *Une Tragédie banalisée: La Faim dans le monde.* Paris: Hachette.

Castilho, Inês. 1987. "Prostituição." *Mulherio* 33: 3–9.

Centro Brasileiro da Criança e do Adolescente Casa da Passagem. 1992. *Meninas de rua do Recife: dimensão, trajetória e sobrevivência.* Recife: Casa da Passagem.

Centro Brasileiro de Defesa dos Direitos da Criança e do Adolescente. 1990. *Relatório do I encontro de meninas do Estado do Rio de Janeiro.* Rio de Janeiro. Mimeographed.

Enfoque. 1990. Buenos Aires. Journal of Amnesty International.

Engelmann, Henri. 1986. *Enfants Perdus du Brésil.* Paris: Fayard.

FASE/IBASE/IDAC/ISER. 1992. *Levantamento de meninas e meninos nas ruas do Rio de Janeiro* (Report on Research Project "Se Essa Rua Fosse Minha"). Rio de Janeiro: Author.

Fedération Internacionale des Droits de L'Homme (FIDH). 1986. *Rapport de Mission: La Prostitution des Enfants au Brésil.* Pp. 105-17. Paris: Author.

Folha de São Paulo. 25 Oct. 1990.

Gonçalves, Zalua de A. 1979. *Meninos de rua e a marginalidade urbana em Belém.* Belém: Salesian Fathers of Pará.

Gomes, Jerusa V. 1988. "Do campo à cidade: as transformações nas práticas educativas familiares." *Cadernos de Pesquisa* 64: 48-56.

IBASE (Brazilian Institute of Social and Economic Analysis). 1988. *Relatório do levantamento de crianças de rua: município de Fortaleza, Ceará.* Rio de Janeiro: Author.

———. 1990. "Levantamento das crianças de rua: Salvador, Bahia." (Axé Project: Terra Nova—National Movement of Street Boys and Girls of Brazil [MNMMR]). Rio de Janeiro: Author.

Küchler, Alita Diana. 1990. "Menina . . . Mãe . . . Mulher." *Revista CBIA* (Brasília) (Oct.): 1-6.

Landers, Cassie. 1988. "A Cry for Help: UNICEF's Response to Street Children in the Third World." *Children's Environments Quarterly* 5(1): 37-42.

Lucchini, Riccardo. 1996. *Sociologie de la Survie: L'Enfant dans la Rue.* Paris: PUF.

Lusk, Mark W. 1989. "Street Children Programs in Latin America." *Journal of Sociology and Social Welfare* 26(1): 55-77.

Martin, Elizabeth. 1991. *Preliminary Findings of Assessment of S-Night Street Enumeration.* Washington, D.C.: U.S. Bureau of the Census.

Movimento Nacional de Meninos e Meninas de Rua. 1991. "Perfil do menino de rua: propostas alternativas." Paper presented at Sixth Brazilian Conference on Education, São Paulo, 6 Sept. 1991. Mimeographed.

O Globo. 29 March 1982.

Pereira Júnior, Almir, and A. Drska. 1992. "Experiência de contagem de meninos e meninas de rua." Pp. 80-105 in *Os impasses da cidadania: infância e adolescência no Brasil,* edited by Almir Pereira Júnior et al. Rio de Janeiro: IBASE.

Ribeiro, Rosa. 1988. *A PNAD como instrumento de trabalho para o estudo da situação do menor no Brasil.* Unpublished manuscript. Nova Fiburgo.

Rizzini, Irene. 1986. "A Geração de rua: um estudo sobre as crianças marginalizadas no Rio de Janeiro." *Estudos e Pesquisas* 1. Rio de Janeiro: Editora Universitária Santa Ursula.

Rizzini, Irene, and I. Rizzini. 1991. "'Menores' institucionalizados e meninos de rua: os grandes temas de pesquisa na década de 80." In *O trabalho e a rua: crianças e adolescentes no Brasil urbano dos anos 80,* edited by Ayrton Fausto and R. Cervini. São Paulo: FLACSO.

Rosemberg, Fúlvia, and Leandro Andrade. 1999. "Ruthless Rhetoric: Child and Youth Prostitution in Brazil." *Childhood* 6(1): 113-31.

Rosemberg, Fúlvia, R. P. Pinto, and E. Negrão. 1987. *A Educação de negros (pretos e pardos) no Estado de São Paulo.* São Paulo: Fundação Carlos Chagas. Mimeographed.

Rossi, P. H., J. Wright, G. Fisher, and G. Willis. 1987. "The Urban Homeless: Estimating Composition and Size." *Science* 235: 1336-41.

Sarti, Cynthia A. 1994. *A Família como espelho: um estudo sobre a moral dos pobres na periferia de São Paulo.* Ph.D. dissertation, Department of Anthropology, University of São Paulo.

Silva, Nelson do Valle. 1992. "Cor e pobreza no centenário da abolição." In *Relações raciais no Brasil contemporâneo,* edited by Nelson do Valle Silva and C. A. Hasenbalg. Rio de Janeiro: Rio Fundo; IUPERJ.

State of São Paulo, Juvenile Affairs Office. 1992 *Casa Aberta.* (Series: Secretaria do Menor: 3 Anos de Experiência.) São Paulo: Secretaria do Menor.

State of São Paulo, Office of Children, Families, and Social Welfare. 1993. *Contagem de crianças e adolescentes em situação de rua na Cidade de São Paulo.* São Paulo: Secretaria da Criança, Família e Bem-Estar Social.

State of Sergipe, Department of Social Action. 1993. *Os meninos e as meninas de rua de Aracaju.* Aracaju: Secretaria do Estado da Ação Social; Fundação Renascer. Mimeographed.

Taçon, Peter. 1981a. *My Child Minus One.* UNICEF document.

———. 1981b. *My Child Minus Two.* UNICEF document.

———. 1981c. *My Child Now: An Action Plan on Behalf of Children without Families.* UNICEF document.

———. 1983. *Regional Program for Latin America and the Caribbean.* UNICEF document.

———. 1980. "Sons and Daughters of the Street." *Ideas Forum* 10: 13–14.

UNICEF. 1992. *As crianças das américas: sobrevivência, proteção e desenvolvimento integral da infância na década de 1990.* Santafé de Bogotá, Colombia: UNICEF.

UNICEF/Brasília. 1984. *1983 Interim Progress Report: The Alternative Services for Street Children Project.* Brasília: UNICEF.

———. 1987. *To Light a Candle: What Was Attempted and What Happened.* Final report of the alternative services for street children project: 1982–86. Brasília: UNICEF.

Universidade Federal do Maranhão, Department of Social Services. *Casa de João e Maria. 1991. Cantagem e mapeamento de meninos e meninas de rua de São Luis, Maranhão* ("Estrela da Rua" project). São Luis: Universidade Federal do Maranhão.

Universidade Federal do Rio Grande do Sul, Department of Social Services. 1983. *Projeto de extensão sobre o atendimento e a educação a meninos(as) de rua.* Report on the census of street children. Porto Alegre: Universidade Federal do Rio Grande do Sul.

9

Standards, Curriculum Reform, and the Educational Experiences of One Homeless Youngster: Some Reflections

Rebecca Newman and Lynn Gillespie Beck

Jeffrey Ricks was a bright energetic 12-year-old.[1] He liked ice cream, loved his younger brothers and sisters, bragged about his father's exploits,[2] clowned frequently in class, and had been described by his teachers as "charming." At the time of this study Jeffrey was a 6th-grader at Jefferson School, his fourth school in that academic year. He was also a resident of the Chalet, a homeless shelter in southern California. This chapter concerns the final weeks of Jeffrey's 6th-grade year as he struggled with a daunting backlog of unfinished classwork and with the year's capstone assignment: the production of a social studies research report on Turkey. By dint of great effort on his part and on the part of his teachers, Jeffrey completed his overdue assignments and his report, a not-inconsiderable accomplishment given the many constraints imposed by his home and school contexts. The work he was assigned arose from a curriculum that conformed to high standards, and it was assigned by hard-working teachers who held high expectations for their students. At the same time, there were grounds for serious concern about his academic future, because his success in completing the work did not indicate any meaningful mastery of the content and processes that constituted the essential core of the assignments. In the case of Jeffrey, the existence of high academic standards not only did not produce meaningful learning, it may even have furthered his academic disadvantages.

Although Jefferson School was located in a very poor neigborhood, Jeffrey's teachers held their students to high standards. In addition, the school made strong, consistent efforts to provide an atmosphere in which all children could learn and to forge connections to the families that it served. Its teachers had not given up on their students; indeed, in an early meeting one of Jeffrey's teachers told us that Jeffrey just hadn't been at Jefferson long enough to understand that *they were going to keep following up on him*. Both his social studies/language arts teacher and his math/science teacher adhered to the full curriculum prescribed by the state and local guidelines. Moreover, convinced that students should not go to junior high school without having had the experience of writing a research paper, Jeffrey's social studies/language arts teacher devoted extensive time in the second semester to guiding students through this experience—the specific assignment being to write a research report on a country other than the United States.

Nevertheless, the conditions of Jeffrey's life, coupled with the inadequacy of available resources in the community and school, made it almost impossible for Jeffrey to do more than go through the motions of completing these assignments. There are, therefore, serious questions about their educational value. In his case, having high standards and dedicated teachers was simply not enough—and Jeffrey's situation is very similar to that of many other students at his school and in this country. In *National Standards in American Education* (Ravitch 1995, cited in Noddings 1997), Diane Ravitch describes three types of standards: *content standards,* which deal with what children should learn; *performance standards,* which define levels of mastery; and *opportunity to learn standards,* which include the resources that schools and states must provide if students are to achieve the desired level of mastery of the prescribed content.

Our national conversation about standards has focused almost entirely on issues of *content* and *mastery,* but for children like Jeffrey the first topic that must be addressed is *opportunity to learn.* Much of the current discussion would seem to suggest that the problems of underachieving students and schools will be resolved by the imposition of high academic standards, a notion that would be laughable were the topic not so serious. Kenneth Howe of the University of Colorado offers an apt metaphor. He writes that in situations where resources are lacking, "better educational standards can eliminate low achievement . . . no more effectively than better nutritional standards can eliminate hunger under famine conditions. Providing the means of attaining the standards is required in each case" (Howe 1995: 22). One may argue about who should determine content and performance standards and what they should include, but for children like Jeffrey, a discussion of content and mastery has little relevance because mastery is so severely constrained by the lack of a meaningful opportunity to do well.

JEFFREY'S STORY

Jeffrey and his family were participants in a study of the educational situation of homeless children. We met Jeffrey and his family in the course of research on the educational experiences of homeless children (Newman and Beck 1993, 1996; Newman 1998). In October of 1995 this research led us to the Chalet, a residential shelter for homeless women and their children that was run by a nonprofit organization. In 2 years of involvement we spent more than 500 hours at the Chalet and at Jefferson School in the course of a study focusing on eight of the families and their 14 school-aged children. We interviewed parents and staff at the Chalet and the children's teachers at Jefferson, and observed and participated in Jefferson classrooms and at the Chalet. We were involved in formal and informal tutoring with Chalet children, conducted 16 arts-and-crafts workshops with children there, and helped develop and operate a homework program. Jeffrey Ricks, his mother Marietta Cardin, and his five younger siblings—9-year-old Helen, 7-year-old-twins William and Wanda, 2-year-old Karen, and baby Raymond—were among these families who allowed us to enter their lives and to participate in and study their experiences with formal schooling.

Jeffrey and his brothers and sisters arrived at Jefferson School in March of the 1995–1996 school year. From the very first day there were problems with all four: Jeffrey, 4th-grader Helen, and 2nd-grade twins Wanda and William. None of the children did well academically, and Jeffrey and the twins were frequently in trouble of one kind or another. At first, both school and shelter were patient. The twins' teachers rearranged their Chapter 1 tutoring schedules in order to accommodate both twins in a special reading group for beginners. Jeffrey's teachers set up a homework contract for him and arranged for after-school help. Chalet staff and one of us met from time to time with their mother Marietta to deal with the children's problems, and we also provided some tutoring support. However, in early May, Jeffrey's teachers pulled one of us aside for an impromptu conference. We were informed that Jeffrey was doing no homework and almost no work in class. He had a huge backlog of unfinished work in all subjects and had barely begun the year's culminating project, which was writing a research report about another country—Turkey, in his case. There was a substantial chance that he would be receiving several failing grades.

Following this meeting we met with Jeffrey's mother, Marietta; then Jeffrey and one of us met with his teachers and devised a plan of action. We began regular after-school tutoring sessions, and Jeffrey's teachers arranged for him to come to school early and to stay late, which required a change in his bus schedule. Chalet staff took on responsibility for monitoring Jeffrey's work in the afternoons when there was no tutoring. Little by little the backlog of work was completed, at least at a minimal level. At the same time, the extent of his educational deficits became clear. He plugged away at division and fractions, but in the course of our work with him it became clear that he did not, in fact, understand multiplication nor have the basic facts memorized; this meant that his grasp of both division and fractions was precarious, at best. His struggles with spelling, vocabulary, science, social studies, and reading assignments revealed large gaps in his general knowledge, which made it difficult for him to grasp and organize the new information being presented. Nowhere was this more evident than in his work on his research report.

Pushed along by all of the people working with him, Jeffrey went through the motions of writing a research report. He colored a flag and drew a map, he copied notes from at least two sources on a set of assigned topics, and strung the notes together to produce a minimally adequate report. It was, however, painfully clear that he did not understand what he was writing, nor, in fact, did he really seem to expect that he *would* understand it. A particularly poignant illustration of this fact occurred on the night he finished the written portion of the report. Jeffrey was sitting in the shelter's tiny office, working on his report. One of us had been conducting an arts-and-crafts session down in the patio, and after arts and crafts ended she went upstairs to check in with Jeffrey and proofread what he had written. It was clear that Jeffrey did not always understand the sentences he had copied, although he seemed to have tried to make sense out of them. One sentence he had written referred to Turkey and made no sense; the word clearly should have been *Europe.* When asked about this Jeffrey explained that his notes did say *Europe,* but he thought that since his report was about Turkey he should change it to *Turkey.* He showed the notes; they did say *Europe.* We tried to explain why the sentence made sense if the word was *Europe,* and no sense if the word was *Turkey,* but he seemed to have only a vague notion of the meaning of the word *Europe* and it was not clear he had enough general knowledge to understand what we were saying. It was abundantly clear that he did not understand the geopolitical relationship between Europe and Turkey. In two other instances, sentences in the report referenced illustrations that were in the original sources from which the notes were copied, but which would not be present in Jeffrey's report. We pointed these sentences out, explaining that he must either eliminate the sentences or change the wording so that the sentences did not convey information that was dependent on illustrations which he didn't have. After some discussion, he seemed to understand.

Jeffrey's story illuminates the dilemmas and complexities of the current emphasis on uniform standards that "specify a common academic core for all students at every grade level" (California Academic Standards Commission 1997: viii), as a means of assuring that all children receive a "world class education." In a 1997 report to the State Board of Education, the California Academic Standards Commission wrote that "standards should be high for all students and reflect academically rigorous content and performance necessary for California's pupils to be comparable to the best in the world" (California Academic Standards Commission 1997: viii). Jeffrey's assignments were consistent with this laudable goal, but the outcomes were not. We may all agree that every child deserves access to a rigorous, challenging curriculum, but it is at best disingenuousness—and at worst demagoguery—to imagine that students and schools will be able to meet such standards unless our society provides the resources needed to accomplish this task. As educational theorist Nel Noddings has written: "It is disheartening that so many adults are willing to prescribe standards that children must meet and yet are so unwilling to dedicate themselves and their resources to meet standards for school delivery" (Noddings 1997: 185–86). Let us turn now to an examination of the way in which Jeffrey's home, community, and school contexts severely constrained his opportunity to meet the high standards his teachers and the educational community held for him.

HOME-LIFE CONSTRAINTS ON EDUCATIONAL EXPERIENCES

Poverty and Family Instability

Jeffrey was born in Chicago, Illinois, when his mother, Marietta, was only 15 years old. He and his siblings had three different fathers. Jeffrey's father lived in Chicago, and he and Jeffrey stayed in touch with one another, but Jeffrey had always lived with his mother. The family had no contact with Helen's father, and neither he nor Jeffrey's father contributed to their children's support. Twins William and Wanda, 2-year-old Karen, and baby Raymond were all children of Raymond Cardin, Marietta's husband, who, when we first met the family, was separated from them and living in a residential substance abuse treatment facility. Although he once worked as a barber, Raymond had not worked steadily for many years. Marietta had held a variety of entry-level jobs, including working as a nursing-home aide and a drug-store clerk. She also attended beauty school but failed to graduate; at the time she came to the Chalet she was in debt to them for unpaid tuition. She had not worked since the birth of 2-year-old Karen, finding that the cost of child care eliminated any benefit from her wages; the family had a long history of reliance on welfare.

In 1989, when Jeffrey was 5, the family moved to Los Angeles so Marietta could care for an ill parent. In 1993, they moved to San Diego, California, then briefly back to Chicago in 1994, returning to Los Angeles the same year. In early 1995 Marietta and her family relocated to Chicago for a brief time, returning to Los Angeles shortly thereafter. In February 1996, she left her husband, fleeing to the Haven, a center for victims of domestic violence.[3] She and her children lived there for a month before coming to the Chalet in March 1996. At that time, Jeffrey, Helen, William, and Wanda were enrolled in Jefferson Elementary School.

Chaotic Home Life

Problems with child care, transportation, and a hectic schedule created chaotic conditions at home. The family's daily life at the Chalet was hectic. The apartment was tiny, and lack of affordable child care and of a car (coupled with a very inadequate system of public transportation) vastly complicated the activities of daily living. The family's schedule was very difficult, and study conditions were poor. For all of these reasons, the children were frequently in trouble at the Chalet, in the neighborhood, and at school. In early May, Jeffrey's mother began training to process medical claims under the auspices of the Job Training Partnership Act program (JTPA). JTPA pays for child care for program participants, but only for care in licensed facilities. Marietta found a licensed program for baby Raymond and 2-year-old Karen, but there were no licensed providers for before- and after-school care of older children in the Chalet's neighborhood. Marietta therefore had to pay for their care herself; it was provided by Yolanda, another resident of the apartment complex.[4] After school and on weekends, much of the responsibility for care of the two youngest children fell on Jeffrey and Helen; it was the only way their mother could get anything done.

Getting the two little ones to child care and herself to school required Marietta to take four buses, meaning she needed to leave the apartment at 6:10 A.M. In the evening she reversed the process, getting home around 6:00 P.M. This schedule required that the whole family get up around 5:00 A.M. The older children could get breakfast at school, but since all four were assigned to "late" reading groups, they would not leave for school until after 8:00 A.M. and needed to eat something before then.[5] They went to Yolanda's apartment at 6:10 A.M., when Marietta left. Theoretically they could do homework or play quietly at Yolanda's; often they went back to sleep, although they cannot have slept very well. The atmosphere at Yolanda's must have been very hectic at that hour. Yolanda had three children of her own to get off to school and a husband to get off to work. In addition, she baby-sat for five other children, all of whom arrived early. By the time Jeffrey and his siblings started class they had already been up for about 4 hours. Before Marietta started her training, she told us she planned to get the children to bed by 8:00 P.M. each evening in order to manage getting them up so early. However, she soon found difficulty maintaining this scheduled bedtime. It was nearly 6:00 P.M. when she got home in the evening; if she maintained the 8 o'clock bedtime, she had only 2 hours to fix dinner for seven, feed and bathe the baby, clean up (or supervise the children in doing so), supervise homework, lay out clothes for the next day, and get six children to bed in one room in an apartment with one tiny bathroom. After that, she had her own homework. Marietta was unable to maintain the bedtime schedule very strictly, and many problems developed. The children's homework had been a problem ever since they arrived at the Chalet, and now she had no time at all to monitor their work and assist them. Jeffrey was clearly not getting enough sleep; as soon as Marietta began school he started falling asleep in class. When we looked for him at the Chalet in the afternoons, we frequently learned that he was asleep at Yolanda's in the midst of an uproar of children, television, and dinner preparations.

Poor Homework Conditions

Jeffrey's home situation made doing homework extremely difficult. There was only one place to work: at the kitchen table, a space usually shared with three siblings during a hubbub of either dinner preparations or cleanup. The table was right next to the front window, so the outside world was a distraction; the TV set was also within sight and hearing. Once Marietta started her job training, homework could not be started at home before her 6 o'clock arrival, and with a 5:00 A.M. rising time, the children were tired by 6:00 P.M. Doing homework at the baby-sitter's was equally difficult; there were usually at least 10 other children there, sometimes more, and the TV was always on. In addition, neither Yolanda nor her husband spoke English, so adult help was unavailable.

The family also had few school supplies. Storage was a problem for Chalet residents even if supplies were given to the children. Most of the older children at the Chalet carried as many possessions as they could in their backpacks (books, decent crayons, toys), fearing that otherwise younger siblings, apartment mates, or other children would use or destroy them—not an unreasonable fear. There were few other resources to support schoolwork: families did not have dictionaries or other resource books; indeed, most families had no children's books of any kind. The public library was too far away to walk to, and families that, like Jeffrey's, lacked cars had no time to take children to the library on a bus. Jeffrey's household was unusual because the family *did* have a small collection of children's books, although no dictionary, newspapers, magazines, or other resources. The neighborhood itself was also singularly lacking in the resources that might have supplemented those of Jeffrey's family—community resources such as church activities, recreational programs, and libraries.[6]

Perhaps most significant of all, the children did not have access to the adult time and attention that is often needed for success with homework. With her large family and difficult schedule, Marietta simply could not oversee and assist with even the twins' simple, easy-to-understand homework, let alone monitor Jeffrey's work on week-long spelling assignments, social studies reports, and the like. Moreover, Helen and the twins were all in greater academic difficulty than Jeffrey. Although in 4th grade, Helen was functioning on a 1st-grade level in reading and about a 2nd-grade level in math. Second-grader William had kindergarten-level skills, and Wanda, too, was below grade level, especially in reading. Since the twins and Helen were virtually unable to read their assignments, it would have required extraordinary personal motivation for them to deal with their homework on their own without regular, firm, sympathetic adult assistance. Lacking this help, they continued to fall behind academically. Jeffrey was better able to *do* the assigned work but exhibited no inclination to do it on his own; without adult monitoring he, too, was falling further and further behind.

SCHOOLING HISTORY CONSTRAINTS ON ACADEMIC SUCCESS

Multiple Schools

Jeffrey had attended at least eight schools during his elementary years, including four during 6th grade—so many that Jefferson was virtually unable to obtain any meaningful academic records for him and his siblings. The scanty records available, combined with Marietta's recounting of the family's many moves, suggested that there may also have been multiple periods during which the children were not even enrolled in school. In fact, there was evidence to suggest they may have missed as much as two months of school in 1995 and 1996 prior to enrolling at Jefferson. Children who change schools frequently are likely to suffer a variety of negative educational consequences. Getting used to a new environment always takes time. Knowing this, teachers are usually inclined to give new students the benefit of the doubt if they initially seem to be low-performing, not wanting to rush to judgment about a student's needs and capacity before the child has had time to settle in. Curricular approaches and school calendars also differ among schools and districts, so children who move frequently may easily miss various sections of the curriculum. Changes between schools with year-round and traditional calendars can also be a problem: Jeffrey and his siblings lost time because they spent part of the 1995–1996 school year in a year-round school. They had a month of vacation in late fall, but would have been in school through the summer. When they came to Jefferson, which is on a traditional schedule, they had vacation again in the summer. Thanks to this change in calendar—and the fact that they made at least one trip back to Chicago and possibly two—they attended as much as two months' less school than their classmates that year.[7]

Lack of School Resources

Jefferson school was, in many ways, the best *possible* place for Jeffrey and his sisters and brother to attend. There were structures in place to support children in academic difficulty, such as a noontime "Homework Shop" and a homework contract system where parents and teachers shared the responsibility for monitoring and communicating about homework. The school staff was very caring and responsive. Jeffrey's teachers made a point of staying after school every afternoon so students could come for extra help and, guessing that Jeffrey was unable to get work done at home, also arranged for him to come to school on the "early" bus each morning and work on homework in the office until it was time for him to start class with the other "late" readers.[8] Jeffrey's very experienced homeroom teacher had weekly written contact with students' parents (via "Happy-" and "Sad-Grams") and did much "scaffolding" for her students—structuring assignments and the classroom environment for success. In addition, there was excellent communication between the school and the shelter. Nevertheless, the school lacked many of the resources needed by its pupils.

Shelters for the homeless are generally situated in poor neighborhoods, and the schools the children attend therefore also tend to be in poor neighborhoods.[9] The Chalet and Jefferson fit this pattern, and the school was a feeder school for the junior and senior high schools with the worst gang problems in the city, according to the local police.[10] Schools in poor neighborhoods are likely to have many high-needs students: children who do not speak English as a first language; children from poverty-stricken families; highly mobile students; and children whose lives have been only marginally different—if at all different—from those of children actually living in homeless shelters.

Jefferson had a high mobility rate; in 1995-1996 it was 36 percent, which means that over the course of a year a typical classroom lost five or six of the pupils who had been there at the beginning, and by the end had gained five or six who were not these at the start. In contrast, in a neighboring district in a more wealthy area, a given classroom could expect to lose or gain only one pupil per year. Jefferson also had large numbers of students with limited English; 25 percent of its classrooms were bilingual. Family incomes in the area were low. Classes were large, usually over 30 pupils. In 1997, 100 percent of the students were eligible for free or reduced-priced meals; in fact, 89 percent were eligible for *free* meals. The school was also inadequately funded. In 1995-1996 the district reported an average per-pupil expenditure of $4,539, about average for California but below the national average and far below the spending levels of many other states; in 1992, California ranked 36th among the states in per-pupil spending (Bureau of the Census 1993).[11]

Assistance Is Not Enough

Particularly in view of the demands on his school's resources, Jeffrey had received an extraordinary amount of help. Given these limitations, it is easy to see why more could not be done for Jeffrey. When a child with a long history of academic problems and few family resources to support him arrives late in the year in the oldest grade in a school where many students have desperate needs and resources are very limited, there are severe constraints on what can be done. A mere 16 pupils from the Chalet were among the school's 841 students. Many of those 841, we can well imagine, were in educational and social situations nearly as precarious as those of Jeffrey and his siblings. In Jeffrey's case, heroic efforts *were* made by both Jefferson staff and the staff of the Chalet; it would be completely unrealistic to suggest that the school could have focused more closely than it did upon the needs of Jeffrey and his family.[12]

CONCLUSION

Jeffrey's story illustrates many of the issues that need to be addressed in our national conversation about standards. It is unlikely that changes in schooling, however far-reaching, could entirely level the academic playing field for students like Jeffrey. However, his chance for success would certainly be enhanced by increasing investment in schools in order better to meet the needs of such students. There are several ways in which schools *could,* given adequate funding, better satisfy the *opportunity to learn standards* so desperately lacking for Jeffrey and other students. If his school had been able to offer a high-quality after-school tutoring, recreation, and academic enrichment program, Jeffrey might have been able to remedy some of his academic deficits and simultaneously get help keeping up with classwork and homework. If counseling had been available to help address his behavioral and attitudinal problems, that, too, would have helped. If such things had been available throughout Jeffrey's schooling, he might not have arrived at Jefferson so woefully unprepared to learn and do what was expected of him.

In addition, Jeffrey was, in some sense, actually disadvantaged by the high *content and mastery standards* dictated by his school's curriculum, and by his teachers' high expectations. His experiences with math assignments and the production of his research report are examples of this problem. Jeffrey was unprepared to benefit from the experience of writing a research report on a foreign country. Had he been given a research topic that built upon learning and skills that he *did* possess, the assignment might well have actually increased both his knowledge of social studies content and his research and writing skills. He was also unready to master the 6th-grade math curriculum. Had he been able to focus on learning the 3rd-, 4th-, and 5th-grade math content and skills that he had not truly mastered, he might, eventually, have been able to learn the 6th-grade curriculum instead of barely getting by with no real mastery. However, teachers are not generally given the authority to make such curriculum decisions, nor the resources for implementing them. If his class had included 20 pupils instead of more than 30, his teachers would have been able to individualize instruction and to devote more time to helping pupils genuinely master content and processes, instead of merely going through the motions. But with more than 30 pupils, many as woefully underprepared as Jeffrey, and with no other support, such as tutoring programs, these options were not available to them.

No matter how much the school had done, however, there would still be the limitations imposed by Jeffrey's family's grinding poverty and the attendant social and personal problems that absorbed so much of the time, energy, and meager resources of his parents and so reduced the time available for him. For the many children like Jeffrey to succeed academically in America's schools, much more than the mere imposition of academically rigorous standards will be needed.

NOTES

1. This and all proper names are pseudonyms. Furthermore, details that might identify the homeless shelters mentioned in this chapter have been altered.
2. Jeffrey's stories concerned his (noncustodial) biological father; he did not get along well with his stepfather, Raymond Cardin.

3. Marietta stated that her husband was psychologically but not physically abusive and that he tightly controlled the children's activities.

4. Yolanda was manager of the non-Chalet apartments in the complex and baby-sat for many Chalet residents and others; one of her daughters, Faith, was a member of the Chalet's staff.

5. To reduce class size for reading instruction, Jefferson's classes were divided roughly in half, into "early" and "late" readers. In the upper grades, early readers arrived at 8:00 A.M. and left at 1:45 P.M.; late readers arrived at 8:45 A.M. and left at 2:30 P.M.

6. See Comer (1984, 1986, 1987, 1988); Natriello, McDill, and Pallas (1990); and Schorr (1989) on the need for home, school, and community cooperation in support of the education of children in poor communities.

7. See Ascher (1991); Beck, Kratzer, and Isken (1997); Cahape (1993); and Nelson, Simoni, and Adelman (1996) for a discussion of the problems associated with high-school mobility.

8. For a definition of "early" and "late" readers, see note 5.

9. See Wolch and Dear (1993) for a discussion of the siting of shelters and other social services for the poor; see also Redlener and Karich (1994) on the location of shelters in New York City.

10. Personal communication with the police department's Director of Youth Services, 6 Aug. 1996.

11. See Hodgkinson (1991) for a discussion of the inadequacy of funding for schools, and Kozol (1991) on funding inequities between wealthy and less-wealthy districts. See Slavin (1997–1998) for a discussion of the capacity of education to reduce social inequity even in neighborhoods such as the one served by Jefferson—given adequate resources, skills, and determination.

12. J. Newman (1988) describes appropriate resources for schools serving highly mobile children. Hodgkinson (1991) provides a similar list for schools serving the children of poverty.

REFERENCES

Ascher, C. 1991. "Highly Mobile Students: Educational Problems and Possible Solutions." *ERIC/CUE Digest* 73 (June) (ERIC Document Reproduction Service No. ED 338 745).

Beck, L. G., C. C. Kratzer, and J. A. Isken. 1997. "Caring for Transient Students in One Urban Elementary School." *Journal for a Just and Caring Education* 3(3): 343–69.

Bureau of the Census. 1993. *Statistical Abstract of the United States: 1993*. Washington, D.C.: Bureau of the Census.

Cahape, P. 1993. "The Migrant Student Record Transfer System (MSRTS): An Update." *ERIC/CRESS Digest* (March) (ERIC Document Reproduction Service No. ED 357 909).

California Academic Standards Commission. 1997. *Language Arts: Reading, Writing, Listening and Speaking Content Standards for Grades K-12.* A report presented to the State Board of Education, October 1. Sacramento, Calif.: The Commission for the Establishment of Academic Content and Peformance Standards.

Comer, J. 1984. "Home-School Relationships as They Affect the Academic Success of Children." *Education and Urban Society* 16(3): 323–37.

———. 1986. "Parent Participation in the Schools." *Phi Delta Kappan* 67(2): 442–46.

———. 1987. "New Haven's School-Community Connection." *Educational Leadership* 44(8): 13–16.

———. 1988. "Educating Poor Minority Children." *Scientific American* 259(5): 42–48.

Hodgkinson, H. 1991. "Reform Versus Reality." *Phi Delta Kappan* 73(1): 9–16.

Howe, K. R. 1995. "Wrong Problem, Wrong Solution." *Educational Leadership* 52(6): 22–23.

Kozol, J. 1991. *Savage Inequalities: Children in American Schools.* New York: Crown.

Natriello, G., E. L. McDill, and A. M. Pallas. 1990. *Schooling Disadvantaged Children: Racing Against Catastrophe.* New York: Teachers College Press.

Nelson, P. S., J. M. Simoni, and H. S. Adelman. 1996. "Mobility and School Functioning in the Early Grades." *The Journal of Educational Research* 89(6): 365–69.

Newman, J. 1988. *What Should We Do about the Highly Mobile Student? A Research Brief.* Mount Vernon, Wash.: Educational Service District 189 (ED 305 545).

Newman, R. L. 1998. "Understanding How Home and School Contexts Constrain Student Outcomes for Homeless Children: Witness to a Cataclysm." Doctoral dissertation, University of California, Los Angeles. UMI Dissertation Abstracts: 9823537.

Newman, R. L., and L. G. Beck. 1993. *Educating Homeless Children in a Suburban California Community: A Snapshot of Research in Progress.* Paper presented at the annual meeting of the University Council for Educational Administration, October.

———. 1996. "Educating Homeless Children: One Experiment in Collaboration." Pp. 95–133 in *Coordination among Schools, Families, and Communities,* edited by J. G. Cibulka and W. J. Kritek. Albany, N.Y.: State University of New York Press.

Noddings, N. 1997. "Thinking about Standards." *Phi Delta Kappan* 79(3): 184–89.

Redlener, I., and K. M. Karich. 1994. "The Homeless Child Health Care Inventory: Assessing the Efficacy of Linkages to Primary Care." *Bulletin of the New York Academy of Medicine* 71(1): 37–48.

Schorr, L. B. 1989. "Early Interventions to Reduce Intergenerational Disadvantage: The New Policy Context." *Teachers College Record* 90(3): 363–74.

Slavin, R. E. 1997–1998. "Can Education Reduce Social Inequity?" *Educational Leadership* 55(4): 6–10.

Wolch, J., and M. Dear. 1993. *Malign Neglect: Homelessness in an American City.* San Francisco: Jossey-Bass.

Part IV: Case Studies of Programs for Homeless and Street Children in the United States, Brazil, and Cuba

10

Restructuring Childhood in Cuba: The State as Family

Sheryl L. Lutjens

The new world order has put Cuba's socialist model of development to a daunting test. Cuban responses include economic reforms that are restructuring ownership, production, and exchange, though official policy discourse steadfastly defends socialist democracy and the revolution's vision of social justice.[1] The 1997 CEPAL study of the Cuban economy recognizes social gains: "It is beyond question that social policy constitutes the terrain where Cuba has most distinguished itself historically, in terms of guaranteeing distributive equity and the well-being of the population, as well as the formation of human capital" (CEPAL 1997: 360).[2] The transformative policies of the Cuban revolution eliminated poverty, malnutrition, high mortality rates, undereducation, child labor, and a host of other symptoms of the prerevolutionary state's neglect of children's basic needs and rights. In assuming new responsibilities for social welfare and Cuba's "human capital," the state in many ways promoted and protected the nuclear family. It also relied upon extended family arrangements and substituted itself in limited cases. In 1997, there were 32 state homes for children without *amparo filial* (family protection) in Cuba. A closer look at the state's role in the care and schooling of these children offers insight into the realities of childhood, family life, and protective policies in a still-socialist Cuba.

The altered circumstances of children in postrevolutionary Cuba include the legal foundations that confer responsibilities and rights. A Family Code was adopted in 1975, and a Code of Childhood and Youth in 1978. The Civil and Penal Codes, documents and programs of the Cuban Communist Party, and the Cuban Constitution (revised in 1992) also define the expected performance of individuals, families, and institutions with regard to children and youth. The Constitution includes a chapter on the family. It declares that the state protects the family, motherhood, and marriage, that the family is the "basic cell of society," and that children have equal rights whether born within marriage or not. The Constitution maintains that "parents have the duty to feed their children and assist in the defense of their legitimate interests and the realization of their just aspirations, as well as to contribute actively to their education and integral development as useful citizens who are prepared for life in a socialist society." According to Chapter V, on education and culture, the mass and social organizations are also expected to pay "special attention to the integral development of children and youth" (Cuba 1992: 18–21).

The particular conditions of the early 1960s directed special attention to children who lacked the care of parents and family. The existing crèches—or *casas cunas* (foundling homes)—were private and religious, with roots in the *casa de expósitos* founded in 1687. The Casa de Beneficiencia y Maternidad—a charity/maternity hospital—was closed and both types of services placed under the Ministry of Social Welfare and then the Children and Women's Department of the Ministry of Public Health. Besides orphans and abandoned infants, the thousands of youth from Cuba's Sierra Maestra who arrived in Havana in 1961 required attention. And as one participant educator explained, a secondary school for children of guerrillas abroad was created in La Chata, the estate of a former president, while in Guanabo, student teachers began their practice with the children left behind in the first wave of postrevolutionary immigration (Ortega 1995). Indeed, between 1959 and 1993, 857,000 Cubans arrived in the United States. This included 14,000 children sent to the United States in the December 1960–October 1962 Operation Peter Pan, because parents feared a rumored transfer of *patria potestad* (parental rights) to the state (Rodríguez Chávez 1994; Reed 1994; Ojito 1998: A1, A14).

History and culture have contributed to contemporary family patterns and practices. In the last Cuban census in 1981, there were 2,351,000 *nucleos particulares* (household units) in Cuba, of which 53.7 percent were identified as nuclear and 32.5 percent as extended families (Alvarez Suarez 1997: 102, 103). The average size had dropped to 4.1 persons, though it varied with color/ethnicity; black Cubans were associated with family units of seven or more, whites and mulattos with four or more, and Asians with single-persons (Catasús Cervera 1997). Other patterns include declining marriage rates, high divorce rates, and a slow rise in the number of consensual unions. The average age of first marriage for Cuban women is the lowest in Latin America, as is the fertility rate (Alvarez Suárez 1997: 104-5).[3] Abortion is legal and widely used, nearly equaling the number of births (Aguilar et al. 1996: 15).[4] The number of female-headed households rose from 14 percent in 1953 to 28 percent in 1981, and to 36 percent in 1995 (Alvarez Suárez 1997: 103; Catasús Cervera 1997: 6). Although women heads of household may be married, one scholar estimates that in the late 1980s virtually all of the 200,000 single parents were mothers (Rosenthal 1992: 166). These characteristics of family structure in Cuba have historical and cultural roots. Single motherhood, for instance, is not an invention of the revolution—it "has always been a feature of Cuban life," according to Smith and Padula (1996: 161)—though problems associated with it were redefined within socialism.

Socialist policies, however, do not fully explain change and continuity in family structures and dynamics after 1959. Cuban scholarship recognizes many factors that affect the functioning of the family, including living conditions, stage of the life cycle, whether the mother works, and class, cultural, or geographical differences (Alvarez Suárez 1997: 104). Cuba's traditional approach to women's equality and the social policies implemented by the revolution have, of course, contributed to the changing realities of family life in Cuba. Yet cultural resilience and economic difficulties have made the nuclear family ideal a contingent one. Assumptions about the proper functioning of families and recognition of old and newer obstacles inform protective policies for children with and without *amparo filial*.

STATE HOMES

Decree-Law 76, January 1984, regulates the system for caring for children without family protection in Cuba. The system includes *hogares* (homes) for children aged 6 through 17 and *círculos infantiles mixtos* (mixed day care centers—CIMs) for those under 6, both aimed at providing care and living conditions similar to those of a family. Decree-Law 76 establishes the foundations for the homes, for adoption of children, and for substitute—foster—families envisioned in Cuban policy; Resolution 48/84 of the Ministry of Education (MINED) provides the complementary dispositions with regard to admission to homes and CIMs, and their organization, control, and supervision (Consejo de Estado 1984; Ministerio de Educación 1984; the description that follows relies on both documents). Similar to one participant's explanation that replacing the missing *cariño* (affection) was the first step taken in the revolution's early efforts, the decree-law presumes that beyond their efficient functioning, homes should provide children with "kindness and affection."

Decree-Law 76 defines two categories of children without family protection: those whose parents have died (orphans); and abandoned minors, those whose parents have been deprived of *patria potestad* or have definitively left national territory, who have been left in hospitals or other places, or who lack parental protection because their parents do not provide for their education, care, and feeding. There are few who meet the letter of the law, however, as explained in 1992 guidelines issued by the National Commission for Prevention and Social Welfare.

In reality, very few children are without family protection in the strict sense of the term. However, a significant number of children exist who develop in a very negative social and familial environment and whose parents and family, for varied reasons, do not care for them. This results in severe deficiencies in their education and the healthy development of their personalities (Comisión Nacional 1992: 1). Thus, "children in situations of social disadvantage"—or at-risk children—are the central, operational concern in working with minors who lack proper family protection, and state policy prioritizes their care and education.

The Ministry of Education implements state policies for children without *amparo familial.* Entry into state homes (*hogares*) begins with the proposal of the Municipal Commission, the Attorney General, the Ministry of the Interior, or any of the institutions under MINED. The mass organizations and neighbors can also initiate the process by referring cases. If there is no *hogar* in the municipality, the provincial level can coordinate placement in another municipality. The municipal office of education thus authorizes enrollment, followed by a study of the case that may last no longer than 30 days. Children receive lodging, round-the-clock care, medical attention, clothing and shoes, school uniform, food, and a stipend. In 1996–1997, 3,000 pesos were invested per child for services, 500 for varied expenses, 360 for clothing, and 518 for food (Perera Robbio 1997: 9).[5] The directors of the *hogares* are to coordinate with and be supported by the political and mass organizations, including the FMC, the youth branch of the party (Unión de Jóvenes Comunistas—UJC), student organizations, the neighborhood Committees for the Defense of the Revolution, and others.

Children who live in *hogares* participate in the formal educational system. Children will attend the primary or secondary school nearest the *hogar,* though secondary students may board in a school in the countryside, returning to the home on weekends as other students do. Children with developmental deficiencies will attend special education schools, though severely disabled children are placed in institutions in the health care system. Directors of homes exercise guardianship (*tutela*) over each child; children leave the home when they are adopted, marry, finish their intermediate studies, are eligible to work and are not studying, or are called for military service. Directors are also responsible for selecting substitute families that will take the child into their homes on weekends. Each child has a case file, and *hogares* and CIMs are attended by social workers, doctors, nurses, and other state agencies.

In 1996, there were 188 children in mixed day care centers in Cuba (see Table 10.1), representing .014 percent of the enrollment in preschool education and .02 percent of the preschool-age population. The reasons for their placement include mothers with AIDS (3), mothers with mental illnesses (24), mothers in custody (47), ill mothers (5), maternal abandonment (60), housing problems (26), improper home (1), orphaned (7), alcoholic parents (1), and neglect (1).[6] Several homes and mixed day care centers were included in a study of adoptions undertaken in Havana in 1992, among them the CIM Los Tavitos. Of the 106 children in the *círculo,* 31 boarded there. One child was in process of adoption by a substitute family and the parents of 2 had been deprived of *patria potestad;* there were 10 cases of lack of housing (in which 3 also lacked adequate attention and 2 were cases of psychiatric illness), 5 mothers who were psychiatric patients, 1 mother had died (and the father was in prison), 9 had been abandoned by their mother, 2 mothers were prisoners, 3 came from inadequate homes, and 1 child was abandoned by a mother with an ill father (González Ferrer and Miranda Sánchez 1993: Attachment 42).

According to ministry figures, at the start of 1997 there were 31 *hogares* throughout the island, caring for a total of 203 boys and 165 girls aged 6 to 16 (see Table 10.2). In contrast to Havana's overwhelming share of reported enrollments in mixed day care centers (61 percent), only 14 percent of the children living in *hogares* were in the capital. The reasons for placement are similar to those noted above, however, including the heavy emphasis on the roles of mothers. For example, in the Presencia de Lenin home in Miramar in 1992, there were 26 children; 5 had been abandoned by their mothers and

Table 10.1   Situation of Children in *Círculos Infantiles Mixtos:* Cuba 1996

Province*	Enroll-ment	Substitute Home	Adoption in Process	Privation in Process	Attention by Family	No Infor-mation
Pinar del Río	10	3	—	1	5	2
La Habana	5	3	1	1	—	1
C. Habana	114	11	6	10	26	76
Matanzas	7	—	—	—	—	—
Villa Clara	5	1	1	—	—	4
Cienfuegos						
Ciego de Avila	6	—	—	—	6	—
Camagüey	14	3	1	1	—	12
Holguín	9	6	7	6	—	2
Las Tunas	3	—	—	—	—	3
Granma	1	—	—	—	—	1
Santiago de Cuba	8	3	1	1	—	4
Guantánamo	5	1	1	—	—	4
Isla de la Juventud	1	1	—	—	—	—
Total	188	32	18	20	37	109

*Sancti Spíritus province is not reported.
Source: "Informe de adopción por provincia," provided by Centro de Documentación e Información Pedagógica, Ministerio de Educación, Jan. 1997.

Table 10.2 Homes for Children without Family Protection: Cuba 1996

Province	Homes	Children	Female	Male	Age 0–6	Age 6–16	Age +16
Pinar del Río	1	10	5	5	—	9	1
Ciudad Habana	3	53	19	34	—	47	6
Habana	2	24	11	13	—	21	3
Matanzas	3	21	8	13	—	19	2
Sancti Spíritus	3	31	17	14	1	17	13
Villa Clara	3	22	14	8	—	17	5
Cienfuegos	1	24	13	11	10	13	1
Ciego de Avila	1	9	5	4	—	9	—
Camagüey	1	13	4	9	—	7	6
Holguín	1	31	8	23	—	27	4
Las Tunas	4	26	12	14	—	22	4
Granma	2	29	13	16	—	23	6
Santiago de Cuba	3	43	21	22	—	32	11
Guantánamo	2	26	11	15	8	16	2
Isla de la Juventud	1	6	4	2	1	5	—
Totals	31	368	165	203	20	284	64

Source: "Informe de adopción por provincia," provided by Centro de Documentación e Información Pedagógica Ministerio de Educación, Jan. 1997.

4 abandoned by both parents, 5 had mothers who were prisoners (and both parents of one were), 7 had mothers who were psychiatric patients or mentally retarded (and another had a father who was), 1 came from an inadequate home, and the parents of 1 had been deprived of *patria potestad* (González Ferrer and Miranda Sánchez 1993: Attachment 42). The director of this home was fêted in the press on Mother's Day 1997, citing "her" 53 children who had passed through the home in the Miramar suburb of Havana where the rich once lived (*Perera Robbio* 1997: 9).

The children in these homes are the responsibility of the state. If the role of the director involves making decisions about substitute families, adoption, and entry and exit from the homes, then it also involves creating and sustaining a homelike atmosphere. The director of the home in Bayamo, created in 1975 and one of three in Granma province, has two children of her own, but Sunday is the only day she spends in her own house. At the time of a January 1997 visit to the home, it counted 50 "graduates" and 9 girls and 12 boys in residence, ranging from 6 to 23 years old (1 studying in the university).[7] The newest were Lázaro and his sister, children with a religious background who had been there for 6 weeks. Speaking openly in front of the children, the director explained that she had no intention of changing their beliefs. Four auxiliaries provide round-the-clock care, though care extends beyond maintenance of the home and the children. Weddings, *quinces* (the coming-of-age parties for 15-year-old women), and birthdays are among the events celebrated in the *hogar;* photo albums and portraits proudly display the "family" history. The *hogar* in Matanzas, capital city of Matanzas province, was once named Flor de la Sierra after the revolutionary heroine Celia Sánchez, but now has no formal name. The director, who had managed the home for 5 years, explained in 1996 that they wanted it to be "more like a home," and other

Figure 10.1 Students from Estado de Cambodia elementary school eat lunch in their school's cafeteria. Prior to the present economic crisis, all Cuban students received breakfast, lunch, and snacks in the morning and afternoons. (Photo: R. A. Mickelson)

children's houses don't have names on them! Three children who lived in the home were in special schools, three in schools for conduct, and two in the university.[8]

There are three homes in Havana, and the apparently small number may be explained by alternative means for caring for children in situations of social disadvantage. An example is the Estado de Cambodia primary school in Miramar.[9] Created September 1, 1974 (the opening of the school year in Cuba), this school's facilities consist of two houses. Due to social problems, approximately 50 of its 334 students in 1995 boarded there. In addition to the director, the school had 18 teachers, 12 pedagogical auxiliaries, 10 cooks, 4 laundry workers, 9 cleaning staff, a gardener, and a barber.

The functioning of one home in Sancti Spíritus is described and analyzed in a study of the home's work since its founding in 1984–1985 (Pérez Valdivia 1995). During the week, the children rise at 6 and leave for school at 7:30 A.M., returning around 4:30 for bath, dinner, and study, TV, or games. Weekend activities include Saturday morning chores, such as cleaning the yard, caring for pets, getting milk and bread, as well as recreation, rest, and reading. The children participate in formal school activities. These range from the school-to-the-countryside program, where secondary students and teachers relocate to rural areas for periods of agricultural work, to the student mass organizations and summer work brigades. Besides birthdays, the home had celebrated two weddings and eight *quinces,* and had been the site of awarding UJC membership. Since its creation, 24 children had lived in the home. Fourteen of the 18 employees had worked in the home since its founding.

The study in Sancti Spíritus focused on the organization of the *hogar*'s work, using improvement in personal characteristics such as cleanliness and attitudes as the measure

Figure 10.2   Estado de Cambodia students sit in their school's courtyard and watch while their fellow students perform a dance for international guests. Their teachers supervise the performance and the audience. Performances of drama, music, dance, and songs are common features of Cuban elementary curricula. (Photo: R. A. Mickelson)

of success. Beginning with general and then monthly meetings, the collective of workers in the home discussed the education and academic performance of the children, as well as their conduct at home and school. Over time they expanded the collective to include the children and realized the "fundamental goal" of creating a system of affective relations "based in love, respect, and organization and efficiency in tasks" (Pérez Valdivia 1995).

Though the study in Sancti Spíritus reports successful behavior change, not all children adjust well to the homes. Children who enter *hogares* usually have conduct problems, noted one director as he distinguished the contrary case of Jorge, who attended a special sports secondary school and later graduated with a law degree (specializing in reeducation of minors). As in the story of "MJ," recounted in the Havana paper *Tribuna,* those who don't adjust are sent to a school for conduct (Lotti 1996: 4–5).

PATRIA POTESTAD

The good functioning of the *hogares* is vital, since some children may pass their childhood in them. Adoption is difficult in Cuba. According to the Family Code, minors may be adopted if *patria potestad* has been extinguished or both parents have been deprived of it. According to the 1995 Cuban Report on Children's Rights, there were 2,125 children in situations of social disadvantage in 1994, but few could be adopted (*Informe* 1995: 18). There are two ways to adopt. The first is indirect, through the *hogar* and its director; the second is direct petitioning to legal authorities. Between 1980 and 1993, there were 640 requests for adoption in Havana City, of which 240 were satisfied—and some 356 petitions then pending (González Ferrer and Miranda Sánchez 1993: 44 and n. 33). Nationwide, there were 859 petitions for adoption filed in the 1985–1988 period (823 resolved, with 631 petitions approved), compared to 230 in Havana (229 resolved, with 187 approved) (González Ferrer and Miranda Sánchez 1993: Attachment 41).

The obstacles to adoption are several. On the one hand, according to the FMC's Secretary of Education, cultural attitudes may tend to make some children "unadoptable." This would include 5-year-or-older males, very black children, or children with severe disabilities; "Families want children like themselves," she explained (Berges 1995). While children who are 7 and older have a voice in their adoption, the study of adoption cited above explains that "in practice there are very few cases of children of this age that are adopted" (González Ferrer and Miranda Sánchez 1993: 112). On the other hand, there are difficulties in depriving parents of *patria potestad*. It can be deprived if parents do not fulfill their duties to the child, if they induce the child to criminal behavior, if they abandon the country and therefore their children, if they display behavior that is corrupt, dangerous, and illegal and thus incompatible with the exercise of *patria potestad,* or if they have committed criminal acts against the child's person (Departamento de Asuntos Civiles 1987: 1). *Patria potestad* can also be suspended with reference to incapacity or absence of parents—authorized judicially, or deprived in criminal sentencing and divorce proceedings. From 1985 through 1988, there were 233 cases filed to deprive parents of *patria potestad* nationwide (and 65 in Havana City); of these, 219 were resolved and 181 petitions granted (compared to 58 resolved and 45 petitions granted in Havana). From 1989 to 1992, 354 cases were filed, 339 were resolved, and 263 petitions granted (González Ferrer and Miranda Sánchez 1993: Attachment 45).

These difficulties are no secret to the system of *hogares* and mixed day care centers, where children often wait years for the resolution of their legal status. Other acknowledged problems include the inadequate development of the substitute family system; often, the families are "preadoptive" and thus do not provide broader support for the system of homes. The system itself is responsible for resolving problems and improving the implementation of state policies that must now respond to the complex effects of the Special Period on the public and private lives of families. The Commissions of Prevention and Social Welfare were asked in 1992 to coordinate better and more quickly the collective work with children in situations of social disadvantage and to facilitate decision making about *patria potestad* (Comisión Nacional 1992). The mass and social organizations are expected to strengthen their support. The Ministry of Education, a crucial actor in the system, is asked to put its teachers, administrators, and others working in the school on the lookout for orphans, abandoned children, or those in a state of neglect.

Neglect can take many forms, including the abandoning of children in the process of illegal immigration. Between 1991 and July 1994, 13,147 rafters (*balseros*) landed in the United States and some 36,200 were thwarted by Cuban authorities; during the *balsero* crisis of August 13–September 13, 1994, some 36,000 arrived in the United States (Rodríguez Chávez 1994: 9–10). In contrast to the Peter Pan exodus in which parents sent their children away, there is evidence that as in earlier periods, some who flee Cuba and the Special Period leave their children behind.[10]

CONCLUSION

The Cuban state cannot resolve all of the problems of families in the Special Period. Material conditions that reflect the economic difficulties of the 1990s affect family stability and children's lives. Resources are not available, for example, to resolve problems of housing (though some 237,000 new housing units were created from 1992 to 1997), to lift household consumption to—or above—the levels of the 1980s, or to provide dollars to the half of the population that has no easy access to them. State policies have promoted specific innovations, however, including a successful campaign to increase breast-feeding; and in the 1990s there has been more emphasis on fathers' obligation to participate in housework, parenting, and childbirth, and the issues of domestic violence are now discussed publicly. The approach to families and their functioning centers on the nuclear family ideal, yet affective, educational, and material factors are included in judging real family practices. In this context, the state's caution in replacing parents with its own authority demonstrates the complexity of restructuring childhood and families, not neglect.

The emphasis on children's education and well-being in Cuban policy reflects a vision of social justice that the state refuses to relinquish. Capitalism is still roundly rejected by Cuban leadership, though they have yet to formulate a formal alternative to the neoliberal model or the socialism of their past. In pursuing recovery through full engagement with the global economy, market relations and a new commercial logic have, in some places and ways, supplanted the mechanisms and dynamics of socialist planning. New actors have surfaced—foreign investors, tourists, the self-employed, workers in the dollarized parts of the economy. The values carried by capitalism's globalized cultural mechanisms also find a place within the painful process of reform in Cuba. The defense of social justice is central to Cuba's adamant refusal to adopt neoliberal solutions for its problems.

The Cuban system of care for children without family protection is a valued, but scarcely visible, part of the educational institutions created by the revolution. Its achievements reflect a commitment to children and "clean streets" that differs sharply from the neoliberal policies that are carving away the infrastructure of childhood elsewhere in Latin America, sacrificing their welfare to the end of healthy private sector profits and foreclosing discussion of parents' needs and children's futures. Where Cuban reforms have ambiguous consequences, as in the relation of tourism to the easy-to-see changes in the Cuban streets, the state's intentions and its actions are crucial. Economic recuperation will help resolve this and other problems; the material conditions of family life matter greatly. Yet in allowing that families—whether nuclear or extended—must perform their roles, the implementation of state policies demonstrates the complicated interplay of inherited cultural practices, gender relations, and social values. The state's ability to control public and private behavior is limited, while its willingness to respect families and to acknowledge their problems may be the most useful predictor of the future of both children and the streets.

NOTES

1. I would like to thank Félix Urquhart Rojas and the Ministry of Education's Center for Documentation and Pedagogical Information for providing information for the preparation of this chapter.
2. Translations from Spanish sources here and below are mine.
3. In 1994, the marriage rate was 10.7/1,000 and the divorce rate was 5.2/1,000.
4. In 1985 there were 83.6 abortions for each 100 births, and 59.4 in 1996. In 1997, the rate was 0.5–0.6 per live birth (*Granma* 1998: 1).
5. In 1984, the stipends were 10 pesos for children in *círculos* and primary education, 15 for basic secondary and youth movement, and 15 for those in higher secondary studies. During a visit to Los Duendecitos CIM in Matanzas in 1996, the author found that the stipend was still 10 pesos.

6. Information provided by Centro de Documentación e Información Pedagógica Ministerio de Educacián, Jan. 1997.
7. Interview, Bayamo, *Granma,* 22 Jan. 1997. According to the municipal director of education in Manzanillo, 22 Jan. 1997, 7 children live in the home in Guisa, while the home in Manzanillo, created in 1979, cared for some 13 children at the start of 1997.
8. Visit by author, 31 Jan. 1996.
9. Visit by author, 29 Jan. 1994; and interview with director by author, 16 Feb. 1995.
10. In a study of failed illegal immigration during the first 2 weeks in August 1993, there were 413 subjects (40 cases); in only five cases were minors present (5.3 percent of the sample), yet more than half of the subjects had conjugal links, while 59.7 percent of those interviewed said they had children (and 67 percent had custody of them) (Martínez 1996: 60-61).

REFERENCES

Aguilar, Carolina, Perla Popowski, and Mercedes Verdeses. 1996. "Mujer, período especial y vida cotidiana." *Temas* 5: 11-17.

Alvarez Suárez Mavis. 1997. "Familia e inserción social." *Revista de Sociología* (Universitat Autònoma de Barcelona) 52: 101-13.

Berges, Célia 1995. Interview with author at National Headquarters, Federación de Mujeres Cubanas, Havana, 21 Feb.

Catasús Cervera, Sonia I. 1997. "Género patrones reproductivos y jefatura de nucleo familiar por color de la piel en cuba." Paper presented at Latin American Studies Association, Guadalajara, Mexico, 14-17 Apr.

Comisión Económica Para América Latina y el Caribe (CEPAL). 1997. *La economía cubana: reformas estructurales y desempeño el los noventa.* Mexico City: CEPAL and Fondo de Cultura Económica.

Comisión Nacional de Prevención y Atención Social. 1992. "Indicaciones para la tramitación, con celeridad y profundidad, de los casos de menores en situación de desventaja social—cuando procede la privación suspensión de la patria potestad." Photocopy.

Consejo de Estado. 1984. "Decreto-ley numero 76 de la adopción los hogares de menores y las familias sustitutas." 20 Jan. Photocopy.

Cuba. 1992. *Constitución de la República de Cuba.* Havana: Editora Política.

Departamento de Asuntos Civiles, Administrativos y Laborales, Fiscalía General de la República, 1987. "Orientación Metodólogica Civil No. 1, Fiscalía General República." 1 Dec. Photocopy.

González Ferrer, Yamila, and Mabel Miranda Sánchez 1993. "La Adopción y la protección de la niñez en Cuba." Thesis, Law School, Dept. of Family and Civil Law, University of Havana.

Granma. 1998. "El Impacto del bloqueo en la salud pública cubana es un acto criminal." 16 Jan., 1.

Informe de la Rrepública de Cuba al comité de los derechos del niño por conducto del Secretario General de las Naciones Unidas en relación con las medidas adoptadas para dar efecto a los derechos reconcidos en la convención sobre los derechos del niño. 1995. Havana, Aug.

Juventud Rebelde. 1997. "Ningún niño está abandonado." 11 May, 9.

Lotti, Alina M. 1996. "'A las alcantarillas no vuelvo,' (I)." *Tribuna,* 27 Oct., 4-5.

Martínez Milagros. 1996. *Los Balseros cubanos.* Havana: Editorial de Ciencias Sociales.

Ministerio de Educación 1984. "Resolución ministerial no. 48/84, organización e ingreso a los hogares de menores y los círculos infantiles mixtos, selección y atención a las familias sustitutas." 13 Feb. Photocopy.

———. 1997. "Informe de adopción por provincia." Centro de Documentación Pedagógica. Jan. Author.

Ojita, Mirta. 1998. "Cubans Face Past as Stranded Youths in U.S." *New York Times,* 12 Jan., A1, A14.

Ortega, Dr. Onelio. 1995. Interview with author at Miramar, Havana, 23 Feb.

Perera Robbio, Alina. 1997. "Madre de cinquenta y tres hijos." *Juventude Rebelde.,* 11 May, 9.

Pérez Valdivia, Gloria. 1995. "Experiencias obtenidas en el trabajo con los niño sin amparo filial." Pedagogía '95: Encuentro por la Unidad de los Educadores Latinoamericanos, Havana, 6-10 Feb.

Reed, Gail. 1994. "Operation 'Peter Pan'—Flight of Fear." *Cuba Update* 15: 1-2, 7-8.

Rodríguez Chávez, Ernesto. 1994. "La Crisis migratoria Estados Unidos-Cuba en el verano 1994." *Cuadernos de Nuestra América* 22: 4-25.

Rosenthal, Marguerite G. 1992. "The Problems of Single Motherhood in Cuba." Pp. 161-75 in *Cuba in Transition: Crisis and Transformation,* edited by Sandor Halebsky and John M. Kirk. Boulder: Westview Press.

Smith, Lois M., and Alfred Padula. 1996. *Sex and Revolution: Women in Socialist Cuba.* New York: Oxford University Press.

11

From Church Basement to Mainstream Classroom: The Evolution of A Child's Place in Charlotte, North Carolina

Maria Grace Yon and Roslyn Arlin Mickelson

A Child's Place is a program for homeless students and their families in Charlotte, North Carolina. Charlotte is a beautiful, clean, prosperous midsize city that is home to the largest bank in the United States. Many organizations, corporations, and individuals generously share their material resources with the destitute poor through their support of A Child's Place. For example, the Sisters of Charity have awarded A Child's Place $118,000 during a 3-year period; A Child's Place received a Chevrolet 15-passenger van as a gift; the Executive Women's Golf Association hosted a golf tournament that raised $14,000 for the program; and the Carolina Panthers (a professional football team) held a bowling and pizza party with the homeless children who attend A Child's Place. Moreover, in 1997, the program's annual fund campaign exceeded its goal.

Among U.S. programs for homeless students, A Child's Place (ACP) is a "jewel box," a beautifully and carefully crafted effort that truly helps children and families that pass through its doors; yet, ultimately it cannot resolve the educational crises these children face and it cannot address the structural foundations of their homelessness (Dewees and Klees 1995: 93; Mickelson and Yon 1995). The story of ACP is a useful illustration of two important points. First, when resources are available, interagency collaborations with public school systems can make powerfully positive interventions in homeless students' lives. Second, despite even the best of programs, the structural conditions that create homelessness and its related human misery remain untouched by such programs.

The purpose of this chapter is to describe the evolution of A Child's Place into an exemplary program for homeless children and their families. Although its origins and early period were difficult, ACP underwent many painful organizational changes and evolved into a highly regarded program. We will describe the three major phases of the program's history. The story of the evolution of ACP is useful for understanding how educators and social services providers—without initial support from the institutions legally responsible for them—came to grips with the problem of increased numbers of homeless children who were not receiving appropriate education. In the late 1980s, although the McKinney Act was in place, no school officials complied with it until pressure from elite citizens and activist social workers forced the issue onto the public agenda.

A CHILD'S PLACE: A TRANSITIONAL PROGRAM FOR HOMELESS CHILDREN

A Child's Place is an interagency collaboration between the Charlotte-Mecklenburg School System (CMS) and a nonprofit social service agency that serves the visible portion of the community's homeless student population, students at risk of becoming homeless, and their families. The goals of the preschool through 6th-grade program are twofold: (a) to locate homeless children and assist them in receiving an appropriate education; and (b) to advocate for the families of these children as they progress toward economic, social, and emotional stability. ACP attempts to meet these goals through the facilitation of homeless students' enrollment in school and the coordination of a variety of social services for them and their families. ACP also seeks to educate the larger metropolitan Charlotte community regarding homelessness and to provide consultations for other school systems.

At present, four component programs comprise A Child's Place. Transient homeless students (those who live in shelters) are mainstreamed at one of two designated schools, Irwin Avenue Open and Nations Ford elementary schools. This program is known as Project MOST (Mainstream Opportunities for Students in Transition). The Charlotte-Mecklenburg School System allocates two extra teachers to Project MOST at Irwin Avenue and one extra teacher at Nations Ford; an extra teaching assistant, a social worker, and an intake assistant are also allocated at both schools. Project MOST employs one volunteer coordinator and one Housing and Urban Development (HUD) worker. While ACP students are placed in regular classrooms upon enrollment, they still receive all the services that have traditionally been a part of ACP—clothing, medical and dental services, school and hygiene supplies, after-school programs, and lunch buddies who

Figure 11.1 The executive director of Charlotte's ACP, Debbie McKone, chats with a homeless student about the child's drawings. (Photo: A Child's Place)

mentor individual children. A family advocate works with the children's parents to assist their search for job and housing stability as well as to help with other social services coordination they usually require.

ACP's second component, Firm Foundations, is an early intervention and prevention program for children whose families are either at risk of becoming homeless or are from stable homeless families; that is, families living in a motel room or doubled up with relatives. Firm Foundations is active in six inner-city CMS elementary schools. Children in these schools are also mainstreamed into classrooms with housed peers. Homeless adolescents typically attend either their original middle and high schools or the ones closest to their current residence. Firm Foundations families receive the services obtained by Project MOST families: assistance in finding permanent housing, clothing, furniture, domestic violence services, and other interventions. In 1997, 255 students and their 146 siblings from 168 families received services from Firm Foundations at six inner-city elementary schools located near critical masses of homeless families. The Firm Foundations Program employs three social workers and is the community's only preventive case management service for families at risk of becoming homeless. The social workers provide case management services to homeless and at-risk families in their home school and provide support services to children and families.

The program's third component is Bright Beginnings, the preschool program serving homeless and at-risk 4-year-olds whose reading readiness is low. Bright Beginnings sites are Double Oaks Preschool Center and First Ward Elementary School. Both schools are surrounded by public housing developments. A fourth component is on the drawing board. In 1998, ACP experienced a sudden influx of identified middle-school homeless students. ACP began providing one-on-one services to them while a formal plan of service is being developed during the current academic year.

As the needs of homeless students and their families have grown, the ACP staff has grown too. The original staff was made up of a part-time volunteer coordinator and a board of directors; it now consists of an executive director, a development director, a program director, five family advocates, one volunteer coordinator, one volunteer assistant, two student liaisons, one assessment specialist, a business manager, and a secretary. The volunteer department handles all volunteers (mentors, tutors, and so forth), all in-kind resources (clothing, medical, dental, and food donations), and all furniture and other deliveries. ACP retains its board of directors who primarily engage in fund-raising activities. ACP administrators manage an annual budget of approximately $600,000. Teachers, teacher aids, and school administrators are salaried employees of the Charlotte-Mecklenburg School System.

DATA AND METHODS

We consider this chapter to be a historical organizational case study. The data we present are drawn from the case study of ACP we conducted over a period of several years (1990–1998). Our involvement with ACP began when we were members of the ACP Board of Directors and the board's research committee. Our data consist of minutes from board meetings, field observations, and interviews of key participants. We recorded field observations during all ACP board meetings, in several board retreats, and in the hallways and offices of the schools. We conducted classroom observations and took extensive field notes. The first author's undergraduate education students who were classroom volunteers kept journals during their in-service at ACP. We conducted in-depth, semistructured interviews with the teachers, teachers' assistants, principals, school district personnel, parents, volunteers, executive director, board members, and ACP's family advocate. Selected individuals involved in ACP were asked to comment upon our initial analyses and interpretations of findings. Their commentaries were incorporated into our final work.

A CHILD'S PLACE IN CONTEXT

In order to better understand ACP's development, it is important to picture the social and historical landscape of the city it services. Charlotte, North Carolina, is a rapidly growing southern city with a greater metropolitan area population of more than 1.3 million people. Approximately 32 percent of the population is African American, 65 percent is white, and the remaining 3 percent is Asian and Latino. Since the passage of NAFTA, the Latino population has grown rapidly. Young families have immigrated to the area to take advantage of the expanding low-wage opportunities in construction and poultry processing.

Charlotte is noted for its history of positive race relations. The city voluntarily desegregated its public accommodations in 1968. In 1971, the U.S. Supreme Court upheld Judge James B. McMillan's ruling in *Swann v. Mecklenburg* and the school system commenced the use of busing to racially balance its public schools.[1] For the next 22 years, the district was a model of school desegregation. In 1993, the use of busing as the primary tool for desegregation was replaced with a system of magnet schools. Currently, students may choose to attend a magnet or they can go to an assigned school. Today, many schools are desegregated by a combination of voluntary busing to magnet schools and mandatory busing of black children into predominately white suburban schools. In the spring of 1999, the original *Swann* case returned to federal court. A group of white parents seeking to return to neighborhood schools sued the school system in order to end court mandated racial desegregation. A return to neighborhood school assignments would all but guarantee that a majority of students would attend racially segregated schools (Mickelson 1998).

The larger metropolitan area is characterized by an active religious community, a spirit of volunteerism, and a great deal of interfaith cooperation (Mickelson and Ray 1994). The Charlotte region is relatively prosperous with a moderate cost of living, a mild climate, and a low unemployment rate. The largest bank in the United States is headquartered in Charlotte. The jobs generated by this sector tend to be in finance, high technology, and skilled services. They typically require levels of education beyond high school diplomas, and there is a shortage of workers in these fast-growth industries.

The creation of so many high-skill jobs has lured many families to the area. This growth resulted in a construction boom that, in turn, attracted many low-skilled workers to the area. Twenty-three percent of the homeless population in the area arrived as a result of relocation, usually to find work. But the unskilled jobs for which most homeless people are qualified pay low wages and are inadequate for acquiring decent housing. As is true across the United States, Charlotte has a severe shortage of affordable housing for low-income families. Moreover, the inadequacy of the area's public transportation system exacerbates the difficulties poor people face as they attempt to gain employment. Following the nationwide trend, 28 percent of homeless families in Charlotte are homeless due to an economic crisis. Twenty-three percent of homeless heads of households blame violence, often associated with either alcohol or drug abuse. Ninety percent of the area's homeless people are single mothers. With little education and few work skills, they cannot provide for their families.

CHARLOTTE'S SAFETY NET FOR HOMELESS FAMILIES

Charlotte has numerous public and private social service agencies that individually and collaboratively attempt to serve the complex needs of the homeless. Public social services available include food stamps, Medicaid, some public housing, mental health services, therapeutic adult day care, screenings for the developmentally delayed, and an array of health services through the city's health department.

Private local services and programs in Charlotte help public agencies meet the crisis needs of the homeless. Emergency housing is provided for hundreds of people each night in several shelters. Food banks and numerous churches provide food for the homeless population. Several church-based programs provide clothing, furniture, and referrals. Day care for younger homeless children is provided at one homeless shelter.

To ensure that shelter residents are aware of and referred to appropriate agencies, private social service organizations have a workable brokering and referral system that operates well within the confines of its limited funding sources. This network of interagency collaboration in the social service sector, then, provides a solid foundation upon which ACP's founders built a collaborative effort to meet the educational needs of homeless children.

PHASE I: THE CHURCH BASEMENT SCHOOL

A Child's Place opened in the fall of 1989 largely through the persistent efforts of three social workers (the founding mothers) who noted that increasing numbers of homeless families with school-age children were arriving in Charlotte in need of services. During the 1987–1988 school year, they observed that rather than attend school, most children remained in the homeless shelters or on the streets during the day. The founding mothers approached school officials with their observations and requested that educational provisions be made for homeless children. Rather than confronting the problem immediately and directly, the school officials requested systematic data to support the claims that (a) there were notable numbers of homeless children in Charlotte who were not attending school and (b) special provisions were needed for them.

Almost a year passed before any action was taken. The catalyst was the response of a powerful city business leader to a television documentary about a successful school for homeless children in another state. As a board member of the city's shelter for homeless men, his interest in homelessness was already piqued. His call to the school superintendent inquiring about the status of local efforts to educate homeless students in the Charlotte-Mecklenburg School District proved to be the impetus CMS needed. Embarrassingly, the superintendent had nothing to report. Soon thereafter, the founding mothers received CMS's cooperation and resources. At about the same time that CMS began to address the educational needs of homeless students, several corporate leaders and an anonymous benefactor donated $75,000, providing start-up funds for the program that would become ACP.

The question remained as to how the educational needs of homeless students could be best met. In its first phase, ACP emerged as a segregated transitional classroom, a model quite different from current educational thinking about mainstreaming children with special needs.[2] The transitional classroom was conceived as a social and educational haven where homeless students could be stabilized until they were ready to move into regular classrooms. The transitional classroom model was chosen for two reasons. First, without a blueprint or a successful model, the social workers drew from their own professional expertise to create A Child's Place. The founding mothers were aware of the extraordinary needs of homeless children for clothing, hygiene supplies, medical attention, nurturance, and attention that would be difficult to meet in a regular classroom setting. Moreover, they realized that in order to educate homeless children, the needs of the entire family must be met as well. Working from a social work paradigm, they reasoned that the needs of homeless children were so great that a special transitional classroom, rather than attendance in regular classrooms, would be the most effective way to deal with the needs of this special population of students. Second, the school system's failure to acknowledge the existence of homeless children left an educational vacuum into which the social workers willingly stepped. School officials initially proclaimed, "We educate those who come to our doors," indicating that they were not in the business of searching out students to place in schools. Even, after the powerful business leader shamed school officials into acknowledging the presence of homeless students, the system's initial response was tepid. By then, social workers—not educators—had taken the leadership role in developing ACP.

The larger community, on the other hand, responded enthusiastically. A downtown Presbyterian church provided space for the transitional classroom. The church seemed appropriate due to its central location and access to shelters, low-budget hotels, and food kitchens. Already known for its community outreach programs, the church provided space for two classrooms, offices, storage, and bathrooms. Students also had access to the playground that was shared with the church's preschool program. The education of homeless children became a pet project of many individuals, businesses, and organizations who donated money, resources, and many hours of volunteer time.

A year after ACP first opened its doors, the Charlotte-Mecklenburg schools met the spirit and letter of the McKinney Act; in 1989 ACP became an official program of the school district. A principal from a nearby school served as the program's administrator. Besides the principal, the school system provided a teacher, a teacher assistant, furniture, school materials and supplies, meals, and transportation on school buses from the shelters and motels. ACP paid the salary of the part-time social worker and the volunteer coordinator.

From the very beginning of ACP's operation, the multiple needs of homeless students made it clear that the program could not exist in isolation. The resources of the school system, social service agencies, grants, and the generous support of local sponsors and contributors were needed for ACP to exist. But collaboration was sometimes difficult. Turf issues arose among the key staff (social workers, educators, board of directors) over differences in rules, regulations, and policies. Each understood the problem of educating homeless children from a different perspective. Furthermore, it was clear to no one which responsibilities belonged to the school system and which ones to the board. In the first year, ACP's board found it difficult to communicate with school officials and to trust that they were concerned with the progress of this program. There was a lack of vision as to what a community and school partnership entailed.

By its second year of operation, it became clear that the program needed a full-time executive director to organize the many tasks necessary to operate ACP. It was also obvious that, with a growing enrollment, a full-time social worker was needed. These two positions, funded with money raised by the board of ACP, were filled by the beginning of the third year.

Meanwhile, in the classroom, the teacher, the assistant, and the volunteers were creating a classroom for approximately 20 homeless students. Dealing with an unfamiliar student population (teacher education programs rarely address the specific needs of homeless children), ACP's educators extrapolated from their professional expertise and intuition to develop strategies for their new students. Their main purpose was to provide the children with a stable environment amidst the chaos that they were experiencing. It was of primary importance that students were fed and clothed and that they felt safe. After this, education could continue.

The newly hired executive director arrived at the beginning of the third year in the midst of confusion and controversy about the purpose and direction of ACP. Her first task was to sort out the issues among the many constituents. She realized the importance of developing a formally stated agreement with the school district in order to clarify its responsibilities. The agreement also helped to define the working relationship of all those involved. It is striking that these tasks were not engaged until the third year of ACP's operation.

In 1992, ACP initiated Firm Foundations. Several elementary schools had large populations of poor and homeless children whose families lived either in welfare motels or with relatives. They required an array of services not provided by the school. ACP's family advocate began to visit these schools and established a resource room in each where children could obtain clothing and school supplies, and families could obtain referrals and other social services.

PHASE II: A SCHOOL WITHIN A SCHOOL

ACP remained at the downtown church for 3 years before moving to Irwin Avenue Elementary School in 1992, a public school 2 miles away. Many people involved in ACP's operation felt that homeless children should not be segregated from other children. Furthermore, they argued that the program would be more efficient with the principal and other resources on-site. Moving to Irwin Avenue Elementary School seemed natural because ACP had already become administratively attached to it. Irwin seemed a good choice because of its racially, ethnically, and economically diverse student population as well as its proximity to shelters and bus routes.

In August 1992, ACP moved from its church basement to Irwin Elementary School. ACP teachers and students occupied a classroom in the school, and the program's office was located in a nearby trailer. The school-within-a-school concept proved to be a difficult time for ACP for many reasons. The needs of ACP continued to have a lower priority for the principal and the school system than other programs. Numerous requests for a second teacher were made but were not fulfilled. It was becoming more and more difficult for one teacher and one teacher assistant to meets the needs of 30 to 35 homeless children from kindergarten through 6th grade.

Finally, after 3 years of requests, in 1994 a position for a second teacher was granted to ACP. After a careful interview with prospective teachers, the ACP staff recommended to the principal a teacher who seemed perfect for the position. Inexplicably, a different candidate eventually filled the second teacher position. That individual was poorly suited for the position and was encouraged to leave the school after about 7 months of ineffective performance.

Although a second teacher had been assigned to ACP, the realities of the classroom became overwhelming as the number of students occasionally increased to 60. There were more intermediate grade (4–6) level students than ever before. The older students seemed to be more affected by homelessness than the younger ones. They brought more behavioral and emotional problems to the classroom, causing chaos and instability on a daily basis. Teachers, not having been trained to deal with the serious misbehaviors, found the work exhausting.

The larger numbers of students also made planning instruction more difficult. Not only were students spread from grades 1 through 6, but there were many achievement levels within those grades. Teachers found it impossible to plan for the academic needs of all the students in every subject level. Furthermore, teachers never knew which students would be attending the following day or how many new ones would arrive. The continual flux of homeless children in and out of ACP made it difficult for teachers to prepare for classroom volunteers in advance. A structured curriculum was difficult to implement for the teacher and the volunteers alike. Because students were assessed only informally as they enrolled, it was unclear whether their academic needs were being met.

In contrast to the school in the church basement, where children were protected from ridicule, at Irwin Avenue School, ACP students were occasionally ostracized. Segregated from other students in their school within a school, they were seen as unusual by some of the other children. Some ACP students interacted only with other ACP students on the playground and in the lunchroom. Furthermore, to some of the ACP students, the school-within-a-school did not seem to be "real school."[3]

The space shortage from increasing enrollment ultimately lead to the mainstreaming of more and more older students into other classrooms at Irwin Avenue School. The ACP staff noted that the older students seemed better adjusted in a regular classroom situation. Their self-esteem and behavior seemed to improve when they were not separated from their age mates. Spreading them out among the classrooms and placing homeless students with teachers who had better classroom management and instructional skills also helped. Importantly, they were not all together in one classroom, "feeding" off each other and bringing shelter problems into the classroom.

PHASE III: THE MAINSTREAMED SCHOOL

In the fall of 1997, A Child's Place began the third stage of its development. The school-within-a-school model was discontinued and replaced with a program that mainstreamed all students in classrooms at their appropriate grade levels. A second school, Nations Ford, joined Irwin as a key site for Project MOST, and Firm Foundations expanded to six schools. The decision to mainstream all homeless students was made for several reasons: (a) the increasing population of students had outgrown the physical space of the school within a school; (b) education experts recommend the mainstreaming of all special needs students; (c) students, especially the older ones, seem to cope better in a regular classroom than in a segregated one; (d) it was becoming increasingly difficult to recruit and retain teachers, teaching assistants, and volunteers in the high-burn-out situation posed by extremely challenging homeless students; (e) it was becoming more difficult to meet the academic needs of the growing number of children with diverse educational needs at many grade levels; and (f) separating homeless students from others violates the McKinney Act.

In 1998 ACP, in partnership with the Charlotte-Mecklenburg Schools, added a new component, Bright Beginnings, for homeless and at-risk preschoolers. It is too early to assess the degree to which Phase III has been successful. Continuing research will enable us to evaluate the social and educational outcomes of ACP's latest transformation.

A CHILD'S PLACE: SUCCESS AMONG THE STRIFE

Throughout the three major phases of its evolution, several aspects of ACP have remained constant. The larger community provided unwavering support. In the early months after

ACP's conception, one board member exclaimed, "It's snowing in our hats," referring to the generous contributions. Today, material and symbolic support continues to flow. ACP remains a favorite project of the middle-class public and of Charlotte's corporate donors. A volunteer spirit also persists. Individuals and organizations contribute many hours serving as lunch buddies, contributing snacks, clothing, school supplies, and gifts. Physicians, dentists, and psychologists donate their services to the children.

While it is both disheartening and ironic to associate the continued existence of a program for homeless children with success, we define A Child's Place as one. Enrollment has increased for two reasons. First, homelessness in the United States has increased because of welfare reform, economic restructuring, and the absence of affordable low-income housing. Second, the program is now a well-established agency among the region's social service resources for homeless people. Agencies and shelters immediately refer homeless children to ACP. Parents report that their children are enrolled in the school the morning after they arrive at shelters (Yon and Sebastien-Kadie 1994). Also, across CMS, teachers and school administrators have learned to recognize the signs of homelessness and make appropriate referrals. In its first year, ACP served 68 children from 43 families (Family Advocate's Report 1989). Each year has brought a steady increase in enrollment. In the 1997–1998 school year, 319 families received services. This number included 497 ACP students and 284 of their siblings. At the time of discharge from ACP, 88 percent of the families secured stable housing; 60 percent of families identified as potentially homeless through Firm Foundations outreach programs were helped to avoid losing their homes; employment or job training among ACP parents (85 percent of whom are single parents) doubled to 66 percent; and children received 3,600 hours of After School Enrichment (Family Advocate's Report 1998).

In an earlier study of Phase I ACP students (Mickelson and Yon 1995), we reported that children appeared to be motivated to attend school and participate in the classroom. Findings suggest that students were motivated because their basic needs for affection, food, shelter, and safety were better met at ACP. Observations indicated that students received the attention and love that they craved from the teachers and volunteers. Students were made to feel safe in the school environment. They did not go hungry while they were in school and received many other material necessities, such as school and hygiene supplies and clothing. More recent research also indicates mainstreamed homeless students are no less motivated. Their basic needs continue to be met and the classroom remains a point of stability in the children's lives. However, systematic research is needed to confirm this finding and to assess children's academic progress.

The school system now accepts more fully its responsibility to educate the homeless children that come through its doors. ACP and the school system have formed a true partnership. In addition to greater support at the school level, the CMS assistant superintendent for student services is a member of the ACP board of directors.

REMAINING PROBLEMS

While ACP has enjoyed success, it still suffers from its relatively low priority in comparison to other programs, projects, and issues that receive greater attention in a large school system. School system officials tend to respond to demands from powerful constituents, sophisticated and articulate middle-class parents, and business leaders. Without powerful parent-advocates, homeless students are at the mercy of philanthropists and activists. This is clear when we examine ACP's history.

Teachers need the help and support of parents when working with homeless children. Homeless parents can be difficult to work with for teachers who have had no training or little experience at working with the homeless population. Most homeless parents are single. Many have an alcohol or drug dependency problem that causes them to be seriously dysfunctional. Some have poor parenting skills. Few attend parent-teacher conferences. The burden of meeting the educational needs of the children then, is left almost entirely to the ACP staff and teachers.

Because ACP serves only 4-year-old preschoolers through 8th-grade students, the population of homeless students in Charlotte-Mecklenburg beyond the 8th grade has not been fully assessed and does not receive full services. Unless they are the older siblings of ACP students, no provisions are being made at the present time for those students.

CONCLUSIONS

ACP, in its ninth year of operation, continues to serve Charlotte's homeless students and their families. Today, the program is institutionalized as an organizational unit of the Charlotte-Mecklenburg schools. The more ACP integrated into the CMS, the better the program became; the clearer its mission, the more directly it served the children, and the less stress teachers and administrators experienced. ACP staff thoroughly and thoughtfully have developed a model program that comprehensively addresses the multiple needs of homeless students and their families. The program also is successful because it has a very powerful set of active allies among middle-class volunteers, child advocates, and generous corporate donors.

We draw several conclusions from our case study. ACP's original model of a separate transitional classroom with extensive interagency collaborative efforts was successful for initially meeting many of the needs of homeless students and their families. That first model gave the program the flexibility to reach beyond the confines of school system procedures to obtain the resources necessary for meeting the needs of homeless children and families, thus enabling the children to reintegrate into a learning environment. As this case study shows, however, the separate transitional classroom, whether in the church basement or as a school within a school, eventually could not meet the educational and social needs of homeless students.

This case study demonstrates the value of incorporating interagency collaborative services into all schools. The needs of the many other poverty-stricken students teetering on the abyss of homelessness also can be met by programs like Firm Foundations. It is important to conceptualize homelessness at the far end of the poverty continuum, not merely as a separate phenomenon. By extending Firm Foundations into more schools, the educational crisis that typically follows homelessness can be averted by averting homelessness itself. Once a family becomes homeless, Firm Foundation's safety net can mitigate some of the devastating effects on the children.

Fortunately for homeless students in the Charlotte-Mecklenburg area, a few key people cared enough to demand appropriate education and services for them. Interestingly, none of the program's founders invoked the Stewart B. McKinney Homeless Assistance Act when ACP opened in 1989. Charlotte-Mecklenburg schools, like most other districts in the nation, had not yet responded to the law although it was already 2 years old (U.S. Department of Education 1990; Yon 1995). The history of ACP suggests that certain education legislation can be ignored in the absence of powerful parental advocates. One has only to compare the social and political dynamics involving the Education for All Handicapped Children Act (P.L. 94–142) to those of the McKinney Act to see this.[4]

None of those involved in the creation of ACP anticipated the myriad problems surrounding the provision of educational and social services for homeless children. The first principal of ACP described the early days of the program as "building a plane while flying it." After 9 years, most of the problems are clear. Many of the solutions are not. Another metaphor captures the current experience of teachers and staff: every day involves "extinguishing multiple brush fires." Today, the school system provides the equipment and support for those on the fire lines.

In the final analysis, it is sobering to consider what a period of economic austerity would mean for ACP. If Charlotte's economy were not booming or if the nation's largest bank were not headquartered there, would the generosity that ACP enjoys continue? What will happen to homeless children in the city when the business cycle takes a downturn? Although ACP is successful in meeting many of the needs of homeless children, it remains no more than a Band-Aid on the problems of homelessness itself. ACP does nothing to stem the underlying causes of homelessness. With the absence of a systematic, long-range, national domestic policy to address the causes of poverty, the reduction of programs for affordable housing, and the demise of the historic federal welfare program, Aid to Families with Dependent Children (AFDC), the problem of homelessness is likely to continue into the future, and so will the need for programs like ACP.

NOTES

1. Following the guidelines established by the court in the *Swann* case, an elementary school is considered Racially Identifiable Black (RIB) if the number of its black students exceeds the district's overall black population by more than 15 percent, while secondary schools are considered RIB if their black student population exceeds 50 percent of the students at any given school. Since CMS adopted its magnet plan for desegregation, the number of RIB schools has increased (Mickelson 1998).
2. The school was segregated in two ways. Not only was it geographically separate from other public educational institutions in the city but also the student body was disproportionately black. ACP's demographics reflect those of the community's poor.
3. Mary Metz (1990) describes the skepticism of many parents and educators who doubt that many innovative programs constitute "real school." She argues that for many people, schools, classrooms, and teachers must conform to traditional organizational forms to be considered genuine, or "real."
4. P.L. 94–142 is the Education for All Handicapped Children Act that mandates appropriate, free education in the least restrictive manner possible for special-needs children. It has resulted in the mainstreaming of many special-needs students into regular classrooms. Parents of handicapped children were instrumental in lobbying for its passage and are relentless advocates for the law's implementation.

REFERENCES

Dewees, Anthony, and Steven J. Klees. 1995. "Social Movements and the Transformation of National Policy: Street and Working Children in Brazil." *Comparative Education Review* 39: 76–110.

Family Advocate's Report. 1989. "A Child's Place: Transitional School for Homeless Children." Charlotte, N.C.: Author.

———. 1998. "A Child's Place: Transitional School for Homeless Children." Charlotte, N.C.: Author.

Metz, Mary. 1990. "Real School: A Universal Drama Mid Disparate Experiences." Pp. 75–92 in *Education Politics for the New Century,* edited by D. E. Mitchell and M. Goertz. London: Falmer Press.

Mickelson, Roslyn Arlin. 1998. "Racially Identifiable African-American Schools, Tracking, and Within-School Segregation in the Charlotte-Mecklenburg School District." Expert Report to the

U.S. District Court for the Western District of North Carolina in the case of *Capacchione v. Charlotte-Mecklenburg Schools et al.,* 1 Dec.

Mickelson, Roslyn Arlin, and Carol A. Ray. 1994. "Fear of Falling from Grace: The Middle Class, Downward Mobility, and School Desegregation." *Research in Sociology of Education and Socialization* 10: 207-38.

Mickelson, Roslyn Arlin, and Maria G. Yon. 1995. "The Motivation of Homeless Children." *International Journal of Social Education* 2: 16-34.

P.L. 94-142, Education for All Handicapped Children Act. 1975. Codified at 20 USC. 1401-1420 (1975, 29 Nov.).

P.L. 100-77, Stewart B. McKinney Homeless Assistance Act. 1987. Codified at 42 USC. 11301-11472 (1987, 22 July).

U.S. Department of Education. 1990. *Report to Congress on Final Reports Submitted by States in Accordance with Section 724(b)(3) of the Stewart B. McKinney Homeless Assistance Act.* Washington, D.C.: U.S. Government Printing Office.

Yon, Maria G. 1995. "The Education of Homeless Children in the United States." *Equity and Excellence in Education* 28: 31-43.

Yon, Maria, and M. Sebastien-Kadie. 1994. "Homeless Parents and the Education of Their Children." *School Community Journal* (winter/fall): 67-77.

12

Projeto Axé:
Educating Excluded Children in Salvador

Fernanda Gonçalves Almeida and Inaiá Maria Moreira de Carvalho

Brazilian society is filled with all kinds of prejudices and hierarchies that engender a culture of exclusion, which underlies social practices at all levels. The result is a stratification of social positions and social rights. There is also an absence of critical public opinion capable of mobilizing society to address the country's age-old poverty in its varied dimensions (Carvalho 1995). It is true that, with the redemocratization of Brazil that began in the 1980s, these problems have become the center of a broad social movement on behalf of marginalized children and youth. That movement achieved some highly significant changes and legal advances—chiefly the passage in 1990 of the Child and Adolescent Statute-Law 8069/90.

The statute was grounded in a radical criticism of the old and bankrupt welfare-oriented and repressive model that had been the basis of government policies and actions. The statute defined children and adolescents as subjects of rights that must be respected because of their special status as developing persons. It adopted a concept of comprehensive protection of children through policies that guarantee the right to life, proper nutrition, education, health, vocational training, dignity, respect, freedom, leisure time, and family and community life, inter alia. The statute attributed responsibility for the effective observance of those rights not only to the family and the state but also to the community and society at large. It gave priority to the formulation and execution of social policies and the allocation of resources to areas related to the protection of children and adolescents, and proposed new structures and modes of serving that population that involve the participation of representatives of the society in their design, implementation, and follow-up.

But few of these provisions have actually materialized. The persistence of the Brazilian economic crisis, together with policies of structural adjustment and the restructuring of the production sector, has exacerbated the pauperization and the exclusion of most of Brazil's population and has penalized its children and youth even more acutely. Workers and families that previously enjoyed a relatively stable living situation have begun to swell the ranks of the homeless, assuming the role of the new poor. And the state's fiscal crisis and tremendous deterioration in the government structure and public services resulted in a vacuum, or in the bankruptcy of policies that ensure access to the aforementioned rights.

The institutional apparatus and its repressive practices have not been deactivated. Despite international trends and recommendations, which argue for mobilizing every possible resource to keep these children and youth in their original environment, internment in residential facilities is still common in Brazil. Furthermore, the increase in the number of street residents—including children and adolescents—the rise in urban violence, and even the sensationalist treatment by the mass media have served to intensify the myths, the stigma, and the violence against that population.

However, there are signs of progress even in this dismal picture. A well-organized and militant contingent of activists is working continuously on behalf of marginalized children and youth. Some cities have begun to develop recreational and cultural programs for the children and youth from poor outlying areas and to combat the violence that affects them. Financial aid to poor families to help them keep their children in school has been implemented in some municipalities. Lastly, there has been special concern about street boys and girls who, in recent years, have become the subjects of innovative and creative programs such as Projeto Axé.

THE LIVES OF STREET CHILDREN IN SALVADOR

Although prejudices and stigma have not been eliminated, research has discredited several myths, such as the one that Brazilian cities are peopled with literally millions of children and youth who have no families, who have been abandoned, and who are on the verge of becoming or already are delinquents. Although the total number of poor and indigent families may indeed be that large, no more than several thousand of their children have taken to the streets. And even among those, about 80 to 90 percent live with (or are in regular contact with) their families, are attending school, and go into the streets only at certain hours to work in some kind of job. Some resort to begging or petty thievery, but in general, their involvement with illegal groups and crime is very low, or nil. They contribute part or all they earn to the household, and when they approach the age of majority, they tend to look for regular jobs. One reason may be that this helps protect them against police repression.

In the city of Salvador, for example, a careful head count found 15,743 street boys and girls (the latter clearly in the minority), of whom 73.1 percent were working and going back home every day, or were strolling or begging (Reis 1993). Others had more tenuous ties with their families. But the typical group of street children, who had lost contact with their families as a result of a deterioration in their family relationships or living conditions, totaled only 630; i.e., 4 percent of the total recorded.[1]

In the majority of cases, the term *street children* is a misnomer. What they really are is young street workers, who seek or create in those spaces opportunities for survival or a chance to help their families in a society that fails to provide the conditions or prospects for a life with some measure of dignity. Others, however, follow a different path. Exposed to all kinds of influences, oppressed by the misery of their poverty and the lack of prospects, facing problems of getting along with people at home, some youth begin to space out their returns to home and family.[2] They end up leaving home—and school too, if they have not already quit—in order to interact more intensely with, and live in, the streets. They gather in small groups, sleep out in the open or in doorways, and become solely responsible for their own survival through the activities that we described earlier. They are at once exploited and learning to exploit others. They get involved with drug use or drug dealing, or embark even more purposefully on the road to delinquency.

These are truly the children who attain the last stage of misery, who lose all sense of limits and the rules of socially acceptable behavior. Their physical condition deteriorates, and they become the target of violence. As is usually the case with poor delinquents, their life spans may not exceed 20-something. Such boys and girls are the main concern of Projeto Axé, an innovative and creative project that gained prominence in the city of Salvador and whose principles have been adopted in other Brazilian cities.

PROJETO AXÉ

The Axé Center for the Defense and Protection of Children and Adolescents (Centro Projeto Axé de Defesa da Criança e do Adolescente) is a nongovernmental organization (NGO) established in June 1990 in Salvador, capital of the Brazilian state of Bahia (Carvalho and Almeida 1994; Centro Projeto Axé de Defesa da Criança e do Adolescente n.d.). The third largest Brazilian city, Salvador has a population of 2.5 million, characterized by an extremely strong presence of blacks, the influence of Afro-Brazilian culture, and the tremendous poverty of the majority of its population.

This project got its start with political and legal support from the National Movement of Street Boys and Girls of Brazil—MNMMR (Movimento Nacional de Meninos e Meninas de Rua), which trained Axé's first instructors. Financing came from Terra Nova, an Italian organization dedicated to cooperation with the Third World. Decisive guidance and influence came from its founder and current president, Cesare di Fiorio La Rocca, an Italian educator who has been working for almost 30 years with childhood and adolescence issues (La Rocca n.d.).

The name chosen for the project has a symbolic meaning that is associated both with the roots of its clientele (almost all of whom are blacks and mestizos, since there is a strong correlation between poverty and skin color in Salvador), and the hopes and dreams of its founders. In *candomblé* (an African religion practiced in Salvador), the word *axé,* of Yoruba origin, means force and power. It is the principle, the force, the energy, that makes things grow and is transmitted to all living beings, thereby assuring that everything comes to pass.

Project Axé staffers explain the presence and the increase in numbers of street boys and girls not from the traditional standpoint of "irregular family situation" or "abandonment" by their families, but as a result of structural conditions in Brazilian society. Specifically, they are the result of the division of that society between a personalized, business-oriented, high-tech world of power and rights, and the world of the dispossessed—who have no food, no work, and no rights, whose identity is lost in the multitude of the poor (Reis 1993).

Projeto Axé believes street children constitute part of that second world, the world of the dispossessed. They do not attend school and have been stripped of their most basic rights. The victims of brutal exclusion, they have lost the most fundamental characteristic of childhood—the ability to dream and desire. It is from this starting point that Projeto Axé attempts to launch a set of actions taken by the "included" in solidarity with the "excluded," as a means of building a more comprehensive citizenship and an ethical basis for life in society. In the words of its leaders, Projeto Axé proposes to serve as an instrument of communication, of mediation between those two worlds.

Principles and Assumptions

Projeto Axé's chosen strategy calls for rebuilding the social unit, supported by an equality of rights, performing a task that seeks to overcome the twin effects of the brutal exclusion described above, restoring a self-esteem that has been lowered by adversity, and building with those children a bridge to their citizenship on the pillars of certain principles and assumptions. Because of their physical deficiencies and cultural differences, the children and youth of the lower classes—especially those who have gone through the traumatic experience of the street—need a high-quality education, grounded in the fundamentals and administered with commitment and professionalism. That is precisely why Axé refuses to accept volunteers and takes great care in selecting and training—and continually retraining—its staff, especially the instructors.

A second—more fundamental—order of principles and assumptions pertains to educational policy issues. Projeto Axé's educational procedures—its "Pedagogy of Desire"—articulates not only the proposals by Piaget but also formulations by Emilia Ferreiro and Paulo Freire, and certain contributions by other theoreticians in education and other fields of knowledge, combined with elements gleaned from the project's own experience.

From renowned Swiss epistemologist Jean Piaget, Projeto Axé took the constructivist principle that the pupil is a subject of intelligence and of knowledge, who is endowed with a structure that is capable of learning contents and constructing bodies of knowledge and of achieving higher-level rational structures, provided he or she is furnished the kind of environment necessary to that development (Piaget 1932).

Projeto Axé uses Emilia Ferreiro's literacy process. The Argentine educator became famous for changing the central axis of the Latin American educational question. Faced with the alarming bankruptcy of schools in South America, Ferreiro proposed a revolution by asking "How do people learn?" rather than "How does one teach?" thereby constructing the psychogenesis of the written language and breaking down the barriers of traditional research in education (Ferreiro 1987, 1990).

Paulo Freire's contribution to the project's theoretical formulation and its practice centers on the ethical question in its broadest sense, including its aesthetic and political dimensions. In Freire's opinion, the educational process must promote an understanding of the world, social integration, and, therefore, the emancipation of the pupil-subject (Freire 1967).

To those notions and principles were added other formulations, including some of a psychoanalytical nature, that deal with the desires to be—especially those that relate to knowledge, to learning, to creating, to positioning oneself vis-à-vis the world. This is because, according to the Axé perception, emotional, cultural, and political aspects linked to the social fabric enter into the learning process. So, instructor and pupil are not to be mistaken for the traditional figures of teacher and student, but rather are connected to a single and indivisible link of cognizance and affectivity that re-creates knowledge in a historically given space/time. They are, in the last analysis, social subjects.

Within Piaget's principles that place the pupil at the center of the teaching/learning process and emphasize cooperation and social exchanges, the program recognizes the potentials and the experience of its boys and girls and tries to take advantage of them. Choices and decisions about actions and activities are constructed jointly by the instructors and the street children as part of a "Pedagogy of Inclusion" that, according to Inaiá Carvalho (1995: 90), "also presupposes that the work to be done is one of constructing the citizenship of the young person."

Projeto Axé emphasizes the need to universalize the generators and receivers of knowledge in order to break up the duality between the world of the excluded and the world of the personalized. With a view to mediating the communication and leaping over the moat that exists between the two worlds that comprise the Brazilian reality, Projeto Axé is a fairly open entity that maintains a broad-based cooperation with various sectors of the local and national communities: businessmen, politicians, and public institutions, entities associated with child and adolescent issues, and cultural groups mainly in the black community.

Practices of Street Educators

The assumptions and principles we have mentioned translate into a series of practices developed in consultation with the children and youth, accumulated during the past 8 years through discussions and the search for alternatives for solving the problems posed by everyday reality. These activities constitute a creative and innovative instructional philosophy in which there are three major stages:

1. **Pedagogical flirting:** Initial contacts with the children and youth are made and street education begins.
2. **Pedagogical romance:** The dialogue has been established and ties are formed between the instructor and the pupil, still in the street.
3. **Pedagogical coziness:** The young person is now integrated into Projeto Axé activities and is making new plans for his life. Usually this means he is moving off the street.[3]

Success in the first contacts with children and the pedagogical flirting phase is not easy to achieve. Those who live on the streets, whether or not in trouble with the law, have internalized a very deep distrust of everything and everyone, especially those that are not part of their world. For that very reason, street instructors need to be well equipped to assess the reality in which those young people live. They must associate an understanding of the processes that created that reality with a familiarity with other experiences and the special culture that is built up in the streets. Furthermore, they do not go out onto the streets to remove the young people from them by force. Instead, they go there to educate, in the hope that at some point in that process, the young person will himself become aware of other possibilities and will prepare to leave the streets and embark on some other kind of life.

That is why pedagogical flirting, as its very name indicates, represents a game of seduction that begins with the presence of the instructors in the streets and plazas where the young people hang out. Instructors usually go out in pairs (one man and one woman). They neither talk nor do anything in particular except arouse the curiosity of the young people who wonder at the presence of such adults in their daily routine—especially because these seem different from the other adults with whom the adolescents have contact: policemen, juvenile court officers, drug traffickers, gays looking for "tricks," and so on.

Curiosity tends to result in an approach. Conversations are struck up, joking occurs . . . the seduction process begins and usually develops into a second phase, the romance. Then the encounters become more regular, trust develops, and a number of activities are arranged, all thought out and implemented jointly by the instructor and his pupils: games, story reading, excursions. The young people feel they are the object of attention, that they are acknowledged and recognized by name; this, to them, is unusual and very positive. The group begins spending more time together and, gradually, activities can be held in enclosed spaces.

From the flirting, to the romance, and to the pedagogical coziness, an educational process occurs that involves continuing discussions and reflections, which help the pupil articulate the significance of his personal and social drama and facilitate his first steps toward recovery of his identity and self-esteem. This happens because the romantic view of the street as a place of freedom, victories, and happy events is a myth not supported by reality. On the streets, one can earn one's living, watch the goings-on in the city, wander around, and play. There are no schedules nor bosses, and each young person seems to be in control of his own body and his own time. But under this veneer of freedom and independence, one also finds hunger, cold weather, aggressive competitors, exploitation, and fellowship with the corrupt and violent side of law enforcement. Life is agonizing, and one's horizon does not extend beyond day-to-day survival, social relationships where individualism dominates, constant fear, and—in the worst case—death itself (Ferreira 1980; Pereira Júnior et al. 1992).

To the majority of those children and youth, therefore, living on the streets is not really a choice, but rather a result of their lack of alternatives. Once the street instructors win their trust during the pedagogical romance phase, usually they express a desire to leave the streets, go back to their families, attend school, and work.[4]

Projeto Axé represents an opportunity that many youth had, more or less consciously, been hoping for. That is why so many demands are made during the pedagogical romance phase, demands that the educator discusses with the pupil and tries to satisfy and that, taken together, become the parts of a new life plan. The following become necessary for that plan to become reality:

- satisfaction of certain of the child's basic needs, such as food, shelter, medical (and sometimes psychological) care, legal protection, protection against violence, assistance with identity documents, and some financial aid to replace what was being earned on the streets;
- an opportunity for the education of which they had been deprived, accompanied by reconstruction of their ability to hope and to dream, their self-esteem, sense of limits, and other conditions; and
- their preparation for life and citizenship, including a return to school and, in the case of adolescents, some vocational training.

With respect to the first of these requirements, Projeto Axé has been providing three meals a day, help with transportation, a weekly allowance of about US$4 in return for participation in educational workshops and other activities, plus a percentage of the proceeds from sales of Axé products. The need for housing is usually solved by a return to the family. Once again, contrary to the prejudices and myths, it has been found that a return to the family is inadvisable in only 5 percent of the cases—usually because of child abuse. When that happens, or if the youths are no longer in contact with the family, they are sent to boardinghouses or rented rooms, subsidized by Axé, until they are ready for greater independence.

Most of the time, however, this is not necessary. Based on our interviews and the testimonies of the Axé educators, we concluded that completely shattered families are very rare. Usually at least one of the parents is sensible, mentally balanced, and open to the possibility of a child's return. In fact, among the 823 adolescents contacted in 1990 who were sleeping in the streets, 768 went back to live with their families. And one of the most meaningful indicators of stronger ties between the educator and the pupil is an invitation by the latter to have the instructor visit his home. Sometimes the return is mediated by the instructor. There are cases of Projeto Axé boys who have assumed the role of head of their families and are reproducing, there, the educational process that they experienced at Axé. Furthermore, Axé has recently started operating a family assistance program.

One of the most common requests is for help in obtaining documents, since most of the young people never had, or have lost, their birth certificates, a document vital to legal and civic existence and life in Brazilian society. Axé takes care of getting these from the courts and government agencies. When violence erupts or problems arise with the police, Axé's street lawyer, who works with the instructors and young people, follows up on these cases and acts as mediator when necessary. Medical attention is provided by public and private clinics and hospitals associated with the program. Axé has a doctor and a psychologist to administer first aid and decide what to do in emergencies.

Drugs are always an issue, since nearly all the young people have used or are using them—mainly marijuana and shoemaker's glue. However, it has been found that 90 percent of the Axé youth are not substance-dependent. The project has been working with experts from the Federal University of Bahia's Drug Abuse Treatment Center. As its name indicates, Projeto Axé's orientation is to avoid abuse of certain substances and the ritualization of their consumption.

Pedagogical Practices

As for the educational process per se, such activities, which take place in semiopen environments, are gradually blended into the street activities until they eventually reach institutional conditions. Education on the streets unfolds as the boys and girls participate in educational workshops, in cultural activities under Projeto Erê (erê is the Yoruba word for child), and in literacy training and the return to school that constitute the objective of Projeto Travessia (Project Passage). They also prepare for entry into the job market—under the adolescent-oriented Projeto Prosseguir (Project Go Ahead). Abandonment of the street, a return to the family, and participation in institutionalized activities and spaces mark the third phase of the Projeto Axé instructional process.

At the educational workshops, girls and boys assist with all phases of the production of a given product, and although there is a concern for the quality and market acceptance of the products, training and preparation for the world of work is the most important aspect. It should be noted that both the establishment of these workshops and the choice of the production activities grow out of collective discussions in which the young people play an active part.

The workshops include a paper-recycling plant, print shop, metalworking shop, an ideas workshop (where toys are made from scrap metal and other cast-off materials), and a fashion workshop (MODAXÉ). The latter was established with assistance from two Italian designers and was inspired by the cheerful motifs of Salvador's Afro-Brazilian culture. All the workshops combine recreation with tasks that improve the ability to concentrate, reinforce motor skills and emotional equilibrium, and form new habits and behaviors.

Projeto Erê includes the instruments, masks, dance, theater, music, and *capoeira* (choreographed kickboxing) workshops. There is also a Circus School, the junior bands, and other activities. Projeto Axé places great importance on participation in cultural activities because of their integrating effect. Axé believes that artistic expression can play a vital role in restoring self-esteem and a sense of community among these children, as well as bringing about a personal restructuring that helps them deal with the shattering experience of the street. This is especially true in Salvador, because, as we have already noted, the strong African influence on the culture there deeply marks both the belief system and the recreational universe of street children.

Joining such groups, linking the recreational with the need for concentration, adhering to group norms, and developing motor skills also leads to the discovery of unsuspected talents and potentials. Performing in the circus, playing in the bands, or modeling in the fashion shows makes young people feel pretty, handsome, strong. They feel and able to express themselves harmoniously or to produce something that will be favorably

Figure 12.1   The musicians from Axé play Afro-Brazilian music in Salvador. Many Brazilian programs for street children incorporate elements of students' African heritage into activities. (Photo: Projeto Axé)

regarded by others. All this contributes most positively to the reconstruction of their identities, the structuring of new habits and behaviors, and the achievement of recognition by their own families and by other segments of society—thus signaling the availability of better alternatives for the future (M. Carvalho 1995; Reis 1993).

Although more than 70 percent of the adolescents in the program are illiterate or semiliterate, the great majority have already been through school and remember the experience as fraught with failures and trauma. Projeto Travessia seeks to teach youth to read and write during a 6-month period. It especially hopes to develop in them a love of knowledge and a taste for asking questions and looking for answers. Literacy, according to constructivist principles, is understood as an individual and collective creation of knowledge—something that stimulates critical thinking, makes children better able to understand the world they live in, and helps them give better answers to their questions and conditions. As we have already said, there is respect for each individual's personal timetable. After teaching them to read and write, attention turns to getting the youth to go back to regular public school. The project also follows up with teachers and administrators in order to facilitate children's integration.

More difficult than the return to school is the matter of vocational training, sought for those who have turned 16. Projeto Axé's intention is to steer them into the formal labor market, and so it signs agreements with public and private companies that can offer a 6-hour workday and pay minimum wage, plus bus and meal tickets. The hope is that the young people can be trained to pursue some occupation and, ideally, be hired by those companies. However, this is a goal rarely achieved,[5] because of the very limited formal job market in Salvador, where unemployment runs at nearly 10 percent among those looking for their first job.

Another problem mentioned by the educational coordinator of Projeto Axé reflects the strength of the deeply rooted ideology and prejudice against manual labor that pervades all of Brazilian society and also affects the young people of the lower classes. Certain trades—mason, electrician, metalworker, and so on—suffer from very low social status, and the youth have adopted those values, even when they could earn more from such work than in certain professions that require an academic background. Projeto Axé is working with its young people and society at large to counter that ideology.

SUMMARY

The Projeto Axé experience inspires certain reflections about the role of NGOs in dealing with crises and social issues in Brazil and in today's world. As we know, these organizations have been the subject of a number of studies (Fernandes 1994) that refer to the existence and relevance of a third sector in contemporary societies, one that is relatively independent and operates rationally and in specific ways with respect to the market and the state. The operative rationale in the market is the profit motive, according to the logic of accumulation. In the government sphere the rationale is that of a battle for political power to gain hegemony and to control the mechanisms of domination. The third sector is said to be characterized by a rationale that is, above all, ethical, concerned about values, and communicative. This is the language used to designate a set of initiatives that were born within civil society—initiatives that are private but have a public side, and which have been dealing with social questions in a flexible and decentralized manner. Those efforts appeal to the public's moral conscience and stress values such as brotherhood, solidarity, social responsibility, participation, and good citizenship.

As an NGO, Projeto Axé has accumulated a wealth of important experiences. In 5 years, what was a small group has grown to a team of 173 employees, 39 of them detailed to the project by state and federal government agencies. More than 3,000 street children and youth have been served, and about 1,000 currently participate in the workshops and other Axé activities. Many of those boys and girls have developed new life plans for themselves; they have gone back to their families and to school, and although they have not overcome poverty, they now enjoy different, better, and more dignified living conditions.

Projeto Axé's theoretical orientations and value system, its flexibility, the creativity and dedication of its leaders, and the team of trained instructors all have made it possible to develop proposals and methods that are much more effective and appropriate than those traditionally employed to rehabilitate the boys and girls of the street. This is true even in financial terms since, like other NGOs, Axé brought to the field of social work a concern for cost-effectiveness that had been foreign to the public service culture. The per capita monthly cost of serving its children is approximately US$100, 83 percent of which is spent directly on the students. This includes three meals a day, clothing, literacy training, transportation, and a weekly cash allowance to replace what the youths used to earn on the street. This cost is far lower than that reported by government agencies caring for street children by confining them in other institutions.

The practices adopted by Projeto Axé, based on the principles of Piaget (1932), Ferreiro (1987, 1990), and Freire (1968, 1997), involve a complex set of procedures that permeate both the individual and personalized spheres and the collective dimension, with its own unique features and rhythms. The recognition of those features and rhythms, and the respect for the adolescents as subjects of the development of critical thinking and of knowledge that will further their independence and integration, has proven crucial to the rebuilding of their mental and emotional structures and identities. It facilitates the search for concrete proposals for overcoming the problems faced by those children and youth and dealing with their exclusion from the rest of society.

In its work with the general public, its cooperation with a network of governmental and nongovernmental agencies (for example, MNMMR, CBIA, the Catholic Church's Ministry to Minors), and its more direct and daily activities, Projeto Axé has helped dispel preconceived and intolerant ideas about street children—that they pose a threat, or that they lack families or guardians. It presents them as a problem that results primarily from social exclusion and other, broader factors that determine the structure of Brazilian society. Above all, Projeto Axé is constructing and proving the viability of an educational philosophy that is capable of offering the children of that exclusion alternatives for their rediscovery and for their critical and competent reentry into the labor market and the life of this society. The Axé experiment now enjoys local, national, and international recognition. The program now advises and trains street instructors for several Brazilian states and even some other countries and has been guiding both public and private organizations in carrying out pilot programs serving street children.

PROGRAM LIMITATIONS

However, an account of Projeto Axé's successes does not tell the whole story. The project also faces limitations and problems, particularly in terms of financial support for its activities and the opportunities for its clientele to rejoin society. While government agencies and services are financed by mandatory taxes, the third sector depends largely on voluntary donations inspired by ethical and moral imperatives to be concerned about others. As we have already said, Axé was founded with funding from an Italian charitable organization and, over the years, has received assistance from UNICEF, Save the Children, Diakonia, the International Labor Organization, and federal, state, and municipal agencies. Sometimes the assistance takes the form of space in buildings or houses, equipment, and temporary assignment of personnel. Axé leaders are continually attempting to diversify the sources of support, especially because there are legal and bureaucratic restrictions on the use of public funds to pay the salaries of nongovernmental organization personnel, the area where Axé is most vulnerable.

However, it is not easy to find new and more diversified sources of funds, especially when philanthropy is not part of the Brazilian business culture. As Fernandes (1994) notes, in Latin American countries, the presence of a populist state that assumes full responsibility for the welfare of its people (although, in fact, not ensuring this), and a culture that views philanthropy and generosity as an individual matter, have kept companies from assuming responsibilities in the social welfare area.

Even so, until May 1995 Axé's payroll costs were being underwritten by a small group of Bahian firms that had been sensitized to the program's purposes and innovative methodology. However, owing to the persistence of Brazil's economic crisis and the financial difficulties associated with the adjustment process, those companies stopped contributing. When the project's financial woes became known, artists, advertising agencies, some companies, and the general public launched a campaign that raised emergency funds to pay off debts and meet immediate expenses. While in the last few years the financial situation has improved, the question of long-term support has not been resolved. The main source of revenue remains public and private contributions.

Furthermore, although there is a strong potential for successful work with younger children, Axé's attempts at social reintegration of older adolescents into the labor market have met with difficulties. Restricted and selective throughout Brazil's history, that market has become even more exclusive in recent years because of the economic crisis and period of economic adjustment, along with the structural transformations that accompany globalization and the downsizing of the production structure. Then too, this market is now demanding a new kind of worker, more versatile, with higher qualifications and a more varied formal education. The Axé youths are still the victim of prejudice against the poor, the blacks, and—particularly—those who have experienced life on the streets of Brazil.

CONCLUSION

This new situation raises the question of relations between the market, the state, and the third sector. Although the market regulates the dynamics and the expansion of economic opportunity, it is not in the market sphere that security and social solidarity will be produced, nor good citizenship made widespread. And although organizations such as Projeto Axé may initiate creative and innovative proposals better suited to the treatment of certain social issues, their scope is still localized and partial, and their funds— usually—limited. Programs of this nature are important, especially in the sense that they harass the administrative powers—they play the role of critic and challenger of government actions and policies.

The truth is that the notion of a third sector makes sense only as a complement to the first and second sectors. Public services rendered by organizations such as Projeto Axé, dispersed in 1,000 different initiatives, will have real impact only if they interact positively with public macrointerventions engineered by the state. Although wider adoption of Axé practices can, on an emergency basis, attenuate the problems of a given segment of the children of misery—those who live on the street—it is obvious that policies in such areas as employment, income, education, health, and job training are indispensable. Those policies must also be aimed at the thousands of children of "discreet disgrace" and their families, so neglected these days. Only then can we envision the achievement of Axé's ultimate objective, as proclaimed by its team of instructors: to cease to exist because it has become completely superfluous.

NOTES

1. A study done in Rio de Janeiro by the Brazilian Institute of Social and Economic Analysis (IBASE) showed that barely 1,000 children could truly be termed *street children,* and another survey, done in Belém, produced similar results.
2. Often the distancing from the family begins because of transportation problems and the distance they must travel to reach their homes, situated on the poor outskirts of the city. And although there are no rigid determining factors or a precise typology of those who tend to remain on the streets, several studies and observations by those who work in programs that serve these children indicate that the ones who remain on the street are usually intellectually better endowed,

less satisfied with the misery endured by their families, or else victims of abuse and violence at home. Remember, too, that the number of street children is very small (Fausto and Cervini 1991).

3. Although the names of these phases may seem funny, Axé participants do not see it that way, but believe they are critical to an understanding of the affective domain that needs to be included in the educational process.

4. Of course there are limits to this success, especially in cases where the young people are heavily involved in drugs and delinquency, or dissatisfied with the (limited and precarious) conditions of community life that will be within their reach. Work with young prostitutes, for example, is hampered by their realization that domestic work is the most immediate alternative offered them by society. They reject such work because of its low wages, low social status, and the requirement for absolute obedience.

5. In a partnership with OAS Construction, Axé managed to get some of its adolescents qualified for construction work that does not require much schooling, such as electrician and carpentry work. The experience was fairly successful; the boys got special treatment and proved to be excellent workers. But despite all the efforts, such success has not been common.

REFERENCES

Alvim, María Roselene, and Lícia do Prado Valladares. 1988. "Infância e sociedade no Brasil, uma análise da literatura." *Boletim Informativo e Bibliográfico de Ciências Sociais,* 3–37. Rio de Janeiro: Vértice/ANPOCS.

Carvalho, Inaiá Ma. Moreira de. 1995. "Direitos legais e direitos efetivos (crianças, adolescentes e cidadania no Brasil)." *Revista Brasileira de Ciências Sociais* (São Paulo) (Oct.): 127–42.

Carvalho, Inaiá Ma. Moreira de, and Fernanda Ma. B.G. de Almeida. 1994. *Os jovens no mercado de trabalho: o caso dos convênios de Salvador.* Brasília: Ministry of Labor/UNDP.

Carvalho, Marco A. C. 1995. "Pedagogia de rua." *Bahia: Análise & Dados* (Salvador) CEI 4 (4) (March): 89–100.

Centro Projeto Axé de Defesa da Criança e do Adolescente. n.d. *Training Center Dossier.* Salvador: Project Axé.

Estatuto da Criança e do Adolescente. Federal Law 8,069 (1990, 13 July).

Fausto, Ayrton, and Rubim Cervini, eds. 1991. *O trabalho e a rua: crianças e adolescentes no Brasil urbano dos anos 80.* São Paulo: Cortez.

Fernandes, Rubem César. 1994. *Privado, porém público: o terceiro setor na América Latina.* Rio de Janeiro: Relume-Dumará.

Ferreira, Rosa Ma. Fisher. 1980. *Menores de rua: valores e expectativas de menores marginalizados em São Paulo.* São Paulo: Justice and Peace Commission of São Paulo; CEDEC.

Ferreiro, E. 1987. *Alfabetização em processo.* Portuguese translation by Sara C. Lima and María do Nascimento. São Paulo: Cortez/Autores Associados.

———. 1990. *Os filhos do analfabetismo: propostas para a alfabetização escolar na América Latina.* Portuguese translation by Maria Luiza Marques Abaurre, 3d ed. Porto Alegre: Artes Médicas.

Ferreiro, E., and A. Tererosky. 1986. *Psicogênese da língua escrita.* Porto Alegre: Artes Médicas.

Freire, Paulo. 1967. *Educação como prática da liberdade.* Rio de Janeiro: Paz e Terra.

———. 1997. *Cartas á Guiné-Bissau: registro de uma experiência em processo.* Rio de Janeiro: Paz e Terra.

La Rocca, Cesare di Fiorio. n.d. *Histórico.* Salvador: The Axé Center for the Defense and Protection of Children and Adolescents. Mimeographed.

Pereira Júnior, Almir, Jaerson Bezerra, and R. Henrique. 1992. *Os impasses da cidadania: infância e adolescencia no Brasil.* Rio de Janeiro: IBASE.

Piaget, Jean. 1932. *The Moral Judgement of the Child.* New York: Harcourt Brace Jovanovich.

Reis, Ana Maria Bianchi dos. 1993. *O Axé da Bahia.* Salvador: The Axé Center for the Defense and Protection of Children and Adolescents. Mimeographed.

13

Breaking the Cycle:
Educating New York's Homeless Children and Their Families

Ralph da Costa Nuñez

O f the many barriers facing America's homeless children, inadequate education is perhaps the most devastating. American Family Inns in New York City provides a comprehensive, education-based residential environment that supports the entire family, offering programs such as the Brownstone School, an accelerated after-school program that supplements homeless children's public school education. Through the various programs it offers, American Family Inns creates the potential for making a real change in the lives of homeless children and their families. This chapter describes this highly effective model that has helped put children in New York City back on the track to educational success.

THE CYCLE OF UNDEREDUCATION

Perhaps the largest single factor affecting the undereducation of homeless children is the undereducation of homeless parents. New York City data are consistent with the national picture: they indicate that most homeless parents have had little access to educational opportunities. The vast majority of homeless parents in New York lack even basic skills: 62 percent do not have a high school diploma, and 60 percent have no work experience of any kind. On average, these homeless parents left school after the 10th grade, and most read at or below the 6th-grade level (Homes for the Homeless 1995). For many, the lack of basic literacy and math skills can make tasks such as completing a school registration form, understanding a report card, or reading a parents' newsletter almost impossible. Children of poorly educated parents suffer on several levels. In addition to having to withstand economic deprivation, they also are at a much greater risk of undereducation (National Center for Children in Poverty 1992: 6). Data from the Children's Defense Fund, the Ford Foundation, and other organizations show that students whose parents have less than a high school education consistently score lower on standardized math and reading tests than students whose parents have graduated from high school (Finlay et al.: 107).

One factor contributing to this correlation is less-educated parents' lack of involvement in their children's schooling (Halpern 1990). Homeless parents in particular tend to keep their distance from their children's education because they often feel ill-equipped academically or were discouraged themselves in school. Even though they maintain the hope that their children will succeed in school, these parents frequently fail to offer appropriate support or encouragement. Because homeless parents frequently feel intimidated by teachers, they may not get involved in their children's studies or school activities. Unfortunately, teachers may misinterpret such reluctance as a lack of interest and can discourage parents further by giving up on efforts to involve them (Jones 1989: 10).

The strong link between parental education and children's success in school means that successful programs must not target either parent *or* child, but should instead work to reintegrate the entire family into the cycle of education. Without the support of parents who are cognizant of the importance of education, homeless children will find it extraordinarily difficult, if not impossible, to succeed in school.

AN EFFECTIVE MODEL FOR EDUCATING HOMELESS STUDENTS

A comprehensive, whole-family approach offers the most promising route to educational success for homeless children. Programs that provide support and schooling in a stable, enriching setting can cement learning as a family value for both parents and children. An increasing number of intergenerational education programs are emerging across the country, offering families with few resources a realistic chance for a sound education. Those programs with the greatest promise are broad, continuous, and intensive (Weiss and Halpern 1990).

Transitional housing facilities are a particularly promising location for effective multitiered educational programming for homeless families. Developed in response to criticisms of the more traditional emergency shelter system, transitional housing usually takes the form of individual apartments where homeless families live for up to 2 years while waiting to secure permanent housing. Transitional housing offers families more security, independence, and privacy than welfare hotels or other types of shelters provided in New York. Transitional housing facilities also offer stability and the opportunity for sustained work over an extended period of time—crucial elements of successful educational programs.

THE AMERICAN FAMILY INNS

One example of a program that builds on transitional housing's potential is the American Family Inns model, currently in operation at four New York City sites. Using the physical structure of the housing facilities, the Family Inns model integrates educational, vocational, and family support services into the residential setting. In a stable, structured environment, parents and children are able to access easily a wide variety of programs, including enriched preschool programs, accelerated after-school education, adult basic education, alternative high schools, job readiness programs for parents, and an intergenerational family literacy initiative. While this chapter will focus on a description of the model's education programs for children, it is crucial to remember that they are located in a residential, learning-based environment that supports the entire family.

On-site children's programming at the American Family Inns is extensive and designed to ensure that children have access to services that will help them succeed in school. All programming is based on the belief that homeless children are not only extraordinarily vulnerable but also resilient and adaptive, ready to succeed as well as any other child, given sufficient support. The continuum of educational services at each Family Inn ranges from infant development to adolescent dropout prevention. Three central components form the core of this effort: preschool programs; accelerated after-school education; and constructive recreational programming. These programs work together to provide what a growing number of researchers recommend but too few policymakers have implemented: continuous, stable, quality education that is family-based and tailored to the individual needs of homeless children (Wood et al. 1990: 111).

The decade-long process of operating, evaluating, and fine-tuning these programs at the American Family Inns has led to encouraging results. Homeless children, who would otherwise accrue alarming developmental difficulties and educational problems, avoid those pitfalls through their participation in Inns programs. In fact, these children flourish. Data gathered from the American Family Inns child education and recreation components reveal that children in these programs achieve significant gains, not only academically but socially and emotionally as well.

EARLY CHILDHOOD EDUCATION PROGRAMS: A JUMP-START ON THE FUTURE

The evidence is clear: participation in a high-quality preschool program holds the potential to influence positively the entire course of a child's education. The nation's foremost study of early childhood education, the High/Scope Perry Preschool Study, found remarkable evidence of the powerful impact preschool programs can have on children's capacity to succeed later in life. Well into adulthood, those who participate in preschool programs as children tend to surpass the achievements of nonparticipants (Schwienhart et al. 1993.) Such successes make clear that a model stressing active learning and parental involvement can have an enormous impact on children's capacity to succeed later in life. Indeed, many thousands of poor children across the country have benefited from high-quality preschool programs based on the High/Scope model.

Despite the clear positive impact of early education on children's development and later educational success, many children in the United States are not enrolled in preschool. This is particularly true of homeless and other low-income children. A 1992 survey of New York City's homeless families found that only 21 percent of their school-age children had attended any school prior to kindergarten. In contrast, more than 60 percent of children from upper-socioeconomic groups and 45 percent from middle-socioeconomic groups had benefited from at least 1 year of preschool (U.S. General Accounting Office 1993).

Not surprisingly, this discrepancy is primarily a function of a family's ability to pay for such programs. While Head Start (a federally financed preschool program) was designed to ensure that low-income children could attend preschool, it has been consistently underfunded and currently serves less than 20 percent of all eligible children. Furthermore, the great majority of existing Head Start programs are part-day, part-year programs only. Homeless children are especially likely to miss out, because local program directors may prefer to maintain continuity in their programs, a goal that precludes placement of children living only temporarily in emergency shelters (National Head Start Association 1993).

In response to homeless children's dire need for an early educational start and the mounting evidence for the effectiveness of early childhood education, the American Family Inns model integrated the highly successful High/Scope curriculum into its own continuum of children's services. Unlike standard child care services, which typically provide only a supervised baby-sitting service and lack educational structure, the American

Family Inns preschool program focuses on developing the physical, social, and cognitive skills of children and places a heavy emphasis on involving the children's families. This preschool program, which includes the Child Development Center, an intergenerational component, and frequently works in cooperation with the Inns family literacy programs, today serves more than 250 homeless children under the age of 6.

CHILD DEVELOPMENT CENTER

The Child Development Center (CDC) forms the centerpiece of the American Family Inns preschool program and serves both infants and preschool-age children. The infant-care component offers children a nurturing environment where they receive critical and engaging stimuli to promote mental and social development. Infant rooms are designed to provide sight and sound stimuli to the youngest infants and to give older infants more advanced psychomotor activities.

The CDC employs a different kind of educational boost for preschool children. For them, the CDC employs a variation of the successful High/Scope curriculum. Developed at the University of Michigan, the High/Scope model is child-directed and promotes involved learning. By using a child's own interests to plan his or her day with the guidance of supportive adults, the activities not only accomplish an immediate goal (such as painting, participating in mock Olympics, or planting vegetables) but also foster a sense of control and initiative in the child. Researchers have found that such activities enrich both the educational and social development of children; they incorporate motor skills activities, creativity, logic, an understanding of spatial relationships, communication, and teamwork (Hohmann et al. 1979).

Central to the CDC's success are efforts to engage parents in their children's education, laying the groundwork for years of involvement and support. Teachers arrange weekly conferences with parents to discuss their child's needs and progress. Parents themselves participate in the infant activities, thereby gaining a greater knowledge of their child's development process, from infancy through the toddler stages. Parents are closely involved in the preschool program as well. They are encouraged to view the CDC not simply as a drop-off service but also as a place where their child will truly learn and develop through a variety of engaging activities, including those that parents can lead in their own homes.

Overall, the Child Development Center has an enormous impact on children, especially when compared to conventional child care. Both quantitative and qualitative assessments indicate that children show rapid developmental, social, and emotional growth in as little as 8 weeks. Teachers using the Child Observation Record (a standard measuring tool) have noted dramatic improvements in children's language skills, attention spans, and their ability to behave cooperatively. Their self-confidence grows, and they become more spirited and alert. Most children also experience growth spurts and weight gain.

THE LEARNING FAST-TRACK: THE BROWNSTONE SCHOOL

One of American Family Inns' most successful programs serves homeless children ages 5 through 13. The Inns' accelerated after-school education program—the Brownstone School—is designed to compensate for the disparity in educational opportunities available to homeless children by supplementing their public school education. Conducted at Family Inns in the South Bronx and Queens after the regular school day, the Brownstone School is based on the premise that children who are behind should not be placed in a "slow lane" or a remedial program to catch up, but rather into the "fast lane," in a program similar to those designed for "gifted and talented" children.

Guided by the accelerated learning educational model developed by Henry Levin, the Brownstone School program emphasizes a low student-to-teacher ratio of five to one, with a high degree of individualization to meet each student's needs. The model stresses active teaching of concepts, analysis, and problem solving, instead of relying on more traditional repetition and drills. Whole-language techniques and theme-based activities keep learning interesting and foster higher-order thinking. Enhancing these innovative teaching techniques and educational programs are interactive learning tools and field work, such as the LEGO-logo computer program for math skill building, a community garden for science experiments, and journal writing for language arts and reading.

These features, coupled with strong student-teacher relationships, allow children in the program to develop enhanced learning ability, greater self-confidence, and a sense of accomplishment. High expectations, deadlines for clearly identified, attainable perform-ance levels, and stimulating instructional materials are also key in this process. Above all, the staff strives to provide a challenging but stable environment that engages children with exciting new educational activities.

Like the preschool program, the Brownstone School sponsors activities to encour-age parents to become involved directly in their children's education. Parents work with teachers and children to develop and complete "learning contracts" based on subject areas chosen by the children. The Brownstone School offers family literacy workshops as well as group field trips and family projects such as working in the community garden and mother-teen workshops. The staff also facilitates greater collaboration between the

Figure 13.1   The Brownstone School offers homeless students the opportunity to com-plete their homework with teachers and aids who can assist them.
(Photo: Homes for Homeless)

parents and the public schools by urging parents to use their children's teacher as a source of advice and by encouraging parent-teacher conferences. Brownstone School teachers frequently accompany parents to these conferences and explore a child's new school with parents when the family moves into permanent housing.

More than 2,000 students have participated in the Brownstone School program since its inception in 1991. These students have consistently reflected the makeup of the homeless family population in New York City and, as such, their experiences with the Brownstone School are telling indicators for the future replicability of the program. Approximately 60 percent of the children are African American, 35 percent are Latino/a, and the remaining 5 percent come from other ethnic backgrounds, primarily white and Asian. The male-to-female ratio is roughly three to two. Almost all live in households headed by single mothers receiving Temporary Assistance to Needy Families (TANF, the new federal welfare program that replaced Aid to Families with Dependent Children [AFDC]) as their primary income. Most families stay at the Family Inns for roughly 9 months, during which time their children are regularly involved in Brownstone School activities.

Overall, these students make extraordinary academic gains. After 6 months of participation, the children's scores in reading can rise from less than 40 percent to 60 percent. Their math scores can more than double, from 23 percent to roughly 50 percent. In addition, many participating students win academic awards from their public schools in reading, science, spelling, and math.

The Brownstone School also has had a positive impact on school attendance. The 92 percent public school attendance rate among students participating in the Brownstone School is almost 30 percent higher than the 63 percent citywide attendance rate for homeless children. Brownstone School students' attendance rate is also higher than the average of 86 percent for all children in New York City. And while 60 percent of the absences attributed to homeless students *not* involved in the program were unexcused, only 35 percent of the absences of participating students were unexcused or unrelated to illness (Homes for the Homeless 1993).

Finally, the Brownstone School also appears to enhance parental involvement in children's education. An astounding 86 percent of Family Inn parents with children in the program visit the school and their child's teacher, as opposed to only 26 percent of parents whose children are not enrolled in the program. Moreover, when parents of Brownstone School students were asked to name the person they would consult about their child's education, nearly all identified teachers from the program. While follow-up to assess long-term parental involvement has not yet been conducted, interviews with 68 homeless mothers of school-age children conducted at American Family Inns have shown that partnerships such as those established at the Brownstone School are likely to motivate parents to continue communicating with their children's teachers in later years, as well as to be more generally involved in their children's education.

Parents get involved even more directly by frequently volunteering for the programs in which their children participate. Equally important, watching and helping their children flourish in educational activities inspires parents to resume their own education. More than half of the parents whose children attend the Inns' accelerated afterschool education program are working toward their own GED.

RECREATION AND CULTURAL PROGRAMMING

Extracurricular activities are essential to round out a child's educational and social development. Social, physical, and artistic activities are especially important for homeless children, who are often consumed by the anxiety and confusion they feel concerning their families. They miss their old neighborhoods and friends and frequently feel unwelcome or uncomfortable in a new school, where they are sometimes taunted and stigmatized for being homeless. Space limitations frequently hamper homeless children and adolescents as well, depriving them of the exercise and exploration so important to healthy development.

To alleviate such stresses and provide enjoyable, supportive activities for children, the American Family Inn includes a recreational component, the Healthy Living Center. These recreation centers serve as hubs for a variety of activities. They furnish critical opportunities for self-expression, social acceptance, accomplishment, and physical exercise for school-age children. The Healthy Living Centers also sponsor preventative programs and offer alternatives to the destructive or violent behavior to which so many of today's poor children fall victim. The only requirement for participation in the recreation center's daily activities is attendance at school. Theater, art, dance, and poetry allow children to build a sense of accomplishment and to express feelings they might not otherwise articulate, from typical adolescent frustrations to those specific to poverty and homelessness. Participation in sports teams, theater companies, and local Boy and Girl Scout troops encourages cooperation and teaches social skills. Workshops and rap sessions on substance abuse, AIDS, pregnancy, and crime help children develop coping and decision-making skills. In addition, the Healthy Living Centers sponsor special outings to popular sports events and theater productions.

Many activities at the Healthy Living Centers directly complement the children's education. Staff offer intensive homework assistance and organize regular trips to local libraries. In addition, children and teens produce monthly newsletters at the centers, reporting on news and events at the Inn, and publishing their artwork and poetry. These publications are part of an overall effort to build community and group support among the children and families staying at the American Family Inns. Collaborations with neighborhood organizations and volunteers serve similar goals. In one such project, nonhomeless teens from surrounding areas participate in Inn activities and provide important links to the community, where homeless families sometimes feel unwanted or isolated.

The Healthy Living Centers also strive to bolster homeless children's self-esteem and sense of identity through activities that explore and celebrate the diverse cultures that make up both the immediate environment and the surrounding neighborhood. Art and dance programs offered in collaboration with local cultural organizations expose children to a rich assortment of cultural experiences and activities.

Finally, like all American Family Inns children's programming, the Healthy Living Centers involve parents. Both individually and in groups, parents meet with staff members to discuss children's attendance at school, contact with teachers, ties with the local schools, and other matters of concern. The staff work to develop trust so that when they notice that a child is experiencing problems, they can work with the parents to address them.

Staff, parents, and children consistently praise the Healthy Living Centers and the many opportunities they offer. Parents are pleased that their children have a healthy outlet for both their energy and the stress of living without a home of their own. Meanwhile, children enthusiastically embrace the centers, frequently participating in as many activities as they can each day.

For homeless children, who spend roughly 12 to 24 months of their lives without a permanent home, programs like the Child Development Centers, the Brownstone School, and the Healthy Living Centers provide vital educational opportunities and creative outlets too frequently absent from their young lives. Such programs also give these children the opportunity to develop relationships and to nurture their capacity for initiative, curiosity, and independence. Above all, the programs work to initiate a broad learning momentum that enhances *future* educational achievement for these children.

By creating a supportive environment centered around education, the American Family Inn model enables homeless children and their families to understand and embrace the value of education. Nothing is more important for these families than the skills and self-confidence that come from education—essential to every aspect of independent living. American Family Inns has the potential to provide this most basic service in an intense, creative, and effective manner.

CONCLUSION

The American Family Inns model is one particularly effective method for intervening in homeless children's lives and setting them on the path to educational achievement. However, the philosophy behind the American Family Inns can be embraced by all service providers working with homeless children. Even a small community-based shelter that recognizes the unique educational obstacles faced by homeless children, provides appropriate programming, and works to involve homeless parents in their children's education can have a significant impact on the future of a homeless child.

The most basic step that a shelter or transitional housing facility can take to improve homeless children's education is to establish a link with the local school system. By maintaining regular contact with school officials, service providers can keep the schools informed of new children moving into the shelters and help with the complicated enrollment and transportation procedures. Service providers also can ensure that a homeless child's teachers know about his or her homelessness and about any special problems, such as a history of abuse, neglect, or ill-health. Building a relationship with the schools can prevent the all-too-common occurrence of homeless children being ignored or lost by a school system that does not know that they exist or does not recognize their special needs.

In addition to acting as advocates for homeless children within the school system, service organizations of all sizes can provide crucial supplementary educational programming. Collaborative relationships between shelters and community organizations, local businesses, and universities can accomplish the same results as an enriched facility like the American Family Inns. An informal intergenerational reading program set up between a senior citizens' home and a shelter can have the same beneficial effects as a highly developed tutoring program. As long as service providers have a thorough understanding of homeless children's needs they can weave together the services required to address them, whether it is through locating after-school programs that will accept homeless children, recruiting local businesses to sponsor recreational activities, or just setting aside a quiet space in the shelter for children to do their homework.

The most crucial step that service providers can take in breaking the cycle of undereducation for homeless children is to focus their resources on programs that involve parents in their children's education. Helping homeless parents return to school or become involved in job training is a critical component of improving children's educational outlook. Family literacy programs, parent-child field trips, and other multigenerational programs are inexpensive but productive investments in the future of an entire family.

Furthermore, even small programs should keep careful data on the progress of their efforts. In this way, service providers can learn valuable lessons from each other. By documenting both the obstacles faced by homeless children and the programs that successfully overcome these obstacles, service providers also can play an invaluable role in public policy debates. It is too often impossible to find these children, let alone provide them with the services they so desperately need. Data provided by those who know can make a crucial difference in how homeless children and their needs are perceived.

Ultimately, the biggest hurdle faced by homeless children as they attempt to become educated is a lack of understanding. The problems facing homeless families are multifaceted, and the life of a homeless child particularly complex. When public officials, educators, parents, and service providers look clearly at homeless children, they can see that the problems of homelessness and undereducation are inextricably linked. This understanding is at the core of the American Family Inns model. It must shape any successful educational program for homeless children.

REFERENCES

Finlay, B., J. M. Simmons, and A. Yang. 1991. *The Adolescent & Young Adult Fact Book.* Washington, D.C.: Children's Defense Fund.

Halpern, R. 1990. "Poverty and Early Childhood Parenting: Toward a Framework for Intervention." *American Journal of Orthopsychiatry* 60 (1) (Jan.).

Hohmann, M., B. Banet, and D. P. Weikart. 1979. *Young Children in Action.* Ypsilanti, Mich.: High/Scope Press.

Homes for the Homeless. 1993. *Access to Success: Meeting the Educational Needs of Homeless Children and Families.* New York: Institute for Children and Poverty.

———. 1995. *An American Family Myth: Every Child at Risk.* New York: Institute for Children and Poverty.

Jones, J. 1989. *Changing Needs for a Changing Future: The Need for Educational Leadership.* New York: National Center for Children in Poverty.

National Center for Children in Poverty. 1992. *Five Million Children: 1992 Update.* New York: Columbia University School of Public Health.

National Head Start Association. 1993. *Head Start: The Nation's Pride: A Nation's Challenge.* Washington, D.C.: Author.

Schwienhart, Lawrence J., Helen V. Barnes, and David P. Weikart. 1993. *Significant Benefits: The High/Scope Perry Preschool Study Through Age 27.* Ypsilanti, Mich.: High/Scope Press.

U.S. General Accounting Office. July 1993. *Poor Preschool-Aged Children: Numbers Increase but Most Not in Preschool.* GAO/HRD-93-111BR. Washington, D. C.: U.S. GAO.

Weiss, H., and R. Halpern. 1990. *Community-Based Family Support and Education Programs: Something Old or Something New?* New York: National Center for Children in Poverty.

Wood, D. L., R. B. Valdez, and A. Shen. 1990. "Health of Homeless Children and Housed, Poor Children." *Pediatrics* 86.

14

Projeto Semear:
Equalizing Opportunities for Adolescents at Risk in Rio de Janeiro

Amelia Maria Noronha Pessoa de Queiroz and Ligia Gomes Elliot

The problems of survival for the Brazilian poor in large urban centers assumed enormous proportions in the 1980s. The desperate conditions of deprived children and youth in Brazil, a country of great disparities, dualities, and inequalities in terms of human development, is exemplified by the city of Rio de Janeiro. Between 1970 and 1991, the population of Rio de Janeiro grew by 67 percent, from 3,281,908 to 5,980,768 inhabitants. This led to major social and economic problems. Of the 1,625,360 households in Rio de Janeiro, 239,680 (12.4 percent) were situated in shantytowns (*favelas*), housing 962,790 people. In addition, there are 177,675 (18.8 percent) living in housing projects consisting of modest houses or small apartments built to house people who had been evicted from shantytowns (Empress Municipal de Informática e Planejamento [IPLAN-RIO] 1992/93).

Although Rio de Janeiro is no different from other Brazilian urban centers, it is seen by many as the nation's capital of violence and abandoned children. It is not surprising, then, that in 1992, 619 institutions and nongovernmental projects devoted to assisting poor children and youth were located there (Valladares and Impelizieri 1991). Those projects and institutions included day care centers and schools, social assistance, human rights advocacy coordination, shelters, residential facilities, vocational training, and alternative education organizations. The latter are intended to support, guide, and educate children and youth on the basis of pedagogical approaches suited to their unique characteristics.

Projeto Semear fits into the category of alternative education organizations.[1] The project is aimed at young people at risk who live in the western zone of Rio de Janeiro in an area called Bangu. Projeto Semear offers basic education, nutritious meals, and some dental and medical care, and gives participants an opportunity to prepare for the world of work. It also houses several who are homeless. This chapter presents a case study of Projeto Semear: it describes the project's history, sponsors, personnel, and resources; profiles the participants; describes the pedagogical theory and objectives of Semear; and, lastly, assesses the impact of the project on its young people.

This chapter is based on years of participant-observation research during which the authors employed naturalistic inquiry techniques (Guba and Lincoln 1985). It draws heavily from Queiroz's 1997 book, *O Caso Semear: A Construçãoda Identidade e a*

Conquista da Cidadania. They also analyzed project documents, such as registration forms, questionnaires, minutes of meetings, and speeches by participants. In addition, they analyzed interviews of the teaching team, former students, and parents or guardians of students. The chapter also uses other relevant data from other studies of Projeto Semear (Penna Firme 1995).

THE YOUTH OF SEMEAR

The project is designed to serve young people who are at risk in terms of their living conditions. Semear's youngsters fit into at least six of UNICEF's (1989) seven categories of marginalized sectors of the population: (a) children and adolescents who are struggling for survival; (b) street children; (c) children and adolescents who have been mistreated and abandoned; (d) institutionalized children and adolescents; (e) children and adolescents involved in armed conflicts; and (f) children and adolescents in need of specific preventive services.

A constant and perverse current runs through the lives of these youth: the absolute inability of parents or relatives to support them. This situation often coexists with family violence bred of frustration at not being able to meet basic needs. Sometimes these children and youth are shoved into the streets to survive. Their search for survival introduces factors that help explain why Semear youth are found in the six categories of at-risk youth identified by UNICEF.

Applicants are required to be between 13 and 18 years of age and either to have been excluded from a regular school or to lag far behind their schoolmates. A birth certificate is the only required document. As of 1999, more than 1,200 adolescents had passed through the program. In 1988, 96 students enrolled; in 1992, 176; and in 1996, the project served 236 young people—60 percent at the farm site and 40 percent in occupational training courses run by the Pastoral do Minor of the Archdiocese of Rio de Janeiro. Currently, Semear's young people come from 32 different communities, most of them in Bangu.[2]

Profile of Semear Participants

In 1996 Queiroz analyzed 701 registration cards from current and former Semear participants in order to develop a profile of the students. Parents' occupations fell into two general categories: low-paying service, and intermittent labor. Most of the adolescents' parents had very low occupational attainment: 19.4 percent of fathers were brick masons; 9.5 percent were drivers; 6.6 percent were auto mechanics; and the remaining fathers were unskilled laborers. Three-fourths of the fathers worked in the informal labor market, meaning that they were unregistered for official social security benefits. Among mothers, 49.6 percent did not work; 35 percent were maids; 11.2 percent were deceased, and 4 percent were dressmakers. And 91.3 percent of the families earned less than one minimum salary (US$100.00)

Most Semear participants did not finish elementary school. All students admitted to the program had previously repeated the early grades in school. Reasons given for leaving school included disciplinary problems, difficulty in learning, entry into the workforce, and pregnancy.

Queiroz found that only 32.8 percent of participants lived with both parents, while most said they lived with only their mothers. The father figure was almost always absent. At the project's first Christmas party, only 3 of the 60 young people in attendance were accompanied by their fathers. This is consistent with prior research on street children.

In their analysis of 16 studies of street children, Rizzini and Rizzini (1991) found that a significant number of families were organized around either the mother or the father.

The authors noted the difficulty of building an identity among Semear students. Many did not know on what day they were born. When they expressed themselves during initial contact with the project, they tended to speak in the third person, referring to themselves as he or she. The fact that these adolescents had to rely on themselves to survive when they had not yet had much schooling or appropriate training and that they were powerless to change the violent conditions in their communities contributed to their feelings of insecurity, impotence, and inferiority. One common consequence of this situation is an expectation of an abbreviated life span. "I don't know whether I will live past age 23. . . . I have nothing to look forward to," said one Semear student. Their expectation of early death and an absence of a time horizon make it hard for these adolescents to plan for their future (Queiroz 1997). "Some came to us because of this [Semear's] wonderful atmosphere, others in search of a better life," recalled one teacher.

Sometimes a child is not accepted by a stepfather or a mother's boyfriend. In an effort to fill an emotional vacuum, these young people often demand attention from teachers and project directors whom they identify as family or mother figures. "They came looking for love and affection," said one of the teachers who has worked with the project since its earliest days.

When the project was first implemented, students' memories of school failures and their problems with learning were reflected in contradictory classroom behavior: at the same time as they refused to attend class, they demanded notebooks and rejected innovative methods that differed from those with which they had become familiar.

In short, the profile of the young people who attend Projeto Semear is marked by the adversities that surround them. They experienced poverty, family disintegration, and a tenuous hold on traditional values. They were emotionally needy and unstable, aggressive, suspicious, and distrustful of society. Their previous school experiences were largely negative, and they left school. Most of them spent their days in the streets either loitering or working for drug dealers. Yet they were able to learn, create, and grow, as this chapter will show.

THE HISTORY OF THE PROJECT

Origins

As with many other philanthropic undertakings directed toward youth at risk, Projeto Semear had its roots in the interest and efforts put forth by the Catholic Archdiocese of Rio de Janeiro. The project is a response to a request from the Pastoral do Menor (Catholic Social Action Project for Youth), sponsored by the Archdiocese of Rio de Janeiro. The Pastoral do Menor sought an educational approach that could be adopted in a rural section of the municipality of Rio de Janeiro for use with a population that was not attending school—the so-called "street children."

Since its conception in 1988, Projeto Semear has faced certain challenges. The first was the planning of the project itself. Initial plans were presented in 1987 to a group of public school teachers who were working at the Curriculum Laboratory of the Rio de Janeiro State Department of Education. This team of educators accepted responsibility for implementing the project, and several of its members are still working on it.

The project was tailored to the community in the selected area. Local community leaders and project staff held discussions over a period of 3 months during which community interests were identified and project objectives were defined.[3] Community leaders most wanted vocational training courses for children. However, these courses had to be tied to basic elementary education because the young people for whom the project was designed had not completed that level of schooling. Other concerns were families' needs for jobs, better medical and hospital care, and housing. Because of the program's pedagogic focus, these were demands that could not be addressed by the Semear. Instead, people were referred to other agencies. In this way, the project staff and community developed an educational approach that included both elementary education and preparation for work. The first challenge—that of developing a project consistent with the needs of the community—was overcome.

The second challenge—finding the needed physical space—delayed the beginning of the project. The staff eventually located a perfect site. Casa do Pobre Nossa Senhora de Copacabana (Our Lady of Copacabana Housing for Poor People), which manages the project for the Archdiocese, borrowed funds from a private bank to purchase an 11-acre farm in Bangu in the western zone of the county of Rio de Janeiro.

The farm is situated at the foot of a mountain, near a nature preserve in the Atlantic Forest. Although located in greater Rio de Janeiro, the site has a rural flavor, an atmosphere quite different from the bustling urban center. About half of its 11 acres are swampy, and a quarter of it is used for horticulture, including a small orchard. The farm was once a private home surrounded by fruit trees, natural vegetation, a groves of banana trees, persimmon trees, and some large mango and jack-fruit trees. The site is an "oasis" within Bangu.

The Bangu neighborhood is divided in two by Brazil Avenue, one of Rio's most important thoroughfares. On the south side are the commercial districts and most of its *favelas*. However, the land on the north side of Brazil Avenue still maintains its rural character and has only a few *favelas*. Bangu is approximately 18 miles from the coast and has a population of about 640,000 people. Access to the coast requires taking two kinds

Figure 14.1 Semear students, their teachers, and their guests (including the authors and the book's editor) gather in the project's common area to discuss that evening's much anticipated July 4, 1994, soccer match that pitted the United States against Brazil in the World Cup finals. (Photo: Projeto Semear)

of public transportation, making it very difficult for most of its impoverished population to go to work in the main business area of the city or to go to the beach.

Funding and Staff

Recruiting expert staff and obtaining financial and material support for the programmed activities through various kinds of partnerships has always been a challenge for the Semear project. Initially, an agreement with the Rio de Janeiro State Department of Education provided nine elementary and junior high school teachers, a woman to prepare snacks, and a janitor. Casa do Pobre Nossa Senhora de Copacabana was responsible for hiring the vocational instructors and the project coordinators and administrators.

In 1992, the federal government began cutbacks in appropriations to many charitable institutions. Federally supported institutions, such as the Legião Brasileira de Assistência (Brazilian Welfare Legion [LBA]) and the Fundação Centro Brasileiro para a Infância e a Adolescência (Brazilian Center for Childhood and Adolescence [CBIA]) were abolished in 1992 and 1995 respectively. This left a gap in assistance to at-risk children and youth and to Semear. Several banks, including the Bank of Brazil and others, donated generously to the project and kept it afloat.

A search for new partnerships and sources of funding was launched. One resource came from a German woman, Caroline Welte. She promoted the establishment of the Children's Mission Fund, a private agency created to back projects aimed at needy population groups. Both the Brazilian and Swiss branches of Caritas, a Catholic relief organization, provided assistance in the early stages of the project in 1993. In addition, a European institution, Monaco Aide et Presence, contributed funds in 1994.

Although the year 1992 began with threats of financial cutbacks, it ended with a visit by representatives of the IDB. The delegation was to select model projects that best serve children who live in extremely difficult circumstances. In July 1993, the Semear team was notified that its project had been included among the first eight selected by the IDB. From 1993 until 1997, Semear received regular funding from the Children's Mission Fund, the Rio de Janeiro State Department of Education, the IDB, and a host of other public and private organizations. Since 1998, funding has come from the state's Foundation for Childhood and Adolescence, the sale of Semear products (chickens and T-shirts), and contributions from other private and public organizations.

THE PEDAGOGICAL PROPOSAL AND ITS OBJECTIVES

Semear operates a "world where there are no *pivetes*" (Vitória 1988).[4] It is a school and a farm that employs a "new way to educate" (Calmon Filho 1988). The program's initial clientele were absolutely unable to afford to attend school. Now they were given the chance to develop themselves mentally, morally, spiritually, and socially, and thus to escape the *pivete* stigma. One objective of Semear is to socialize young people who have been marginalized by society. The socioeconomic conditions of the families and nearby communities create a difficult climate for adolescent development.

The theoretical convictions of the Rio de Janeiro public school teachers who conceived Semear underlie the program's operations. Its approach follows three courses of action: recreation, academics, and initial preparation for work (Teves Ferreira 1993). The approach had been thoroughly discussed with local community leaders before the final version was implemented. Participation, consciousness-raising, and liberation (from their oppressive living conditions) are the guiding principles of the Semear project. Participation helps the children become familiar with the project, its objectives, and its goals so they can make suggestions for improvement, share decision making with the project's staff, and take an active part in implementation of proposals developed by mutual agreement. The concept of participation also extends to relationships among students: "Participation not only allows a child the right to have a voice; it is equally valuable in enabling children to discover the rights of others to have their own very different voices" (Hart 1995: 42).

Raising the consciousness of the children means helping them understand the context of their own lives and how to fight to transform them. As Freire suggested:

> Since men do not exist outside the world, outside of reality, the movement must begin with the man-world relationship. Consequently, the starting point must always be within men, in their "here and now" which constitute the situation in which they find themselves—sometimes immersed, sometimes emerged, sometimes inserted. (1980: 82)

This "man-world" interrelationship is brought to life in the project through the dialogue between students and their instructors. It is up to the educator to develop the students' interests, to enrich their relationship with the world, to help them take the best possible advantage of the tools available during the process of acquiring knowledge. This will permit young people to enter society with a wider and more comprehensive range of opportunities for a decent life. This procedure enables students to become independent and to put forth efforts toward freeing themselves from their substandard living conditions. They begin to discover and build their own identities, and to participate actively in the transformation of society while promoting their own well-being.

Through intense practical and theoretical interaction with the project team, Semear's design underwent a true reconstruction during its implementation. The program was officially accredited by the Conselho Estadual de Educação do Rio de Janeiro (Rio de Janeiro State Education Council). This means that young people enrolled in the project are eligible to receive elementary and junior high school completion certificates. Because of the way the curriculum is structured, Semear's instruction is not tied to the graded system found in official public schools. Instead, the Semear approach has fewer but broader objectives. It is more selective about content and keeps the subject matter pertinent to the students' daily lives. Simultaneously, Semear supplements clients' limited social experiences.

The process of critical appreciation in weekly assemblies attended by all participants has permitted a continual evaluation of the activities and, when necessary, their restructuring. Those assemblies afford the young people a chance to assess their own experiences in the project and to develop their capacity for self-criticism. This process is one result of the democratic approaches adopted at Semear.

CURRICULUM

Elements of Semear's curriculum include instruction in basic subjects (Portuguese, math, social studies, hygiene, physical education, and art); courses in farming methods (growing fruits and vegetables and raising chickens); and practical work in knitting, crocheting, serigraph printing, tailoring, electricity, and music (Secretaria do Estado de Educação do Rio de Janeiro 1989). In an effort to preserve Brazil's roots, cultural activities emphasize Afro-Brazilian dancing and *capoeira*.[5] Workshops fill young people's days from 9:00 A.M. to 4:00 P.M.

The study of Portuguese and mathematics is basic to the educational approach at Semear. In teaching Portuguese, the project attempts to develop reading skills through comprehension and writing, starting with the basics so that the young people can have access to the various linguistic ways of explaining the world. The Portuguese language is the vehicle for discussion and study of a variety of texts from many sources (books, newspapers, magazines) in other fields of knowledge, including geography, history, social studies, and even science and math. Contrary to the practice in regular public schools, no textbooks are used. The students record what they learn in their notebooks.

Mathematics is taught by activating the adolescents' cognitive structures, using knowledge they have already acquired. The curriculum is minimal, and its content was determined by polling experts as to the kind of math skills needed in daily life. Comprehension is essential. The teacher does not move ahead to the next topic until he learns through evaluation that the students have understood and assimilated the points already covered.

Science focuses on the development of good hygiene habits and basic principles for achieving good health. Social studies teachers use the daily experiences of their students as the starting point for their classes. They then reach to a wider field of study encompassing the students' city, their country, and the world. In physical education, the principle of having fun links participation and esprit de corps as paths to socialization. Because of its success with its clientele of students with histories of educational failures, the Semear curriculum still serves as the basis for the curriculum used in the *supletivo* courses (supplementary schooling for those who left school early) offered by the State of Rio de Janeiro (Secretaria do Estado de Educação Rio de Janeiro 1989).

PREPARATION FOR WORK

Workshops develop and nurture positive attitudes toward work. Students are prepared for work through courses in serigraphy, electronics, computing, photography, tailoring, machine knitting, agriculture, and poultry raising. The courses provide opportunities for the initial contacts that may lead to future employment. Farming practices were chosen because the site is in a rural area. At the outset, the young people rejected the chance to work in the fields. Now it is one of the preferred activities because students have developed an appreciation and respect for agriculture and ecology.

The project staff is fully aware of the problems the young people will encounter in the formal job market. Therefore, preparation for work is not limited to manual practice. Students learn to persevere, to attend to the task at hand, to be creative, to cooperate, to accept others, to accept criticism, to be self-critical, and to make decisions. They learn skills in handling tools, the theoretical knowledge of the activity being performed, professional zeal, and responsibility—in short, all the qualities that will enable them to learn future tasks more easily and to adapt themselves socially to their field of work.

Proceeds from the sale of goods produced in the workshops are earmarked for the support of the project. Initially, it was hoped that all the shops would generate a profit for pupils, but this proved not to be possible. Semear sells its chickens to the headquarters of its administrative overseer, Casa do Pobre Nossa Senhora de Copacabana, and at a butcher shop near the project; and sells its T-shirts to retailers. Surplus farm products not needed to feed project participants are distributed to them to take home to their families, thereby enriching the diets of people who rarely eat vegetables.

The purpose of the electrical shop is to get the students started in this occupation by teaching them to do minor repairs and simple domestic installations. After the students finish the course, they are referred to the Archdiocese's Projeto Integração, Rio-Criança Cidadã, Projeto Pleitear, and various units of the army. These programs offer practical training in occupational skills like auto mechanics or electronics. Students are guided to available jobs by the Archdiocese's Project-Center of Job References.

Figure 14.2   As do many female participants in Brazilian programs for street youth, Semear girls are taught to sew and tailor clothing. Boys are often taught silk screening, sewing, and tailoring, as well as other skills. (Photo: R. A. Mickelson)

TEACHERS AND STAFF

When a teacher is first selected to work at the project, priority is given to familiarizing him or her with the particular kind of student Semear serves, including the circumstances in which they live. The teacher is given a report that describes adolescents with the same kind of problems as Semear children (Mucchielli 1979; Redl and Wineman 1965). Only later are aspects of educational theory discussed. In this way, the teachers become aware that their primary role is to educate the students for life, not to try to drill into their heads the excessive volume of subject matter required by the curricula of traditional schools.

To carry out its pedagogical plan, the project now employs a team of teachers assigned by the Rio de Janeiro State Department of Education. They work in project administration (overall coordination, management, and pedagogical supervision); five work as classroom teachers, and three work as physical education teachers. The five teachers in the workshops, a secretary, a financial affairs assistant, the couple who serve as "house parents" at the group home that is located within the Bangu property, and the food preparers are all hired by the project's administrative overseer, Casa do Pobre Nossa Senhora de Copacabana. In addition to two volunteers (one for landscaping and another who does arts and crafts with the children) and college interns is a community leader, Madalena Vieira, who has been with the project since it started. Madalena's nickname—"mother of all the children"—conveys her importance to Semear. She is the link between Semear and the communities where the program's youth live. After working for 2 years as a volunteer, in 1989 she became a food service employee of Semear.

THE IMPACT OF PROJETO SEMEAR

Since it began, Semear has faced many challenges. But faithful to the metaphor implicit in its name, the program has begun to harvest the fruit of its labors. The data presented in the following sections are based on Queiroz's study of the project (1997). She constructed a group of indicators to assess the impact of the program and triangulated these outcomes with findings from projective tests administered to participants. Data were analyzed in light of theories of adolescence, especially those in situations of risk (Erikson 1972, 1968; Mucchielli 1979; Redl and Wineman 1965, 1957; and Winnicott 1995, 1984).

Student Opinions

The high regard in which the youngsters hold the project is illustrated by the increases in enrollment and the continuous inquiries about vacancies from people who "have heard good things" about the project.

Further evidence of Semear's acceptance and credibility is its penetration into the communities from which its participants come. These are neighborhoods with frequent drug traffic and turf warfare that have been closed off to access by outsiders. However, neighborhoods have begun to admit institutions endorsed by Semear. For example, the Children's Mission Fund was able to open a day care center, two social assistance offices, and two medical referral centers in those communities—the latter coordinated by former project interns.

Institutional Recognition

Another indicator of Semear's credibility is its selection as a site for research and internships for students at the Federal University of Rio de Janeiro and other institutions of higher education. The continued funding Semear receives from many international and national organizations is further evidence of its accomplishments.

Literacy

All the illiterate students who remained with the project learned to read and write. Between 1992 and 1998, 71 students out of 1,000 (7 percent of total enrollees) completed their junior high education and are working; 40 (4 percent of the total) are in high school.

Once students overcome the problems that prevented them from keeping up with the kind of instruction given at regular schools, they begin attending school outside the project, usually equivalency evening courses at public schools. These are designed to make up for the deficiencies in schooling the young people typically exhibit.

Work Outcomes

Every year, between 60 and 70 young people referred for apprenticeships outside of Semear through the Pleitear and Integração projects gain employment. Unfortunately, many are still in the informal market, because it is very hard to find a "registered" job. A variety of factors contribute to this: a shortage of money to pay commuting costs and buy clothes, and the nationwide shortage of jobs due to Brazil's economic situation.

Administrators of the program began to record information about former students only in 1997. Consequently, little formal data exists regarding most graduates' work histories. However, there are notable exceptions. For example, 27 young people have been employed outside of Semear at the Bank of Brazil, under an agreement with the Pastoral do Menor. There, working in the formal labor market, Semear students have won praise from their instructors for their ability to adapt and for their conduct. This praise demonstrates their newly acquired ability to integrate themselves into society.

Self-esteem

The most important impact on the students is related to the promotion of self-esteem, greater trust in the teachers, and the establishment of better teacher-student interaction. Fostering self-esteem among the participants of the project has not only helped build a positive sense of identity but also developed and strengthened the emotional ties to the Semear project.

It is worth recalling that, according to Semear staff, when the young people entered the project, they were not only aggressive and rebellious but also fearful about starting work, and they had no expectations for the future. "They harassed me frequently," said one teacher, "not because they didn't like me . . . but because they wanted to eliminate the bad stuff they had inside, in order to make room to receive other stuff. . . . Now, when they provoke me, fight, or start hitting each other, they often look at me later and say 'I love you.'"

The authors found that the sense of a job well done, one of the methods employed to promote self-esteem, brings the students pleasure and makes them proud to be part of the project. "Now they . . . want to work, they like farming, they try to get into courses that make the work easier, and a lot of them are working," declared one of the teachers. "Now Semear is a success," said one community leader, referring to the young people's achievements in the shop courses.

Cultural Outcomes

The results achieved by those who participate in the Afro-Brazilian dance group, known as Renascer da Africa (Africa Reborn), demonstrate the artistic and cultural talents of Semear youth. The group has given shows at the National Museum of Fine Arts, the Carlos Gomes Theater, the Brazil–United States Institute, the American School, and other sites. Occasionally, the City of Rio de Janeiro pays for shows. In the area of recreation, the young people have been exposed to new experiences and expanded their spheres of free expression by visits to museums, trips to the theater, the movies, and participation in athletic events.

Juveniles and the Law

Of the approximately 1,200 young people who have enrolled in Semear in the past 10 years, only 6 percent are now involved in illegal activities; 41 died in their communities during armed conflicts between rival drug lords or as victims of stray bullets. "In the project, the young people are shown that there are alternatives to joining in the drug traffic," said one teacher, María Amelia.

Oral histories of participants and community leaders indicate that *drogueros* (drug dealers) have praised students who took the initiative of enrolling in Semear. They say that Semear students gain an opportunity in life that they wouldn't have elsewhere and that the lack of similar opportunities led the drogueros to the world of crime.

Teachers

The teachers expressed the opinion that "today's group of students is quite different" but "we have changed, too." The Semear project has had an impact on the professionals who work there. Teachers feel more mature and ready to deal appropriately with project participants; many have gone back to school for additional training. "Recognizing the lack of knowledge needed to deal with the new reality, I began to look for theoretical references to help me in my work—I read about Summerhill, I read Makarenko," said Angelo, one of the teachers. Lea, the director, observed, "Semear is giving me more courage to face these challenges as a professional." Once afraid of the "new and unknown" represented by the project, its clientele, and its educational approach, teachers endured self-criticism of their own shortcomings—truly an exercise in intellectual humility. Now this team of educational professionals cites as among the most important effects of the project on their own lives a willingness to make a conscious effort to meet the needs of the young people and to develop a healthy affective relationship between teachers and students.

SUMMARY AND CONCLUSION

The entire range of changes that have occurred in the young people who participated in the Semear project can be summarized in a single, concise, statement by Coordinator Maria Helena:

> They have changed, certainly. Even their posture, the way they relate to others, the way they seek out opportunities. I think they have changed their view of the world, their view of their relationship with other people, with authority figures, although some have taken the wrong path and gotten lost. They have changed the way they demand things [and] their behavior.

An analysis of Semear's pedagogical praxis indicates that through its activities, the project channels unhealthy impulses and develops fine relationships between instructors and students in a democratic environment that provides opportunities for students to complete tasks in time frames that depend on individual ability. Moreover, through Projeto Semear, young people come to believe in their own ability and to accept responsibility for their actions. They gain chances to experience in daily life the social, civil, moral, and spiritual values that contribute to personal growth, integration into society, and, certainly, the conquest of citizenship.

There have been many benefits for most of the 1,200 at-risk adolescents who entered Projeto Semear since it opened its doors in 1988. For them, the seeds of the program are beginning to bud. This chapter presented the scope of the program and how it approached the social and educational problems faced by these desperate youth. Nevertheless, in the city of Rio de Janeiro there are many more youth whose families earn less than two minimum salaries per capita and who live in situations of high risk but do not participate in Semear.

The project's work has social and economic limitations because of Brazil's structural problems related to the lack of housing, good health services, and employment opportunities. But most of all, the critical situation of the world's and Brazil's economy has worsened income disparities and chances of gaining employment in the formal sector of the economy. Nonetheless, the history of Semear goes on. Semear continues to open its doors to any youngster who is searching for schooling and life beyond the *favelas* and the streets.

NOTES

1. The Portuguese verb *semear* means to sow seeds.
2. The term *community* refers to the subdivisions or neighborhoods within Bangu. Each is characterized by strong cohesion and a sense of belonging among those who live there. Many communities are rivals in the fight to control the drug traffic in Bangu.
3. These leaders were people from different walks of life in the community who were interested in discussing common problems and finding solutions. During the first phase of the Semear project, those leaders were appointed by the Pastoral do Menor and by the presidents of local residents' associations.
4. *Pivete* is a word designating delinquent, mischievous street children.
5. *Capoeira* (kickboxing) is an Afro-Brazilian game of attack and defense that is also practiced as a sport. Brazilians also consider *capoeira* to be a martial art.

REFERENCES

Calmon Filho, Milton. 1988. *Jornal O Globo-Zona Oeste,* 12 June, 10.
Empress Municipal de Informática e Planejamento (IPLAN-RIO). 1992/93. Rio de Janeiro: Author.
Erikson, Erik H. 1968. *Identity: Youth and Crisis.* New York: W. W. Norton.
———. 1972. *Identidade: juventude e crise.* Translated by Alvaro Cabral Rio de Janeiro: Zahar
Freire, Paulo. 1974. *Pédagogie des Opprimés.* Paris: François Maspero.
———. 1980. *Educação e mudança.* Rio de Janeiro: Paz e Terra.
Guba, E., and Y. Lincoln. 1985. *Naturalistic Inquiry.* Beverly Hills, Calif.: Sage.
Hart, Roger A. 1995. *Children's Participation: From Tokenism to Citizenship.* Florence: UNICEF/International Child Development Centre; Spedale degli Inocenti.
Instituto Brasileiro de Geografia e Estatística (IBGE). 1996. *Anuário estatística do Brasil.* Rio de Janeiro: Author.
Mucchielli, Roger. 1979. *Comment ils devienent délinquants.* Paris: Les Editions ESF.
Penna Firme, Thereza. 1995. *Capacitação de recursos humanos e fortalecimento institucional das entidades integrantes do programa de atenção a menores em circunstâncias especialmente difíceis.* Final Report. (mimeographed). Rio de Janeiro: IDB, Cesgranrio Foundation.
Queiroz, Amelia Maria Pessoa de. 1997. *O Caso Semear: a construção da identidade e a conquista da cidadania.* Rio de Janeiro: Nova Fronteira.
Redl, Fritz, and David Wineman. 1957. *Children Who Hate: The Disorganization and Breakdown of Behavior Controls.* New York: The Free Press.
———. 1965. *Controls from Within: Techniques for the Treatment of the Aggressive Child.* New York: The Free Press.
Rizzini, Irene, and I. Rizzini. 1991. "Menores institucionalizados e meninos de rua: os grandes temas de pesquisa da década de 80." Pp. 69–90 in *O Trabalho e a rua: crianças e adolescentes no Brasil urbano dos anos 80,* edited by Ayrton Fausto and R. Cervini. São Paulo: Cortez.
Secretaria de Estado de Educação do Rio de Janeiro. 1989. *Proposta alternativa de ensino de primeiro grau: modalidade supletiva.* Departamento Geral de Ensino. Rio de Janeiro: Imprensa Oficial.
Teves Ferreira, Nilda. 1993. *Cidadania: uma questão para a educação.* Rio de Janeiro: Nova Fronteira.
UNICEF. 1989. *Lineamientos para la aplicación de guia metodologico para analisis de situación de niños en circunstancias especialmente dificiles.* Preliminary version. Bogotá, Colombia: Guadalupe.
Valladares, Lícia, and Flávia Impelizieri. 1991. *Ação invisível, o atendimento a crianças carentes e a meninos de rua no Rio de Janeiro.* Rio de Janeiro: IUPERJ.
Vitória Gisele. 1988. *Jornal do Brasil,* 6 June.
Winnicott, Donald. 1984. *Deprivation and Delinquency.* London: Tavistock Publications, Ltd.
———. 1995. *Privação e delinqüência.* São Paulo: Martins Fontes

15

The "Magnet School" for the Homeless:
A Worst-Case Scenario

Jean Anyon

As I entered the second-grade classroom there was a strong smell of urine. The windows were closed, and there was a board over the glass pane in the door. The teacher yelled at a child from her desk, "I'm going to get rid of you!" Some children were copying spelling words from the board. Several of them jumped up and down in their seats. Most were not doing their work; many were leaning back in their chairs, chatting or fussing.

The children noticed my arrival and looked at me expectantly; I greeted them and turned to the teacher, commenting on the broken pane of glass in the door. She came over from the desk and said, "Jonathan put his hand through the window yesterday— his father passed him on the street and wouldn't say hello. Jonathan used to live with him, but since he started living with his mother, the father ignores him."

"These kids have hard lives, don't they," I said. At that, she began a litany of the troubles of the children in her class: Derrick's father died of AIDS last week; one uncle had already died of AIDS and another was sick. One girl's father stole her money for drugs. On Monday a boy had been brought to school by his mother, who said that the boy had been raped by a male cousin on Thursday, but that "he was over it now." The teacher was trying to get the boy some counseling. Two boys were caught shaving chalk and "snorting" the dust. One boy had a puffy eye because his mother got drunk after she got laid off and beat up the kids while they were sleeping; last night he had hit her back, while she was sleeping.

At this point, I interrupted the teacher to say, "It's really stuffy in here. Why don't you open a window?" "I can't," she replied, "because I have some children [points to a tiny girl] who like to jump out of school windows."

This chapter describes a ghetto school located in Newark, New Jersey.[1] In this city with a substantial homeless population, the school system had at the time of my research (1991–1993) few provisions for its homeless students. McKinney Act money provided funds for an after-school program for 2 years in two schools. Marcy School, the site of my research, was designated The Magnet School for the Homeless on the grant application for McKinney Act funding. This chapter summarizes characteristics of the school milieu and discusses the history of the city in order to document the political and economic trends and decisions that led to the present situation. Marcy School illustrates the central point that children who are homeless experience what most poor children in America experience: slipshod, sometimes abusive education.

A GHETTO SCHOOL—THE "MAGNET SCHOOL" FOR THE HOMELESS

Marcy School is located in an inner-city minority ghetto. I call on the concept of *ghetto* to highlight the extreme poverty and destitution of the children in America's inner cities. The definition of ghetto that I will use draws from William J. Wilson, who describes a ghetto as an inner-city neighborhood in which more than 40 percent of the inhabitants are poor. Most inhabitants of such neighborhoods are African American (and increasingly Hispanic) and typically are economically, culturally, and politically isolated from the mainstream, despite their usual proximity to city hall and downtown shopping districts (Wilson 1987, 1995).

Marcy School exists in such a neighborhood. Census data from 1990 show that, in the census tract in which the school is located, 45 percent of all persons have incomes below the poverty level; of female-headed households with related children under 18 years of age, 66 percent are below the poverty level; of female-headed households, with related children under 5 years of age, 82 percent are under the poverty level. According to the 1990 census, the per capita income was $7,647 in the census tract in which the research site is located. Per capita income in the city of Newark was $9,437; per capita income in the state of New Jersey was $24,936, which was 33 percent higher than the national average. In 1990, New Jersey was the nation's second-wealthiest state.

All but 3 of Marcy School's 500 students, and 78 percent of the students in the school district, are poor and qualify for free lunch. During the period of this research, between 5 and 20 percent of the students in the school were officially unhoused. Teachers stated that many more were unofficially homeless, bunking with relatives or friends. The student body's racial composition was 71 percent African American, 27 percent Hispanic, and 2 percent Asian and white.

The social context of this school, then, is of an impoverished minority ghetto, with all the attendant problems of unemployment, underemployment, drug abuse, child abuse and neglect—stressful, danger-filled, often chaotic lives lived close to the bustle of the downtown business district, but far from the mainstream of American middle-class society.

The McKinney Act was designed to help schools like this one attend to the special needs of the homeless children among its students. However, other than its curious name, The Magnet School for the Homeless, and an after-school program that provided homeless students no benefits beyond custodial child care, there was little if any programmatic effort to assist homeless children. With the exception of some teachers who personally brought them clothes and soap, homeless children were treated the same as the other poor students who attended Marcy School. Homeless children were teased by other students. This school is emblematic of the worst education America has to offer her poor and homeless children.

ATTEMPTS TO IMPLEMENT EDUCATIONAL REFORM IN MARCY SCHOOL

Preceding, as well as during, the period of the study, the school was a focus of massive efforts at reform, with 28 improvement projects underway in the building between 1989 and 1993. Almost all of these projects were carried out in the school by white professionals. Projects had managerial collaborators from the city's corporate giants,[2] who had committed money although only a few of their representatives were ever present in the school.

The after-school tutorial and mentoring program that gave Marcy School its name, The Magnet School for the Homeless, was started by a psychology professor and two graduate students from a nearby university. During the 10 months in which I worked with teachers in their classrooms as a staff developer, I observed that the milieu in both the school and the after-school program for the homeless children was characterized by the following four attributes:

1. *Sociocultural differences among the white, professional or business executive reformers, on the one hand, and the teachers and parents, on the other.* These differences lead to miscommunication and mistrust and only minimal success on joint efforts at reform. For example, a series of meetings between two retired white executives (who had volunteered to assist the parent group improve its efforts to get more parents involved) and the school's parent group came to naught. The leader of the parent group said, "They're just white men tryin' to tell us what to do." And one of the executives said, "Nobody here [in the school] wants to do *anything* [other than what they are currently doing]."

2. *Sociocultural differences between a white, middle-class curriculum presented in textbooks written in standard English, a dialect of English spoken neither by students (who are marginalized from the mainstream in a ghetto neighborhood), nor by many of the teachers (who were themselves reared in working-poor and minority neighborhoods).* This disjuncture between the languages spoken and the texts contributed to mathematical and scientific confusion between math and science textbooks and classroom conversations, and in reading, to alienation on the part of students from much of the reading materials. The confusion and alienation reduced student comprehension and therefore academic performance as well.[3]

3. *An abusive school environment in which teachers' and administrators' interactions with students were commonly characterized by degrading comments and outright psychological (and sometimes physical) abuse or degradation that the parents did not have the social power to prevent.* This environment is apparently not confined to the school I observed. In 1995, the district as a whole—with only 4 percent of the state's students—reported more than 40 percent of all incidents of abuse by school employees reported to the state by school systems. The abusive school environment created an oppositional student culture and a refusal by many students to cooperate during class—and often, during standardized testing. This opposition to instruction and evaluation led to diminished accomplishments on the part of the students.

4. *An almost universal feeling of resignation on the part of school personnel regarding student failure because of the enormity of the students' social predicament and because of the history of failure of reform in the district during the last 30 years (Trachtenberg 1978; Anyon 1997).* The expectations of failure were accompanied by explanations expressing the belief that even if the students did learn to read and write, or even if the reforms did work, it would not be enough "to do any good," and "there would be no jobs" available for students later anyway, so what was the use? The emiseration of the students' lives and the lack of a receptive economy seemed to impinge on reform by producing a profound antipathy to the effort needed to make curricular and other educational changes.

These four phenomena, which I attribute in large part to the social context of poverty and racial marginalization in which Marcy School is embedded, impinged upon successful implementation of the after-school tutorial and mentoring project and other educational reform attempts. For example, the tutorial and mentoring for homeless children devolved into an after-school snack and "free-time" session, with one aide and 50 children. According to a teacher involved, no educational activities actually took place, although the program was funded through the McKinney Act with money earmarked for educational programs for children like those in Marcy School.

HISTORICAL FOUNDATIONS OF FAILED EDUCATIONAL REFORM

As the above summary suggests, I believe the social context of a school impinges on educational improvement efforts in inner-city ghetto schools. To understand how this happens, we need to assess everyday economic and political phenomena for their normally unremarked educational consequences. It also means that we need to examine what economic and social trends have caused the ravishment of the environment in which the inner-city ghetto school is located. In the following section I sketch a brief analysis of this history. To this end, I will take the four characteristics of school life during the reforms I studied and show how each problem results in important ways from noneducational economic, political, and social phenomena and historical trends.

Sociocultural differences, mistrust, and suspicion between white professionals and executives engaged in reform, on the one hand, and low-income black parents and teachers, on the other, result from the separation and alienation in U.S. society between blacks and whites, and between poor people of color and whites from professional and corporate backgrounds (Orfield and Ashkinaze 1991; Hacker 1992).

There are historical reasons why this great gap in experience, language, and belief exists. In Newark, for example, as in most other older American cities, important history includes the following: during the last several decades of the nineteenth century, wealthy industrialists and owners of businesses lived near their factories and shops in the downtown areas of the developing cities. Close by lived the workers—immigrants from Ireland, Germany, and the British Isles. Between 1900 and 1920, most elites moved to the surrounding countryside, and with the installation of a network of trolley connecting the city and the countryside around 1890, the middle classes began to leave as well. European immigrants continued to pour into the inner cities and moved into the older wooden houses, now in disrepair. After World War II, many business and manufacturing firms left the inner city for the developing suburbs. During the same years, hundreds of thousands of rural, impoverished southern blacks—most of whom were sharecroppers idled by the mechanization of agriculture and tobacco—arrived in the northern and midwestern cities. The only landlords who would rent to them were in the deteriorating sections in the central cities abandoned by the last wave of white immigrants, now ensconced in the suburbs.

As Kenneth Jackson has shown in his book, *Crabgrass Frontier* (1985), the creation of roads, sewage lines, and new homes in the new suburbs after World War II was heavily financed by the federal government—while the cities received few improvement funds. Even black veterans could not get the federally guaranteed home mortgage loans in the suburbs that whites were able to acquire, and so were forced to remain in the deteriorating cities. The federally sponsored redlining of city neighborhoods in which blacks lived and of the neighborhoods in which whites and blacks lived together led to the refusal of federally insured banks and real estate companies to grant insured mortgage or home improvement loans to people in these neighborhoods.[4] This resulted in huge areas of America's inner cities in which homeowners could not receive loans to buy or improve their property. These properties soon became rentals with absentee landlords and minority tenants.

Beginning in 1937, and continuing until the middle of the 1960s, housing rehabilitation (urban renewal) of the resulting slums created low- and middle-income housing—almost all of which was segregated. These federal and local policies contributed to the extreme residential segregation in older northern and midwestern cities. When combined with historical occupational segregation in the U.S. economy, housing segregation resulted in blacks (and other minorities) and whites living in different places and not knowing each other. The minority inner-city resident (usually poor) is now almost completely alien to the white resident of suburbs (only 12 percent of suburban residents are black, and many of them live in low-income suburban enclaves).

The media contribute to fear among suburban whites and resentment among city blacks by emphasizing black crime but not white-collar crime. Suburban whites come to fear the inner-city minority residents, and the ghetto residents resent and are suspicious of whites for their alleged and real privileges. This suspicion and mistrust finds expression in the dynamics of educational reform projects when—as in the reform effort in which I participated—former executives attempt to tell low-income parents from housing projects how to attract other parents to the reform effort, or when white middle-class psychologists from affluent suburbs try to tell black teachers (most of whom are from working-class or working-poor backgrounds) how to "cooperate" with each other; parents and teachers often resent and ignore the advice.

The sociocultural differences between curricular reforms and students' language and experience arise from the same disjunctures discussed in the previous section, except that these disjunctures are also a manifestation of the fact that white upper- and middle-class experiences are represented, cataloged, and transmitted in the texts, because that is the culture and experience of the dominant group (Anyon 1979). That the story of World War I, the expansion of the railroads, industrialization, and the Rockefellers does not reverberate with the experience of children and youth in the ghetto does not need elaboration. Many ghetto youth—for all their bravado and street "smarts"—have often never been outside of the neighborhood, never been on an elevator, never been on a train, to a restaurant (except a fast food outlet), or to a doctor's office.

Similarly, the tests they regularly take are written in white standard English. However, inner-city dialect is spoken by almost all the children in the inner-city school I studied—blacks, Hispanics, and the few poor whites who attended. It is also spoken by many of the city's black teachers. There are cultural attitudes of difference and pride involved in speaking black dialect (when, for example, one is fluent in standard English as well), but a good deal of the pronounced use of inner-city dialect by the students in Marcy School results in difficulty navigating texts and the tests.

An abusive classroom and school environment in which both white and black teachers and administrators may degrade and otherwise psychologically abuse the students also arises from complicated causes, and can have various meanings. It is my view that the systematic degradation of the impoverished minority ghetto students, wherein they are treated as if they were of little or no worth, arises, in part, from the perceived low status of the children and adults. Perceiving low-status persons as if they were barely human has roots not only in the social and economic facts of little social power but also in the characteristics of past colonial relationships.

Albert Memmi, Franz Fanon, and Paulo Freire have each demonstrated how, in colonial societies, white colonists generally view colonized people of color as subhuman or substandard in an unconscious way—thus keeping them the "other" and separate from the colonial self. This view of the native permeates social interchange among the groups. It serves to maintain the white colonialists' sense of superiority, and the natives' belief in the validity of their own situation of oppression (Memmi 1965, 1968; Fanon 1967; Freire 1970; Said 1979).

These theorists have also pointed out that in many cases members of the colonized group who have climbed from the bottom of the social hierarchy into the lower-middle or middle classes also view those natives still on the bottom as subhuman or degraded, or of very little worth. This phenomenon, it seems to me, operates in ghetto schools like Marcy School where black teachers systematically see the children as the "other," and abuse these "natives"—the impoverished minority students. For white teachers, on the other hand, it is the dominant societal view they express—poor children are difficult to teach, not good students, and of little social value.

Another factor contributing to the view of impoverished ghetto students as of little worth is the dependency that poverty in modern America enforces. Unable to be self-supporting, an impoverished family may crack under the weight of despair, drugs, and alcohol. In the absence of other options (such as decent jobs, nondehumanizing medical care), dependency on government programs often ensues. Many in the U.S. middle class (both minority and white) view this dependency with disdain and disgust. Teachers' comments to children that they were "disgusting" or "like animals" may reflect this view (Anyon 1995, 1997).

Teachers' and administrators' expectations that the reform will fail arise in part from past experience in the school system. The district has been attempting to upgrade the achievement of students in its inner-city schools since 1970 (Trachtenberg 1978; Anyon 1997). School personnel are cynical about the efforts of the Newark Board of Education, which they describe as "chaotic" and "full of graft," and that it "doesn't really care about the kids." The history of Newark's government and education systems is, like that of many other older U.S. cities, one of extensive patronage. Because of this history of political patronage (in operation since the late nineteenth century)—Germans, whose dominance gave way to the Irish machine, then to Jewish dominance in the thirties, then to the Italian machine aided by the Italian mafia in the sixties—African Americans have dominated the patronage and graft only since 1980s. Currently, because of the large number of political appointees, there are unqualified workers at all levels of the Newark school system. A recent state evaluation found that incompetence, lack of qualifications, and mismatched skills were rife at all levels of the school system (New Jersey Department of Education 1993).

Many employees at the board of education and in the schools are long-term residents of the city and themselves attended the city's schools. In the absence of other employment opportunities in Newark, these residents depend upon the schools for their jobs. In this way, the system, with all its faults, becomes "their" system, and they defend and support it for reasons that any dependency on an employer creates (see Marion Orr's [1998] discussion of the same dynamics in Baltimore, Maryland).

There is a further dimension of the expectations of failure of reform. And that is that—as many teachers and administrators stated in interviews—even if the reform were to succeed, it would not positively affect students' futures, because Marcy School's students have overwhelming life problems that the reforms do not touch. The attitudes shared by students and staff are summed up in the following quote: "Even if they [the students] do learn to read and write, there aren't any jobs [for them]."

POVERTY, HOMELESSNESS, AND SCHOOL FAILURE

The economic reality of few jobs for the students and their parents is painfully apparent to everyone associated with Marcy School. Why try? Why work hard? There will be no reward for such effort (see MicKelson 1990 for a general discussion of the effects of these attitudes on school performance). The economic decline and of recent economic isolation of America's cities are root causes of the failure of school reform, and of the poverty, homelessness, and other social dislocations described in this chapter and by other scholars (Kozol 1992; Wilson 1996; Massey and Denton 1995).

Moreover, during recent decades, the U.S. economy changed fundamentally, penalizing the city's residents even further. Deindustrialized, based no longer on manufacturing but heavily reliant on services and new financial, technical, and information jobs, the newly globalized economy has produced a wage structure that reflects the bifurcated occupational structure: most new jobs are either low-paying service jobs or high-income professional, managerial, and technical jobs. As middle-class positions become more scarce, even the middle classes are beginning to feel the results of these economic developments.

The trends that began in the 1920s (but temporarily halted during World War I) as manufacturing and skilled jobs relocated to the suburbs, and recently to other countries, have left skilled and unskilled workers in inner cities with few jobs other than temporary, part-time ones in the low-wage service sector. Currently, in the cities there is little employment for high school graduates that pays a wage significantly above the poverty line. Students, teachers, and administrators in Marcy School know this. Their knowledge of the kind of economic future that awaits residents is likely to have produced a culture of resignation that can overpower good intentions, good deeds, and educational improvement projects.

CONCLUSION

The miseducation of homeless and other children in Marcy School is emblematic of the worst American public education has to offer its poor. The neglect that homeless students suffer is but one end of a continuum of miseducation frequently perpetrated against poor inner-city children. And that is the central theoretical point of this case study. Children and families marginalized by a transforming political economy are likely to receive increasingly marginalized services, including public schooling. The homeless are merely the most marginalized.

It seems to me that educational reform is affected in significant ways by the "noneducational" events and processes originating in the political, economic, and cultural environment. When you trace the history of a school system such as the one I studied, you can see that during the period of industrialization (1850-1917) when the city was producing substantial profits for its financial classes, and when the students were perceived as having a potential contribution to that profit as workers, even though the population was poor and immigrant, the schools were bustling with nationally renowned administrators and nationally reported innovations.

The city of Newark, like many other cities in the United States, is now economically moribund. Newark's ghetto is separated from postindustrial skilled and high-paying jobs. Importantly, the student population is perceived as having no potential profitable economic role. The schools reflect these perceptions and conditions. The fact that the parent and student populations are perceived as deficient, impoverished, or dysfunctional minorities lends a legitimacy to the condition of the schools and the failure of reform to reverse the educational decline.

I suggest that the structural basis for failure in inner-city schools—and the failure of educational reform projects such as the one for homeless children in Marcy School—is political, economic, and cultural in nature. This must be changed before meaningful school improvement projects can be successfully implemented. I maintain that the only solution to educational resignation and failure in the inner city is the ultimate elimination of poverty and racial degradation. The solution to the problem of the failure of educational reform for poor and homeless children in the ghetto ultimately depends upon the elimination of the ghetto.

NOTES

1. This chapter is based on my book, *Ghetto Schooling: A Political Economy of Urban Education* (1997).
2. I (one of the white professionals) participated in the reform during 1991–1993 primarily as a staff developer. I carried out workshops in cooperative learning in several of the eight target schools in the district. I worked at least 1 day per week during the 10 school months in Marcy School's teachers' classrooms (see Anyon 1994, 1995, for further descriptions of this work). In addition to the more than 200 hours spent with teachers in their classrooms, I also attended reform team meetings during the school year and spent numerous hours talking with teachers at these meetings. During the year I spent 21 lunch periods "hanging out" with students in the cafeteria and the asphalt yard; I also chatted with them frequently in the classrooms and halls. Between 1991 and 1993, I formally interviewed the assistant superintendent, his staff, 24 of 25 classroom teachers at Marcy School, the members of the school-based support team, both school administrators, the school's drug counselor, 15 parents, and 25 students. I read numerous school and district reports and other documents (such as state reports) pertaining to the schools and the reform initiative. I also examined the curriculum materials in use and those prepared by the state but not in use.
3. In 1987 Eleanor Orr demonstrated fundamental ways black dialect can interfere with mathematical thinking in educational contexts where mathematical thinking is governed, in textbooks and in most pedagogy, by standard English language and forms of thought. She argues that not only do the subtlety of differences and the lack of familiarity with terms impede mathematical understanding but also the outright conflict of black dialect terms with standard English terms interfere. Orr demonstrates that the grammars are distinct, the lexicons overlap, and—significantly—the unconscious rules that govern syntax in black dialect often conflict with and interfere with standard English (Orr 1987).
4. *Redlining* refers to the now-outlawed practice of literally drawing a red line on a map around areas where minorities lived in high concentrations. The redlined portions of a city were used to identify areas where the federal government and financial institutions refused to make loans.

REFERENCES

Anyon, Jean. 1979. "Ideology and U.S. History Textbooks." *Harvard Educational Review* 49: 361–86.

———. 1994. "Teacher Development and Reform in an Inner City School." *Teachers College Record* 96: 14–31.

———. 1995. "Inner City School Reform: Toward Useful Theory." *Urban Education* 30: 56–70.

———. 1997. *Ghetto Schooling: A Political Economy of Urban Educational Reform.* New York: Teachers College Press.

Fanon, Franz. 1967. *Black Skin, White Masks.* New York: Grove Press.

Freire, Paulo. 1970. *Pedagogy of the Oppressed.* New York: Herder and Herder.

Hacker, Andrew. 1992. *Two Nations: Black, White, Separate, and Hostile.* New York: Charles Scribner's Sons.

Jackson, Kenneth. 1985. *Crabgrass Frontier: The Suburbanization of the United States.* New York: Oxford University Press.

Kozol, Jonathan. 1992. *Savage Inequalities.* New York: Crown.

Massey, Douglass, and Mary Denton. 1995. *American Apartheid.* Chicago: University of Chicago Press.

Memmi, Albert. 1965. *The Colonizer and the Colonized.* Boston: Beacon Press.

———. 1968. *Dominated Man.* Boston: Beacon Press.

Mickelson, Roslyn Arlin. 1990. "The Attitude-Achievement Paradox among Black Adolescents." *Sociology of Education* 63: 44–61.

New Jersey Department of Education. 1993. *Newark Public Schools: Level III External Review.* Trenton, N.J.: Author.

Orfield, Gary, and Carol Ashkinaze. 1991. *The Closing Door: Conservative Policy and Black Opportunity.* Chicago: University of Chicago Press.

Orr, Eleanor. 1987. *Twice as Less: Black English and the Performance of Black Students in Mathematics and Science.* New York: W. W. Norton.

Orr, Marion. 1998. "The Challenge of School Reform in Baltimore: Race, Jobs, and Politics." Pp. 93–117 in *Changing Urban Education,* edited by Clarence Stone. Lawrence: University of Kansas Press.

Said, Edward. 1979. *Orientalism.* New York: Pantheon.

Trachtenberg, Paul. 1978. "Pupil Performance in Basic Skills in the Newark School System since 1967." Pp. 235–43 in *Newark, 1967–1977: An Assessment,* edited by S. B. Winters. Newark: New Jersey Institute of Technology.

Wilson, William J. 1987. *The Truly Disadvantaged: The Inner City, the Underclass, and Public Policy.* Chicago: University of Chicago Press.

———. 1996. *When Work Disappears.* Chicago: University of Chicago Press.

16

Programa Curumim:
A Program for At-Risk Children in the Industrial Heartland

Murilo Tadeu Moreira Silva

Our car drove along the wide boulevards of the central business district through the city's industrial sector until we reached the edge of Belo Horizonte. The vistas changed from skyscrapers, to industrial plants, and then to barren hills dotted with squatters' homes. In the distance, the huge red and white striped roof of the Curumim facility appeared at the edge of the favela. *The cheerful, open tent-like structure seemed appealing against the stark and shabby* favela *homes. The Curumim grounds included a fenced in swimming pool, a garden, and a makeshift soccer field. First, my daughter and I visited the director's modest office. Then we toured the kitchen and met the cooks, two motherly women sweating as they stirred huge steaming vats of food. In the classroom, we found a young teacher leading about 25 attentive youngsters uniformed in their Curumim shirts. In the recreational area, a group of about eight boys presented a* capoeira *demonstration. Two preteen girls, both named Maria, watched with us. When we departed, the one wearing hot pink lipstick embraced me and gave me a kiss on both cheeks.*
—R. Mickelson, field notes, July 14, 1994

Programa Curumim targets young children living in difficult situations who are apt to be attracted into the streets. Curumim—the name comes from the Tupi Indian word *kuru' mi,* which means "child"—serves children age 6 to 12. It tries to ensure children the right to be children and to experience this important phase in their development as individuals in a manner that is playful, but at the same time educational. The program is sponsored by the government of the state of Minas Gerais, which operates Curumim through its Secretaria de Esportes, Lazer e Turismo (Department of Sports, Recreation, and Tourism). Conceived in the early 1990s, it was designed to deal with the abandoned children and adolescents on the outskirts of Belo Horizonte, the state capital. In practice, Curumim operates as an intervention that prevents young adolescents from entering the life of the streets. Most are not abandoned by their families; they are merely suffering from the stress of poverty (Secretaria de Esportes 1991).

Currently, there are 140 centers around the urban areas of the state of Minas Gerais. Twenty-seven are in Belo Horizonte, and 113 in other towns and cities. Each center serves between 150 and 180 children at one time, and since its inception, an estimated 22,000 children have participated in the program. About 30 percent of the centers have the program's distinctive red-and-white-striped tentlike edifice; the other 70 percent are housed in more traditional buildings.

Objectives of the Curumim Program

The program's goals are to foster, through recreation, sports, arts and crafts, and educational enrichment activities, the personal and social development of children and adolescents who are in difficult circumstances. Several other aims include: providing educational and social guidance for their families; preserving the emotional and sociocultural ties between the children and their families; arranging for adolescents' enrollment in school (or return to the classroom), continued attendance, and success of young people in the school system; and referring adolescents to vocational training courses. Referrals to vocational courses are made, but not very frequently; in fact they are sporadic. In addition, the program ensures balanced nutrition by serving a meal at the beginning or end of the day. Some centers serve snacks when the children arrive, since it is not unusual for them to have left home without eating anything. Access to local medical services is facilitated; the kinds of accidents that commonly occur among children—cuts, fractures, and so forth—build a relationship between the centers and local clinics or hospitals. These depend upon the presence of factors other than the mere participation of a child in Curumim.

DEMOGRAPHICS OF MINAS GERAIS: TARGET POPULATION

The state of Minas Gerais is one of the wealthiest in Brazil. The level of poverty and destitution there is far less than in other industrial states, like São Paulo, and far less than in the impoverished Northeast. Belo Horizonte, its capital and largest city, has 2,020,161 inhabitants (IBGE 1997). The state's name in English means "general mines," suggesting the nature of the area's industrial economy as well as its history. The racial composition of the city's residential population reflects its prosperity. In a country where race and class are tightly linked, the more prosperous citizens of Belo Horizonte are more European/white than Brazil as a whole (Velloso and Calvalcanti 1991; IBGE 1988). About one- half of the city's population is considered white (*branca*), 6 percent is black (*preta*), another 43 percent is brown or mestizo (*parda*), and a small number are indigenous or of Asian descent (IBGE 1997).

The greater Belo Horizonte area boasts one of Brazil's most important industrial and commercial hubs. This ought to have a positive impact on the city's poor, but such is not the case. The tremendous wealth generated in the Belo Horizonte area simply deepens even further the gulf that separates those who are prosperous from those living in misery.

The heavy concentration of income and the lack of a commitment by either the government, the society, or the business community to solve social problems exacerbates the poverty and problems faced by these population groups. Isolated initiatives have been taken by some companies that have made contributions through programs and partnerships. However, their impact is slight because the dimensions of the problems are so large.

The urban communities served by the Programa Curumim are composed principally of migrants from other parts of Minas Gerais. These people were driven from the countryside, escaping horrendous living conditions that had deteriorated due to several factors: extremely low wages; loss of crops to drought or floods; exploitation by employers; and poor distribution of land. This situation has been exacerbated by the perpetually postponed agrarian reform, the violence sparked by disputes over land, and the government's disheartening farm policy. Because of the difficulties that farmers face in obtaining financing, and the high interest rates that prevent small farmers from modernizing their operations, their products are less competitive and they frequently default on loans.

The migratory flow from impoverished rural areas to the urban regions caused *favelas* to spring up in the areas around Belo Horizonte. There, families live in improvised dwellings built of castoff materials scavenged from construction sites or from whatever flimsy materials they can somehow acquire. Usually illiterate or only semiliterate, lacking any skills or trade, they have little chance of competing for a spot in the already saturated labor market, so they become part of the mass of the city's unemployed or underemployed. They make their living from odd jobs or menial work. Even when they manage to find steady employment, their earnings are insufficient to meet even the minimum needs of their always large families. The women in these families, when not working at home, are frequently employed as domestics. Another segment of the population on the outskirts of Belo Horizonte is composed of natives of the city who were displaced by floods or evicted from illegally occupied real estate. In short, they are the by-products of poverty created by the city itself. Seeing no alternative, these groups occupy the outskirts and hillsides of the city. There is also a growing number of homeless people driven into the streets when they cannot afford the cost of living in the shantytowns.

GUIDING PRINCIPLES

The founding Curumim Educational Psychology Team, included an educational theorist, a psychologist, and an art teacher. The team decided to employ theoretical models that have been recognized as valuable for the conduct of a solid, critical, and democratic instructional and educational effort. They concluded that, even considering the socioeconomic background of the target children and adolescents, Curumim could offer the kind of high-quality assistance that would give the children a chance to assimilate, through the four program activities, contents vital to strategies for living.

Instructors were recruited from university schools of human sciences, the communities, or even from the civil service. They were trained to develop a new pattern of democratic educational management. The training of these instructors emphasized the need to acknowledge the child as the agent of his own history and to realize that the appropriation of the basic instructional content makes a huge contribution to the emancipation of the lower social classes from which most Curumim pupils come. Consequently, the education of these children must be an exercise of freedom, so as not to oppress, but rather, to liberate them by respecting their culture and beliefs, and by encouraging their independence and critical thinking.

On this point, Curumim's inspiration came from the teachings of Paulo Freire: all responsible socioeducational actions must be committed to the transformation of the lives of poor children, their families, and their communities. It follows that there is yet another requirement: understanding the process by which children acquire knowledge. This is indispensable if the instructor is to promote and facilitate the learning process while keeping in mind the age and stage of (cognitive and emotional) development of the child, so as to make the learning process compatible with them. Adopting a constructivist posture in daily contacts with the children and during the instructor training became an important feature of the technical and scientifically based training of the Curumim teaching staff. Moreover, instructors must be socially committed to the project's goal of reducing inequalities and democratizing knowledge.

Another aspect emphasized by the Curumim Educational Psychology Team was the need to become familiar with the phases in the emotional development of a child. These are used as a guide for selecting the educational activities. Several kinds of organized games or play activities had to be adopted for one age bracket or replaced in another, in light of the conclusions reached after the study of the cognitive processes and the phases of emotional development. Knowledge of child development is also used as preparation for the kind of questions about sex that the teams at the Curumim centers are frequently asked by the children and adolescents. Psychoanalytical knowledge proved to be important in understanding and dealing with problems. The Curumim educational psychology team gives the educators an overview of the problems that they may encounter. However, all centers have at least one psychologist who can intercede when an instructor believes he/she is not ready to deal with more serious problems involving learning disabilities and aberrant behavior.

OPERATING A CURUMIM CENTER

Establishing a Curumim Center

At the beginning of the program (1991–1992), experts identified critical zones in the city of Belo Horizonte and then began their diagnostic studies. Later, other communities contacted the department to express an interest in establishing a center after having heard reports about the program. Theoretically, the establishment of a center must be preceded by a diagnostic study, a phase that involves gathering information about the community where it is to be installed. In principle, before a center is implemented, officials verify that the locality is indeed economically needy. They visit the homes in the community with the instructors, observe the habits, customs, beliefs, and economic status of the residents, and find out where the people originally came from. Funds to establish a program are transferred under a cooperation agreement for construction and maintenance of the centers. The agreement provides for partnerships with other municipal governments when the center is to be built outside the state capital city. While officials recognize that familiarity with the community for which a center is planned is important, unfortunately, consultation with the community has not been standard practice. It turns out that political decisions tend to prevail over the actual, diagnosed, needs of local residents.

In metropolitan Belo Horizonte, the Department of Sports, Recreation, and Tourism not only builds the facility but also recruits, hires, and trains the teaching staff. Financing from other federal and state agencies pays for food and uniforms. The four planned activities:—sports, recreation, arts and crafts, and educational enrichment—take place in relays, two per half-day session (Secretaria de Esportes, Lazar e Turismo 1991). The children are welcomed, readied, and divided into four groups, each headed by an instructor. Each center has one director, a cook, and a teaching staff whose size can vary from one center to another. Instructors and pupils are encouraged to hold a meeting before beginning the activities, in order to reach a consensus as to whether the children prefer supervised play or an organized game. Plans are completely flexible, although clear, well-defined rules govern the center's operation. Groups of children take turns helping in the kitchen, organizing the cleaning crew, and performing other tasks to maintain the center—but these matters, too, are agreed on with the students.

Center directors and the teaching staff meet daily to discuss problems, consider specific cases, read reports and memos, and handle other matters. Almost all centers are able to call on at least one psychologist, or professor or student of psychology, although there is no specific position on the Curumim organization chart for either a psychologist or an educational theorist.

The duties of the psychologists, as defined by their professional association, emphasize work with the community as being the most important aspect of their performance, in addition to routine referrals made with the supervision of the instructors.

Skits and plays, puppet shows, choral performances, and musical shows are frequently staged by the children. However, activities are not restricted to the center site. Field trips are made to the theater, points of ecological interest, and cultural and recreational events. Competitions among centers in a "Curumim Olympics" bring the athletics year to a close.

Facilities

The facilities and equipment used in the program are based on extremely simple and practical patterns inspired by community parks and the circus. The roof of the Standard Curumim Building is painted in red and white stripes. The building consists of a sheet-metal roof supported on the outside of its four corners by four rooms built of unfinished cement block, with cement floors. Two of the rooms are used for program activities; the other two are used as the kitchen and dressing area. The large central space under the roof is used for cultural activities (plays, lectures, music recitals) and, when it is raining, for recreation. A multipurpose athletic field is located next to the main building. Construction methods and structural features can be adapted to the specific site where a Curumim center is to operate. Some centers have extra space that include a small vegetable garden cultivated by the children, with the help of community volunteers.

Figure 16.1 Curumim's distinctive red-and-white tentlike edifice is built adjacent to a *favela* in Belo Horizonte. The building is supported in each corner by rooms that serve as a classroom, a program office, a kitchen, and a dressing area. The large space under the tent is used as a dining and meeting area and for student performances. (Photo: Curumim)

The Semi-Constructed Curumim Facility was designed for smaller spaces. In an effort to ensure at least a minimum covered area, it has one activity room, a dressing area, kitchen, and bathrooms. It features the same red-and-white striped roof. The Integrated Curumim Facility appears to be the most viable and economical option, because it uses a building that already exists in the community, such as an association's clubhouse or a sports field that can be adapted to make it compatible with Curumim activities. This would seem to be the ideal mode, since it requires few resources and serves immediately to involve the community in a partnership, thus facilitating incorporation of Programa Curumim into its host community. The Department of Sports, Recreation, and Tourism is responsible for making needed physical improvements to these integrated facilities and adapting the space to the program.

Teacher Training

A programmatic content for an instructor training course has been developed through trial and error, and through the criticisms and suggestions of the instructors and program experts. Its format is as follows:

- basic concepts about a child's emotional development, including a description of the phases in the structuring of the libido and other concepts formulated by psychoanalysis;
- basic notions of cognitive development, based on the theoretical constructs of psychogenesis;
- discussion of the ideas advanced by noted educator Paulo Freire, through debates on the role of the instructor who is committed to the transformation and liberation of the students and their community;
- summary of the historical evolution of assistance programs in Brazil and their philosophical approaches: repressive/correctional, welfare-oriented, and educational, as well as the political implications of these programs;
- the legal foundations of the Programa Curumim (the 1989 United Nations Convention on the Rights of the Child, the Constitution of Brazil, the Child and Adolescent Statute, and Minas Gerais State Law No. 8,502; Secretaria de Esportes, Lazar e Turismo 1991);
- the functioning of the Programa Curumim, its organizational structure, architecture, and objectives;
- workshops in arts and crafts, recreation, sports, and educational enrichment;
- methods for integrated planning of these activities, featuring a single content for the four activities scheduled for a given day;
- one or two days of practical experience as interns at a center, so that the instructor can observe the activities and choose the one to which he or she will dedicate time, depending on his or her individual skills and specific knowledge;
- group dynamics that enable the instructors to be exposed to a variety of personal and professional experiences, making them more sensitive to the realities faced by pupils and instructors;
- debates and discussions about educational, political, and economic topics (including current events), the day-to-day problems of running a center, and the submission of criticisms and suggestions to the Educational Psychology Team, as well as instructor self-evaluation and reports of their visits to various centers.

The training course lasts eight 4-hour days. There are 30 to 50 instructors in each group.

THE IMPACT OF PROGRAMA CURUMIM

Assessing the impact and social "reach" of Programa Curumim remains a challenge, one that people have postponed facing. The program has no data or reliable information that would permit a substantiated and detailed assessment, which would enable us to visualize its evolution or qualitative progress. The figures furnished by the program show the number of children served by each center, but they are of no use in understanding or qualitatively evaluating Curumim or drawing conclusions as to the likely number of children whom the program has kept off the streets.[1] After 4 years of operation, Programa Curumim has not evolved in qualitative terms. Unless its impact and social reach can be measured, there is no way to evaluate it.

PROBLEMS WITH CURUMIM

Despite the absence of systematic evidence about the impact of the program, operations during the past few years have indicated a number of problems with staff, pedagogy, administration, community relations, and the ideology of the program. The quality of a program such as Curumim exhibits certain vulnerabilities that merit special attention.

Staff

Instructors could be selected on the basis of criteria agreed on in advance by the Educational Psychology Team, with a view to hiring people who are compatible with Programa Curumim's approach and objectives. The acceptance of staffers who have no preparation and no commitment to the socioeducational work with children and adolescents who are in difficult circumstances results in practices that are ineffective and not at all constructive. It is not unusual for such instructors to resign after a few months on the job, leading to a new call for interns and the holding of another training course to restaff the centers. This adversely affects service and increases the cost of the program.

Human resources and the amount of their compensation are the aspects that most directly compromise the quality of a program the size of Curumim. The low salaries attract apathetic instructors who are not necessarily dedicated to the task of carrying out a truly transcendental educational effort. Another point that impairs quality is the absence (on the organization chart of the institution that conducts the program) of qualified experts to supervise and monitor the instructors. Instructors who have not been properly trained and who harbor feelings of guilt very often reproduce welfare-oriented, repressive, and authoritarian values and standards, thus hampering the qualitative progress of Programa Curumim.

Another discouraging factor is that the time spent at Curumim is not formally recognized as an internship for university students. What could be a supervised internship under a psychologist or educational theorist becomes a professional experience that does not earn students any curriculum credit.

Instructional Issues

Among Curumim instructors there is no consensus as to the proper role of educational enrichment. Opinion is divided as to whether students should do their (school) homework at Curumim. The controversy on this point has hurt the children. This is a case in which we must remember that Curumim is supposed to be child-based. From the ideological and philosophical standpoints, a great many of the instructors have no clear

Figure 16.2   Curumim students and their teacher in their classroom. All students wore a Curumim T-shirt, but there were no papers, books, or pencils visible on students' desks, and only a few books were evident in the classroom. (Photo: R. A. Mickelson)

perception of certain aspects that, mistakenly, permeate their educational practices. This makes them either mere "domesticators" of children and adolescents, or monitors who spend their time playing with the children.

Homework is meant to be done at home, but often homes lack the proper environment. Because many houses do not have a table, chair, or lighting, someone needs to show the children how to do their homework under these circumstances.

Community Involvement

Several communities have been hostile to Curumim centers, and the result has been poor attendance. This shows that the community was not consulted and their consent about the desirability of building a Curumim center in their "space" was not sought.[2] Even though the program's approach seeks to ensure the involvement of and mutual efforts between Curumim, the family, community, schools, and private companies, work with these other institutions has not been carried out systematically. At the same time, members of some communities develop a welfare-oriented expectation of obtaining food, clothing, medicine, plots of land, building materials, and jobs. They are not challenged to examine if their present living conditions can be transformed and their difficulties overcome.

It has also been observed that some children disappear after attending Curumim for a while. Others cannot accept some of the basic rules of Curumim: hours, uniforms, adherence to their assigned shift, inasmuch as they are going through a period of detaching themselves from their homes and the community and are on their way into the streets. This is distressing to the teaching staff, since it indicates that the strategies employed are not sufficient to prevent this situation from developing and are not affecting the complex set of contributing factors. Physical and mental abuse, privations, street habits that have already become ingrained, disintegration of the family, and abandonment by parents are some of the factors that force children and young people into the streets to find alternative ways to survive. Therefore, they stop attending the Curumim center.

Partnerships need to be encouraged, so that the community and larger society becomes fully involved with Curumim. This means opening up new possibilities for placing young apprentices in local companies. The Curumim Program needs these links to other alternatives for placing these young people, such as vocational courses and companies that would accept adolescents as apprentices. Once they reach the program's maximum age of 12 and find there is no alternative, there is a risk that they will head for the streets.

Administration of the Program

In general, the programs waste public funds and frustrate the target populations (Costa 1991: 16–19). People start to question the intentions, integrity, and effectiveness of the programs and to see them as just another vote-getting maneuver. Problems of an institutional political nature work against partnerships with the local community and its institutions; program managers have little regard for partnerships with entities that assist children and adolescents. The welfare-oriented and narrowly focused view of its practices and attitudes, which perceives poor children as needy and therefore maladjusted since they live in a reality that is different from that of the middle-class instructor, is still deeply rooted among program managers and teaching staff.

Class Conflict

Initially it was thought that interns or university students would become good teachers or instructors. But in time, Curumim's leadership reached the conclusion that simply having a college degree did not mean someone would be a suitable teacher or instructor. Experience showed, however, that since they came from the middle class, university graduates identified with values different from those of the children. The two groups were strangers to each other in social terms. Working with children demands theoretical knowledge and technical training, but this does not necessarily mean that it requires a university education. So it was decided to give preference to candidates from the community since, at some centers, the cooks came from the local area and this facilitated their relationships with the children; they knew the children's family history.

This point brings out another aspect. For a university student, the salary or grant is too low in terms of their standard of living. However, an instructor recruited from the community would find it quite reasonable. However, hiring local workers means overcoming enormous bureaucratic and political obstacles, which have prevented execution of part of this project.

It was observed that college student instructors were obsessed with discipline, cleanliness, and other reference factors to which impoverished children are not accustomed. The clients have never been exposed to that universe, so systematized in rituals. As a result, the instructors would impose codes of behavior on the children, and the children in turn would rebel by shouting obscenities that intimidated and offended the instructors.

Ideological Issues

Initially, during the training courses, the candidates were inspired by appeals to Christian principles as the only guide to social work, and it was considered that all a Curumim instructor needed to do was know how to play with the "needy" children. Those premises distorted the seriousness and social commitment that a government action project must have.

Christian ethical and philosophical principles cannot eliminate the need to understand the emotional and cognitive development of the children to be served, to take advantage of the wealth of experiences that social work has accumulated, and to recognize the state's responsibility to guarantee, promote, and defend the rights of the children and adolescents, rights enshrined in both federal and state legislation.

Brazilians must not forget that religion has been and is still being used to control and exploit excluded population groups and to convince them to tolerate their indigence. This observation is not a Marxist allusion. While one should not dismiss the monumental contribution that churches have made to social work (Costa 1991), teaching the poor to be complacent about their misery is still a daily and despicable practice. In a similar vein, publicity about the program conveys the impression, not unusual, that the program is a panacea and the solution to the problem of impoverished children. This misconception creates expectations among the general public that do not correspond to reality and require the achievement of profound changes in our society.

OUTLOOK FOR THE FUTURE

Curumim has by no means exhausted its potential for overcoming the serious obstacles to a socioeducational, participatory, and democratic effort. Curumim has made some progress. The frenzy to achieve an integral education such as found in the First World cannot be supported by state governments that have been bankrupted by their own administrative incompetence. In this respect, Curumim holds out the prospect of a viable and simple route that can easily be maintained if we ensure the quality of the human resources and if we continue to battle for permission to hire instructors from the communities—since they bring knowledge of the culture and living conditions of the pupils—to work alongside the college students and technical staffers in a continuing exchange of contents and experiences.

Community work is an insignificant, or nonexistent, part of the Brazilian. Years of dictatorship not only demobilized social movements; it shaped technical personnel who are incapable of working with communities. Perhaps the Educational Psychology Team that designed Curumim was a bit naive in its intentions; however, there still has been no attempt at mounting a genuine experiment in which the community and its associations or institutions would assume some responsibilities in center management. The lack of a clear view of the problem and the absence of systematic and supervised community work by technical staff who are qualified for the specific type of work has compromised the program. The community must come forward and express its opinions, not only on its problems but also on the most likely solutions.

The experience with the Curumim Center at Ventosa should be closely studied, since Curumim collaboration with a facility operated by the Christian Fund can be regarded as a success. Curumim Ventosa's 1993–1994 *Monthly Attendance Record for Children and Adolescents* provides evidence of success (Curumim Ventosa 1994). The relationship between the Christian Fund and the local community had developed and deepened during years of hard work, international sponsorship of children, and assistance in medical, social, and educational areas. Curumim took advantage of those references, put down roots in the community through these partnerships, and progressed further with them. The existing educational enrichment program, administered by the fund, has remained under fund supervision. Comparing the *Monthly Attendance Record for Children and Adolescents* with those from other centers, it became clear that the Ventosa unit had the highest truancy admissions rate and was highly sought out by the community. In fact, there was a waiting list for admission to the center. According to the report cards for the students who attended Curumim, the rate of success in school is about 78–82 percent. Meetings scheduled with families were attended by more than 80 percent of families. Another Curumim center, which has collaborated with the Salesians, serves to confirm that partnerships are beneficial and can produce qualitative advances in the service provided.

Curumim's responsibility is enormous; it must avoid retracing the ideological path already taken. The ideological path refers to the assistance programs that have been more a form of social control than of actual alternatives for personal and social advancement leading to independence for children, young people, and their families. Such a path excludes millions of Brazilians and causes them to tolerate the shameful misery of their lives. Just as urgent as trying to rescue children from the horrors of the street through programs such as Curumim is the need to reduce poverty, battle for democratic and transparent administration, and fight for payment of decent salaries to competent and dedicated professionals.

The Curumim educational psychology team still holds out the hope for a democratic, ethically correct, and technically oriented socioeducational effort. Until then, Curumim remains a source of hope of what can yet be achieved, without the frenzy of some extravagant marketing campaign. It is a viable, tangible, and feasible alternative method of assistance, packaged in a responsible approach that was developed out of a serious and scientifically based socioeducational effort.

NOTES

1. Figures from the *Monthly Attendance Record for Children and Adolescents* are updated daily by the instructors with general information on children and young people. They give clues to a center's diligence and reflect the position of a particular center vis-à-vis other centers' average attendance.
2. The Morro Alto center in the town of Vespasiano, part of metropolitan Belo Horizonte, is one example. It was shunned and vandalized by the residents, who refused to accept it. Some time later, thanks to a coordinated effort by the Curumim team, the community, and local government agencies, Curumim took a different approach. It integrated itself into the community and became part of the local landscape.

REFERENCES

Brazilian Institute of Geography and Statistics. (IBGE). 1988. *Pesquisa nacional por amostra de democílios* (PNAD). Rio de Janeiro: Author.
———. 1997. *Censo demográfico.* Sistema IBGE de Recuperação Automática (SIDRA).
———. 1991. *Anuário estatístico do Brasil.* Rio de Janeiro: Author.
Costa, Antonio Carlos Gomes da. 1991. *De Menor a cidadão.* Brasília: Ministério da Ação Social, CBIA.
Curumim Véntosa. 1994. *Monthly Attendance Record for Children and Adolescents, 1993-1994.* Belo Horizonte: Author.
Secretaria de Esportes, Lazer e Turismo. 1991. *Manual de implantação do Curumim.* Belo Horizonte: Author.
Velloso, João Paulo dos Reis, and Roberto Calvalcanti de Albuquerque. 1991. *National Forum on the Foundations of Modern Development.* Belo Horizonte: Nobel.

Part V: Marginalized Children and Youth: The Social and Educational Needs of the Most Disadvantaged Children

17

Improving Education for Homeless Students with Disabilities in the United States

Lori Korinek, Brenda T. Williams, Virginia L. McLaughlin, and Chriss Walther-Thomas

Students who are homeless constitute a unique subset within today's school population; those among them who also have disabilities face even greater challenges. Appropriate support models for students with disabilities who are homeless are almost impossible to find. While data are difficult to gather, it appears that few of these students receive ongoing special education support. Most appear to slip through the cracks of public education. This chapter examines the unique characteristics of students with disabilities who are homeless, the legislative mandates for serving them, and promising practices for overcoming institutional and educational obstacles that continue to impede their access to educational opportunities. The practices that are most promising—collaborative relationships at multiple levels, staff development, and social and instructional support for students—are important for educating all homeless students but absolutely essential for the success of homeless students with disabilities.

Students who are homeless manifest a wide range of emotional, social, and academic difficulties commonly seen in students qualifying for special education, including depression, aggression, regression, low frustration tolerance, inattentiveness, poor achievement, low self-esteem, and language and cognitive delays (Anderson et al. 1995; Bassuk 1985; Grant 1990; Heflin and Rudy 1991). While many of these problems may be predictable reactions to homelessness, disabilities can be expected among students who are homeless just as they exist among children and youth in general. Homelessness compounds the challenges presented by disabilities. Although there are no current and reliable estimates of the number of students who are homeless and who qualify for special education, Bassuk (1985) reported that 29 percent of the students she sampled had been in special education. School-age individuals with disabilities who are homeless have a legal right to access special education services to meet their needs, and schools have a legal and ethical obligation to help them. To do this effectively requires an expanded "continuum of care" that integrates school programs with community services for students and their families (U.S. Department of Housing and Urban Development 1995).

LEGAL BASES FOR EDUCATING HOMELESS STUDENTS WITH DISABILITIES

The Stewart B. McKinney Homeless Assistance Act (P.L. 100–77) of 1987 was the first federal legislation specifically to address the educational needs of children and youth who are homeless. The McKinney Act and subsequent amendments mandate equal access to the same free, appropriate, public education for students who are homeless consistent with the services provided to other children and youth who are residents of their respective school districts. These services include preschool programs, special education and related services, compensatory education, programs for students with limited English proficiency, meal programs, before- and after-school care, extended school year opportunities, vocational education, and programs for students who are gifted and talented. The McKinney Act also states that homelessness alone should not be a sufficient reason to separate students from the mainstream school environment.

The Individuals with Disabilities Education Act (IDEA 1997) guarantees students with disabilities, including those who are homeless, the right to a free, appropriate public education in the least restrictive environment. Many students who are homeless manifest learning, behavioral, and health disabilities that would legitimately qualify them for special education (Bassuk and Rosenberg 1990; Heflin and Rudy 1991; Rescoria et al. 1991), yet accessing special education and related services (e.g., counseling, physical therapy, speech) presents additional challenges beyond getting students to school.

DISABILITIES AMONG HOMELESS STUDENTS

IDEA defines a "child with a disability" as a child who has been evaluated according to the act as having mental retardation, a hearing impairment including deafness, a speech or language impairment, a visual impairment including blindness, serious emotional disturbance, an orthopedic impairment, autism, traumatic brain injury, other health impairment, a specific learning disability, deaf-blindness, or multiple disabilities, and who, because of that impairment, needs special education or related services (IDEA 1997). The most prevalent disabling conditions among school-age populations are learning disabilities, speech and language impairments, mental retardation, and emotional disturbance (U.S. Dept. of Education 1998). The characteristics associated with these disabilities are often similar to those exhibited by students who are homeless, and distinguishing the effects of homelessness from those of a disabling condition is difficult. Many legal disability definitions contain criteria (e.g., persistent over time; not due to environmental, economic, or adaptive behavior deficits) that make it difficult for transient students to qualify for services under these categories. While common reactions to homelessness should not automatically be deemed to be the results of disabling conditions (Korineket al. 1992), certainly the circumstances of homelessness exacerbate negative effects of disabilities. For these students, there is an increased need for special education in order for them to be successful both in and out of school, yet their homelessness may interfere with accurate diagnosis.

LEARNING CHARACTERISTICS

Special learning needs in the areas of physical, cognitive, communication, academic, and behavioral-emotional development are associated with each of the disability categories identified in IDEA. In addition, students who are also affected by poverty, homelessness, and negative attitudes toward cultural differences experience the cumulative, adverse effects of these influences on learning and educational success (Williams and DeSander 1999). A primary characteristic of students with disabilities is underachievement when compared to their typical peers. A Children's Defense Fund report, *Poverty Matters* (Sherman 1997), indicates that children who are homeless or constantly moving from one dilapidated place to another have lower reading and math scores and suffer numerous serious and long-lasting consequences: poor health, missed school, and emotional damage. In addition, these children have more than triple the average risk of lead poisoning, a common problem among those who live in old housing that causes neurological damage linked to lower IQ and long-term behavior problems. Homeless students with special needs, regardless of their categorical identification, present teachers with challenges in addressing unique learning characteristics and needs. Some characteristics commonly observed in this population are described below.

Perceptual and Information-Processing Problems

Students often have specific problems processing auditory or visual information. For example, some will have difficulty in recognizing the sounds of language (phonological awareness), or recognizing letters, numbers, or words (visual perception). Memory deficits—difficulties storing and retrieving information that has been learned—are also evident.

Disorders of Attention

Students with attention problems may have difficulty focusing when a lesson is being presented, short attention spans, poor concentration, and high levels of distractibility. They may also demonstrate impulsive behavior and increased, nonpurposeful movement (hyperactivity).

Poor Motor Abilities

Delays in this area involve difficulty with gross motor abilities and fine motor coordination. Some children exhibit spatial orientation problems, general awkwardness, or clumsiness. Handwriting and the ability to complete written tasks that must be copied from the board or textbook are affected by delays in motor skill development.

Failure to Develop and Mobilize Cognitive Strategies for Learning

Some learning problems stem from students' inability to identify effective strategies for completing tasks (Ellis and Lenz 1996). Many students with disabilities do not know how to organize for learning and studying because they have not developed active and self-directed learning styles. Delays in this area are also referred to as metacognitive deficits. They interfere with students' abilities to plan, monitor, and evaluate the efficiency and effectiveness of strategies that they have chosen to complete academic assignments or engage in social interactions (Rivera and Smith 1997).

Inappropriate Social Behavior

Students who have not learned how to act in social situations often find it difficult to establish satisfying relationships and to make and keep friends. Social skills deficits are especially challenging for students who are homeless and change schools frequently. Many of these students do not possess the skills required for interpersonal interactions or do not use these skills effectively. This lack of social competence lowers social status and affects lives while at school, at home, and on the job.

Limited Motivation

School failure may result in not only academic deficits but also motivational difficulties. After repeated experiences with failure, many students come to expect failure, attributing it to external forces beyond their control. Such students may be afraid to respond, take risks, or actively engage in learning. Some come to believe that they cannot succeed due to a lack of ability. Eventually, such individuals meet their own lowered expectations. This situation is called *learned helplessness*.

These characteristics affect students' learning as well as their adjustment to school. The assessed educational needs of students who are homeless and have diagnosed disabilities should influence how individual instructional programs are developed. Evaluation of current delivery systems reveals obstacles to effective programming for such students. These barriers are identified below.

OBSTACLES TO APPROPRIATE EDUCATION AND SERVICES

With few advocates to help them, students with disabilities who are homeless have severely limited access to appropriate educational services. A recent survey of state coordinators for homeless services (Anderson et al. 1995) revealed that special education was one of the most difficult services for students without homes to access. The special education process itself may present obstacles to service delivery. Qualification for special education and related services requires progression through a series of steps mandated under IDEA and intended to protect student and parent privacy, confidentiality, and due process, while identifying specific problems that justify special education. Movement from referral for assessment for special education through a disability eligibility determination legally may take 65 administrative days (approximately 3 to 4 months) to complete, even with full parental involvement. In the face of limited parental involvement, the short-term enrollment patterns typical of students who are homeless, and the increased resources required by students with identified disabilities, educators and administrators may be reluctant to pursue special education services for these students, despite the legal mandates.

In addition to residency, health, and transportation barriers, frequent and often unpredictable moves impede the transfer of formal school records. Consequently, transitions from one school to another often lack meaningful instructional and social continuity. Students face the prospect of starting over again and again with teachers, peers, placement tests, classroom rules, and instructional materials. While this is a difficult task for any student, for homeless students with additional learning and behavioral problems, it can prove insurmountable without extra support. In addition, teachers who notice these difficulties in performance may attribute them to frequent absenteeism and homelessness, rather than to a true disability.

PROMISING PRACTICES

Most students who are homeless, including those with identified disabilities, are likely to be served in general education programs. Many of the support structures and practices already in place in effective schools enable educators to respond quickly and appropriately to the special needs of these students. Programs that are characterized by strong collaborative relationships, responsive administrative systems, effective staff development, and provision of appropriate instructional and social support are best positioned to serve students with disabilities who are homeless.

Developing Collaborative Relationships

Schools that openly embrace an ethic of care and shared responsibility for *all* students are best able to serve students with disabilities who are homeless. When families, teachers, and service providers work together as a team, students have the benefit of more creative and coherent programs to meet special needs. Collaborative relationships are also critical in providing a network of support to help both families and professionals persist in their efforts when the odds seem overwhelming (Walther-Thomas et al. 1999).

Collaboration with Families

Family involvement in the educational process is particularly critical for students with disabilities who are homeless. IDEA mandates the active participation of parents or legal guardians in securing special education services. When a student is suspected of having a disability, the parent or guardian must give written permission for their child to be assessed for special education or related services. If the child or adolescent is found eligible, the parent or guardian must be involved in the development of the Individualized Education Program (IEP) for the student. The IEP is a written document that must include a statement of the student's present level of performance; annual goals and short-term instructional objectives; special education and related services he or she will receive; a statement describing how much the student will participate in general education programs; dates of services; and the criteria, methods, and time lines for evaluating the student's progress.

Once the student's IEP is developed, a committee that includes the parent or guardian must determine where the student will most appropriately receive the services outlined in the IEP. The school must be as close as possible to the child's temporary home or the school district must provide or pay for transportation to and from school. Every school district must provide a continuum of services so that every student with a disability can receive an appropriate program. This continuum includes general education classes with special support, separate special education classes, a combination of general and special classes, special day schools, hospital services, and residential schools.

Parents and guardians are important sources of information about their child's functioning and the educational programs experienced in other settings. When homeless students have already been identified as having disabilities, families may have copies of evaluation reports and IEPs from previous schools. Even when these documents are not available, families may provide names of teachers or other contact persons who can expedite the transfer of records and communicate information to the receiving program.

Viewing families as partners in the special education process requires focusing on their unique strengths and coping resources. The goal is to empower families to develop their own skills in order to negotiate educational and community systems more effectively (Dunst et al. 1993). Professionals need to recognize the grave concerns that families have at this time. Basic survival demands often preclude their significant involvement with the schools, and lack of participation should not be interpreted as lack of interest. Professionals must also respect cultural and economic differences that influence expectations, attitudes toward disabilities, and daily experiences of students and families. Insensitivity by teachers or administrators intensifies feelings of isolation and may alienate parents or guardians when the schools most need their active involvement to secure and implement special education services. When families feel valued and respected and perceive the schools as truly committed to serving their children, they are more likely to participate in educational programs.

Collaboration among School Professionals

Effective education for students with disabilities who are homeless requires a high level of collaboration among the professionals who serve these students and their families. Fortunately, many of the structures already in place to encourage collaborative planning and problem solving can offer support for homeless students with disabilities. Departmental or grade level team meetings may provide an initial forum for discussion of special needs, classroom accommodations, and available resources. When teachers have concerns about particular students, they may seek assistance from a principal, supervisor, or appropriate specialist (e.g., special educator, counselor, psychologist).

Many schools now have assistance teams to support teachers in their work with students who have academic or behavioral problems. Teachers may request assistance and then meet with the team of three to five peers to target specific intervention goals, brainstorm alternative strategies, and develop action plans to serve students more effectively. Teachers who work most directly with students remain the primary contacts and retain responsibility for follow-through.

Another form of collaboration well suited to serving students with disabilities who are homeless is team teaching or coteaching. Two teachers, most typically a general educator and a special educator, share responsibility for planning, delivering, and evaluating classroom instruction. This ongoing interaction affords teachers opportunities for early recognition of individual student needs, generation of creative ideas for instructional adaptations, delivery of more intensive and flexible lessons, and continuous monitoring of student performance. Coteaching and the other collaborative arrangements described thus far are available within the general education program. Students with disabilities can access more extensive supports and program modifications through the special education process described earlier.

Collaboration within Communities

Because schools and shelters tend to be central in the network of human service agencies providing assistance to families who are homeless, they often exert leadership in promoting interagency collaboration to integrate services and to deliver them in inclusive settings. The challenge for education leaders is to initiate a forum for communication among community agencies (e.g., Social Services, Mental Health) and nonprofit organizations (e.g., Salvation Army, Red Cross, church-sponsored shelters) who share responsibility to serve families who are homeless. Some shelter programs have in-house staff members who are designated as school liaisons. Liaisons can help ensure effective communication among families, schools, and agencies. They can facilitate prompt student enrollment and can assist with the transfer of important school records such as previous assessment data, IEPs, and special education placement information. In addition, informed shelter staff members can offer student residents ongoing encouragement about school activities and projects, promote regular attendance, and offer homework assistance. Unfortunately, some shelters, already burdened by enormous demands and limited staff, may be reluctant to participate in school identification and tracking programs. Schools should work with shelters to encourage cooperation and participation. For example, McKinney funds can be used to establish homework and reading areas within shelters that can offer student residents school supplies, books, educational games, and tutorial assistance.

Less formal support can also be mobilized at the community level. Civic groups, churches, sororities and fraternities, retired citizens, and college students often serve as mentors to provide children and youth with special attention and support. These community members may deliver individual tutoring, homework assistance, transportation to after-school activities, access to libraries and computers, enrichment activities, and coaching in vocational and self-advocacy skills.

Designing Effective Staff Development

A well-developed, ongoing, multidimensional program of staff development experiences should be designed to facilitate within-school and within-district awareness, understanding, and capability to respond to identified needs of homeless students, particularly those with disabilities. Ongoing staff development activities should be designed for all administrative, instructional, and support staff, who need to be aware of their respective roles in assisting homeless families. Topics should include: legal and procedural issues related to students with disabilities who are also homeless (e.g., enrollment, exiting, referral, eligibility, parental rights, transfer of records); "red flags" that would indicate that a student is homeless and might require additional consideration and support; positive, accepting communication skills with families and external agencies; methods for prioritized assessment and placement in specialized educational support programs; and strategies for instructional, academic, and extracurricular support. These staff development programs should enable staff to respond to the following six priorities established by the U.S. Department of Education for meeting the special educational needs of students who are homeless (Cavazos 1990): (a) remediation and tutoring of basic skills; (b) support services including counseling; (c) after-school and extended day services to provide basic needs and recreation; (d) awareness training for personnel; (e) educational assessment, screening, and placement; and (f) program continuity and stability.

DEVELOPING SOCIAL AND INSTRUCTIONAL SUPPORT

For students who are homeless and uprooted repeatedly, new schools are often traumatic experiences (Johnson 1992). For students who also have disabilities, new school traumas are complicated by many other academic and social problems (e.g., limited skills, poor self-confidence, low self-esteem, a history of past school failures). Academic and social adjustment problems make it difficult for many to settle into new schools quickly and make the most of the available learning time. The McKinney Act stipulates that available funds can be used to develop programs and services that facilitate social and instructional support for these students.

Developing Social Supports

Inclusive learning communities facilitate student adjustment by providing an array of social supports. Students are afforded learning experiences that foster peer interaction, teamwork, choice making, and group decision making (Sailor et al. 1989). Staff members model behaviors that demonstrate their commitment to these concepts. Offering choices in peer partners, response modes for demonstrating learning, and projects of interest enhances student control, motivation, and opportunities for interactions.

Advance preparation of students and staff members ensures better support for students with special needs. It reduces the likelihood that homeless students with disabilities will feel isolated in schools because peers and teachers lack skills and understanding. In supportive schools everyone learns about issues of concern in their communities (e.g., homelessness, disabilities, poverty). They develop skills so they can support affected community members appropriately (Thousand et al. 1994; Tower 1992). All students, including those with disabilities, should have opportunities to perform helper roles (i.e. coach, buddy, tutor, team leader). This helps ensure that students who receive special support are not socially stigmatized by well-intentioned efforts (Johnson 1992). Cross-grade-level support systems facilitate opportunities for assistance in many areas. Older students who may lack age-appropriate academic or social skills may be effective academic and social skills mentors for younger students. Other well-known support models include buddy systems (Falvey et al. 1992), peer tutoring (Greenwood et al. 1989), and cooperative learning groups (Putnam 1993). Programs should also emphasize instruction in self-advocacy to help students with disabilities understand and explain their conditions and access needed assistance.

Providing Instructional Support

At the classroom level, a number of accommodations can be instituted to respond to the varied learning characteristics of students, with disabilities who are homeless. For these students, appropriate adjustments make the critical difference between academic success and failure; between meaningful participation in educational experiences and continued frustration and alienation in school. The vast majority of accommodations for students with disabilities also benefit other students who are homeless or at risk for learning or behavioral difficulties.

Organizational Strategies

The organization of the classroom environment and instruction is central to success for special needs students, who often appear disorganized as a manifestation of their disabilities—a characteristic exacerbated by homelessness. Clear, consistent daily class schedules, rules, and routines (e.g., for turning in homework, securing materials, asking for assistance) help students with disabilities know what is expected and provide a source of stability during the schoolday. Calendars for monitoring projects; folders or notebooks for recording assignments, organizing papers, and taking notes; and copies of the daily/weekly assignment schedule assist students in organizing and participating in classroom activities. Extra materials (e.g., school supplies, textbooks, lunch money) for use when students are unable to bring their own prevent embarrassment and allow students to complete classroom tasks along with their peers.

Instructional organization is also critical for students with disabilities who frequently exhibit attentional, memory, or perceptual difficulties. Outlines of material to be covered; visual aids such as diagrams or charts showing relationships among key concepts; and study guides for lessons, units, or chapters focus students' attention and study. A set of class notes, models of completed assignments, and folders for blank copies of assignments assist students and teachers in tracking missed instruction when students are absent.

Materials and Methods Adaptations

Many students with disabilities demonstrate sensory or perceptual difficulties and preferences for certain modalities (e.g., visual, auditory, kinesthetic) in which they learn best.

Using a multisensory approach that incorporates a variety of modalities increases the chances that students with varying preferences will be successful. Including "hands-on" activities in which learners can manipulate items helps focus their attention, increase memory, and enhance understanding of abstract concepts. Incorporating movement into activities when possible and alternating periods of seatwork with more active tasks improve concentration and meet the needs of students who may seem overly active.

Other classroom accommodations for students with disabilities involve changing the way information or skills are presented. For many students with disabilities, typical pacing of classroom instruction fails to provide them with the repetition and practice they need to master concepts. When the rest of the class moves on to higher-level concepts and skills, their difficulties are compounded. Educators can assist students with disabilities through the use of additional examples and models of skills and concepts, use of simpler language to explain material, and frequent checks for understanding. Regularly providing students with specific feedback regarding aspects of tasks performed correctly and exact procedures for correcting mistakes is critical. Previewing lessons and summarizing key points to close lessons help to emphasize essential learning. Memory devices or mnemonics can be used to aid retention.

Task directions are frequently challenging for students with perceptual and learning difficulties. Clarifying directions by presenting them one step at a time, giving oral as well as written directions, and simplifying the language to match students' reading level are helpful accommodations. Materials for students with disabilities can be modified to make important features of the learning task more noticeable by highlighting, underlining, or color-coding key directions. Increasing the space between items and using larger print assist students with visual difficulties. Additional practice on skills can be provided through peer tutors, classroom volunteers, computer software, and audio- or videotaped materials. Educational games also provide necessary repetition in a motivating manner and afford opportunities for social interactions.

Task Alterations

Beyond accommodations for students with disabilities who are homeless suggested above, changes in the tasks being required or in the criteria for success may be appropriate for some students. For example, students with fine motor problems who have difficulty completing assignments in the time allotted may be more successful with fewer problems/questions or increased time. A classroom "buddy" may be assigned to take notes or to record the student's dictated responses. Oral responses into a tape recorder may be allowed. Aids such as word banks, calculators, or spelling lists for tasks typically completed from memory may be appropriate. Complex tasks can also be broken down into simpler parts to be completed sequentially. On occasion, the student may be given an easier task related to the class assignment (e.g., work on a prerequisite skill) or use easier reading materials that cover the same content. Collaboration among the teacher, specialists, student, and family helps to ensure appropriate accommodations for students with disabilities who are homeless.

CONCLUSION

Numerous factors mitigate against students with disabilities who are homeless receiving an education, let alone special education, to address their needs. Bureaucratic and educational obstacles are compounded by limited resources and poor communication systems across schools, organizations, and agencies. These barriers often impede opportunities for the sharing of resources, knowledge, and skills among care providers necessary for delivery of the free, appropriate public education to which students are entitled. Given these roadblocks, many professionals have recognized the need for better teamwork at all levels (e.g., classroom, school, school district, community agency, state organizations). Effective programs are based on ongoing collaboration between students, teachers, administrators, related services professionals, families, community members, and others to provide a network of social and instructional support for students with disabilities who are homeless.

REFERENCES

Anderson, L. M., M. I. Janger, and K. L. M. Panton. 1995. *An Evaluation of State and Local Efforts to Serve the Educational Needs of Homeless Children and Youth.* Washington, D.C.: U.S. Department of Education.

Bassuk, E. L. 1985. *The Feminization of Homelessness: Homeless Families in Boston Shelters.* Unpublished manuscript. Cambridge, Mass.: Harvard Science Center.

Bassuk, E. L., and L. Rosenberg. 1990. "Psychosocial Characteristics of Homeless Children and Children with Homes." *Pediatrics* 85: 257-61.

Cavazos, L. F. 1990. *Report to Congress on the Education for Homeless Children and Youth Program for the Period October 1, 1988 through September 30, 1989.* Washington, D.C.: U.S. Department of Education.

Dunst, C. J., C. M. Trivette, A. L. Starnes, D. W. Hamby, and N. J. Gordon. 1993. *Building and Evaluating Family Support Initiatives: A National Study of Programs for Persons with Developmental Disabilities.* Baltimore: Paul H. Brookes.

Ellis, E. S., and B. K. Lenz. 1996. "Perspectives on Instruction in Learning Strategies." Pp. 9-60 in *Teaching Adolescents with Learning Disabilities,* 2d ed., edited by D. D. Deshler, E. S. Ellis, and B. K. Lenz. Denver: Love.

Falvey, M., J. Coots, and S. Terry-Gage. 1992. "Extracurricular Activities." Pp. 229-237 in *Curriculum Considerations in Inclusive Classrooms,* edited by S. Stainback and W. Stainback. Baltimore: Paul H. Brookes.

Grant, R. 1990. "The Special Needs of Homeless Children: Early Intervention at a Welfare Hotel." *Topics in Early Childhood Special Education* 10(4): 76-91.

Greenwood, C. R., J. Delquadri, and R. V. Hall. 1989. "Longitudinal Effects of Classwide Peer Tutoring." *Journal of Educational Psychology* 81: 371-83.

Heflin, L. J., and K. Rudy. 1991. *Homeless and in Need of Special Education.* Reston, Va.: Council for Exceptional Children.

Individuals with Disabilities Education Act (IDEA) Amendments. 1997. P.L. 105-17, 20 U.S.C. 1401 et. seq.

Johnson, J. F. 1992. "Educational Support Services for Homeless Children and Youth." Pp. 153-76 in *Educating Homeless Children and Adolescents: Evaluating Policy and Practice,* edited by J. H. Stronge. Newbury Park, Calif.: Sage.

Korinek, L., C. S. Walther-Thomas, and V. K. Laycock. 1992. "Educating Special Needs Homeless Children and Youth." Pp. 133-52 in *Educating Homeless Children and Adolescents,* edited by J. H. Stronge. Newbury Park, Calif.: Sage.

Putnam, J. W. 1993. *Cooperative Learning and Strategies for Inclusion.* Baltimore: Paul H. Brookes.

Rescoria, L., R. Parker, and P. Stolley. 1991. "Ability, Achievement and Adjustment in Homeless Children." *American Journal of Orthopsychiatry* 61(2): 210-20.

Rivera, D. P., and D. D. Smith. 1997. *Teaching Students with Learning and Behavior Problems.* 3d ed. Boston: Allyn & Bacon.

Sailor, W., J. L. Anderson, A. T. Halvorsen, K. Doering, J. Filler, and L. Goetz. 1989. *The Comprehensive School: Regular Education for All Students with Disabilities.* Baltimore: Paul H. Brookes.

Sherman, A. 1997. *Poverty Matters: The Cost of Child Poverty in America.* Washington, D.C.: Children's Defense Fund.

Stewart B. McKinney Homeless Assistance Act. 1987. 42 U.S.C.S. § 11301–11472 (1989).

Thousand, J. S., R. A. Villa, and A. I. Nevin. 1994. *Creativity and Collaborative Learning: A Practical Guide to Empowering Students and Teachers.* Baltimore: Paul H. Brookes.

Tower, C. C. 1992. "The Psychosocial Context: Supporting Education for Homeless Children and Adolescents." Pp. 42–61 in *Educating Homeless Children and Adolescents: Evaluating Policy and Practice,* edited by J. H. Stronge. Newbury Park, Calif.: Sage.

U.S. Department of Education (ED). 1998. *Twentieth Annual Report to Congress on the Implementation of the Education of the Handicapped Act.* Washington, D.C.: Author.

U.S. Department of Housing and Urban Development (HUD). 1995. *HUD Makes Largest Award of Homeless Funds—Nearly a Billion Dollars—to More Than 200 Communities.* News release, 10 July. Washington, D.C.: Author.

Walther-Thomas, C., L. Korinek, V. McLaughlin, and B. T. Williams. 1999. *Collaboration for Inclusive Education: Developing Successful Programs.* Boston: Allyn and Bacon.

Williams, B., and M. DeSander. 1999. "Dueling Legislation: The Impact of Incongruent Federal Statutes on Homeless and Other At-Risk Student Populations." *Journal of Just and Caring Education* 5:34-50.

18

Children of Undocumented Immigrants:
An Invisible Minority among Homeless Students

Ana Huerta-Macías, María Luisa González, and Linda Holman

Homelessness among children, including those in foster or institutional care and those who are immigrants and refugees, is one of the five forces likely to affect adversely the lives of young people during the 1990s (Scales 1991). The challenges and needs of homeless families are well documented in the literature (National Coalition for the Homeless 1989; First 1998; González 1992). Similarly, the demographic changes resulting from immigration policies have brought substantial attention to the growth of the immigrant population and its implications for our economy and schools. An immigrant is traditionally defined as a person admitted as a permanent resident of the United States (Vialet 1996). However, this term refers to undocumented individuals as well as those legally admitted to the United States. The issues surrounding homelessness among the undocumented immigrant population have not been addressed in the literature. Yet, this group of homeless individuals faces even more severe and complex circumstances in the struggle to survive than do homeless individuals who are U.S. citizens. This chapter addresses those issues faced by homeless undocumented immigrants in a Southwest border community with a large influx of immigration from Mexico. We begin by providing a historical perspective of Mexican migration to the United States and describing the diverse situations of homelessness that undocumented immigrants experience. The chapter will then discuss the social and educational problems of undocumented homeless children. A case study that which illustrates the problems will be presented next, followed by a description of how the schools can function as safe havens for undocumented youth and their families.

MEXICAN MIGRATION TO THE UNITED STATES: A HISTORICAL PERSPECTIVE

The National Research Council (1997) estimates that between 1,000,000 and 1,100,000 immigrants, both legal and illegal, enter the United States every year. The majority of these immigrants live in six states: California, New York, New Jersey, Texas, Florida, and Illinois. Assuming that immigration continues at its present level, the U.S. population will grow to 387 million people by the year 2050, and immigration will account for two-thirds of that growth. Immigrants of Hispanic ancestry will grow from the current 27 million to 85 million by 2050, and will account for 26 percent of the U.S. population.

Mexicans comprise one of the subgroups of Hispanic immigrants and also the single largest group of immigrants to the United States (National Clearinghouse for Literacy Education 1997). A chance at a better life continues to entice many Mexican immigrants, who often risk their lives to enter the country when documentation for immigration proves difficult to obtain. Indeed, during the single decade of the 1980s, the Arizona Farm Workers estimated, based on interviews with migrant workers, that 300 people died trying to enter the country through the deserts of southwest Arizona (Annerino 1996). However, this figure is not inclusive of other border states and represents only a portion of the total incidents.

Those migrants who make it into the country safely arrive with few, if any, material resources. Fix and Passell (1997) indicate that immigrant poverty increased strikingly during the past decade; the number of poor immigrant households grew by 42 percent, while the number of native households in poverty grew by 11 percent. Schwartz (1996) states that immigrant youth are twice as likely as natives to live in families with an income in the lowest quartile. The lack of documentation for immigrants compounds the problem because without any, they are prohibited from legal employment in the United States.

Because of the increased enforcement of immigration laws along border areas, moreover, many of the workers moved to urban areas (*El Paso Herald-Post* 1997). This high immigrant density, along with the lack of government response to the need for increased low-cost housing, created a situation in which these families had only one recourse: they moved in with extended family members or friends until they could find affordable housing. This combination of factors has contributed to the high poverty rates among immigrant households, and because immigrants who are not documented often do not seek public services for fear of deportation, they are at even greater risk of homelessness. Immigrant families living in extended family circumstances or in substandard housing qualify as "homeless" under the McKinney Act and, therefore, may be categorized as homeless immigrants. The following describes five diverse settings in which homelessness occurs.

One possible setting finds documented immigrants living with documented family members in extended households. Documented immigrants living with documented family members in extended family households generally reside in crowded living conditions; however, they have the best situation of the five groups. Members of the extended family provide assistance in obtaining services, working through red tape, dealing with language and cultural differences, and child care and supervision. Emotional support and less fear of deportation are also benefits to these individuals. The positive factors for immigrants living in this setting may be offset by a lack of privacy and feelings of dependency upon others.

Another living arrangement is where undocumented immigrants live with documented family members in extended family households. Undocumented immigrants living in this type of situation have many of the benefits of immigrants living in the first setting in terms of assistance and emotional support. However, increased fear of deportation and separation from their family members, as well as difficulties in obtaining employment due to their undocumented status, tend to result in these individuals' classification as part of the "invisible" homeless and the perpetuation of an overcrowded impoverished setting.

Undocumented children living with documented parents or other relatives constitute another homeless situation. Immigrant children in this circumstance are somewhat more fortunate than the second group described above. These children, as a result of *Plyler v. Doe* (1982), cannot be denied admission to school on the basis of their undocumented status. If legal adoption is a possibility for this child, then citizenship may result. However, if legal adoption is not feasible, upon reaching adulthood, this person must face the economic, social, and societal barriers to obtaining employment or higher education in the United States. On the other hand, this same individual may find it difficult to survive in the country of which he is a legal citizen (because, for example, of the threat of political oppression or the existence of an economic catastrophe).

Another setting involves families in which one parent is documented, another undocumented, and the children may or may not be documented. Families in this situation are particularly challenged because the documented parent has all the power in the relationship, with deportation as an imminent threat for the undocumented parent. The undocumented adult in this setting is completely dependent on the other and, again, is part of the "invisible" homeless. Children of this family may live in fear of being separated from a parent and from one another. As the undocumented adult has limited employment opportunities, the income level in this home is likely to be minimal.

The last setting involves families, all of whom are documented, living in substandard housing. They are considered homeless under the law. Many live in border area communities known as "gateway communities," where recent immigrants find temporary housing with family or friends. Their plight grows with the demolition of existing low-income housing, as few large inexpensive housing projects have been built since the 1970s. Older housing typically is not in compliance with current building regulations. By spending little to comply with laws governing sanitation, zoning, and safety, allowing overcrowded conditions, and having rents paid in cash (possibly on a per-head basis), unscrupulous landlords profit significantly. Even documented immigrants are hesitant to engage in a dispute with the landlord; undocumented immigrants virtually have no rights in these situations (Nielsen 1988).

NEW LAWS AND CONTRADICTORY POLICIES

The *Plyler v. Doe* ruling states "that undocumented children and young adults have the same right to attend public primary and secondary schools as do U.S. citizens and permanent residents." Like other children, undocumented students are obliged under state law to attend school until 12th grade (ERIC Digest 1990). As a result of *Plyler,* public schools may not:

> deny admission to a student during initial enrollment or at any other time on the basis of undocumented status; treat a student differently to determine residency; engage in any practices to "chill" the right of access to school; require students or parents to disclose or document their immigration status; make inquiries of students or parents that may expose their undocumented status; nor require social security numbers from all students, as this may expose undocumented status. (National Coalition of Advocates for Students 1998)

However, under the Immigration Reform and Immigrant Responsibility Act of 1996, "international" students will be unable to attend public schools in the United States. "International" students in grades kindergarten through 8th will be allowed to attend only private U.S. schools, and "international" students in grades 9 through 12 can attend U.S. schools for only 1 year, with prepaid tuition (Lee 1997).

With the new laws, schools may have to determine whether or not a student is an "international" student, and schools may be asked to require proof of documented status to enroll children. If enforced, these practices will ultimately have a "chilling" effect on documented, as well as undocumented, children who seek an education. Educators will, in fact, be asked to become de facto agents of the Immigration and Naturalization Service, thus violating *Plyler v. Doe.* Currently, however, some schools are playing a crucial role in assisting homeless immigrants, particularly those who are undocumented, in their struggle to survive. The following describes the issues surrounding assistance for the undocumented and the central role that a border school and the surrounding community have played in this effort. The discussion is developed through the case study of an undocumented parent and her children, who were homeless upon arrival to the school.

SOCIAL AND EDUCATIONAL PROBLEMS SPECIFIC TO HOMELESS IMMIGRANTS

While homelessness in itself is problematic, there are additional social and educational issues that impact the situation when undocumented immigrants are involved. One of these issues is the lack of citizenship or residency status. Not having citizenship or residency precludes many families from accessing those social services that would otherwise be available, including assistance from city, state, and federal agencies. Often the only help for families without citizenship or without a social security number comes from private organizations such as churches and local community groups. This help, moreover, is often highly limited because few resources are available from these organizations.

The inability to communicate in English, coupled with the unavailability of bilingual personnel at all assistance centers, is another problem. This language barrier often precludes homeless immigrant families from accessing resources that might be available to them. Filling out forms in English, for instance, presents a major obstacle—as does the inability to explain their economic and social situations to the English monolingual "gatekeepers" often found at the various agencies.

Another problem specific to undocumented homeless immigrants is a lack of knowledge about the schooling system and about American society as a whole. Because these families come from a country where the educational system functions quite differently from the American system, these families are often lost when it comes to enrolling children in school, meeting vaccination requirements, or finding avenues of communication with school personnel. Families face an additional related difficulty when they attempt to obtain birth certificates and other important documentation from their country of origin (Mexico, in this case). Because the family may have moved frequently, these records are difficult to obtain. They may be in several different locations throughout Mexico; or they simply may be nonexistent—at least in the format required by American schools; or the family may not be able to pay any required fees for obtaining such documents. The process of obtaining legal records becomes an insurmountable task when one considers that Mexico is a struggling, nontechnological country and as such the government system is unable to provide or transfer records on demand.

Perhaps the single greatest factor differentiating the plight of homeless undocumented immigrants from other homeless immigrants is the constant fear of deportation. This fear is triggered when an employer (or prospective employer), a spouse, a neighbor, or other angry individual reports immigrants to the Immigration Naturalization Service (INS). The fear that one or both parents, or that some or all of the children, will be deported terrifies and torments these families day and night. This factor precludes their seeking assistance from other more capable individuals in any of the situations described above (for example, when enrolling children in school or accessing social services). The anti-immigrant sentiment currently evident in the United States places additional attitudinal and emotional barriers to obtaining public assistance. Bartolomé and Macedo, for instance, write that the cultural condition in the United States "has had the effect of licensing institutional discrimination whereby both legal and illegal immigrants materially experience the loss of their dignity, the denial of human citizenship, and in many cases, outright violent and criminal acts committed by those institutions responsible for implementing the law" (1997: 231).

The children's behavior in the classroom is highly affected by all of these factors. They sense the fear and the constant anguish and torment present in their families. These children are often silent in the classroom. They appear timid when spoken to and often look very tired; some of them have slept very little during the night because of crowded, noisy, and substandard conditions at home. These students, to be successful, need time, patience, and teachers who are knowledgeable about their plight and how to create learning environments that address their psychosocial as well as linguistic and academic needs (González and Huerta-Macías 1997).

The drama that unfolds on a daily basis in the struggle to assist undocumented immigrant homeless students evolves from these highly complex issues. Situations develop whereby the families become victims of systems and bureaucracies that, by their very nature, can be highly impersonal, rigid, and merciless. The following case study illustrates some of these problems and how the school provided a safe haven for parents and children.

REACHING OUT TO THE UNDOCUMENTED HOMELESS: A STUDY OF A BORDER SCHOOL

Isabel Mercado came to the United States by walking across the border along with her three children, Jose, Gabriela, and Carmen. Isabel was raised in Ciudad Juárez, Chihuahua, Mexico, with her parents, both of whom were highly educated and provided a comfortable home. However, they both died and left Isabel an orphan at the age of 12. Isabel then went to live with her grandmother, who passed away 3 years later, leaving her alone. After living on the streets, she became pregnant and had her first child, Jose, at age 15. She later married and had two additional children, Gabriela and Carmen. Because of physical abuse, Isabel left the marriage. She took her children, crossed the border, and decided to start a new life in the United Sates. Thus, at the age of 19 she took her three children, the oldest of whom was 5 years old at the time, crossed into El Paso, Texas, and made her way 45 miles north to Las Cruces, New Mexico.

In Las Cruces she moved in with distant relatives and enrolled the children in the neighborhood school. She and the children subsequently bounced from place to place, living with other families as long as they would take them. After the last family asked Isabel to leave, her family became homeless. The school first became aware of the situation when Gabriela indicated to her teacher that she could not possibly do homework because her family was living in a car. At that point, the principal was notified and the appropriate staff was alerted as to the situation. The school maintained very close ties with a Title I social worker, Ms. Gómez, who provided assistance with referrals and follow-up in such cases. From that point on, Ms. Gómez served as a liaison between the family and the school, and between the family and public assistance agencies.

Ms. Gómez began by meeting with the parent, learning about her situation, and then driving her to the appropriate places to seek the needed shelter, clothing, and food. Although there are several public service agencies in the city, most of them require a social security number or citizenship in order to provide assistance. In this case, none of the family members had social security numbers; thus, help in the form of public housing, food stamps, income support, and even overnight shelters was not accessible to them. A few other agencies did not require a social security number (i.e., residency status); however, other criteria—such as some form of steady income—also precluded the family from receiving help. Ms. Gómez took Ms. Mercado to the few agencies and to a church organization that she knew had no criteria with respect to documentation or income. Through the church, the family was given a one-time gift of $50. Another agency provided them with a box of food with the understanding that the family could not request food more than once per week. Another center directed by a border health fund provided medical check-ups and dental care for the children; the stipulation here was that the school had to vouch for the family and verify that they were in need. Throughout all of this, Ms. Gómez drove Ms. Mercado from place to place, advocating, translating, assisting with the paperwork that had to be filled out, and communicating with school personnel as needed, with other families, and with landlords as she tried to find a modest, safe place in which the family could live.

At the school, the children's teachers were all apprised of the Mercado family situation. The teachers then provided flexibility with homework assignments. They were careful to assign the appropriate amount of homework, allowing the children to stay after school to complete it. Additionally, each of the children was paired up with a "buddy" whom they knew would be a good friend and help them feel comfortable and not out of place within the school. Fees for field trips and other school activities were waived for them, or were paid by Ms. Gómez's office. The school keeps a supply of toiletries as well as clothing and uniforms to be used in such cases. The children were thus provided with items such as toothpaste, a toothbrush, soap, and shampoo. They were also given some clothing and two school uniforms; the extra uniform would ease the pressure of having to find washing facilities overnight when the uniform was dirty. The cafeteria staff assisted by carefully monitoring to make sure the children had their daily breakfast and lunch. With respect to their education, the children were placed in bilingual education classes, providing native language support necessary for them to learn academic subject matter and acquire proficiency in English.

A network of families existed within the school, including volunteers, PTA members, classroom aides, and so forth, that also assisted families in need. Through this network, Ms. Gómez was able to find some work for Isabel; she cleaned houses one or more days a week for $20 to $30 per day. It is common for undocumented immigrant women to take on housecleaning, child care, and maid work at lower than minimum wage. In time, Isabel also found a small place where she could stay: two large rooms divided into a living area, a sleeping area, a kitchen, and a bathroom. Although it had broken windows, a stove that did not always work, and no heat, it was within walking distance of the school. Over time, when she was not working during the day, Isabel volunteered many hours at the school, so that the teachers and other staff came to rely on her for everything from classroom assistance to yard patrol to office work. She was warmly welcomed by all of the staff and other families; a sense of mutual friendship and trust developed.

The school community was there for her whenever a crisis erupted. During the winter, for instance, various families donated items, including a heater, to help Isabel make her home more comfortable. On another occasion, the PTA collected used household items that were given to her. Isabel then had a garage sale and used the money earned to help her pay the rent. The school community was very careful to help her maintain her dignity and self-esteem; thus a project like the garage sale gave Isabel some ownership to the money that she raised by cleaning, fixing, and selling the items herself. Likewise, when other gifts were presented to her by the PTA or teachers, it was "in appreciation" of the many hours of volunteer time that she provided in helping the staff. Most importantly, the school was very careful about following up on the family to make sure that things were running smoothly. A phone call was made to Ms. Gómez as soon as it was determined that one of the children was absent. She would then contact the family to make sure that everything was all right.

However, lack of citizenship still precluded the Mercado family from receiving basic entitlements such as food stamps and public housing. At 27 years old, Ms. Mercado met a young man, whom she married. He was an American citizen and had recently applied for sponsorship of his wife and the children. Meanwhile, Isabel worked and scraped enough money to help with the citizenship application process. (This process is long and difficult, not only because there is a 2-to-3-year waiting period but also because the $1,000 penalty for living in the United States without documentation, plus the $130.00 fee for the application, puts a tremendous hardship on a family that is already struggling to survive on a day-to-day basis.)

Isabel continued to volunteer at the school, to work as jobs arose, and to care for her children as best as she could. She became the backbone of her family—keeping them together, seeking assistance when that last bag of food had been used, helping the children with their schoolwork, and taking them for medical and dental care as needed. She became very active in helping other families who were in her situation; having experienced the process of seeking help, she knew where to send the families for help and what would be required. However, she continued to live with the terrifying dread that any day, any time, she and/or her children could be deported and her life and the progress she had made in the United States lost—probably forever. Her children, as they attended school and went about their daily work, keenly sensed the precariousness of the situation and they too lived in fear. Thus, this family and others like them faced not only homelessness and poverty; in addition they lived 24 hours a day with the psychological tensions that the lack of documentation brought to their lives. Social workers, such as Ms. Gómez, faced and lived with the reality of having to do illegal work in order to help these families.

SCHOOLS AS SAFE HAVENS AND FAMILY ADVOCATES

The school community is a vital link in programs that assist immigrant undocumented homeless families in finding adequate food, shelter, health, and educational services. It is through the school that the social worker is available and able to target her efforts on the many families, regardless of citizenship status, who have come to the city in search of a better quality of life. Most of these families in the Southwest borderlands are of Mexican descent and many are recently arrived immigrants. While their family circumstances are varied, they all share a history of poverty, as well as a strong desire to stay in the United States despite the many obstacles that they have to overcome.

After immigrant parents eke out a living doing the menial and below-minimum-wage jobs that American citizens will not take—such as working as maids, dishwashers, gardeners, seasonal workers—by the end of the month they are unable to provide the basic necessities for their families. This is why Ms. Gómez, as the school district's social worker, spends much of her time searching for and connecting these families to the few social agencies and centers that can help them with food, shelter, clothing, and health care without regard to citizenship status. Much of her time is also spent communicating with government agencies, such as the INS, so that she may be able to provide accurate information and assist her clients with legal procedures such as establishing residency, fulfilling citizenship requirements, and filling out the multitude of forms involved in these processes. Ms. Gómez as well as the other school staff—including teachers, counselors, principals, cafeteria staff, custodians, and families—are that critical link which is so vital in assisting immigrant families, whether undocumented or documented. Among the services the school community provides to immigrants are clothes for the children, including uniforms; referrals, as needed, for assistance from private agencies and centers; and information on the legal rights of parents, inside and outside of the schools. The schools also serve the families by sensitizing teachers, counselors, cafeteria staff, and other school personnel to the issue of homelessness; placing children in a bilingual education program; assisting children with school assignments after school; assuring that the children get a free breakfast and lunch; communicating closely with the social worker who coordinates all efforts for assistance in finding food, shelter, clothing, medical and dental care, and employment; providing transportation to the various agencies and centers; assisting with filling out paperwork; brokering with landlords and other entities; assisting in requesting documentation as needed (such as birth certificates) from Mexico; providing them with assistance in communicating with INS personnel; and most significantly, advocating for the families.

In these ways, the school community provides the advocacy and caring that are so critical in determining whether these students and their families will survive and, eventually, succeed in a culture that is foreign, usually uninviting, and often hostile to them. Contact with school personnel whom the family can trust is critical. School personnel become the strong and consistent link with the community, and they foster an integrated, safe, and nurturing learning environment for homeless undocumented immigrant students and their families.

Ms. Gómez is thankful that she can focus on assisting these families for "who they are, and not where they come from." The system, she feels, has failed them by focusing not on where they are or where they need to be, but rather on whether they have that piece of paper identifying them as citizens. While other poor and homeless families have legal rights under the McKinney Act, undocumented immigrants have only the right to schooling; their undocumented status precludes their receiving almost all resources that an American citizen or legal resident has a right to receive. Churches and other private organizations are the only other recourse. Private organizations, however, are few in number and have very limited resources, making them unable to provide for the many families in need. Consequently, essential and necessary services are denied to these families, thus virtually leading them into a life on the streets—often exposing them to violence, criminal activity, and danger for all involved. Ms. Gómez is grateful that her hands are not tied, as they are for others who work outside the school in helping families in need. The day that school personnel, such as herself, are asked to withhold their support from families who are undocumented, she says, is the day she will quit her job.

CONCLUSION

Homeless undocumented immigrants face even more severe and complex circumstances than homeless documented immigrants or U.S. citizens as they struggle to survive and create a better world for themselves and their families. For these families there appears to be only one safe system that can be their haven when all else looks threatening. It is the school community that can open its doors to engage parents, families, and children by building trust and helping them lead productive lives in the United States.

REFERENCES
Annerino, J. 1996. "Where Dreams Die: John Doe Mexican." *Arizona Republic,* 8 Sept., H2–H3.
Bartolomé, L., and D. Macedo. 1997. "Dancing with Bigotry: The Poisoning of Racial and Ethnic Identities." *Harvard Educational Review* 67: 222–46.
El Paso Herald-Post. 1997. "'Typical' Immigrant No Longer a Migrant." 7 Aug., A–7.
ERIC Digest. 1990. *Undocumented Children in the Schools: Successful Strategies and Policies* (EDO-RC-90-4). Charleston, W.V.: ERIC/CRESS.
First, J. M. 1998. "Immigrant Students in U.S. Public Schools: Challenges with Solutions." *Phi Delta Kappan,* 205–10.
Fix, M., and Passell, J. S. 1997. *Immigration and Immigrant Students: Setting the Record Straight.* Washington, D.C.: The Urban Institute.
González, M. L. 1992. "Educational Climate for the Homeless." Pp. 194–211 in *Educating Homeless Children and Adolescents,* edited by J. H. Stronge. Newbury Park, Calif.: Sage.
González, M. L., and A. Huerta-Macías. 1997. "Mi Casa es Su Casa: Building Trust in Border Communities." *Educational Leadership* 55: 9–12.
Lee, L. 1997. "School's Out: Immigration Reform Keeps Many Mexican Students out of U.S. Schools." *El Paso Herald-Post,* 17 July, 1A–4A.
National Clearinghouse for Literacy Education. 1997. *One-Tenth of U.S. Population is Foreign Born* (NCLE Notes) 6: 3.
National Coalition of Advocates for Students. 1998. *School Opening Alert.* Boston: Author.
National Coalition for the Homeless. 1989. *American Nightmare: A Decade of Homelessness in the United States.* Washington, D.C.: Author. (ERIC Document Reproduction Service No. ED 317 645.)
National Research Council. 1997. *Executive Summary: The New Americans: Economic, Demographic and Fiscal Effects of Immigration.* http://www2.nas.edu/new/2152.html
Nielsen, J. 1988. *Immigration and the Low-Cost Housing Shortage: The Los Angeles Area's Experience.* Washington, D.C.: Center for Immigration Studies. (ERIC Service Document Reproduction No. ED 301 499.)
Plyler v. Doe. 457 U.S.202 (1982).
Scales, P. C. 1991. *A Portrait of Young Adolescents in the 1990s: Implications for Promoting Healthy Growth and Development.* Carboro, N.C.: Center for Early Adolescence. (ERIC Service Document Reproduction No. ED 346 990.)
Schwartz, W. 1996. *Immigrants and Their Educational Attainment: Some Facts and Findings.* (ERIC Document Reproduction ED402398.)
Vialet, J. 1996. *Immigration Fundamentals: CRS Report for Congress.* Washington, D.C.: Congressional Research Service; The Library of Congress.

19

Hungry Hearts:
Runaway and Homeless Youth in the United States

Marc Posner

Sometimes we see them. We see them in hot pants and halters in New York City, tapping on automobile windows, asking drivers if they want a "date." We see them in Los Angeles, waiting for a sexual rendezvous that will bring them 25 dollars or dinner and a place to sleep. Sometimes we don't see them. We don't see them being smuggled into friends' basements. We don't see them sleeping under a plastic tarp in the woods. And, we don't see them living as concubines in migrant labor camps. And, sometimes we see them, but we don't recognize them. We don't recognize them because they look like the other teenagers talking to their friends in malls and on street corners. But unlike other teenagers, they cannot go home to a meal and a bed. They are runaway and homeless youth. They are among the poorest of America's poor. They lack not only money and homes, but positive peer relationships, families, and the other social supports that most Americans can take for granted.

The cultural changes of the 1960s brought with them a transformation of the stereotype of the runaway youth. Norman Rockwell's young boy with his belongings tied in a handkerchief on the end of a stick became the rebellious, overprivileged middle-class teenager who left home, with its restraints and responsibilities, for the freedom and adventure of urban youth ghettos and rural communes. While there may be a germ of truth in this stereotype, the limited research indicates that many of the runaways of the 1960s were fleeing family conflict and abusive homes. And, like the runaways of today, many of them became victims of violence, sexual exploitation, and the abuse of alcohol and other drugs (Deisher et al. 1969).

The Runaway and Homeless Youth Act (originally authorized as part of the Juvenile Justice and Delinquency Act of 1974) defines a runaway youth as "a person under 18 years of age who absents himself from home or place of legal residence without the permission of parents or legal guardians" and a homeless youth as "an individual who is not less than 16 years of age and not more than 21 years of age; for whom it is not possible to live in a safe environment with a relative; and who has no other safe alternative living arrangement."

According to the federal definition, runaways include teens who, after an argument with their parents, storm out of the house to spend the night with their grandparents and adolescents who sneak out to spend a night with their friends swimming in the pool of a vacationing neighbor. Such episodes do not reflect the family conflict, alienation, and risk behavior characteristic of the chronic runaway, young people who spend a substantial amount of time out of their parents' homes, unsupervised by responsible adults, and growing more estranged from their parents as well as peers, schools, and other social supports. Researchers and practitioners often divide these youth into three categories:

1. *runaway youth* who leave their homes (or institutional placements), usually because of conflicts with parents (or guardians);
2. *throwaway youth* who are forced from, or locked out of, their homes by their parents or step-parents; and
3. *homeless youth* who feel they no longer have a home to which they can return, either because of irreconcilable differences with their parents or because they have lost track of their family's whereabouts. Homeless youth should not be confused with "homeless children," who are part of homeless families. Homeless children live with their families, in shelters, cars, or on the streets. Homeless youth are not only homeless but also family-less.

Most of the research on runaway youth focuses on a narrower group than "federal-definition runaways." These are the young people that practitioners and researchers refer to as "chronic runaways" or "runaways, throwaways, and homeless youth." They are estranged from their families and spend substantial periods living in places other than the family home (or court-approved placement). These youth, whom we will refer to as "runaways," are the focus of this chapter.

WHY THEY RUN

Families from which children run—or from which they are expelled by parents—are often characterized by an inability to communicate and peacefully resolve conflicts: both the typical conflicts that arise during adolescence and more serious conflicts resulting from family dysfunction. As conflicts accumulate and intensify, family life becomes intolerable and the youth leaves home, or is physically locked out (or taken to a social service agency or police station) by parents.

A significant number of families from which children run are subject to problems more serious than an inability to communicate. Many of these families have histories of violence, criminal activity, and the abuse of alcohol and other drugs by both parents and children. A majority of chronic runaways have left homes in which they are physically abused (National Network of Runaway and Youth Services 1991; Administration for Children, Youth, and Families 1990). A substantial proportion were sexually abused (Powers et al. 1990; Rotheram-Borus and Koopman 1991). Young people who have been sexually abused tend to leave home more often and stay away for longer periods than other runaways. They are less trusting of adults and social service institutions (who often return them to abusive homes) and thus avoid contact with social service agencies or runaway shelters. The psychological consequences of sexual abuse (and the desperation to avoid their homes) often puts these youth at risk of further sexual exploitation while out of the home (Kurtz et al. 1991). They are at greater risk of abusing alcohol and other drugs (McKirnan and Johnson 1986). That, in turn, elevates their risk for sexual exploitation, violence, unintended pregnancy, depression, and infection with HIV or other sexually transmitted diseases (Kral et al. 1997).

A disproportionate number of runaway or homeless youth are gay, bisexual, or lesbian (Stricof et al. 1991; Yates et al. 1988). These young people are often subject to ostracism by family, peers, and other adults (such as teachers) at a period in their lives when they are in need of increased support to come to terms with a sexual identity not yet accepted by mainstream society.

An unanswered question is why some youth will leave homes characterized by severe conflict or emotional, physical, and sexual abuse, while others with similar home lives will continue to live with their families. Researchers and practitioners continue to explore the reasons that children can respond so differently to similar family environments. We know that single parent or blended families are especially prone to the stresses that can lead to a child running away or being thrown out of the home. Fewer than one-third of all runaway youth come from families in which both biological parents were present (Finkelhor et al. 1990; Administration for Children, Youth, and Families 1990). However, consensus has been reached on two points. The first is that once a young person has spent a substantial amount of time out of the home (or "on the street"), he or she is so alienated and distrustful that specialized programs are required to reconnect these young people with society (if not their families of origin). The second is that, with increasing levels of urban violence and new and more deadly drugs, life outside of the home is so dangerous that programs are needed to provide an immediate refuge to young people who feel they need to, or are forced to, leave their homes or families and spend time "on the street" (Posner 1994,1993).

WHO THEY ARE

Numbers

Best estimates indicate that, at any given time, about 500,000 young people are living out-of the home in unstable and unsupervised environments (Finkelhor et al. 1990). Other estimates place the runaway population at anywhere from 400,000 to 2 million. These discrepancies in data reflect the difficulty of accurately counting a population that is, by nature, secretive, as well as the differing definitions used to count these youth. Many agencies serving runaway youth are not federally funded and do not submit data. And many runaway youth do not come in contact with either type of agency. Thus, the federal reporting system fails to count a fairly substantial number of runaways (Administration for Children, Youth, and Families 1990).

Age

The average age of runaways is usually reported to be 14 or 15 years old (National Network of Runaway Youth Services 1991; Administration for Children, Youth, and Families 1990). The age at which children start to run away from home is largely a product of child development. Children under the age of 11 or 12 are generally afraid to leave home. During adolescence, a child's desire for self-autonomy escalates. Adolescents characteristically rebel against parental authority. This can create an intolerable level of conflict in families with poor communication and negotiation practices. Adolescence also brings about changes in the nature of incest and sexual abuse. Children who have been sexually abused since they were very young may begin to object to this treatment as they enter adolescence. And, as girls develop during adolescence, they may attract the attention of a sexually predatory stepparent or sibling.

Institutional and legal forces also influence the age of the runaway populations. Unaccompanied young children on the streets at unusual hours are quickly noticed and apprehended by the police. Parental fear of criminal neglect or abuse charges also play a role. A parent who may not report a 16-year-old who has left the home will report the absence of a younger child. Parents are unlikely to lock a very young child out of the house during a family conflict. These factors work together to limit severely the number of runaways under the age of 12 (Posner 1994, 1993).

The upper age limit of the runaway population is a legal, rather than developmental, phenomenon. Most federally funded runaway programs must exclude children older than 18. Many states set the age of emancipation even lower. In some jurisdictions, a 15-year-old can legally leave home. Programs for homeless families often exclude boys over the age of 13 or 14, forcing these children to remain on the street when their mother and siblings seek shelter. When youth living on their own are counted as "runaways," and when they are counted as "homeless adults," is the consequence of rather arbitrary legal definitions.

Gender

Studies done at shelters often conclude that runaway girls outnumber boys by about 10 percent (National Network of Runaway Youth Services 1991; Administration for Children, Youth, and Families 1990). This may be a function of the number of young girls fleeing sexual abuse. Or it may be a reporting phenomenon. Girls tend to seek help at shelters more often than boys. They also tend to be interdicted by police or social workers, who see them as more in need of protection than their male counterparts.

Family Socioeconomic Status

Although the often-repeated statement that "children run away from homes of all income levels" is certainly true, it conceals the fact that the majority of runaway youth are from working-class and lower-income homes (National Network of Runaway Youth Services 1991). While families at every economic level experience problems, the lack of income and resources in poorer families places an additional stress upon their members. Although the abuse of alcohol and other drugs, spousal abuse, and the physical and sexual abuse of children cut across class lines, these problems also affect lower-income families more than others. Lower-income families also have fewer resources to muster to combat the causes of social and economic stress than their wealthier counterparts. Middle- and upper-income families can afford counselors (for both children and parents), as well as summer camps, private schools, and private inpatient mental institutions to separate parents from their children and reduce family stress. Although putting a child into a private school or inpatient mental institution sometimes unfairly places the blame for family dysfunction upon a child, it is an alternative to having that child turn to the streets.

Alternative living opportunities for children from lower-income homes are usually state institutions or foster care homes. About half of all runaways have spent time in foster care or group homes. (Olson n.d.; Ryan and Doyle 1986). Victims of sexual abuse or of homophobia do not necessarily find alternative placements to be any more supportive, or any safer, than their homes. One study found that 40 percent of runaways who have spent time in residential placements report that they were sexually or physically assaulted in that setting (Olson n.d.). Given the realities of an inadequate foster care system, and the behavioral habits of the young people placed in such settings, it is no surprise that a substantial percentage of runaway youth have fled from foster care or group homes.

Race, Ethnicity, and Immigration

Twenty years ago, most programs for runaway youth reported that their clients were white. Since the late 1980s, the runaway population has tended to reflect the ethnic and racial composition of its community (Posner 1994, 1993; Administration for Children, Youth, and Families 1990). The changing face of the runaway population also reflects changes in minority communities. For example, African Americans traditionally have often resolved generational conflicts by sending children to live with extended family members, especially grandparents. This has become less of an option as older generations die and ties with extended families and "the South" loosen. At the same time, the creation of an impoverished underclass, characterized by families with single mothers or transient step-parent surrogates, living in small apartments in neighborhoods plagued by alcohol, drugs, and social fragmentation, contributes to the types of family stress and conflict that result in youths running away, or being expelled, from their homes (Posner 1994, 1993).

Immigration has also contributed to the ethnic and racial diversity of the runaway population. Impoverished immigrant families (especially undocumented immigrants) are subject to high levels of economic, as well as cultural, stress. Children who immigrated at a very young age (or are the first generation born in this country) assimilate America's bad habits, notably the abuse of alcohol and other drugs. All of these factors create stress and intensify conflict within families. Since many immigrant families are extremely mobile, changing residence, moving from city to city and sometimes back and forth to their country of origin, it is easy for children and families to lose track of one another during runaway episodes (Posner 1994, 1993).

LIFE AWAY FROM HOME AND ON THE STREETS

Until fairly recently, children and adolescents in the United States could obtain legal work on farms and factories. Although this work was unhealthy and underpaid, it provided young people with a way to survive apart from their families. While the passage of child labor laws improved the lives of adolescents in general, it also ended the possibility of legitimate economic independence for adolescents. Runaway youth survive as best they can. They are fed by relatives and friends, eat in shelters and soup kitchens, beg for money on the street, and engage in drug dealing and petty crime. Runaway youth generally cannot even provide themselves with a subsistence income and are generally ill-housed, underfed, and in poor health.

The Search for Shelter

The lives of most chronic runaways involve a series of runaway episodes, extended stays with the other parent (in the case of divorced spouses), relatives, or friends, or in foster care, residential, or juvenile justice facilities. Youth who run from, or are thrown out of, their homes return when they get cold, hungry, and disillusioned with their newfound freedom. This pattern can keep a family together until the youth is old enough to find a job and live independently. However, some children develop a "runaway career." As the youth grows older and more accustomed to life on the street he or she stays away from home for longer periods of time (Palenski and Launer 1987). Parents also grow less tolerant as a youth ages, and they gain confidence in their child's ability to survive outside the home. In some cases, the youth will no longer return home (or the parents will no longer allow the child into the home) unless forced to by police or the courts.

Often, a runaway will begin his or her "career" by staying with friends, relatives, or, in the case of divorced parents, the noncustodial parent. However, the behavioral patterns learned by these youths in their homes eventually make them unwelcome. After exhausting these options, runaways live where they can. When they can scrape together enough money, runaway youths will band together and rent rooms in cheap hotels. They will spend time in runaway shelters, foster placements, and with older young people who have apartments. At worst, they live in makeshift camps under overpasses, in county parks or wooded areas, or simply spend the nights walking city streets, huddled in doorways, or sleeping anywhere they can find a place in which they feel they are relatively safe from predators and the police.

Most runaways stay within 10 miles of their homes; only 25 percent go further than 75 miles from their homes (National Network of Runaway and Youth Services 1991; Finkelhor et al. 1990; Administration for Children, Youth, and Families 1990). While runaways are thought of as being an urban phenomenon, children leave home at about the same rate in urban, suburban, and rural areas (General Accounting Office 1989). While local authorities may claim that their town or county does not have a "runaway problem," experienced practitioners maintain this is simply because authorities do not know how to recognize runaway youth.

Physical and Mental Health

All runaways spend a great deal of time outdoors. Many runaway programs are either shelters that are only open at night or drop-in centers that only provide services during the day. Few runaways can afford a long-term stay in even the cheapest hotel. Runaways are exposed to the elements. They are always hungry. Their food often comes from dumpsters behind restaurants or groceries. When they can afford food, they make the same poor nutritional choices made by their more affluent peers: fast food hamburgers, snack cakes, and soda. They do not have access to bathrooms or baths. They lack warm clothing and anything resembling proper medical care. They are malnourished and suffer the effects of exposure. Many of them fight persistent colds, viral infections, and

Figure 19.1   Berkeley, California, has long been a magnet for people seeking an alternative lifestyle. Continuing that tradition, these runaway and homeless adolescents hail from all over the United States. They hang out, panhandle, socialize, and sleep on Telegraph Avenue, a few blocks from the entrance to the University of California. (Photo: Nick Lammers/Oakland Tribune)

digestive problems. The majority of runaway and homeless youth abuse alcohol and other drugs (National Network of Runaway Youth Services 1991; Administration for Children, Youth, and Families 1990). And they suffer the medical consequences of these habits. In the world of the runaway youth, alcohol and other drugs are used to "self-medicate" to alleviate the pain of survival sex, prostitution, exposure to the elements, and hunger. At the same time, alcohol and drugs compound these problems and siphon what little money runaways manage to obtain away from more constructive uses, such as food or clothing.

The world of the runaway is often violent. Physical and sexual assault are prevalent, especially among runaways who work as prostitutes (Robertson 1989; Olson n.d.). The margins of society through which runaways move are places with scarce resources. Runaways are often the prey of adults, and younger, more recent runaways, become the prey of older, more experienced ones. The use of alcohol and other drugs contributes to the violence of this world. In recent years, street gangs have added to the danger. Unlike runaways, gang members are organized, armed, and predatory. As gangs expand their turf, the neighborhoods in which runaways are even marginally safe contract.

While fleeing their homes may resolve immediate family conflicts, the conditions of life out of the home do little to improve the emotional lives of runaways. Psychological problems are endemic among runaway youth (National Network of Runaway Youth Services 1991; Administration for Children, Youth, and Families 1990). In some cases, these problems were at the root of the family conflicts that caused them to flee their homes. In many, mental health problems are the consequence, rather than the cause, of family conflict. This is especially true of the victims of physical or sexual abuse. Runaways, both before and after they leave their homes, are characterized by depression and suicidal thoughts. Many have attempted suicide (National Network of Runaway Youth Services 1991). The alcohol and drugs they use to cope with their lives exacerbate their emotional problems. Their transitory lifestyles and lack of trust of adults reduce their willingness to seek professional help.

Sex and the Street

Most runaways are sexually active (Kowaleski-Jones and Mott 1998; Rotheram-Borus and Koopman 1991). They are unsupervised at a time in their lives when they are undergoing physical and emotional changes of adolescence. Sexual acceptance is also a way of trying to boost the low self-esteem that often results from family conflict (and physical or sexual abuse). This sexual activity leads to elevated rates of HIV and other sexually transmitted diseases (Robertson 1989), as well as unintended pregnancy (National Network of Runaway Youth Services 1991; Administration for Children, Youth, and Families 1990). Few receive proper and consistent medical care for these or other conditions.

While chronic runaways can certainly form strong, supportive, and even loving bonds with their peers and other members of marginal cultures with whom they interact, evidence suggests that "street families" are not necessarily any more functional than the families from which these children fled. Relationships formed on the streets, although sometimes supportive, are often transitory and exploitative. "Boyfriends" are often pimps. "Friendships" can turn violent in disputes over scarce resources: food, money, or drugs. Many runaways have learned to be social isolates, not fully trusting peers, and very suspicious of adults. There is little reason that children from families characterized by conflict and violence should spontaneously produce more positive relationships in the even more unstable environment of "the street."

Contrary to the popular myth perpetrated by sensational television shows and exploitation movies, only a minority of runaways engage in explicit prostitution (Stricof et al. 1991; Yates et al. 1988). This proportion increases in some urban areas (such as New York City and Los Angeles) where as many as 25 percent of chronic runaways may turn to prostitution (Victim Services Agency 1987). Both male and female runaways turn to this method of surviving on the street. There is evidence that a large proportion of, if not most, adult prostitutes begin as teenage runaways.

A larger number of runaways engage in what practitioners call "survival sex," explicitly or implicitly trading sex for food or a place to live, often with older men. While these men are sometimes thought of as "boyfriends," there is little doubt that these liaisons are economic in nature (Stricof et al. 1991; Robertson 1989). Youth who have been sexually abused in their homes are far more likely to engage in prostitution and survival sex than other young people. They are already sexually active, even if this activity was forced upon them. They do not want to return home and face resumption of their sexual abuse. Prostitution or survival sex gives them the illusion of being in control of their own lives, as well as the illusion of being loved or wanted. Both forms of sexual activity carry risks. Surveys indicate that the bulk of young prostitutes have been raped or assaulted.

EDUCATION AND RUNAWAY YOUTH

Runaways are trapped in a world between adolescence and adulthood. They are excluded from much of that world to which their peers have access. Their most primarily exclusion, of course, is from family and home. But exclusion from family usually breaks the social bonds connecting youth and children to other social institutions that could play a healthy and helping role in their lives. The most primary of these institutions is the school.

School provides children and adolescents with more than an academic education. The contemporary American school is a place that readies children for a vocation, providing health, mental health, and nutritional services. Extracurricular activities encompass a broad range of athletic, intellectual, and artistic pursuits. Perhaps most importantly schools strive to help children grow and mature in an environment of positive peer relationships supervised by caring adults who act as positive role models for children and adolescents.

The bond between runaway and homeless youth and school is fragile. The problems encountered by these children in their home often adversely effect their behavior at school. They bring the behaviors learned in their conflict-ridden and chaotic homes to school. These behaviors do not contribute to learning nor to positive relationships with their peers or teachers. While some children attempt to remain in school while they are out of the home and on the streets, most do not. Their lives are taken up in a search for food and shelter. They often are malnourished, dirty, and tired from staying awake through the night. Even the most motivated teenager is likely not to attend school under such circumstances (Posner 1996).

In most cases, runaway and homeless children and adolescents will cycle through their schools as they cycle through their homes. This often leaves them perpetually behind their classmates in both their academic and social development. In addition, the hard lessons of the street (and their home lives) often cause these children to be stereotyped as "bad" or "delinquent" by peers and staff, reinforcing their sense of social isolation and making the school an uncomfortable and unwelcome place (Posner 1996). As the bond between the child and his or her family grows ever more fragile, so does the bond between the child and the school—and with it the child's relationships with positive peer and adult role models. Eventually, both these bonds break, leaving these youths without the support systems and social attachments available to most adolescents. At the same time, their legal status as minors bars them from living independently in the adult world.

THE LONG-TERM CONSEQUENCES OF RUNNING AWAY

We know remarkably little about what happens to runaways after the age of 21. Runaway programs are not funded to conduct long-term follow-up with their clients. The transitory nature of these youths (and the families from which they come) makes it exceedingly difficult for research projects to track and document them for more than a few months. Few studies of adults, either mainstream, homeless, or institutionalized, have attempted to explore the issue of how many of them experienced runaway episodes when younger. We can understand that runaways who manage to reintegrate into mainstream society might not reveal these experiences (even if anyone thought to ask).

Thus, we do not know how many chronic runaway youths return to their families and how many stay homeless into adulthood. We do not know how many manage to transcend their predicament and find jobs and places to live. We do not know what happens to those youth who return to their homes, who stay on the streets until they reach the age of emancipation, or who enter foster care, group homes, or transitional living programs.

We do not want to underestimate the resiliency of the human spirit. It is possible that some runaways transcend their hardships and achieve stable, healthy, adult lives. But limited studies of former runaways reveal substantial levels of emotional problems, problems at school and work, abuse of alcohol and drugs, and marital problems (Olson et al. 1980). Studies of children (including runaways) raised in environments characterized by conflict, sexual or physical abuse, and the abuse of alcohol and other drugs find that many of them replicate these attitudes and behaviors as adults and pass them on to their children as a harsh legacy of their own youths (Plass and Hotaling 1995).

Yet much of what happens to runaway youths as they enter adulthood is only speculation. It is a tragic irony that runaway youths, of whom we often catch only fleeting glimpses, completely disappear when they reach the age of 21, leaving little behind except the knowledge that they will not be the last generation to spend their troubled formative years at the very edge of our collective peripheral vision.

REFERENCES

Administration for Children, Youth, and Families. 1990. *Annual Report to the Congress on the Runaway and Homeless Youth Program.* Washington, D.C.: U.S. Department of Health and Human Services.

Deisher, R., V. Eisner, and S. Sulzbacher. 1969. "The Young Male Prostitute." *Pediatrics* 43: 936–41.

Finkelhor, D., G. Hotaling, and A. Sedlak. 1990. *Missing, Abducted, Runaway, and Thrownaway Children in America: First Report: Numbers and Characteristics: National Incidence Studies.* Washington, D.C.: Office of Juvenile Justice and Delinquency Prevention, United States Department of Justice.

General Accounting Office. 1989. *Homelessness: Runaway and Homeless Youth Receiving Services at Federally-Funded Shelters.* Washington D.C.: Author.

Juvenile Justice and Delinquency Act of 1974. (Public Law 95–415; 88 Stat. 1109). 42 U.S.C. 5601 et seq. As amended.

Kowaleski-Jones, L., and F. L., Mott. 1998. "Sex, Contraception, and Childbearing among High-Risk Youth." *Family Planning Perspectives* 30: 163–69.

Kral, A. H., B. E. Molnar, R. E. Booth, and J. K. Watters. 1997. "Prevalence of Sexual Risk Behaviour and Substance Use among Runaway and Homeless Adolescents in San Francisco, Denver, and New York City." *International Journal of STD and AIDS* 8: 109–17.

McKirnan, D., and T. Johnson. 1986. "Alcohol and Drug Use among 'Street' Adolescents." *Addictive Behaviors* 11: 201–5.

National Network of Runaway and Youth Services. 1991. *To Whom Do They Belong? A Profile of America's Runaway and Homeless Youth and the Services that Help Them.* Washington, D.C.: Author.

Olson, L. N.d. "Treating Street Youth: Some Observations." *Juvenile Justice and Delinquency Prevention Profile.* Unpublished manuscript.

Olson, L., E. Liebow, F. Mannino, and H. Shore. 1980. "Runaway Children Twelve Years Later: A Follow-up." *Journal of Family Issues* 1: 165–88.

Palenski, I., and H. Launer. 1987. "The 'Process' of Running Away: Redefinition." *Adolescence* 22: 347–62.

Plass, P., and G. Hotaling. 1995. "The Intergenerational Transmission of Running Away: Childhood Experiences of the Parents of Runaways." *Journal of Youth and Adolescence* 24: 335–48.

Posner, M. 1996. "Recognizing Signs of Stress Is the First Step in Keeping Kids from Living in the Streets." *Harvard Education Letter* 12(1): 6–8.

———. 1994. Unpublished research for Project Protect.

———. 1993. Unpublished research for The Runaway Risk Reduction Project.

Powers, J., J. Eckenrode, and B. Jaklitsch. 1990. "Maltreatment among Runaway and Homeless Youth." *Child Abuse and Neglect* 14: 87–98.

Robertson, M. 1989. *Homeless Youth in Hollywood: Patterns of Alcohol Use: A Report to the National Institute of Alcohol Abuse and Alcoholism.* Berkeley, Calif.: Alcohol Research Group.

Rotheram-Borus, M., and C. Koopman. 1991. "Sexual Risk Behaviors, AIDS Knowledge, and Beliefs about AIDS among Runaways." *American Journal of Public Health* 81: 208–10.

Ryan, I., and A. Doyle. 1986. *Operation Outreach: A Study of Runaway Children in New York.* New York: City of New York Police Department.

Stricof, R., J. Kennedy, T. Nattell, I. Wesifuse, and L. Novick. 1991. "HIV Seroprevalence in a Facility for Runaway and Homeless Adolescents." *American Journal of Public Health* 81: 50–53.

Victim Services Agency. 1987. *The Streetwork Project and AIDS.* New York: Author.

Yates, G., R. MacKenzie, J. Pennbridge, and E. Cohen. 1988. "A Risk Profile of Runaway and Non-runaway Youth." *American Journal of Public Health* 78: 820–21.

20

Civic Invisibility, Marginality, and Moral Exclusion: The Murders of Street Youth in Brazil

Martha K. Huggins and Myriam Mesquita

Sixteen-year-old Jefferson was shot to death in the entryway to his family home in a poor district on the periphery of Brazil's largest city. He was one of thirty poor children murdered in São Paulo, Brazil, just in July 1991 alone. Jefferson, like many other murdered youth, did not know his father; he lived with his younger siblings and mother, a washer woman, in a one-room cardboard, stucco, and wood structure. He dreamed of earning enough money to add a room where he could entertain his friends. But Jefferson's dream was an illusion; his earnings for his family had always been well below subsistence level.

Jefferson had begun working when he was seven, mostly in the informal sector, where he pieced together a meager income gathering scrap metal and cardboard, selling fruit, washing windows, and helping out a fishmonger and a stone mason. Jefferson had been looking for a "regular job"—one covered by minimum wage and social security legislation. But his search had been in vain, for, as his mother explained, "employers don't hire draft-age boys." (Arruda 1991: 21)

Jefferson's story puts a human face on Brazil's young murder victims; the majority are poor black or dark-brown males between 15 and 17 years old. These are the youth most likely to die at the hands of a stranger. Girls of all ages are less likely to be murdered by strangers; most often, girls are killed by a family member or close family associate. This chapter focuses on youth murdered by strangers in Brazil.

EXCLUSION AND MURDER: A THESIS

This chapter focuses on victim-generating sociostructural situations and the social creation of victims in Brazil. Rather than concentrating on individuals' predispositions or overt motives for murdering Brazilian youth, or the victims' specific alleged misbehavior and threats, or on some generalized culture of violence, we identify the conditions that make particular kinds of Brazilian youth into social problems and symbolic assailants— adolescents whose assumed social and physical characteristics render them criminal without their necessarily having committed a crime.

Our thesis states that modern Brazilian social structures powerfully shape poor Brazilian youths' vulnerability to being murdered by strangers. Such youth come from segments of Brazilian society most marginalized socially, economically, and politically. Their origins render them civic and political nonpersons—outside the moral universe of "good citizens." Since the excluded are seen as nonentities and expendable, harming them appears acceptable. Thus, in Brazil, where civic invisibility is combined with their high social visibility as symbolic assailants, some youth are rendered vulnerable to murder. In this chapter, we will examine the sociocultural conditions that foster civic invisibility, social visibility as symbolic assailant, moral exclusion, and murder of street youth.

STUDYING MURDERED YOUTH

Martha Huggins's 3 years of field research in shelters and outreach programs for "abandoned" street children in São Paulo and Recife—two of Brazil's biggest cities—provided an opportunity for exploring the lives of poor Brazilian youth. Myriam Mesquita, who has spent 13 years studying violence against poor youth, was one of the researchers for *Vidas em risco* (MNMMR 1991), a groundbreaking study of youth homicides in Brazil. She has since conducted extensive doctoral research (Mesquita 1996) on homicides of youth in Brazil through the use of Brazilian morgues and police records. Primary and secondary data have come from human and children's rights agencies and groups, from Brazilian newspaper reports, and from the published statistics of UNICEF Brazil.

These sources reveal great variation in statistics on youth homicides. For example, Rio de Janeiro Military Police statistics for 1991 indicated that 196 youth had been assassinated in that year. The governor's office of Rio de Janeiro State announced that 245 youth were murdered that year. The Brazilian National Street Children's Movement's (MNMMR) regional coordinator for Rio de Janeiro State said that in 1991, 340 youth were murdered there (*Jornal do Brazil* 1991a: 5).

Clearly, official statistics carry no guarantee of statistical reliability or validity. Indeed, Brazil's statistics from the 1980s and 1990s on youth murders are thought to underestimate by up to one-half the annual number of youth homicides in Brazil (Dimenstein 1991; Mesquita 1993; MNMMR 1991). In the first place, most figures include only Brazil's largest cities—São Paulo, Rio de Janeiro, Salvador da Bahia, and Recife—failing to include youth murders in other Brazilian cities and in rural areas. Second, even statistics for the most populous urban areas do not include the bodies dumped in well-hidden graves. They also fail to count the murders recorded as "traffic accidents" or "suicides." Third, the families of murdered children often fail to report these murders, fearing perpetrators' retaliation (Dimenstein 1991; Huggins 1991; MNMMR 1991). Finally, pressure is especially strong to distort or undercount the killings where agents of the state are involved. Yet in spite of such problems, researchers and human rights activists still know a great deal about youth homicides in Brazil.

Based on our knowledge of each data source, we reduced data unreliability by selecting the least biased of several sources. Because of the possible bias associated with any single data source, the best research strategy was to use at least two sources whenever possible—cross-checking each against several others or calculating the mean between them. We found older statistics that could be checked against each other and compared them with newer information. While the data available on youth murders in Brazil are far from perfect, they do provide a reliable profile of victims and their murderers. This is a foundation for analyzing youth murders within a broader sociostructural context.

STATISTICS ON YOUTH MURDERS

In all of Brazil between 1988 and 1991, more than 7,000 poor children and adolescents were murdered—the vast majority by strangers. In São Paulo municipality between 1970 and 1990, reported murders of youth climbed 1,440 percent (*Estado* 1992), an increase greater than for adult homicides and outpacing São Paulo municipality's overall population growth, especially in the municipality's 15-to-17-year-old population—the age group most likely to be murdered by strangers (Mesquita 1993: 89; CPI-Menor, 1993; *Jornal do Brasil* 1991b: 1-4). Between 1992 and 1997, just in São Paulo municipality alone, 1,634 youth were assassinated. This rate, even if lower than during the previous 2 decades, is still higher than for adult homicides (*Estado* 1997: C-3).[1]

Instead of youth murders decreasing during Brazil's transition from military rule to formal democracy (1985 to the present), overall there was a steady increase in this violence, especially in the late 1980s and early 1990s. For example, for all of Brazil between 1985 and 1992, the number of children and adolescents officially recognized as murdered grew 161 percent, while adult murders increased by only 76 percent (*O Globo* 1993: 10). As for increases in absolute numbers of youth homicides, in 1988 in Rio de Janeiro, São Paulo, and Recife, one youth was killed on average every 2 days; the next year, four poor youth were murdered in these cities every day (MNMMR 1991).

In Rio de Janeiro, in Brazil's affluent Center-South region, there was a 50 percent increase in youth murders between 1992 and 1993 (*O Globo* 1993: 10). In Brazil's impoverished Northeast during the first 9 months of 1994, there were slightly more than 15 youth murders monthly in Pernambuco state—50 percent higher than the monthly average for the prior 6 years (*Serviço Brasileiro de Justiça* [SEJUP] 1994).

SOCIOLOGICAL PROFILE OF MURDER VICTIMS

The social image of murder victims is that they are poor, idle youth without family and that they are criminals who are dangerous to themselves and others. Although some street youth engage in petty theft, they are not necessarily as personally violent as their stereotypes. For example, in 1991, according to Brazil's national news weekly *Veja* (1991: 32-35), in São Paulo City's central plaza, Praça da Sé, children committed more than 32,000 thefts and robberies annually—or up to three thefts per child daily. Most were not associated with violence. Moreover, in three major Brazilian cities in 1991, up to two-thirds of the murdered youth did not have police records (Mesquita 1990, 1991, 1993, 1996; MNMMR 1991). In a 1994 Rio de Janeiro study of 336 murdered youth, 95 percent had no criminal record (SEJUP 1994). While many street youth involved in common crime may escape being caught by police, the image of their criminality does not match the realities of their lives. This discrepancy suggests the need to examine the facts about the lives of murdered youth that challenge media and social stereotypes.

Income

Precise economic information on Brazil's murdered youth is unavailable, but the great majority of youth murdered by strangers are either very poor—totally dependent on their own meager substandard earnings—or are children of Brazil's low-paid and often unemployed working class (*Estado* 1997: C-3). Poverty structures a young person's vulnerability to murder by a stranger—especially when combined with their skin color and gender, as will be seen (CPI-Menor 1992; Dimenstein 1991; Mesquita 1993; UNICEF 1991).

Occupation

Data from three of the largest Brazilian cities demonstrate that at the time of their murders, most of the young homicide victims were full-time workers, although poorly paid (Mesquita 1990, 1991, 1993; MNMMR 1991). In Brazil's biggest cities, many poor children toil well in excess of 40 hours a week (Campos 1991; Fukui 1985; Rimbaud 1980). Like the adults in their families, the majority of working urban youth must survive in Brazil's urban informal economic sector—the small-scale, unlicensed activities (many in ambulatory street sales) that pay no government taxes, lack social security and health protection, and do not receive the minimum wage, as low as it is. In fact, Brazil's informal sector employs about 60 percent of all urban workers (Greenfield and Prust 1990; Kowarick 1994).

Family Status

More than a third of the murdered youth in three Brazilian cities lived with birth family or in some kin-based residence; many others visited kin frequently, despite the stereotype that they had lost all connections with birth family and other kin (Mesquita 1990, 1991, 1993; MNMMR 1991).

Age

Eighty percent of Brazil's young murder victims are between 15 and 17 years old, a far greater proportion than this age group's percentage of the Brazilian youth population (Brazil Network 1992; CPI-Menor 1992; Dimenstein 1991; GAJOP 1991b; Mesquita 1993; SEJUP 1994; UNICEF 1991: 111). In São Paulo State, for example, 15-to-17-year olds constitute 16 percent of the population, yet they make up 80 percent of the known youthful murder victims (CPI-Menor 1993; Mesquita 1993: 89).

Gender

Young males are murdered by strangers in much greater numbers than their proportion in the Brazilian population. This general trend shows up in São Paulo State, where in 1989 one girl was killed for every six boys; in 1990–1991, one girl was murdered for every five boys (Mesquita 1991, 1993), even though the gender distribution of São Paulo's overall population is 50.4 percent male, 49.6 percent female (Instituto Brasileiro de Geografia e Estatistica [IBGE] 1992) At the same time, the younger the murder victim, the more likely she is to be female (Mesquita 1993; MNMMR 1991).

Color

In Brazil, the vast majority of youth murdered by strangers are dark-skinned. For example, data on youth murders between 1984 and 1989 in 16 Brazilian states indicate that 52 percent of the victims were "black" (i.e., listed as *negros,* or *pretos*—the darkest among Brazil's many-graded color rankings) (*Jornal do Brasil* 1990). A consensus is emerging among most Brazilian researchers and human rights workers that black youths are murdered in much greater proportions than their numbers in the Brazilian population (Brazil Network 1992; *O Globo* 1993; Huggins 1991; Mesquita 1996, 1993; Penha-Lopes 1994; SEJUP 1994; UNICEF 1991: 111). For example, in São Paulo, 50 percent of victims are "black" although only 25 percent of the population is considered *negros,* or *pretos* (IBGE 1992). Data from Salvador, in Brazil's state of Bahia, show that in 1990, where dark-skinned Brazilians made up about 68 percent of the population (IBGE 1992; Mesquita 1993;

MNMMR 1991), 87 percent of young murder victims were dark-skinned; only 7 percent were white. In Rio, 56 percent of the youthful murder victims were dark-skinned, compared to only 39 percent of the city's population (IBGE 1992; *O Globo* 1993: 10).

PERPETRATOR CHARACTERISTICS

For the majority of youth murders in Brazil, the perpetrator will never be officially identified. For example, the data for São Paulo indicate that between September 1990 and August 1991, in 78 percent of the youth deaths the murderers were unknown to the police; in such cases most researchers make the assumption that the perpetrator was a police-linked extermination group (Mesquita 1991, 1993, 1995). The older youth, mostly males, were likely to have been killed by such strangers—the private "rent-a-cops" and off- or on-duty police—whether acting alone, or as part of a "death squad," or as a lone-wolf "justice-makers" (*justiceiros*) (*Folha de São Paulo* 1991; GAJOP 1991a, 1991b; *Jornal do Brasil* 1991b; Mesquita 1991, 1995). Interestingly, these perpetrators are also likely to have low incomes and live in slums.

The youngest murder victims—usually girls—were most likely to be killed by family or close family associates, not by strangers (GAJOP 1991a, 1991b; Mesquita 1991). In most Brazilian cities where youth murders are reported, young girls are much less likely than boys to be murdered by an extermination group, except where they are in close physical proximity to a young male marked for murder (Dimenstein 1991; GAJOP 1991a: 24–25). One explanation for the lower probability of young girls'death from an extermination group is that Brazilian male stereotypes about women "protect" some young women from murder. According to this thesis, a paternalistic ethos presumably insulates young girls from assassination by male strangers (CPI-Menor 1992: 23; Dimenstein 1991). Of course, such protection is often associated with physical abuse by these young women's male associates.

A related hypothesis about young women's lower probability of being an extermination group's victim is that young girls are less likely to be considered criminally dangerous and thus less likely to be murdered by strangers, including death squads. Another hypothesis is that young girls' commodification as prostitutes provides "protection" from death squad assassination. As one Recife City street prostitute explained, "We have a body to sell; we serve men" (quoted in Dimenstein 1991: 22). A final reason is that in urban Brazil, poor female youth—due to their predominant social and work roles in house cleaning, child care, or prostitution—spend more time indoors than boys. Being indoors seems to insulate girls from murder by strangers while increasing their vulnerability to death at the hands of a family member, close family associate, or intimate non-relative. Thus, while life on the streets heightens the social visibility of stigmatized, outcast youth, "deviant" prostitutes who serve men indoors are spared this fate, suggesting that gender role definitions affecting physical location of work powerfully structure the vulnerability of Brazilian youth to murder by a stranger.

MURDER MOTIVES

As for why some Brazilians murder poor youth, a simplistic answer would be that the murders grow out of Brazilians' socialization within a distinctive Latin American "culture of violence" (see Wolfgang and Ferraucti 1967). But the United States has its own "culture of violence"—with up to 12 youth homicides a day (Children's Defense Fund [CDF] 1993)—without a *characteristically* Latin American culture of machismo. The increasing numbers and proportions of youth murders in such non-Latin countries as India, where the pre-dominant targets are outcast youth (*Chicago Tribune* 1986; *New York Times* 1992), also suggest that more than a Latin American culture of violence shapes some Brazilian youths' exceptional vulnerability to murder. A global "culture of violence" does not do much to explain the increases in violence against Brazilian youth.

One motive behind youth murders is profit: many murderers receive a fee for serv-ices rendered. Prospective victims are auctioned off to the lowest bidder; some urban shop owners and commercial associations have assassination teams on retainer. In July 1991, the going rate for killing a street youth was just half that month's adult minimum wage (*Estado de São Paulo* 1991). It is ironic that a street youth is worth more dead than the child's labor would earn in 2 weeks even at an (unlikely) adult level.

Many business people see "street children" as bad for business: the glue sniffers and pilferers are said to scare away shoppers and suppress sales. Besides, the poor youth who toil in Brazil's informal sector—particularly those who hawk the same goods as the rent-and-tax-paying shops, and at lower prices—are considered unfair competitors. Thus some merchants or their commercial associations pay police, rent-a-cops, and extermi-nation groups to kill annoying children (Boletim 1993; Dimenstein 1991; Huggins 1997, 1998; GAJOP 1991a, 1991b; Mesquita 1991; MNMMR 1991). And while it is true that hired guns and extermination groups are paid very little by U.S. standards, even these earnings are helpful in an economy with few jobs and low salaries—especially for state Militarized Police, who make up a large portion of the perpetrators. Their earnings are so low that they must often live in the same slums as the people they control (Huggins 1997). Another motive behind the youth murders is Brazilians' frustration with the for-mal justice system, including its inability to control "dangerous" youth. It seems to legit-imize vigilantism that Brazil's 1990 Juvenile Code (Estatuto da Criança e do Adolescente [ECA]) requires giving any juvenile alleged law-breaker the same legal rights as adults—including not taking away their freedom of movement unless the person arrested is caught in flagrante or where there is a judicial order for arrest. Once charged, a youth has the right to a court-appointed attorney, to confront his/her accuser, and to have parents or guardians present at proceedings (NEV 1993).

This potentially lengthy process—combined with the fact that there are insufficient facilities for incarcerating even convicted lawbreakers—has led many Brazilians to charge that the 1990 juvenile code fosters juvenile crime by tying the hands of the police and other officials. Since the system "protects" juvenile lawbreakers, the only recourse is to murder them.

Potential murderers are motivated by the fact that most killers enjoy immunity from punishment. The murders continue because murderers get away with them. There is an absence of public pressure to do something about the killings: many Brazilians are un-interested in the murders; many others support this violence. For example, in July 1993, when the state government of Rio de Janeiro set up a special telephone line for securing confidential information about the murderers of a group of 7 male street youths (who had been gunned down while sleeping with a group of 39 other street youth at Rio's Candelária Cathedral), twice as many people called in support of the murders as con-demned them (Penha-Lopes 1994: 16). The murderers might not have even been caught and brought to trial had there not been an international outcry about this massacre. Even-tually, eight police from an off-duty death squad were tried. Among the eight—the major-ity were Rio Militarized Police—as of November 1998, 5 years after the massacre at Candelária Cathedral, only two had been found guilty and sentenced; three had won acquittal; three were still on trial.

Figure 20.1 The mass murder of sleeping street children on the steps of Rio's Candelária Cathedral garnered international attention. Most murders of street children are much less visible to the world. Neighbors comfort each other after finding the body of a young male victim of a death squad in the Baixada Fulminense *favela* close to Rio de Janeiro. (photo: J. R. Ripper/Impact Visuals)

In fact, the Brazilian state is very unlikely to respond to most violence against the poor. For example, one study of all "suspicious deaths" (read: "unsolved murders of the poor") in São Paulo State between 1982 and 1986 disclosed that police investigated only 1 percent of the cases (Mesquita 1990, 1991: 8). A police inquiry was opened up in only 20 percent of the cases of youth murders (*Folha de São Paulo* 1991). Between 1986 and 1992, even where a perpetrator was identified, police began investigations in only 36 percent of such cases. Even then, only 20 percent of the youth murderers known to the police were actually found guilty and punished (Dimenstein 1991: 40).

MURDER STRUCTURE: MARGINALITY AND EXCLUSION

Violence against poor youth must be seen within the context of class and racist exclusion. The poorest 50 percent of Brazilians divide up barely 15 percent of the national wealth, while the richest 10 percent hold more than half the nation's wealth. Almost half of all Brazilians earn less than 2 dollars a day; 44 percent of the Western Hemisphere's poorest are in Brazil, which is also the richest country in the region (Agencia Ecumenica de Notícias e Serviço Brasileiro de Justiça e Paz [AGEN] 1993).

Many poor adults who are in competition with poor youths for any piece of the system's spoils attempt to distance themselves from youths of very similar social and economic status by stereotyping them as morally different—as "deviant" and "criminal."As a consequence, the supposedly more respectable poor Brazilians can see themselves as the hardworking honest poor. By doing so, a segment of the poor attempts to differentiate itself in social space vis-à-vis a group of despised and deviant "others" (see Caldeira 1992).

Economic conditions in the 1980s and early 1990s were especially propitious for such intraclass stereotyping. By the early 1990s, there had been almost a decade of roaring inflation, stunted wages, and massive worker layoffs. Not only did the urban informal sector expand to absorb some of the newly laid-off workers, but it also experienced changes in class composition. Recession hit hard the previously somewhat better-off, more-privileged salaried and unionized adult (primarily male) workers, who increasingly sought income in the informal sector. For example, in greater São Paulo in 1991, almost half the city's new informal-sector workers had recently held regular jobs in industry (42 percent), in services (19 percent), or in commerce (15 percent) (*Jornal da Tarde* 1991). As these workers entered the informal sector, they took the jobs of the poorer Brazilians who had traditionally survived there—youth, blacks, the elderly—pushing down these workers' already meager earnings and intensifying the competition for economic survival between different sectors of the Brazilian poor.

Racism was very much a part of this intraclass struggle. In spite of traditional discourse in Brazil about "racial democracy," the darkest Brazilians have the least education, live in the most precarious housing, hold the worst jobs, get the lowest pay (even for the same jobs as lighter Brazilians), die youngest, and hold very few elected posts or high positions in business, government, or the military (see especially Dzidzienyo 1972; Caipora Women's Group 1993; Fiola 1990). Racism structures the probability of being among Brazil's poorest and then having to live on the streets; it promotes marginality, moral exclusion, and vulnerability to murder.

For example, visible ethnicity powerfully structures who among poor youth is most likely to be murdered, primarily through cultural images of crime and criminals. A Brazilian popular saying is, "If a white man is running, he must be an athlete; if a black man is doing the same, he must be a thief" (Penha-Lopes 1994: 14). According to Penha-Lopes (1994), black men in Brazil's urban public spaces are more likely to be searched by police or become the object of police violence (see also Barcellos 1992). In 1994, the leader of Salvador da Bahia's Olodum music group (featured on Paul Simon's *Rhythm of the Saints* album) was shot by police while rushing with his suitcase through a Brazilian airport: apparently police assumed that a black man with a suitcase must have stolen it from a tourist (Penha-Lopes 1994: 8–9). Likewise, poor, dark-skinned male adolescents on the streets are transformed into "symbolic assailants," rendering them "dangerous" outsiders who do not deserve the consideration applied to a society's moral community.

Another important mechanism driving youth murders in Brazil is fear of crime. Yet it must be emphasized that this fear has a complicated relationship to the amount of known crime. As Mark Fishman (1978) has pointed out for New York City, sometimes fear of crime more powerfully shapes public and government reactions to presumed deviants than the actual extent of criminality. Thus, the violence against poor Brazilian youth and the public's acceptance of youth killings may be the result of how the public perceives a segment of the youth population—as symbolic assailants—and not simply a product of these youth's actual criminality.

Within the Brazilian context, poor youth are candidates for murder because they are seen as without family or other "civilizing" connections—in effect, feral. Media discourse in Brazil routinely links negative images about poor youth to urban criminality. For example, when the Brazilian press reports on the murder of a poor child—commonly referring to the victim as a *menino de rua, menor,* or *pivete*—an image is evoked of a glue-sniffing, familyless, dirty, thieving, dangerously violent delinquent. This is the "street child" who gets media attention; these are the children whom many Brazilians—and foreign tourists—want out of "their" public spaces, the ones reserved for "proper" civic actors. These are the children that Brazil can presumably do without.

According to Caldeira (1992), this demonizing of Brazil's urban poor grows out of images about how poor urban dwellers live. Their precarious squatter slums are culturally configured as "residences, but not 'proper' residences"—the *favelas* are "on a usurped terrain" and inhabited by people who "do not pay city taxes . . . do not have an official address, and . . . are not property owners" (Caldeira 1992: 83). Like most stereotypes, the truth about slums is distorted by negative exaggerations. In the process, the brutalizing realities of *favela* life are turned against the poor, placing them in a liminal social status that is *in* Brazilian society but not really *of* it—at least not belonging to the parts of society reserved for "respectable" Brazilians (see Scheper-Hughes and Hoffman 1994). Since slums exemplify all that is dangerous and bad about Brazil, *favela* residents are, by definition, criminal (Caldeira 1992: 84).

A SOCIOLOGY OF EVIL

Negative stereotypes about poor youth provide a foundation for youth murders in Brazil by drawing symbolic parentheses around "proper" society and its "good" citizens, excluding from equal treatment those who do not fall within the group's moral universe. Stereotypes offer a quick formula for differentiating the "good" and "conforming" poor who stay in their places from the deviant poor who make "improper" use of social spaces reserved for "true" civic actors (see Scheper-Hughes and Hoffman 1994). As outsiders without a fixed legitimate social status, Brazil's poor are easily morally excluded and thus rendered candidates for violence.

In her original elaboration of this thesis to explain crime in Brazil, Caldeira (1992) posited that, in Brazil, "evil"—which is the opposite of "reason"—is what does not make sense, and what takes advantage of people's state of precarious rationality. This offers a plausible explanation for poor teenage boys' greater vulnerability to being murdered: they have been transformed into adult "unworthy" poor and thus beyond the influence of reason.

CONCLUSION

Through an elaborate process of social scapegoating, the poor Brazilian youth who are killed each day are often conceptualized as deviants, rather than victims. This transformation of violence victims into criminals is most likely to occur where the violence against them is perceived as apolitical and anomic; where victims are marginalized, socially stigmatized, and rendered relatively powerless vis-à-vis their victimizers and the larger social system. This, in turn, provides fertile soil for a "culture of denial" (Cohen 1993: 103) that helps socially neutralize violence (Sykes and Matza 1957) against poor youth. Brazilians' (a) deny that any injury really occurred: "Poor youth commit violence against each other; their murder is only an extension of violent lives"; (b) dehumanize the victims: "Street youth are feral discards of under-socialized parents"; (c) appeal to a higher good to justify the murders: "Street youth are dangerous social evils that threaten the very fabric of Brazilian society," as Brazil's military claims; and (d) reject state culpability for youth murders: "Their murderers are lone-wolf killers who are merely settling accounts in the only way they know how." This discourse helps foster the invisibility of youth murderers and their victims; justifies violence against victims; morally excludes them; and exempts state agencies and organized society from responsibility for the violence.

In fact, youth murders are part of the rational organization of Brazilian society. Like most stereotypes, the Brazilian image of poor urban youth as dangerous street children individualizes youth murders and mutes social consciousness about the relationship of these murders to such structurally rooted social problems as inflation, unemployment, debt, hunger, and brutal wealth inequalities. Such stereotypes avert thinking about the sociostructural conditions that throw some Brazilian children onto the streets. Blaming the victim ignores the fact that youth are on the street because their families have no resources to send them to school, and that there are insufficient schools for them to attend in any case (*Miami Herald* 1994). It disregards the fact that children live and work on the streets because they do not have adequate food, social space, or sanitary conditions at home, and thus must survive in even more unsafe and unsanitary public spaces in order to help support their families.

Recognizing poor families' pain at having their children captured by the streets and by its drugs and violence, we can ask what better and more permanent solutions to youth homicides might be found if we were not distracted by the assumption that the victims of this violence are part of the social problem, rather than one of its symptoms.

NOTES

1. These statistics are kept by a unit (Grupo Especial de Investigação sobre Crimes Contra a Criança e o Adolescente) of the São Paulo Civil Police homicide division (*Estado de São Paulo* 1997). We can assume that these data, like other police statistics, underestimate the number of youth murdered in São Paulo.

REFERENCES

AGEN. 1993. *Agencia ecumenica de notícias e serviço brasileiro de justiça e paz.* News Agency, Number 99 (30 October). http://www.oneworld.org/sejp//gg.htm.

Arruda, Roldão. 1991. "Violência liquidou em julho 30 menores nas ruas de São Paulo." *Estado de São Paulo,* Aug. 4, 20–21.

Barcellos, Caco. 1992. *ROTA 66.* São Paulo: Editora Globo.

Boletim, C. 1993. "Boletim de recortes sobre Candalária." Brasília: Ministério Público Federal Procuradoria Geral da República, Assesoria de Communição Social.

Brazil Network. 1992. *Children without a Future.* Washington, D.C.: Author.

Caipora Women's Group. 1993. *Women in Brazil.* New York: Monthly Review Press.

Caldeira, Teresa. 1992. *City of Walls: Crime, Segregation, and Citizenship in São Paulo.* Ph.D. dissertation, University of California at Berkeley.

Campos, Maria Machado Malta. 1991. "Infância abandonada o piedoso disfarce do trabalho precoce." In *Massacre dos innocentes,* edited by Jose de Souza Martins. São Paulo: Ed. Hucitec.

Chicago Tribune. 1986. "Med Schools Fear Skeleton Pinch." 15 June, 6–3.

Children's Defense Fund (CDF). 1993. *The State of America's Children.* Washington, D.C.: Author.

Cohen, Stan. 1993. "Human Rights and Crimes of the State: The Culture of Denial." *Australian and New Zealand Journal of Criminology* 26 (July): 97–115.

CPI-Menor. 1992. "Destinada a investigar o exterminio de crianças e adolescentes no Brasil." *Relatório Final.* Brasília: Camâra dos Deputados, Mar.

CPI-Menor, S. P. 1993. "A comissão parliamentar de inquérito para investigar o menor." São Paulo: Assembléia Legislativa, Oct.

Dimenstein, Gilberto. 1991. *A guerra dos meninos: assassinatos de menores no Brazil.* São Paulo: Editora Brasiliense.

Dzidzienyo, Anani. 1972. "The Position of Blacks in Brazilian Society." Pp. 162–85 in *The Fourth World: Victims of Group Oppression,* edited by Ben Whitaker. New York: Schocken.

Estado de São Paulo. 1991. "Exterminio do menor é negado por comerciante." 19 Aug.

———. 1992. "Assassinatos de menores aumentam 1, 440%." 5 May, Cid.-1.

———. 1997. "247 Menores foram matados na capital em 97." 2 Nov., C-3.

Fiola, Jan. 1990. *Race Relations in Brazil: A Reassessment of the Racial Democracy Thesis.* Amherst: University of Massachusetts, Monograph Series.

Fishman, Mark. 1978. "Crime War as Ideology." *Social Problems* 26 (June): 531–43.

Folha de São Paulo. 1991. "CPI culpa policias por morte de crianças." 7 Dec., I-10.

Fukui, Lia, et al. 1985. "A questão do trabalho infantil na grand imprensa paulista na década de 70." *Revista de estudos pedagógicos* 66 (152): 28–46

GAJOP. 1991a. *Grupos de exterminio: a banalização da vida e da morte em Pernambuco.* Olinda, Brazil: GAJOP.

———. 1991b. "Levantamento de homicídios de crianças e adolescentes." Jan.–Sept.

O Globo. 1993. "Violência contra menor aumenta 50% no Rio." 2 Nov., Rio-10.

Greenfield, Sidney, and Russell Prust. 1990. "Popular Religion, Patronage, and Resource Distribution in Brazil." Pp. 123–145 in *Perspectives on the Informal Economy,* edited by Estelle Smith. Washington, D.C.: University Press of America.

Huggins, Martha K. 1991. *Vigilantism and the State in Modern Latin America.* New York: Praeger.

———. 1997. "From Bureaucratic Consolidation to Structural Devolution: Police Death Squads in Brazil." *Policing and Society* 7 (4): 207–34.

———. 1998. *Political Policing: The United States and Latin America.* Durham, N.C.: Duke University Press.

Instituto Brasileiro de Geografia e Estatística (IBGE). 1992. *Anuário estatístico do Brazil.* Rio de Janeiro: Author.

Jornal da Tarde. 1991. "Camelôs os novos filhos da crise economica." 5 Nov., Cid.-18.

Jornal do Brazil. 1990. "ONU prequisou morte de menor em 16 estados." 8 Apr., I-8.

———. 1991a. "Assassinatos de crianças." 23 Nov., Cid.-5.

———. 1991b. "CPI aponta 7 mil assassinatos de crianças nos ultimos anos." 6 Dec., I-4.

Kowarick, L. 1994. *Social Struggles and the City: The Case of São Paulo.* New York: Monthly Review Press.

Mesquita, Myriam P. De Castro. 1990. "State and Society: A Violation of the Right to Life." Unpublished paper presented at the University of Coimbra, Portugal, July.

———. 1991. "Assassinatos de crianças e adolescentes no estado de São Paulo." São Paulo: Documentação Gráfica, NEV/USP.

———. 1993. "Assassinatos de crianças e adolescentes no estado de São Paulo." *Revista crítica de ciências sociais* 36: 81–102.

———. 1995. "Homicídios de crianças e adolescentes: uma contribuição para a administração da justiça criminal em São Paulo." São Paulo: Ministério Público do Estado de São Paulo/UNICEF.

———. 1996. *Vidas sem valor: um estudo sobre as homicídios de crianças e adolescentes e a atuação das instituições de segurança e justiça (São Paulo, 1990-1995).* Ph.D. dissertation, University of São Paulo, São Paulo, Brazil.

Miami Herald. 1994. "Resource-Rich Brazil Failing Its Children: A School System in Chaos." 14 Mar., 1–4A.

MNMMR. 1991. *Vidas em risco.* Rio de Janiero: Movimento Nacional de Meninos e Meninas de Rua.

NEV. 1993. "Os direitos humanos no Brasil." São Paulo: USP/NEV/CTV.

New York Times. 1992. "Hundreds Tortured to Death in India, Rights Group Says." 25 Mar., A-7.

Penha-Lopes, Vania. 1994. "An Unsavory Union: Poverty, Racism, and the Murders of Street Youth in Brazil." Unpublished manuscript.

Rimbaud, Christine. 1980. *53 Millions d'Enfantes au Travail.* Paris: PLON.

Scheper, Hughes N., and Daniel Hoffman. 1994. "Kids Out of Place." *NACLA* 27, (6).

Serviço Brasileiro de Justiça (SEJUP). 1994. "Rio de Janeiro." *Peacenet* 155 and 156 (17 and 24 Nov.)

Sykes, G., and D. Matza. 1957. "Techniques of Neutralization. A Theory of Delinquency." *American Sociological Review* 22: 664–70.

UNICEF. 1990. *O Trabalho e a rua: crianças e adolescentes no Brasil urbano dos anos 80*. Rio de Janeiro: UNICEF.

———. 1991. *Bahia: suas crianças e adolescentes o que está acontecendo?* Salvador, Brazil: UNICEF.

Veja. 1991. "Meninos de rua: os filhos da miseria e do crime." 29 May, 32–35.

Wolfgang, Marvin, and Franco Ferraucti. 1967. *The Subculture of Violence: Towards an Integrated Theory in Criminality*. London: Tavistock.

Part VI: Conclusion

21

Children on the Streets of the Americas:
Implications for Social Policy and Educational Practice

Roslyn Arlin Mickelson

Figure 21.1   In 1994, Semear student João Roberto dos Santos Rosa held the world in his hands. (photo: R. A. Mickelson)

The lives of homeless and street children in the Americas are filled with light and shadow, hope and despair. The light and hope exist in each child's human potential as well as in the existing laws, programs, and policies that form the architecture for educational and social change. The shadow and despair come from the grinding poverty that emiserates their lives, and the harsh neoliberal prescriptions for economic growth that have influenced governmental policies in the Americas during the last 2 decades.

271

Relationships among the governments, civil societies, and economic forces in and among Brazil, Cuba, and the United States shape the contours of the lives of homeless and street children. The comparative case studies and policy analyses presented in the previous chapters enable one to see how the differences among the three nations' political economies and their governments' domestic policy choices have profound consequences for children's education, health, and social welfare.

It is now possible to return to the questions prompted by my reflections on the Brazilian, Cuban, and U.S. children I encountered in 1994. What are the commonalities and differences in the life circumstances of homeless and street children in the three countries? How are differences in child well-being and education affected by broad political and economic trends and globalization forces, and how does domestic policy in each country mediate these processes? What educational and social policies are necessary to address street and homeless children's immediate needs and to effect long-term changes in their lives and their societies? Drawing upon the findings and arguments in the case studies and policy analyses in the previous chapters, I found the answers to my questions share several broad themes.[1]

Diversity

The lives of children on the streets of the Americas are quite varied. Some have homes, some have families, others have neither. Some children participate in comprehensive programs that provide surrogate families, or informal education; others receive formal education in comprehensive programs that address a constellation of their needs. The differences among Brazilian, Cuban, and U.S. homeless and street children's circumstances are a matter of degree and detail, not of kind. What children on the streets share is extreme poverty.

The Structural Nature of Poverty

Homeless and street children are members of marginalized classes. The interaction of global economic restructuring with the Brazilian, Cuban, and U.S. political economies exacerbates long-standing internal stratification dynamics. The spatial (concentration of power and control of financial nerve centers in global cities) and technical (information systems, computers, communications) aspects of globalization intensify the income and wealth polarization associated with the mobility of capital and production processes.

Structural Adjustments and Income Polarization

Neoliberal structural adjustments contribute to increased income polarizations within and among nations (Carnoy 1999; Lustig 1996). They exacerbate the extant structures of inequality, increasing the pressures that lead children to work and live on the streets. International political and business leaders are now beginning to acknowledge the unnecessary suffering neoliberal prescriptions for fiscal discipline and reform have brought to people in developing nations like Brazil. Surveying the forces of global capitalist economic integration and domestic economic disintegration across emerging markets, the world financial and political leaders meeting at Davos, Switzerland, in early 1999 questioned the wisdom of structural adjustment medicine for ailing economies. Even the IMF and other financial managers of the global crisis are beginning to advocate a kinder, gentler austerity—one that does not abandon the poor and the unemployed (Sanger 1999).

This reevaluation of structural adjustment notwithstanding, the burdens of imposed austerity combined with the legacies of government corruption and inefficiencies, plus the weight of the external debt burden, make it extremely difficult for the Brazilian state to control its economic future, or provide public education and other vital social services to the majority of citizens. Sheryl Lutjens and others (Cardoso and Helwege 1997; Eckstein 1994; Thorp 1998) describe Cuba's situation as comparably bleak, but for different reasons: the U.S. embargo and the demise of the USSR and the Eastern European trading block, together with mistakes committed by the government; a continued dependence on sugar; dollarization; and the repercussion of expanded tourism have crippled the Cuban economy. The reemergence of street children in Cuba may foreshadow a nascent crisis that is even more disturbing than other domestic problems of the last decade. And in the United States, neoliberal domestic policies, such as welfare reform, contribute to the plight of poor children and their families.

Race and Gender

Race and gender intersect every dimension of street and homeless children's lives, including their access to education and the type of education they receive. For example, in Brazil, while there are fewer street and homeless girls and adolescents, females are at greater risk than males due to the gendered division of labor in the informal economy and the dangers they face as sexual targets, especially those who are sex workers. Martha Huggins, Myriam Mesquita, and Fúlvia Rosemberg document how adolescent males are at greater risk for violence in Brazil. Marc Posner notes that in the United States, runaway adolescents are disproportionately females, most likely victims of sexual abuse. Homeless adolescent males in the United States face their own unique obstacles to survival. Many end up on the streets because they fall through the gaps in the shrinking safety net; they are too young for men's shelters, but too old for family shelters.

The stain of racism seeps down to the streets as well. In the three Americas, race and social stratification are linked such that poorer Brazilian, Cubans, and North Americans are disproportionately people of color. Among nonwhites, those with the darkest skins can suffer the greatest discrimination. While street and homeless children come from all racial and ethnic groups, children perceived to be *criollo, branco,* or white are less frequently found on the streets or in homeless shelters.

Arguably, the most abused and exploited children are child sex workers. Adults' taste for child prostitutes, long entrenched in Brazil, is rapidly reappearing in Cuba in conjunction with increased international tourism. Among domestic elites and foreign tourists in Brazil and Cuba, *las mulattas,* or child prostitutes, are the most desired (Fusco 1998; Longo 1998; Montgomery 1998). In the global sex economy, *las mulattas* represent the intersection of gender and race with the exploitation and abuse of street children. However, as Fúlvia Rosemberg cautions us, it is important to expose and condemn its exploitive and abusive nature without exaggerating the scope of the problem.

The Role of Education

Education offers poor children hope and literacy; without education, there is poverty with little hope. For ethical, moral, and developmental reasons, both formal and informal educations are essential for homeless and street children who have few resources or social networks with which to make their way in the globalizing economy and society. The emerging informational economy requires a particular kind of educated workforce. This suggests that those without education essentially will be not only marginalized but also irrelevant—and relegated to the informal sector.

If we cannot make an argument for children's education on moral grounds, then we must rely on utilitarian ones: countries with children living or informally working in the streets cannot prosper, grow, or be democratic or fully civilized. Educational systems can serve individual and national ends if they are designed with human dignity, not merely with technical or economic development goals as their centers of gravity. But, as Fernando Cardoso once argued, for hope to survive it is necessary to associate social justice and freedom with a political instrument (1993: 151).

A Dual Approach

Short-term microlevel interventions—such as formal and informal educational programs, collaborations between state and civil society (NGOs, religious organizations, civic organizations, unions, firms)—as well as long-term macrotransformations of structures of inequality and oppression are necessary. In the long term, the interventions that will have the greatest effects are those that attack all aspects of the structure of inequality (Wilson 1998).

Necessary Actions

A number of actions are necessary to reduce the numbers of, and eventually to eliminate, street and homeless children in the Americas. The necessary legal foundations are already in place; as Yvonne Rafferty and Steven Klees and his colleagues note, all that is needed is to comply with them. The Brazilian and Cuban constitutions guarantee children the right to a childhood that includes the protection of the state in all realms of life if families cannot provide safety and sustenance. These fundamental rights include education (Brasil 1988; Cuba 1992). Brazil's Child and Adolescent Statute further guarantees these rights to all children irrespective of their life circumstances. In the United States, the McKinney Act (1987) guarantees homeless children the same.

Moreover, throughout Brazil and the United States, there are innumerable programs in place that begin to do this. As the chapters in this book have shown, the organization and institutional architecture to address the short-term needs of homeless and street children already exist. Yet, as Irving Epstein, Steven Klees, Irene Rizzini, and Anthony Dewees argue, perfectly good programs fail to solve the problems homeless and street children face, because they ignore the political rationality that maintains, and often exacerbates, inequality. Even the most carefully designed and comprehensively delivered programs potentially affect the lives of only a few homeless and street children, while the conditions that produced their plight remain untouched.

We are left then with the question of *what to do*. As an alternative to the technical/rational approach that seeks to "fix" programs or schools so that they can better educate poor children, or the human capital model that seeks to "fix" children's educational and skills deficits so they can compete more successfully in the same economic system that generated their plight, is a political action model in which social movements give voice and power to excluded groups, who then pressure the state for meaningful reform and action (Carnoy and Levin 1985; Easton et al. 1994).

Social movements that pressure governments to act in ways that meaningfully address the conditions of homeless and street children are consistent with the work of Amartya Sen, whose scholarship in the areas of social choice, welfare economics, and poverty earned him the Nobel Prize in Economics in 1998. His work unites social choice theory and economic development theory to address how distributions of societal welfare and collective decisions (public policy in democratic states) can be consistent with individuals' welfare. Poverty is a distributional issue intimately connected to a society's values. Social programs involve political and ethical choices, not merely technical, fiscal, or monetary decisions (Royal Swedish Academy 1998). Cuba's superior educational outcomes reported in the recent UNICEF study of educational achievement in 15 Latin American countries illustrates the proposition that excellent education can be provided to all citizens *if* the resources and values of a society are truly bound to this goal (Casassus et al. 1998).

The Role of the State

Sen's work, then, brings us back to the fact that governments mediate the processes of global capitalist economic restructuring through their domestic policy choices. Governments not only mediate the production of wealth through their fiscal and monetary policies but also mediate the effects of market forces and income inequality on citizens' lives. Western European and U.S. governments have done so to varying degrees for much of the twentieth century.

This duality is at the heart of the tension between generating economic growth *and* greater equity that has perplexed nations in the Americas throughout the twentieth century. The challenge of achieving both growth and equity is nicely captured in Brazilian economist Fernando Fajnzulber's dilemma of the "empty box." His four-cell typology represents the relationship between growth and equity. In the postwar period, there have been cases of Latin American countries experiencing no growth but more equity; countries with economic growth but less equity; and countries with neither greater equity nor economic growth. But in no case did a country experience rapid economic growth and more equity (Fajnzylber 1990; Thorp 1998: 239). During the early 1980s Cuba experienced some growth and greater equity (Cardoso and Helwege 1998; Eckstein 1994), but that conjuncture was short-lived. The cell in Fajnzylber's typology representing Latin American countries experiencing both fast growth and increased equity essentially has been an "empty box." Certainly the United State's own economic history during the last 5 years of the century reflects aspects of the dilemma of the empty box. Despite soaring corporate profits, the proportion of American children who are poor has not changed.

There are small signs that policymakers, at least in some countries and in certain international institutions, have come to see the potential complementarity between growth and equity along with increased productivity and greater democratic participation (Thorp 1998: 281). Such a paradigm shift is very hopeful. In the meantime, there are a host of micro- and macroeducational and social policies needed. I now turn to a discussion of these policies.

EDUCATIONAL PROGRAMS FOR STREET AND HOMELESS CHILDREN

All children share the same profound needs for sustenance, shelter, safety, affection, education, and opportunities for creativity and play. Poor children have difficulties meeting some or all of these needs; street and homeless children encounter the greatest obstacles. The policy analyses and case studies presented in this book offer a set of common lessons regarding how collaborative programs can best assist homeless and street children to meet their needs. The lessons that emerge are consistent with the conclusions reached by Easton and his colleagues in their 1994 review of 100 programs for street and working children from 20 countries.[2] The lessons from the American case studies also are similar to the findings reached by Sally Power and her colleagues, who investigated educational opportunities for homeless children in London (Power et al. 1997). Table 21.1 summarizes key characteristics of these lessons and indicates which characteristics appear in the various programs for homeless and street children discussed in the previous chapters.

Table 21.1 Characteristics of Educational Programs for Homeless and Street Children

Characteristics of Programs	Case Studies								
	ACP	Axé	Brownstone	Chalet School	Curumim	Estado de Cambodia	Gateway School	Marcy School	Semear
1. Adapts to characteristics and needs of children	•	•	•	•	•	•	•		•
2. Program design respects children's need to work	•	•			•				•
3. Involves children and parents in program design	•	•			•		•		
4. Offers comprehensive, integrated services	•	•	•	•	•	•	•		•
5. Cultural bridges to children's lived realities; street educators	•	•			•				
6. Informal, flexible, critical pedagogy	•	•		•	•	•			•
7. Flexible, practical curriculum that can prepare for reentry to formal schooling	•	•	•		•	•	•		•
8. Educates the public about homeless and street youth	•	•			•				
9. Professional development provided to educators	•	•		•	•	•	•		•
10. Collaboration among state, NGO, or civil society (e.g., church)	•	•			•		•		•
11. Provided by state								•	
12. Provided by an NGO			•	•					

The common lessons that appear in Table 21.1 lend themselves to more specific courses of action that can be divided broadly into recommendations at the micro- and macrolevels. I consider micropolicy recommendations to be those that concern (I) educational programs, and (II) curricular and instructional design issues. Macrolevel recommendations address educational and social policy (III).

I. Features of Successful Educational Programs

- Education is only one component of successful programs. The needs of homeless and street children are multiple and linked to their family's and community's problems. Before children can engage in learning, their more immediate needs for safety, food, and shelter must be addressed. Therefore, in collaboration with other organizations—frequently NGOs or state agencies—a successful program provides shelter, medical care, food, and a range of other services. If the program does not offer these directly, then it works with organizations that may be able to provide needed services.
- As several scholars have argued in this volume, it is imperative to target the needs of children; generic programs are not effective. Successful interventions adapt to the specific characteristics of street and working children and the diverse context in which they live. For example, programs distinguish between homeless families and street children; and children *of* and children *on* the street; program services include children's real or fictive kin; they pay attention to the special needs of girls and to the fact that many street children are sexually active.
- Successful programs pay attention to the reality that many children in developing countries need to work; if they don't work, then they don't eat. In all countries, most children will work later in their lives. Incorporating workforce education into programs can serve dual purposes of developing students' workforce skills while luring them back to school for literacy training. Programs may offer stipends for their participation and loss of income from the streets (for example, Projeto Axé). Work training or apprenticeship programs that teach literacy and numeracy offer students more than a potential bridge from the informal to the formal economy; they impart literacy that is critical for citizenship (Stromquist 1997).
- Involvement of the children and their families in program development enhances the likelihood of the program's success (for example, Semear, Curumim, Gateway School, A Child's Place, and the Brownstone School). Design and implementation of programs in this way create ownership among those for whom the program is intended. Programs conceived and imposed on communities by outsiders are rarely successful. The more grassroots or community based, the greater the program's success.

II. Lesson for Curriculum and Instruction

- All programs for homeless and street children have an explicit educational component. Most students in programs for homeless and street children have had bad experiences with formal education. In order to heal this rupture, schools and programs need to reengage children's attention. Ultimately, they must entice them to return to the educational process. Successful programs bridge the culture gap and overcome the distrust of schools and adults that children often have. In Brazil, this is often done by street educators. Almeida and Carvalho describe the techniques and multistage approaches used successfully by Projeto Axé.

- For many street children and homeless children traditional education has not worked. At least initially, they need more of a critical education approach that offers flexible instruction, rather than traditional pedagogy. Constructivist, whole language, and Freirian conscientization approaches are more suitable, at least initially. At the same time, it is clear most homeless and street children are severely behind in formal literacy and numeracy skills.[3] They require serious educational remediation so that they can close the gaps in their literacy and numeracy levels. The Brownstone School's use of Accelerated Learning and the Chalet's and Curumim's use of tutoring after school are examples of this remediation in action.

- Flexibility regarding nontraditional approaches to curriculum is necessary, too. Curriculum has to be immediately relevant, while it must also offer some kind of credential or certification that can lead to jobs in the formal economy. Additionally, some homeless and street students will be able to transition from informal and nontraditional programs into formal education. This possibility must remain viable. Easton and his colleagues recommend a graduated approach that begins with informal education that provides survival skills and moves through business skills and aptitudes (so many children already engage in retail and service work), on to activities to promote self-confidence, and ultimately moves students into the formal curriculum where they gain access to "official knowledge."

- Access to official knowledge is important for several reasons. First, if homeless and street children are ever to progress through the formal school system to higher education, then they must learn the official curriculum. Programs cannot offer only alternative curricula that preclude this possibility, however slight. Second, most students—even those who have failed in traditional schools—desire "real school." Mary Metz uses this term to describe the common script shared by generations of parents and students as to what should be taught in school and how it ought to be conveyed by teachers (1990). A Child's Place and Semear students explicitly requested "real school" from their teachers. The challenge, then, is to design curricula and instruction that simultaneous provide "real school" as well as engaging, flexible, innovative, practical, and emancipatory experiences for homeless and street youths. A well-designed holistic curriculum can meet the challenge.

- Programs need to educate the public about homeless and street children in order to dispel harmful stereotypes that further erode these children's chances of obtaining an education. In the case of Brazilian street children and North American runaways, stereotypes increase street children's chances of being murdered. ACP, for example, incorporates community education into its formal program. Several others in the United States and Brazil do as well.[4]

- At the beginning of each day, educators need to have an arsenal of techniques, resources, strategies and—most of all—reasons to engage in the difficult work of teaching homeless, poor, and street children. Teachers must have strategies to deal with the dilemma of "Monday mornings," Paul Willis's (1977) metaphor for the imperative teachers face when they walk into their classrooms day after day while they work for larger structural and cultural transformations. Although many of the professional educators who work with homeless and street children in both formal and informal settings are caring and competent professionals, they are not always knowledgeable about their students' unique needs. Silva's discussion of the class conflict between Curumim educators and their students is illustrative of this dilemma. At the same time, street educators who are more knowledgeable about their students' lives may not have the professional background to be effective teachers. Professional development is extremely important, particularly when educators and students come from different social classes and have different cultures. Professional development must include sensitivity and awareness training about the implications of children's backgrounds for their educational and social needs as well as provide teachers with a host of strategies to use.

III. Lessons for Macroeducational and Social Policy

- To date, in both developing and developed countries, globalization has pushed governments away from equity-driven educational reforms. But according to Carnoy, states have much more political and financial space to condition, or what I have termed mediate, the ways that globalization influences educational policies (1999). Democratic social movements in support of greater access to quality education for all children, but especially for street and homeless youth, are needed to pressure governments to respond in more equitable ways to the educational dimensions of the emerging global economy.
- We cannot educate children out of homelessness any more than we can educate people out of poverty. If all people in the Americas are well educated, then there are still not sufficient opportunities for them to earn living wages (CDF 1998; Connell 1994; Easton et al. 1994; Gallagher 1998; Natriello et al. 1990; Sassen 1998; Wilson 1996). This is true for the United States and Brazil. Cuba *has* educated its citizenry very well, yet it is still a poor nation. Clearly solutions to poverty must be sought elsewhere.
- While the solutions to poverty are being developed elsewhere, the state plays an important role in mediating the effects on people of macroeconomic restructuring, loan contingencies of international financial institutions, and the flow of international capital in and out of emerging markets. This role requires decisive government actions to ensure all people have the minimal necessities of life. This means coordinating the emerging global capitalist economy with an aim to producing better jobs, higher wages, a cleaner environment, a more equitable distribution of resources and quality of life, and greater democratic participation in society.
- NGOs and the state have complementary roles to play in this process. NGOs often fill the gaps left by government and private sector inaction or neglect. NGOs perform a vital function in piloting new approaches to problems, but government is needed to set the social policy framework, to pay for the programs, and to disseminate successful innovations initiated by NGOs. For example, the curriculum for students at risk developed by Projeto Semear has been disseminated widely by the state of Rio de Janeiro.
- In the long term, the problem of poor and street children cannot be resolved or prevented from recurring without reform of both formal and informal education. Brazilian public education—where most children are schooled—is seriously flawed. While the majority of U.S. children receive good educations, those in inner-city or rural areas generally do not (Anyon 1997; Connell 1994; Kozol 1991; Natriello et al. 1990). And as we see from the case studies, homeless and street children often receive the worst educations of all. At best, we can design a series of "jewel box" programs (the term Easton et al. use for comprehensive and successfully implemented programs) for homeless and street youth. But with this approach, we only assist the few who pass through the programs' doors. In the end, targeted programs for homeless and street children are unlikely to have a lasting impact on children's lives or their societies unless the programs are part of

a broader agenda for social justice because, as James Gallagher (1998) observes, education is a weak treatment.

- We can no longer think of policy solutions for children that reflect local, state, or even national boundaries. For centuries, people seeking better lives have taken profound risks, moving entire families across nations and continents. Globalization of the world's economy, in fact, intensifies migration of people within and among nations.[5] Poverty and homelessness are associated with the movement of people who come from rural areas to urban centers, or who cross international frontiers in hopes of a better life. Both domestic and international patterns of migration disabuse us of any lingering illusions that we can fix our local problems and ignore the rest of the nation or the hemisphere. Pedro Vicente's Guarani-speaking children who sell palmettos and beg on the streets of São Paulo to earn their living, Isabel Mercado's children who crossed the Rio Grande River from Ciudad Juárez to El Paso, and Marietta Cardin's four children who moved from Chicago to Los Angeles all illustrate the dynamics of migration as well as the conditions faced by immigrant children who work and live on the streets of the Americas.

CONCLUSION

The continued presence of homeless and street children on the streets of the Americas is a visible reminder that the disease of poverty has been neither contained nor eradicated. The presence of homeless and street children within sight of the skyscrapers, museums, and luxury apartments of great North and South American cities exposes the contradictions between the concentration of wealth and the intensification of poverty that accompany globalization. Homeless and street children are harbingers of a looming social crisis facing the Americas.

Solutions to social crises frequently involve education. It is simplistic, though, to suggest that education alone can redress social inequalities that bring children to live and work in the streets. While providing quality education to homeless and street children is a moral imperative, it is hardly adequate for ensuring them a better life. Jean Anyon's powerful metaphor in *Ghetto Schooling* (1997) aptly exposes the Sisyphean shortcomings of such an approach: educating homeless and poor children without tending to the social conditions of their lives is akin to cleaning the air on one side of a screen door. Appreciating the larger implications of this insight is one of the challenges facing educators and citizens of all the Americas.

NOTES

1. Very few of the case studies in this book reported formal evaluations of their program. This is not unusual. Easton and his colleagues note that, in general, there are a limited number of evaluations of programs for homeless and street youth. Those that exist tend to be done by internal evaluators and tend to be somewhat promotional. Easton and his colleagues suggest that judgments of the success of a program should not be based on whether it eradicates the problems of street and homeless children. To do that, a program would have to grapple with poverty's embeddedness in a nation's political economy and the global economic order. Nor should evaluations of a program's success hinge on whether it guarantees a different life to its clients. Rather, a determination of a program's success should be based on whether it initiates the beginning of significant change in children's lives (1994: 2).
2. I want to acknowledge my debt to the scholars at the Center for Policy Studies in Education at the Florida State University, whose UNICEF-sponsored study of programs serving street and

working children in 20 countries is one of the most comprehensive and rigorous investigations of programs ever completed. Because my findings and conclusions resonate with theirs, I have adapted their framework to present mine.

3. Meg Sheffield's *Maths in the Street* is a fascinating Open University film that depicts the mathematical proficiencies and dexterities of street children in Brazil. It shows how children working in the informal economy complete complex mathematical operations in their heads. These operations include converting foreign currency into Brazilian currency, factoring in the daily fluctuations in exchange rates in the currency due to inflation, calculating the cost of the various quantities of merchandise being purchased, and then making change in Brazilian currency. At times, they also had to estimate the weight and volume of merchandise before presenting customers with the price of the goods. The street children are highly successful in this. The film showed that when the same children were in their elementary school performing a paper and pencil test of comparable mathematical operations, they were completely baffled and could not answer any questions correctly.

4. During my visit to São Martinho, a program for street children in the heart of Rio's commercial district, I attended a professional development seminar about street children given by the program's director to approximately 40 off-duty law enforcement personnel. His lecture lasted about 2 hours, and we then toured the program's nearby group home, where street girls and adolescent women lived, many of them with their infants. During the seminar, the director spoke passionately about the plight of street children, how they come to live and work on the streets, and how, contrary to stereotypes, the vast majority are not criminals. The officers peppered him with harsh questions that betrayed their skepticism of his analysis, as well as their view of these street children essentially as pests, delinquents, or worst, criminals. I wondered to myself if any of these officers moonlighted as assassins. As we began to file out of the room to tour the group home, the police officers suddenly stopped and circled around a colleague whose tooth had just broken and who was in obvious agony. I was struck by the contrast between their unforgiving, harsh attitudes toward street children and the utter tenderness and compassion they openly exhibited to their colleague.

5. One of the racist undersides of globalization involves the array of state responses to the undocumented immigration of Third World citizens seeking employment opportunities in developed nations. In this context Nobel laureate Amartya Sen was, as he describes it, treated like any other Third World traveler when he arrived at the Zurich Airport in February 1999 to give a talk at the World Economic Forum. Americans and Europeans enter Switzerland without visas, but not Indians. Although the Harvard professor and master of Trinity College in Cambridge produced his identity cards and the letter of invitation from the Swiss Embassy in London promising him a visa at the airport, he was held for more than an hour until police were satisfied that he was financially solvent and would not stay on to work as an illegal alien (Uchitelle 1999).

REFERENCES

Anyon, Jean. 1997. *Ghetto Schooling: A Political Economy of Urban Educational Reform.* New York: Teachers College Press.

Brasil. 1988. *Constituição do Brasil.* 8 Oct.

Cardoso, Fernando Henrique. 1993. "North-South Relations in the Present Context: A New Dependency?" Pp. 149–60 in *The New Global Economy in the Information Age: Reflections on Our Changing World,* edited by Martin Carnoy, Manuel Castells, Stephen S. Cohen, and Fernando Henrique Cardoso. University Park: Pennsylvania State University Press.

Cardoso, Eliana, and Ann Helwege. 1997. *Latin America's Economy: Diversity, Trends, and Conflicts.* Cambridge: MIT Press.

Carnoy, Martin. 1999. *Globalization and Educational Restructuring.* Paris: International Institute of Educational Planning.

Carnoy, Martin, and Henry Levin. 1985. *Education and Work in the Democratic State.* Stanford, Calif.: Stanford University Press.

Casassus, Juan, Juan Enrique Froemel, Juan Carlos Palafox, and Sandra Cusato. 1998. *First Comparative International Study.* Report of the Latin American Laboratory of the Quality of Education.

UNESCO-Santiago: Regional Office for Latin America and the Caribbean, Nov. http://ns.unesco.cl/lab/estudio.htm.

Child and Adolescent Statute. 1990. Federal Law 9.069.

Children's Defense Fund. 1998. *The State of America's Children: Yearbook 1998.* Washington, D.C.: Author.

Connell, R. W. 1994. "Education and Poverty." *Harvard Education Review* 64: 125–49.

Cuba. 1992. *Constitución de la República de Cuba.* Havana: Editora Política.

Easton, Peter, Steven J. Klees, Sande Milton, George Papagiannis, Art Clawson, Anthony Dewees, Hartley Hobson, Bayard Lyons, and Judy Munter. 1994. *Asserting the Educational Rights of Street and Work Children: Lessons from the Field.* Report submitted to the Urban Section UNICEF, New York. Tallahassee, Fla.: Center for Policy Studies in Education.

Eckstein, Susan Eva. 1994. *Back from the Future: Cuba under Castro.* Princeton, N.J.: Princeton University Press.

Fajnzylber, Fernando. 1990. *Industrialization in Latin America: From the "Black Box" to the "Empty Box": A Comparison of Contemporary Industrialization Patterns.* Santiago, Chile: Economic Commission for Latin America and the Caribbean.

Fusco, Coco. 1998. "Hustling for Dollars: Jineterismo in Cuba." Pp. 151–66 in *Global Sex Workers,* edited by Kamal Kempadoo and Jo Doezema. New York: Routledge.

Gallagher, James. 1998. "Education, Alone, Is a Weak Treatment." *Education Week,* 8 July, 60.

Kozol, Jonathan. 1991. *Savage Inequalities.* New York: Crown.

Longo, Paulo Henrique. 1998. "The Pegação Program: Information, Prevention and Empowerment of Young Male Sex Workers in Rio de Janeiro." Pp. 231–39 in *Global Sex Workers,* edited by Kamal Kempadoo and Jo Doezema. New York: Routledge.

Metz, Mary. 1990. "Real School: A Universal Drama Mid Disparate Experiences." Pp. 75–92 in *Education Politics for the New Century,* edited by D. E. Mitchell and M. E. Goertz. London: Falmer Press.

Montgomery, Heather. 1998. "Children, Prostitution, and Identity: A Case Study from a Tourist Resort in Thailand." Pp. 139–50 in *Global Sex Workers,* edited by Kamal Kempadoo and Jo Doezema. New York: Routledge.

Lustig, Nora (ed.). 1996. *Coping with Austerity: Poverty and Inequality in Latin America.* Washington, D.C.: The Brookings Institution.

Natriello, Gary, Edward L. McDill, and Aaron M. Pallas. 1990. *Schooling Disadvantaged Children: Racing against Catastrophe.* New York: Teachers College Press.

Power, Sally, Deborah Youdell, and Geoff Whitty. 1997. "Refugees, Asylum Seekers, and the Housing Crisis: No Place to Learn." In *Refugee Education: Mapping the Field,* edited by J. Rutter and C. Jones. Stoke-on-Trent, Eng.: Trentham Books.

Royal Swedish Academy. 1998. Press Release: 1998 Bank of Sweden Prize in Economic Sciences in Memory of Alfred Nobel to Professor Amartya Sen, Trinity College, Cambridge, U.K. (citizen of India). http://www.nobel.se/announcement-98/economics98.html

Sanger, David E. 1999. "Markets are Freer Than Politicians." *New York Times,* 21 Feb., WK5.

Sassen, Saskia. 1998. *Globalization and Its Discontents.* New York: Basic Books.

Stewart B. McKinney Homeless Assistance Act. 1987. P.L. 100–77.

Stromquist, Nelly P. 1997. *Literacy for Citizenship: Gender and Grassroots Dynamics in Brazil.* Albany: SUNY Press.

Thorp, Rosemary. 1998. *An Economic History of Latin America in the Twentieth Century.* Washington, D.C.: Interamerican Development Bank.

Uchitelle, Louis. 1999. "Demeaning a Nobelist." *New York Times,* 7 Feb., BU2.

———. 1998. "The Role of Environment in the Black-White Test Score Gap." Pp. 501–11 in *The Black-White Test Score Gap,* edited by Meredith Phillips and Christopher Jencks. Washington, D.C.: The Brookings Institution.

Wilson, William J. 1996. *When Work Disappears: The World of the New Urban Poor.* New York: Alfred A. Knopf.

Willis, Paul. 1977. *Learning to Labour: How Working Class Kids Get Working Class Jobs.* Westmead, Eng.: Saxon House.

Afterword

Several years ago, I worked as an external program evaluator for a NGO that provided residential treatment for substance-abusing pregnant adolescents and adults in Charlotte. Some clients were homeless; most were merely poor women and girls. Taped to the wall in the main office was a yellowing rectangle of paper offering the staff a parable intended, I suppose, to encourage them through yet another difficult day:

> Walking along a beach carpeted with thousands of starfish washed ashore by the tides, a man encountered a young boy who was tossing one after another back into the sea. "Why are you wasting your time throwing a few fish back into the ocean?" asked the man. "Can't you see there are so many, that what you do makes no difference?" The boy replied softly, "It makes a difference for this one," and he threw another starfish back into the water.

I recalled that maudlin tale from time to time as I completed this book because it seemed so apt; while relatively few children benefit from them, the "jewel box" programs discussed in this volume may make a difference for those who pass through their doors. But I also recalled the wisdom of Jean Anyon's metaphor about the futility of urban school reform absent structural change.

I am left to reconcile these two contradictory truths: "jewel box" programs for homeless and street youth are both absolutely necessary and woefully insufficient. I conclude that we must undertake both short- and long-term strategies. We must immediately provide humane and necessary social and educational services to poor children. A number of the programs described here—Projeto Axé, Projeto Semear, A Child's Place, Estado de Cambodia—offer useful, though imperfect, collaborative models of comprehensive services for homeless and street children. But none of the programs—or even the high-minded legislation enacted during the last decade—can stop children from turning to the streets either to work or to live when they perceive no good alternatives (Mickelson 1990; Ogbu 1998). Even the best programs seek to educate or change—to improve—the children or their families so they can better function in the same society that sent them to the streets.

At the end of the day, as R. W. Connell (1994) observes, educational problems are essentially political problems. Domestic policies reflect values and choices. The long-term solutions to the situations facing the homeless and street children described in this book lie in eradicating poverty, in fighting racial and gender oppression, and in developing democratic social movements that demand economic growth with equity. Educating the most marginalized of our children—those who are homeless or live and work on the streets—may just be one of the best ways to begin.

REFERENCES

Connell, R. W. 1994. "Education and Poverty." *Harvard Education Review* 64: 125–49.
Mickelson, Roslyn A. 1990. "The Attitude-Achievement Paradox among Black Adolescents." *Sociology of Education* 63(1): 44–61.
Ogbu, John U. 1998. "The Study of Community Forces: Some Theoretical and Methodological Issues." Address to the Graduate School of Education, Harvard University, Cambridge, Mass., 11 Dec.

Contributors

Fernanda Gonçalves Almeida is a doctoral candidate in education at the Universidade Federal da Bahia, in Salvador da Bahia. She is a researcher at the Center for Human Resources at the Universidade Federal da Bahia, where she coordinates a project aimed at integrating children at risk into society. She teaches at the Pontifícia Universidade Católica do Salvador (Catholic University of Salvador).

Jean Anyon is professor and chair of the Department of Education at Rutgers University, Newark. She is also director of the Rutgers Institute for Outreach and Research in Urban Education. She received her Ph.D. in cognitive psychology in 1976 from New York University. Anyon is the author of *Ghetto Schooling: A Political Economy of Urban Educational Reform*. She is a nationally recognized expert on urban schools and has published numerous articles on race, class, and inner-city school reform.

Lynn Gillespie Beck is the dean of the School of Education at Pacific Lutheran University in Tacoma, Washington. Prior to this, she was professor and program chair of the Department of Administration and Educational Leadership at the University of Alabama. She is the author of six books, including *The Four Imperatives of a Successful School* and *Ethics in Educational Leadership Programs: Emerging Models* (with Joseph Murphy). Her teaching and research focus on ethics and educational leadership, school reform, and the preparation of educational leaders.

Inaiá Maria Moreira de Carvalho holds a Ph.D. in sociology from the Universidade de São Paulo. She teaches at the Universidade Federal da Bahia (UFBA) and was the coordinator of research for the Office of the Dean of Research and Post Graduate Studies at UFBA. Her research and teaching interests include urban poverty, social movements, and politics.

Anthony Dewees received a Ph.D. from Florida State University in 1998. He is currently the impact evaluation specialist in the Woman/Child Impact office of Save the Children (U.S.). His interests and prior work deal with programs and policies concerning children and youth in developing countries.

Ligia Gomes Elliot received her Ph.D. in education from the University of California at Los Angeles, in 1980. She was professor and researcher at the School of Education of the Universidade Federal do Rio de Janeiro (1981–1995). She worked as an assistant in the Office of Instruction of the Rio de Janeiro State Department of Education from 1981 to 1990. At present, she is director of the Evaluation Center of the Fundação CESGRANRIO.

Irving Epstein is associate professor of education at Illinois Wesleyan University. He has published widely in the field of comparative education and has edited *Chinese Education: Problems, Policies, and Prospects*. From 1989 to 1998, he served as an associate editor of the *Comparative Education Review*. Children's rights issues, including the education of street children, have been one of his principal research interests.

María Luisa González earned her doctorate from New Mexico State University, where she is currently serving as the academic department head in the Educational Management and Development Department. She has worked as an evaluator-researcher and as the principal of an inner-city school that received congressional recognition as one of 15 exemplary schools in the nation for homeless and at-risk populations.

Linda Holman is principal of Hillside Elementary School in El Paso, Texas, a school that is 91 percent Hispanic and serves a substantial immigrant population. A campus-level administrator for 10 years, Dr. Holman completed her doctorate in educational management and development at New Mexico State University in 1993. Her published work has appeared in *Educational Leadership, Phi Delta Kappan, Texan Researcher*, and several practitioner-related journals.

Ana Huerta-Macías received her doctorate from the University of Texas at Austin in 1978. She is currently an associate professor in the Department of Curriculum and Instruction at New Mexico State University, where she coordinates the TESOL (Teaching English to Speakers of Other Languages) program. She has published widely in the areas of family literacy, TESOL, sociolinguistics, and bilingual and immigrant education. Most recently, she coedited *Educating Latino Students: A Guide to Successful Practice.*

Martha K. Huggins received her Ph.D. in sociology from the University of New Hampshire in 1981. She is now the Roger Thayer Stone Distinguished Professor at the Union College in Schenectady, New York. Huggins has been visiting professor at the Universidade Federal de Pernambuco (1975–1977), the Universidade de São Paulo (1991), and the Universidade de Brasília (1993). She has conducted scholarly research in Brazil for 23 years and has published numerous articles and books about crime, the police, and extralegal violence. Her most recent book is *Political Policing: The United States and Latin America.*

Steven J. Klees is a professor in the Department of Educational Policy, Planning, and Administration at the University of Maryland. He received his Ph.D. from Stanford University and has subsequently taught at Florida State University, Cornell University, Stanford University, and the Federal University of Rio Grande do Norte in Brazil. He also was a Fulbright Scholar on two occasions at the Federal University of Bahia, Brazil. His research interests center on issues concerning the political economy of educational policy and social change.

Lori Korinek is a professor of curriculum and instruction with an emphasis in special education at the School of Education at the College of William and Mary in Williamsburg, Virginia. She teaches courses and conducts staff development in the areas of learning disabilities, behavior disorders, curriculum development, and instructional strategies. Her current research and writing projects involve team problem solving and collaborative service delivery for students with special education needs.

Sheryl L. Lutjens is associate professor of political science at Northern Arizona University. She received her Ph.D. from the University of California, Berkeley, in 1987. Her research interests include: political participation; theories of the state, power, and democracy; feminist political theory; and Cuba. Her publications include articles on Cuban education, Cuban women, and current reforms in Cuba. Her recent book is *The State, Bureaucracy, and the Cuban Schools: Power and Participation.*

Myriam Mesquita, who received her Ph.D. in sociology from the Universidade de São Paulo in 1996, has conducted research for 10 years on violence against Brazilian street youth. As research coordinator at the Universidade de São Paulo's Nucleus for the Study of Violence, she collaborated on the groundbreaking *Vidas em risco,* the first published empirical study of the murders of Brazilian street youth. She expanded these studies nationally as a researcher for UNICEF in Brazil and is now examining a range of problems as an independent researcher.

Virginia McLaughlin is currently Chancellor Professor of Education and dean of the School of Education at the College of William and Mary in Williamsburg, Virginia. Her teaching, research, and staff development efforts focus on curricular development, program evaluation, and collaborative service delivery. She publishes regularly on the topic of inclusion through collaboration.

Roslyn Arlin Mickelson is professor of sociology and adjunct professor of women's studies at the University of North Carolina, Charlotte. She was visiting professor at the Universidade do Estado do Rio de Janeiro (1994) and visiting scholar at Stanford University (1998–1999). Her areas of interest include the political economy of schooling and relationships among race, ethnicity, gender, class, and educational processes and outcomes. She has published widely on minority students' achievement and the education of homeless children in the United States.

Nelly Moulin received her Ph.D. in education from the University of California, Los Angeles, in 1980. She was a professor of curriculum and society at the Universidade do Estado do Rio de Janeiro (UERJ) until 1998. Currently, she is the coordinator of the Graduate Program in Education at the Universidade Salgado de Oliveira (UNIVERSO) in Rio de Janeiro. Her research interests include distance learning resources and organizations. Her latest publications are texts for distance learning, evaluation, and the organization and administration of centers for distance learning.

Rebecca Newman coordinates before- and after-school and tutoring programs at a public high school in Santa Ana, California. She is associated with the School-Age Care Project of the University of California, Irvine. She received her Ed.D. from the University of California, Los Angeles, in 1998, and is the author of *Educating Homeless Children: Witness to a Cataclysm*. She has authored several publications dealing with the problems of homeless families.

Ralph da Costa Nuñez is president/CEO of Homes for the Homeless and president of the Institute for Children and Poverty, the research division of Homes for the Homeless. Dr. Nuñez who serves as professor at Columbia University's School of International and Public Affairs, earned a Ph.D. in political science from Columbia in 1978. He is the author of *Hopes, Dreams, and Promise: The Future of Homeless Children in American* and *The New Poverty: Homeless Families in America*.

Vilma Pereira holds a Ph.D. in education from the University of California, Los Angeles. She is professor of methodology of teaching at the Universidade Salgado de Oliveira (UNIVERSO) and Universidade do Estado do Rio de Janeiro (UERJ) where she specializes in math education and evaluation. Before assuming her position in the academy, she worked at the Brazilian Center for Childhood and Adolescence (CBIA), where she investigated the lives and education of street children. In the 1980s, she worked on adult literacy for UNESCO and authored numerous reports and publications on literacy.

Marc Posner is senior research associate at the Education Development Center, Inc., in Newton, Massachusetts. He holds a bachelor's degree in philosophy from Boston University, a masters in political science from Rutgers University, and a Ph.D. in politics from Brandeis University. He is the author of *Nowhere to Run: HIV Prevention for Runaway and Homeless Youth* and *Working Together for Youth* as well as a number of articles and book chapters on youth, education, and public health.

Amelia Maria Noronha Pessoa de Queiroz received her Ph.D. in education from the Universidade Federal de Rio de Janeiro in 1996. She was the coordinator of Projeto Semear from 1987 through 1993 and presently serves as its general coordinator. She was a specialist at the Curriculum Laboratory (1979–1987) and director of the Office of Instruction (1988–1990) of the Rio de Janeiro State Department of Education. From 1994 to 1997 she coordinated the Program in Attention to Minors in Especially Difficult Circumstances for the Inter-American Development Bank. She is the author of *O Caso Semear*.

Yvonne Rafferty is an assistant professor of psychology and a policy analyst at the Children's Institute, Dyson College of Arts and Sciences, Pace University in New York. She received her Ph.D. in 1987 from the State University of New York, Stony Brook. She is a recognized national expert on the impact of homelessness on children, including their educational needs and legal rights. As an action researcher, she has used her research and knowledge base to advocate on the national and local levels for more equitable and humane social policies for homeless children.

Irene Rizzini received her master's degree at the University of Chicago (School of Social Service Administration) and her Ph.D. in sociology from Rio de Janeiro Institute of Research (IUPERJ). She is currently the director of CESPI (the University of Santa Ursula Center for Research on Childhood) and professor at the Department of Social Policy at the Rio de Janeiro State University. Prof. Rizzini serves as the vice president of the Advisory Board of Childwatch International Research Network (Norway). She is the editor of *Olhares sobre a criança no brasil: séculos XIX e XX (Images of the Child in Brazil: 19th and 20th Centuries*, 1997), and the author of *O século perdido: raízes históricas das políticas públicas para a infância no Brasil (The Lost Century: The Historical Roots of Public Policies on Children in Brazil*, 1997).

Fúlvia Rosemberg holds a Ph.D. in psychology and is a researcher at Carlos Chagas Foundation (Fundação Carlos Chagas) in São Paulo. She is professor of social psychology at Pontifícia Universidade Católica de São Paulo (Catholic University of São Paulo). Her primary publications concern child care. She is the author of *Creches e pre-escolas no Brasil* and *Creches e pre-escolas no hemisferio norte* (both with Maria Malta Campos).

Murilo Tadeu Moreira Silva holds a bachelor's degree in psychology, has done postgraduate studies in human resources, and is currently pursuing a master's degree in public policy at Fundação João Pinheiro, Escola de Governo do Estado de Minas Gerais. He is the technical assessor for the Secretariat of Labor and Social Assistance for Children and Adolescents in Belo Horizonte, Minas Gerais.

James H. Stronge is Heritage Professor and area coordinator of educational policy, planning, and leadership at the College of William and Mary in Williamsburg, Virginia. His primary research interests include personnel issues in education and educational policy analysis. His current focus is on organizational issues in educating homeless students. He serves as state coordinator for the Virginia Homeless Education Program and is the author of numerous articles and chapters on the topic. He is the editor of *Educating Homeless Children and Adolescents: Evaluating Policy and Practice.*

Chriss Walther-Thomas is an associate professor in educational policy, planning, and leadership with an emphasis in special education at the School of Education at the College of William and Mary in Williamsburg, Virginia. Her current research and writing projects include coteaching, instructional planning, and leadership in the development and maintenance of inclusive education programs.

Brenda T. Williams is associate professor of educational policy, planning, and leadership in the School of Education at the College of William and Mary in Williamsburg, Virginia. Her primary research interests include critical success factors for special education leadership, strategies for involving families and community members in the educational process, multicultural education, and alternative education.

Maria G. Yon is associate professor of education in the Department of Reading and Elementary Education at the University of North Carolina, Charlotte. A former elementary school teacher, she received her Ed.D. from Virginia Tech University in 1987. Her research interests are effective teaching, learning to teach, and the education of homeless children.

Glossary

abertura   the political opening that preceded the fall of the Brazilian military junta during the 1980s

axé   a Yoruba word, meaning force and power

balseros   people leaving Cuba for the United States on rafts

barrios   poor neighborhoods

Bel-India   a characterization of Brazil as a country, because it has both the wealth of Belgium and the oppressive poverty of India

branco/a   white, referring to light-skinned Brazilians

Bretton Woods institutions   the International Monetary Fund and the World Bank were born at a 1944 conference held at Bretton Woods, New Hampshire

candomblé   a syncretic religion that combines African and European beliefs and rites and is practiced in Salvador, Bahia, and elsewhere in Brazil

capoeira   an Afro-Brazilian sport that combines choreographed dance and martial arts

Candelária Cathedral   site of the infamous 1994 massacre of sleeping street children in Rio de Janeiro

cariños   affection

cariocas   residents of Rio de Janeiro

casas cunas   Cuban foundling homes

Casas Abertas   "open houses," a program for street children in São Paulo

casco histórico   historic section of Old Havana

círculos infantiles   Cuban day care centers for working mothers

círculos infantiles mixtos   Cuban mixed day care centers for children under 6 (CIMS)

clientelismo   a widespread system of public corruption; a political spoils system that guides the administration of Brazilian education and other public services, whereby political supporters of public officials are rewarded with jobs, contracts, and other favors

conscientization   the process by which education enables a person to gain a tranformative self-awareness and liberatory political consciousness, introduced by Paulo Freire

contagem de crianças e adolescentes em situação de rua   census of children and adolescents in street situations

Copacabana   a prosperous beachfront neighborhood in Rio de Janeiro

crianças e adolescentes de rua   children and adolescents who claim the streets as their principal residence (children and adolescents of the street)

crianças e adolescentes na rua   children and adolescents who use the streets as a place of work or recreation, occasionally sleeping on the streets, but who maintain ties with their families (children and adolescents on the street)

criollo/a   designation for light-skinned Cubans

desvinculados   youth who are neither studying nor working

dollarization   the introduction of the U.S. dollar as legal currency in the Cuban economy

drogueros   drug dealers

erê   Yoruba word for child

Estatuto da Criança e do Adolescente   the 1990 Children and Adolescents Act, which defines the rights of Brazilian children and the obligations of the state and their families toward them

favelas   urban squatter slums, usually built on hillsides of Brazilian urban areas

fazenda   plantation estate

Gini coefficient   a measure of the extent to which the distribution of income among individuals or households within an economy deviates from a perfectly equal distribution. A Gini coefficient of 0 indicates a perfectly equal distribution, while one that is 100 represents a perfectly unequal one.

Head Start   a U.S. federally financed preschool program designed to ensure that low-income children have the opportunities to attend developmental preschool

hogares   group homes where Cuban children without families live

homeless youth   as defined by the Runaway and Homeless Youth Act, an individual is homeless who is not less than 16 and not more than 21 years of age and for whom it is not possible to live in a safe environment with a relative and who has no other safe, alternative living arrangement

household income   the sum of the total weekly earnings of all persons living in a household

human capital   the notion that individuals who invest time and money in education, training, and other skills and competencies increase their productivity and value to employers; variations in pay are considered by some economists to reflect variations in levels of human capital; other economists note that human capital theory cannot account for racial and gender differences in returns to the same education and experience

jeitinho   a crafty or clever solution to an everyday or common problem

jiniterismo   prostitution

justiceiros   "justice makers," the lone assassins who commit the murders of Brazilian street children

kuru 'mi   Tupi word for child

low-income housing ratio   the number of households living below the poverty line divided by the number of affordable housing units available.

maquiladores   Mexican factories near the U.S./Mexico border

meninos/as de rua   street children

mestizo/a   a person of mixed race, usually including indigenous peoples of Latin America

mocambos   huts in the woods that were originally used by refugee slaves

monetarism   an orthodox approach to economic stabilization that typically involves cutting budget deficits, supporting free-trade policies, and eliminating price controls (among other measures)

McKinney Act   the Stewart B. McKinney Homeless Assistance Act of 1987, P.L. 100–77, establishes the rights of homeless children to free, appropriate education in the least restrictive environment possible

Movimento Nacional de Meninos e Meninas de Rua   the National Movement of Street Children, founded in 1985 to defend the rights of Brazilian street children

mulatta   a woman of mixed racial origins who, in some contexts, is sexually objectified, especially by foreign tourists seeking exotic sex workers

negro/a   black, referring to dark-skinned Brazilians

neoliberalism   a laissez-faire approach to capitalism that involves dismantling of government programs and regulations, cutting social welfare spending, and instituting greater privatization

niños de la calle   street children

nucleos particulares   household units

Operation Peter Pan   the sending of Cuban children to the United States during the period Dec. 1960 to Oct. 1962; following the revolution, some parents feared the rumored transfer of their parental rights to the state

paladares   restaurants in private homes in Cuba

pardo/a   brown, referring to brown-skinned Brazilians

patria potestad   parental rights

pater familia   male head of household

pivetes   a derogatory term designating delinquent, mischievous children

poverty line   the amount of money the federal government calculates as the minimum necessary for acquiring the basic necessities

preto/a   black, referring to dark-skinned Brazilians

quaternization   the process by which a developing Third World nation becomes so poor it joins the Fourth World

quince   the coming-of-age celebration held for 15-year-old women in Cuba and other Latin American countries

real   Brazilian currency introduced in July 1994 in conjunction with an economic reform plan that pegged the currency to the U.S. dollar

rightsizing   reducing the size of a firm or bureaucracy's labor force in order to cut costs, also referred to as downsizing

runaway youth   as defined by the Runaway and Homeless Youth Act, a person under 18 years of age who absents him- or herself from home or place of legal residence without permission of parents or guardians

semear   to sow

senzala   slave quarters

structural adjustments   neoliberal economic policy contingencies that the IMF and the World Bank attach to loans to Third World countries

Terra Nova   an Italian organization dedicated to cooperation with the Third World

tutela   guardianship

welfare hotel   old hotels in large U.S. cities that have been used as housing for poor families on public assistance

Index